THE FINNISH FRONT LINE

THE FINNISH FRONT LINE

KEKKONEN, KENNEDY, AND KHRUSCHEV'S COLD WAR SHOWDOWN

GORDON F. SANDER

CORNELL UNIVERSITY PRESS
Ithaca and London

First published 2025 by Cornell University Press

Printed in the United States of America

Library of Congress Cataloging-in-Publication Data

Names: Sander, Gordon F., author.
Title: The Finnish front line : Kekkonen, Kennedy, and Khrushchev's Cold War showdown / Gordon F. Sander.
Description: Ithaca : Cornell University Press, 2025. | Includes bibliographical references and index.
Identifiers: LCCN 2024051209 (print) | LCCN 2024051210 (ebook) | ISBN 9781501781308 (hardcover) | ISBN 9781501781339 (epub) | ISBN 9781501781322 (pdf)
Subjects: LCSH: Kekkonen, Urho, 1900–1986. | Finland—Foreign relations—Soviet Union. | Finland—Politics and government—1945–1981.
Classification: LCC DL1135.5.K44 S26 2025 (print) | LCC DL1135.5.K44 (ebook) | DDC 948.9703/3092 [B]—dc23/eng/20250121
LC record available at https://lccn.loc.gov/2024051209
LC ebook record available at https://lccn.loc.gov/2024051210

To my longtime friend and colleague, Michael Franck, and my beloved brother Elliot G. Sander and cousin Roger Widmann, without whom this book would not have been possible

Contents

Map 1. Post–World War II Finland. Daniel Huffman.

Map 2. Metropolitan Helsinki of the Kekkonen era. Daniel Huffman.

MAP 3. The USSR, Finland, and Sweden. Daniel Huffman.

Acknowledgments

The decade-long journey to bring *The Finnish Front Line* to port and fruition involved two stellar transatlantic crews, all of whom deserve my unalloyed thanks: the first one behind *Citizen Kekkonen,* the original 2022 WSOY Finnish language volume, and the second exemplary one behind this significantly revised and updated Cornell University Press English-language edition.

First, spotlighting the five members of my Finnish crew, I would like to thank, in order of service:

—Tomas Sjöblom. My first assistant, Tomas, performed the crucial, and occasionally crazed, task of helping to arrange the first round of interviews for *Citizen* and recording and transcribing the interviews.

—Mau Vuori. My longtime assistant Mau Vuori, who also assisted me with my prior Finnish tome, *The Battle of Finland*, about the Winter War, translated over one hundred articles about Kekkonen from Finland's leading newspaper and paper of record, *Helsingin Sanomat.*

—Heidi Silvennoinen. Heidi had the immense job of both reading and summarizing Kekkonen's journals, which she performed with grace, dispatch, and distinction.

—Alec Neihum. A talented journalist in his own right, Alec, who first "signed up" with the Kekkonen Corps in 2017, has the honor of being my longest-serving assistant. A partial list of the tasks Alec performed for *Citizen* includes finding and translating numerous Finnish texts for me, sourcing the manuscript, and generally helping me keep my balance during the latter three years of the first leg of this epic literary/historical odyssey.

—Vuokko Schoultz. An up-and-coming historian, this charming and resourceful young lady had the thankless task of finalizing the myriad source notes for the book, which she executed flawlessly and without complaint (even though she had ample excuse to execute me).

—Henry Mannberg. Henry, a brilliant young historian who I happened to meet after a visit to Tamminiemi, where he has been working as a guide for several years, had the challenging and complex job of checking the myriad facts in the book and serving as my biographical and literary quality control chief as the *Citizen* caravan raced (and occasionally stumbled) to the finish line. Henry is also working with me on my next—and fourth—volume of Finnish history, *In the Shadow of the Peace*, the sequel to *The Battle of Finland.*

A hearty—and heartfelt—*kiitos* to all you gals and guys! I literally could not have done it without you. *Kiitos kiitos! Tack tack!*

Back in Latvia, where I am currently based, I am grateful to my first two research and personal assistants, Dace Saukuma and Ieva Kalvane, for performing numerous hair-pulling bibliographical tasks associated with this book, as well as keeping the faith.

Continuing my Finnish roll call, I wish to thank Timo Kekkonen, Kekkonen's grandson, for granting me three lengthy interviews, which gave me special insight into his grandfather. This is not an authorized biography nor, to his credit, did Timo ask to review the manuscript as a condition of his cooperation. *Kiitos kiitos!*

Close behind in the ranks of the Finns, I am deeply grateful to my dear friend Michael Franck, the noted documentarian to whom this tome is co-dedicated, whom I have known since the early 1990s when my Finnish "thing" began and have worked with on numerous projects over the years. Micce was kind enough to arranged for numerous of the interviews for this book, including with Joiko Loikkanen, UKK's longtime friend and assistant, and Ambassador Jaakko Iloniemi.

I am much obliged to my friend and colleague Henrik Meinander, Finland's greatest contemporary historian, who was kind enough to sit for numerous lengthy interviews for the book and who was also kind enough to review it.

My friend and colleague, journalist Yrjö Länsipuro, who also has served in several capacities for the Finnish Foreign Ministry, including chief spokesperson, has my deep gratitude for both connecting me with several of Kekkonen's former staff and allowing me to interview him myself, as well as vetting the manuscript.

I am also very grateful to Kekkonen's former chief of staff, Ambassador Jaakko Kalela, for granting me several long interviews, followed by a salvo of copious and very helpful letters of clarification, as well as connecting me with various other members of Kekkonen's former staff, including General Juha Engstrom, the president's last aide-de-camp, and his former chief of staff, the late Kauko Sipponen, who were also kind enough to sit for interviews.

I am indebted to Pekka Lahteenkorvva, head archivist at the Kekkonen archives, for welcoming Tomas and me to the archives and providing various documentary assistance over the years.

Many thanks to Sauli Niinisto, the former president of Finland, and a great man in his own right, for the privilege of interviewing him on the subject of his predecessor and his interest in the project.

Words cannot express my thanks to my brilliant and long-suffering friend and editor, Joni Strandberg, who had the foresight to commission *Citizen Kekkonen* in the first place, and the above and beyond patience to wait for the oft-delayed manuscript. I hope and trust that the words herein I provided will suffice. It certainly has been a long and winding road. Thanks for hanging in there, Joni!

Speaking of WSOY, I am also intensely appreciative of the successive efforts of my learned and exacting copyeditor, Elias Salimen, as well as those of his estimable successor, Anssi Makinen.

Back in my homeland, my cousin, advisor, and occasional proofreader, Roger Widmann, deserves a big mention in dispatches for his abiding help and support. So does my brother, Elliot, who has followed this project with interest since its inception and to whom I owe my original interest in Finland. I am honored to dedicate *The Finnish Front Line* to them, along with Micce.

Other friends on both sides of the Atlantic to whom I indebted for tips, information, and other forms of moral or material support are Ian

Bourgeot of the estimable Arkadia International Bookshop, Aarne Hallama, Marvin Kalb, David Kirby, Lasse Lehtinen, David Kirby, Stephen Kinzer, Lasse Lehtinen, Ron Liebkind, Jouni Molsa, Stephen Schlesinger, and my two beloved departed friends, Ami Hasan and Christian Moustgaard, my original two Finnish godfathers, who cultivated and grew my (still) raging Fennonphilia.

Fast-forwarding to the equally stellar crew who helped me bring this version of my Finnish *obra maestra* to life and give it a second life that it deserved in the broader, English-speaking world, I must hasten to thank Elina Ahlback of Elina Ahlback Agency of Helsinki for "adopting" *Kansalainen Kekkonen*, as the original Finnish version was called, and finding a home for it at Cornell University Press—which also happens to be my home press and the publisher of two of my previous books, *Serling: The Rise and Twilight of Television's Last Angry Man*, and *The Frank Family That Survived.*

Kiitos kiitos Elina!

Mahinder Kingra, editorial director of Cornell University Press and my long-standing friend, has my deepest gratitude for acquiring *The Finnish Front Line* along with my brilliant editor, Sarah Grossman, who helped me revise and update the original book, such that is now essentially a new book and worthy addition to the American annals, as well as Finnish ones.

I also am indebted to the editorial staff at Cornell University Press who were responsible for the lapidary work on *The Finnish Front Line*, including Susan Specter, Katy Bond, and Ange Romeo-Hall.

Too, I am deeply grateful to the two Latvian assistants, Anna Sicova and Laura Lasma-Boreiko, who proofed the revised manuscript. *Liels paldies* ladies!

Ditto to my current assistant, Marta Gulbe, who suffered me during the final (mutually) hair-pulling stretch of the final push to get the revised manuscript off my desk and off to Sage House and on its way into the hands of our wonderful readers. Thanks, Marta!

And last but not least, I would like to award a posthumous White Rose to my beloved late mother, Dorrit Hilde Sander, who was still alive when this book was originally conceived amid the snows of Helsinki during the winter of 2013 and gave it her blessing and support, as she did to my entire Finnish corpus, before she joined Kekkonen in that Tamminiemi in the sky in 2014, and, who, along with Lieutenant Colonel Kurt Sander, my late father, endowed me with the *sisu* that got me to the finish line a second time.

THE FINNISH FRONT LINE

Introduction

> On the eve of your departure for Novosibirsk, I am sending you this private message so that you not be in doubt of the position of the United States . . .
>
> —Top secret message from President John F. Kennedy that Ambassador Bernard Gufler delivered to President Urho Kekkonen of Finland on November 21, 1961 before he flew to Siberia to meet Nikita Khrushchev about the Note Crisis

The history of the early Cold War and its associated crises—the first Berlin crisis and the Berlin airlift in 1948, the second Berlin crisis in 1961 and the stand-off at Checkpoint Charlie, the 1962 Cuban Missile Crisis—is well known.

There is one crisis, however, that coincided with the second Berlin one, and in some ways foreshadowed the Cuban Missile Crisis, particularly in the way US president John F. Kennedy reacted to it, which has been forgotten: the so-called 1961 Fenno-Soviet Note Crisis. That watershed, which also was the most serious political crisis in modern Finnish history since the Soviet invasion of Finland of 1939, which initiated the Winter War, was triggered on October 30, 1961, when Andrei Gromyko, the Soviet foreign minister, handed a peremptory demarche to the Finnish ambassador Eero Wuori.

In language that recalls the Kremlin's anger at Finland's recent historic decision to join NATO, thus bringing the so-called special relationship between the two neighbors to a final acrimonious end, the note called attention to "revanchist" NATO member West Germany's putatively increased military activities and proposed—really demanded—that the military staff of both countries begin consultations as called for by the Fenno-Soviet Treaty of 1948.

A great shock, and front-page news around the world, many Finns and their friends in the West feared that the note presaged the establishment of a Soviet military presence on Finnish soil and the de facto end of Finnish independence, even a reprise of 1939. The battalion of Western journalists, or "news vultures" as Finns called them, who once again descended on Helsinki, as they did twenty years before seemed to expect as much.

At the time the sixty-year-old Finnish president, then at the end of his first term, and in the midst of a contested campaign for a second one—also the last time Urho Kekkonen would have significant opposition during his quarter century reign—was in the Hawaiian Islands at the tail end of his much-ballyhooed visit to the United States. The highlight of his trip, the first by a Finnish president, was the two-day meeting at the White House two weeks before with his American counterpart, Kennedy, then at the end of his own tumultuous first year in office. At the meeting Kennedy pressed Kekkonen, the Western leader who had the best relationship with the Soviet Union's imperious and impulsive leader, Nikita Khrushchev, with whom he had just nearly come to blows over Berlin, for insight into the Soviet leader's motives and behavior, including vis-à-vis Finland as well as the "special relationship," which mystified the American. It also mystified Kekkonen, as he, in a moment of candor, confessed.

At the same time Kennedy tried to use Kekkonen, or UKK, as Finns knew him, to send a message of America's determination to his putative Soviet friend. The message evidently did not hold, as Khrushchev decided to test Kennedy's resolve a year later by placing those missiles in Cuba. The meeting, one of the most fascinating and revealing of both presidencies—as well as virtually the only one of the hidebound Finnish president's for which there is an accurate stenographic record—is analyzed at length herein; as is the equally revealing and somewhat bizarre one he had with Dean Rusk, Kennedy's bellicose secretary of state, in which Kekkonen confided his apparently genuine belief that the Soviet Union was actually winning the Cold War.

The closely watched confab culminated with a statement underlying Washington's recognition of Finnish neutrality, the most important objective of Kekkonen's trip. It was that statement that irked Moscow, as well as the unabashed amity with which Kennedy and his wife Jackie greeted the Finnish leader and his wife, Sylvi, which likely lit the fuse to the crisis that exploded two weeks leader.

In the meantime, Khrushchev had set something else off, by way of flaunting Moscow's military muscle and disdain for the West: the

60,000-pound so-called Tsar Bomb. The device, the most powerful nuclear device ever created and tested, was detonated the very same morning that the explosive note to the flustered Finnish ambassador to Moscow, Eero Wuori, was delivered. The explosion was principally timed to coincide with the twenty-second Congress of the Communist Party of the USSR. Khrushchev's decision to simultaneously drop the high-tonnage note on Kekkonen and Finland while the former was still in the United States was no accident, however. Clearly, he also wanted to send a message to the Finnish president, as well as the West: *Hands off Finland!*

That was a message that Kennedy, the ardent Cold Warrior and Fennophile, who had once headed the Help Finland chapter at Harvard during the Winter War, and who hoped to pull *Suomi* (Finland) out of the Soviet sphere of influence and closer to the West, chose to ignore. Three tense weeks later, after the shaken Finnish president had returned to Helsinki and before the latter had agreed to fly to Siberia to meet with Khrushchev and resolve the Note Crisis, as it was already being called, Kennedy sent a top secret message of support to Kekkonen in which he pledged that the US was prepared to go to the mat for Finland and do everything short of going to war in order to help preserve its independence if things went awry at the Siberian conclave and the Kremlin went ahead with his demand for joint military discussions.

It is the delivery of *that* fateful top secret note from the White House—on a certain level, this book is a history of demarches, secret and otherwise—by Kennedy's ambassador to Helsinki, Bernard Gufler, to Kekkonen at Tamminiemi, the presidential mansion, on the evening of November 19, 1961, which kicks off this book, a historical biography of Finland's eighth president, Urho Kaleva Kekkonen, and my third work of Finnish history.

Kekkonen, Kennedy, and Khrushchev: For three momentous weeks in November 1961 the fate of the Cold War devolved on the words and actions of these three leaders. Would Finland become the next front of the simmering East-West conflict? There certainly was a good chance of that happening as the beleaguered Finnish president flew off to meet Khrushchev in distant Novosibirsk, carrying with him the hopes of the Free World.

Kekkonen, Kennedy, and Khrushchev. Of course we all know the latter two, or think we do.

But who was Kekkonen? How did this former attorney and intelligence officer wind up becoming the five-term "strongman of Finland," as he has been called. How and when did the "special relationship" between Helsinki and Moscow begin and how did the one-time *Russkie*-hater wind up becoming its symbol? And how and why, during the Note Crisis, did Finland, the country known as Europe's odd man out, come to play a featured role in the Cold War?

In order to answer these questions, we must revisit Finland's checkered political and geopolitical history during the 1940s, as well as Kekkonen's own journey during that tumultuous decade. To be sure, few countries had as topsy-turvy a history a decade as Suomi did during the 1940s. When the decade began this country of three million was locked in battle with the Neighbor to the East, as Russia has traditionally been known, following Joseph Stalin's shock decision to invade its former grand duchy in November 1939. Against all odds, Finland was also winning—or apparently winning—after its fast-moving ski troops decimated an entire Soviet decision in the frozen uplands of eastern Finland at a place called Suomussalmi.

At the time, America's sister republic across the waves was the toast of the West. Brave Little Finland, she was called. The epic David and Goliath battle between the USSR and Suomi, which some consider the first chapter of World War II, and Finns still consider their country's finest hour was front page news. "Finland is America's Sweetheart," observed Christopher Isherwood, the English playwright, then in exile in California, in his diary, as then stalwart neutral United States staged Ice Capades and raised millions for the hard-fighting Finns, but did little else.

Inevitably, the fortunes of the *Talvisota* (Winter War) turned against the vastly outnumbered Finns, after Stalin, who had underestimated the latter's *sisu* and the tensile strength of Finnish society, realized his mistake, revised his tactics and personnel, made sure to attire them properly in winter wear, and launched a new offensive, which succeeded in breaking the vaunted Mannerheim Line, forcing the bloodied and beleaguered if not yet bested Finns to capitulate, bringing the epic 105-day war to an end.

The price of peace was severe: According to the Peace of Moscow, which the future president and Kekkonen's mentor Juho Paasikivi helped negotiate, the Finns were forced to give up 10 percent of their territory, including the province of Karelia and the beloved city of Viipuri, shattering the nation and making some sort of rematch all but inevitable. That took place under murky and still controversial circumstances a year later when Adolf Hitler made the fateful and fatal decision to invade the USSR, and Finland joined the fight as cobelligerents, as Finns called themselves, reconquering Karelia, helping the Germans maintain the siege of Leningrad and becoming a pariah in the West. The following conflict was called the Continuation War.

Now it was Berlin's turn to fête their northern quasi-allies. Hitler even flew to Finland to help celebrate Mannerheim's seventy-fifth birthday (to the latter's surprise). But the German dictator's true purpose was to ensure that Finland would remain allied with Berlin and dissuade the Finns, who were already beginning to wonder about the wisdom of the Faustian deal they had made with the Germans, from sending peace feelers to the Soviets and their Western allies.

That is exactly what they did six months later, after the Nazis' defeat at Stalingrad. In March 1943, shortly after that pivotal battle, while Finnish troops were heavily engaged with the Soviets, Edwin Linkomies formed a new cabinet with a view toward making peace with Moscow, an objective which both Paasikivi and Kekkonen supported. Of the two, the latter made the furthest political about-face since the war. In March 1940, Kekkonen, a veteran politician who had previously served as minister of justice and other cabinet posts, was one of only two members of *eduskunta*, the Finnish parliament, who voted against accepting the draconian Moscow Peace Treaty. The staunch nationalist, who had fought with the German-backed Whites against the Soviet-backed Reds during the 1918 Finnish Civil War, wanted to keep on fighting the hated *Russkies*, as the Finns used to call the Russians, even if it meant battling Stalin's forces at the gates to Helsinki. By 1943, however, Kekkonen, who spent the bulk of the Continuation War as director of the Karelian Evacuees' Welfare Center, a position that allowed him to see and reflect on the personal cost of war up close, had become something of a pacifist, as well as a realist. Like Paasikivi he also recognized and accepted that Germany had already lost the war, and favored Finland's withdrawal from the bloody three-year-long see-saw contest, in which over 60,000 Finns died.

With Gustaf Mannerheim, the Finnish commander-in-chief and his troops still committed to the fight—not to mention the Germans, who stationed nearly a quarter million troops in Finland—this was easier said than done. Secret peace negotiations were conducted intermittently in 1943 and 1944 between Finland, the Western Allies, and the Soviets but no agreement was reached. In the meantime Stalin decided to force Suomi to surrender with a bombing campaign against Helsinki, which only served to remind Finns of the murderous surprise attack which had started the *Talvisota* in November, 1939 and did little to advance the cause of peace.

Meanwhile, Finnish armed forces, bolstered by a generous supply of German *pänzerfauste* (portable antitank weapon), which Hitler's foreign minister, Joachim von Ribbentrop, gave President Risto Ryti in exchange for a personal guarantee that he would *not* seek a separate peace with Berlin, kept on fighting. And so they did, with mixed success, through 1944. The Battle of Ilomansti, the last battle of the Continuation War, actually was a Finnish victory, resulting in the destruction of two Soviet divisions. Still, once again the writing was on the wall. Its resources exhausted, Helsinki now sought to exit the three-year-old war-within-a-war.

In August, President Ryti resigned and Gustaf Mannerheim was appointed by the Parliament to succeed him. The venerable field marshal, who has been called the Father of Finland, promptly annulled the agreement his predecessor had made with Ribbentrop, enabling his government to sue for peace with Moscow again.

The Kremlin's peace terms arrived on August 29, 1944. They were harsh. First, Finland was required to return to the borders agreed to in the 1940 peace treaty, as well as cede the 3,500-square-mile municipality of Petsamo in eastern Lapland. It also forced Finland to grant a fifty-year lease at Porkkala, on the country's southern Baltic coast, for a naval base it wanted to establish there. Additionally, according to the final protocol signed by Paasikivi, who was now prime minister, Finland was forced to pay reparations of $300 million in gold, or the equivalent of $6.24 billion in 2025, to be paid in the form of ships and machinery—a burden that many felt would sink the country's devastated economy, but instead kick-started its shipbuilding industry, laying the foundation for the "Finnish miracle," as its remarkable postwar reconstruction has been called.

The armistice included several other painful clauses. To its chagrin, the defeated country was required by the Allied Control Commission to apprehend and put on trial those wartime leaders, including Ryti, the former president, ex-prime minister Linkomies, Väinö Tanner, the former foreign minister, and five others who it deemed responsible for "influencing Finland into getting into a war with the Soviet Union and the United Kingdom." The latter actually declared war on Finland in 1944. Washington had avoided the last step—but only barely.

Finland's tortured wartime relationship with the United States is personified by the dramatically reversed fortunes of its ambassador to Washington, Hjalmar Procope. In 1939, at the height of the Winter War, the dashing envoy was the toast of Washington and perhaps the capital's best known foreign diplomat. Five years later, in June 1944, when the Continuation War was still raging and Finland had come to be seen as a pariah nation, Procope was declared persona non grata and forced to leave the country. Last but not least, according to the terms of the 1944 armistice, the Finns were required to expel the sizable German forces still stationed on its territory.

The guests were not cooperative. The result was the bitter Lapland War, the third and final of the three wars Finland engaged in during the Second World War. The Finns succeeded in evicting their former allies, but not before the incensed *Wehrmacht* razed much of Finland's snowbound northern province, including the provincial capital of Rovaniemi, embittering the local populace. The Lapland War ended in April, 1945, when Finnish soldiers raised the Finnish flag at the three-country cairn between Norway, Sweden, and Finland.

Thus ended Suomi's tortured and tortuous odyssey during World War II and the first half of the 1940s. On the positive side, the country could claim that it had survived the global storm without losing its independence, unlike most of Nazi Germany's allies or "cobelligerents," as the Finns still preferred to be called. Additionally, Helsinki, along with Moscow, was the only capital of a combatant nation on the European continent that was not occupied.

But Brave Little Finland was hardly America's sweetheart anymore. And, though technically independent, that independence came along with an enforced, politically and spiritually burdensome relationship with Moscow, which felt that it had veto power over Finnish foreign policy. The coercive nature of that relationship was confirmed in 1947 when, under Soviet pressure, Finland declined to accept economic aid from the Marshall Plan. From Washington's point of view, Finland was now a war orphan. Good luck!

That was fine with Kekkonen, who felt that the only way to ensure Finnish sovereignty (or what remained of it) was to do everything possible to eliminate Soviet suspicions and create the conditions for bilateral trust. "The Finnish nation stands at the beginning of the new political path determined for it," he declared in a radio speech in September 1944, following the armistice. That path would not be an easy one, he stated, nor one that others would easily understand. "Broad, ready-built roads are closed to us," he continued. "We must construct a new national course through marshland and mountains." The self-assured former lawyer, who already showed signs of the authoritarian personality that would mark his quarter century long presidency, made it clear that he was the person best suited to lead the Finnish nation forward on that path.

Two months later, in November 1944 the rising magnifico was reappointed minister of justice, a post he was to hold for two years. One of Kekkonen's responsibilities during that fraught time was to oversee the war responsibility trials that the Soviets had forced on Helsinki. Paasikivi, his mentor, who became president in the summer of 1946 upon the resignation of the ailing Mannerheim, intensely resented the mandatory trials. Kekkonen, his protégé, had no problem with them, however. The Soviets, included the dread Andrei Zhdanov, who were installed at Helsinki's landmark Hotel Torni, along with their British colleagues on the Allied Control Commission, intently overseeing the hated trials, took note of Kekkonen's cooperative attitude. Here was a man to watch and with whom they could do business with.

When Paasikivi, or the Old Man, as the venerable septuagenarian statesman was known, became president, Kekkonen's party, the Agrarian League, enthusiastically proposed him for prime minister, however the move was thwarted by the opposition of the Finnish People's Democratic Front, the communist front, which remembered Kekkonen's Russophobe days and distrusted him. Instead Kekkonen became deputy speaker and speaker of the *eduskunta* (parliament). He never relinquished his ambition to rise to the captaincy of the Finnish ship of state, however. The difference between his attitude toward Moscow and that of Paasikivi, whom the Russians also liked, was a matter of degree not of kind. Paasikivi, too, also firmly believed that Finland's interests required bilateral trust, and his foreign policy during the decade when he was president, from 1946 to 1956, was successfully directed toward that end.

Nevertheless there were limits to how far The Old Man would go to assuage Moscow. When Stalin proposed a Treaty of Friendship, Cooperation and Mutual Assistance in February, 1948—the same time the Allies were forming NATO—Paasikivi approved the general idea, while at the same time trying to ensure that the treaty codifying Finland's "new" path, was drawn up on the basis of an outline provided by Helsinki. Article 2, the problematic clause that Moscow would invoke thirteen years later during the Note Crisis whereby Moscow could insist on mutual military consultations and essentially call Helsinki on the mat whenever it felt like it, was the Soviets' idea. There was not much that Paasikivi could do about that, or for that matter, the Treaty of Paris of the prior year, which reduced Finland's regular armed forces to a minimal defensive force (although the Finns continued to maintain large reserves.) After all, Finland *had* lost the war.

Paasikivi had no qualms about stifling a possible communist coup during the spring of 1948, like the ones which had taken place in the other Eastern European countries that had fallen under Stalin's steel-tipped umbrella, or with drawing the line with Moscow. Would his protégé, Kekkonen, who had already begun flaunting his access to the Kremlin, have as much spine? He wondered. "Kekkonen at the present moment is the man who would be the best president after me," Paasikivi confided to his diary in 1950, after he was elected president by the grateful Finnish nation in his own right. One of his opponents was the rising Urho Kekkonen, whom he beat by a considerable margin. "But he [Kekkonen] ought to restrain his ambition," Paasikivi wrote. "He places too much emphasis on Russian support. Amongst his own people he has no support except in his own [Agrarian] party." "But," the Old Man emphasized, "the president of Finland is not and must not simply be a Russian governor. Kekkonen ought to seek support from his own people." Nevertheless Paasikivi overcame his qualms and made Kekkonen his prime minister that year.

Thus ended Finland's wild and wooly 1940s. By this time, of course, the Cold War between the United States and the Soviet Union was in high gear and the battle lines between the Free World and the communist one, including the areas where Washington was prepared to contest Soviet influence, beginning with Berlin, where the NATO allies had thwarted Moscow's attempted stranglehold of West Berlin with their massive airlift, had basically been drawn.

Finland, as Dean Acheson, President Harry S. Truman's secretary of state, made clear, was not one of those areas. Acheson articulated the US line toward Finland in a memo he sent his boss, Truman, in response to a query from the latter whether Washington ought to get more involved with Suomi. "It would be most dangerous," Acheson advised the president in 1950, at the start of the Korean War, "to make any efforts in the direction of Finland that would produce a reaction on the part of the Russians."

In the meantime, America's one time "sweetheart" more or less disappeared from the front pages and the consciousness of the American public. If the bastion of Sibelius and *sisu*, now firmly within Moscow's sphere of influence, was not entirely a lost cause, it was basically off America's political and psychological map, although it continued to be featured in travel magazines: After all, Santa Claus still lived there. That basically was Washington's attitude towards Finland for the next decade, up until the Note Crisis of 1961.

Meanwhile, Urho Kaleva Kekkonen had become president. After serving four times as prime minister under Paasikivi, Kekkonen was elected on his second try for the post in January, 1956, if only barely, beating his Social Democratic rival, Karl-August Fagerholm by a mere two electoral votes. Fagerholm, who had headed two prior governments, and Kekkonen had a complicated relationship. They were also co-fathers-in-law. Nevertheless there was no love lost between the men.

There was about to be less. As the results showed, Kekkonen had garnered more support from the Finnish people than he had earlier, as Paasikivi had urged, if only marginally. However, unlike his beloved predecessors he was still a polarizing figure, with the populace divided between those who adored him, and those who despised him. As such, he reminded some American observers of their own great, polarizing Franklin D. Roosevelt.

Kekkonen certainly had Russia's support. In late 1955, Moscow agreed to abrogate its lease on its naval base at Porkkala, which had been a thorn in the Finnish soul. The popular move, clearly designed to help Kekkonen win the election, may well have put him over the top, and he never forgot it. At any rate, the new president had no qualms about being a latter-day Russian governor general as his predecessor and mentor had feared. Like Kekkonen, Paasikivi also premised his presidency on winning Moscow's trust. The Old Man, however, who spoke fluent Russian—something which his protégé did not—refused to kowtow to the Kremlin.

Kekkonen had no such reservations. Indeed, his statements and actions during the first four years of his first term seemed designed to assure the First Secretary of the Communist Party of the USSR and the other members of the Politburo that he was the person best suited to "manage" the contentious Finns, who still harbored a certain resentment for their former enemies, for Moscow—as well as vice versa. This difficult balancing act entailed maintaining a discreet silence about Moscow's excesses. Kekkonen was mum about the brutal way with which Moscow suppressed the Hungarian Revolution, which coincided with his first year in office, including the execution of the prime minister Imre Nagy. The obsequious manner with which he greeted visiting Soviet potentates, like Kliment Voroshilov, the chairman of the presidium of the CPSU (Communist Party of the Soviet Union), who had helped oversee Stalin's invasion of Finland during the *Talvisota*, did not go unnoticed either.

The worst fears of the Western diplomatic community, particularly those of the US ambassador, John D. Hickerson, were further confirmed during the so-called Night Frost crisis. That half-year-long political tempest, which presaged the Note Crisis, began in August 1958, when the Kremlin, which hitherto had had a hands-off policy toward Finnish domestic politics, changed its mind after the formation of a new pro-Western government headed by none other than Fagerholm. The new cabinet included members of the right wing of Fagerholm's party, the Social Democrats, a definite *nyet-nyet.* There was no change in Finland's foreign policy per se. Nevertheless this was too much for the Central Committee, which saw in the new government the long hand of its bête noire, Tanner, the Social Democratic chairman, one of the defendants in the war responsibility trials, whom the Russians still reviled. Now the Kremlin decided to get involved, expressing its distinct displeasure with Fagerholm III, as the new government was called, in various ways.

First, in October, the USSR withdrew its long-time ambassador, Viktor Lebedev, without advance notice. Suddenly, too, the Soviet Navy came calling in the form of a sudden "courtesy visit" from the hulking Sverdlov-class cruiser *Ozrdzhonikidze*, which spent several weeks lurking ominously off Helsinki harbor, in view of the presidential palace. At the same time, Moscow suspended its scheduled bilateral trade talks with Helsinki, throwing the Finnish economy into limbo.

Meanwhile, I. V. Spiridinov, the secretary of the presidium of the Supreme Soviet, the Soviet equivalent of the American chamber of commerce, made it abundantly clear what Moscow's line regarding its neighbor-cum-client state was. Be in no doubt, the high-ranking apparatchik declared in *Tass*, "Finland firmly belongs in the Soviet sphere of influence and those interests determine Finnish policies." Regarding Finland's foreign policy, Spiridinov, noting that the international situation was becoming increasingly tense, stated that the USSR "must know that Finland must not serve as a "springboard for NATO countries," menacingly alluding to the sword of Damocles Moscow held over its former adversary's head, the clause of the 1948 Fenno-Soviet treaty under which it was entitled to call for joint military discussions. Put simply: Moscow was watching. *Got the message?*

Hickerson, the US ambassador, certainly got it. "It is now clear that the Soviets are engaged in a many-faceted pressure campaign against the present Finnish cabinet," he cabled Washington in October. Frustrated by the State Department's standing hands-off line on Finland, Hickerson urged his superiors to get more involved in the "game" over Finland, as he put it, lest the US risk seeing the country further absorbed into the Soviet orbit. Kekkonen also certainly got the message. The flummoxed president, shocked by the sudden crisis and threat to his presidency, did everything he could during the affair to bring Fagerholm's government down, badgering him and his ministers by phone and in person.

Meanwhile, across the ocean, the US government was rousing itself to get more in the "game" over Finland, as Hickerson had urged. One of those who agreed with the ardently anticommunist Hickerson was Gerald Smith, the assistant secretary of state for policy planning. "No overall objective of [US] foreign policy has a higher priority than reducing or preventing the expansion of the area subject to Soviet domination," Smith asserted in a memo to Christian Herter, the acting secretary of state, who was filling in for the ailing John Foster Dulles.

With the exception of Iran, Afghanistan, and Turkey, Finland is the only nation in the world free of foreign domination that possesses a common border with the USSR. The Finnish situation presented a clear test of Western ability in assisting a free nation to withstand Soviet political and economic pressures. Ad interim, the Finnish "situation" grew more parlous. In November Moscow dropped the boom by halting payments on the dozens of ships it had ordered, leading to mass shipyard layoffs. In the event, Hickerson's and Smith's pleas to help Finland were of no avail. Returning to his post, Dulles rejected his subordinates' urgings to get more involved in the "game" over Finland and northeastern Europe, authorizing only a smaller loan for Helsinki in the unlikely case of a total Soviet economic blockade, nothing more. "While we share your hope that assurances of US sympathy may help bolster Finland to resist Soviet pressure," he messaged Smith, "we do not wish any US offer to create a situation in which [the] US and USSR would appear in economic struggle over Finland." In December, the cabinet finally capitulated and resigned, to Kekkonen's relief, and the dismay of Hickerson and his allies in the State Department. The "game" for Finland was over for now, at least as far as Washington was concerned.

In January 1959, the still shaken Finnish president made a "secret" trip to Leningrad to meet Khrushchev to confirm where he and Finland stood vis-à-vis the Kremlin. No hard feelings, the latter told the apprehensive Finn. The "night frost" that he had imposed on Fenno-Soviet relations—Khruschev's phrase—was just a test, really. As long as he and Finland continued to toe the line, including giving a wide berth to Tanner and his *menshevik* ilk, he need not worry about a repeat. And incidentally could he please do something about muzzling the feisty Finnish press?

No problem, replied Kekkonen, who promptly gave a manifestly disingenuous radio speech to the nation in which he rationalized the Kremlin's strong-arm tactics and told the Finnish press to put a lid on it—or else—which it more or less did. Thus Finnish self-censorship, one of the unspoken codicils of the special relationship, along with Article 2, and one that lasted for another thirty years, until the fall of the USSR.

The reason why the USSR had lowered the boom on Finland, Kekkonen explained, was because the former no longer trusted the latter. Everything had to be done in order to regain the Soviets' trust. There was that word again: trust. It also popped up again in an interview Kekkonen gave Werner Wiskari, *The New York Times*'s Stockholm correspondent in early 1959. Contrary to what some critics supposed, the top Finn told Wiskari, Finland was free to do what it liked, but "naturally we take into account the fact that our vital interests require that our neighbor trust us." At the same time, in case anyone was wondering, he also pointed out, "the Soviet Union has not attempted to dictate to Finland what course it should take in either internal or in external affairs." But, of course, it just had done exactly that: sometimes the job of hostage president required a bit of acting. And Kekkonen knew his lines.

As far as Hickerson, the disheartened American ambassador, was concerned Kekkonen's obsequious "secret" pilgrimage to Leningrad confirmed his worst fears about the "pliable"—the embassy's favorite adjective for describing him—Finnish president, along with his fears for Finnish democracy. According to the downhearted envoy, whose four-year tour began shortly before Kekkonen was inaugurated, the Machiavellian president's principal motivation was to "further his own personal ambitions and personal spites."

As Hickerson and his fellow Fennophiles saw it, the game was up for Finland, as far as the US was concerned, unless (a) the apparent latter day Russian governor general showed more spine, and (b) the bigger geopolitical contest between the US and the USSR, i.e., the Cold War, caused Washington and the next White House administration to revise its calculations vis-à-vis America's former sweetheart and seek to pull it closer its side of the East-West fifty-yard line.

That is basically what happened over the next two years, through Finland's next great political crisis, the Note Crisis of the fall of 1961. The truth was that John Hickerson had underestimated Kekkonen somewhat. Of course the Finnish leader was ambitious. He never denied that. He also could be petty. But, above all, he was a patriot. As his long-time aide Jaakko Iloniemi told me, "Everything Kekkonen did he did for Finland." Of course, added Iloniemi, who was also ambassador to Washington, like Charles de Gaulle and other historical autocrats, "he also thought he *was* Finland. But he was first and foremost a patriot."

To be sure, Iloniemi maintains, the pliability his former boss displayed towards the Kremlin, particularly during his first term, was fueled by his megalomania, but also by his fierce determination to protect Finnish sovereignty. Kekkonen, too, also had more character than his critics alleged or supposed. That much became clear, or clearer, in September 1960, when Khrushchev decided on the spur of the moment to pop by to help his friend celebrate his sixtieth birthday. Delighted by the gesture, the surprised president decided to use the occasion to make clear to the Soviet premier, as well as the world, his true feelings about the differences between their two countries and respective political systems, as well as his countrymen's willingness to fight for theirs, once again, if necessary.

"There are those who say that living in a peaceful way as a neighbor to the great Soviet Union will change Finland into a communist state," Kekkonen declared to Khrushchev at a luncheon at the Soviet embassy the day following the latter's arrival with his entourage at Helsinki Central Station, as several thousand schoolchildren hastily gathered by the SKDL, the Finnish People's Democratic League, the CPSU's Finnish sister party, cheered on. However, Kekkonen continued, as his Soviet friend and sometime sauna mate listened on in deferential silence, "I am convinced that even if the whole of Europe turns communist Finland will remain traditionally democratic if this is the will of the people, as I believe it is." "The leaders of the Soviet Union know," Kekkonen continued for good measure, "that we will defend our own system in any circumstances because we think it is better for us." The *Times* of London, among others, was impressed. "It is sometimes said," the British paper opined later, "that Kekkonen gained more by the few words he said that day than by anything else as President."

That evening it was Khrushchev's turn to speak his mind at Kekkonen's official public birthday celebration at the Finnish National Theatre. After acknowledging Finnish neutrality, the volatile Soviet premier seized the moment to denounce NATO, including its putative role in the armaments race, notably West Germany's reported desire to obtain nuclear weapons, as well as Finland's Nordic neighbors, Norway and Denmark, for joining the organization in the first place—shades of things to come!

"As the Russian spoke," *The New York Times* reported, "Mr. Kekkonen's head sank to his chest." The headline on the front page of next day's paper said it all:

> PREMIER STUNS FINNISH HOSTS WITH ATTACK ON THE WEST—HITS NATO ROLE

So much for Finnish neutrality.

However, as it turns out, the opera was not over, nor was that weekend's entertainment. At the bibulous dinner the birthday boy hosted that evening at his house, he made it clear that there were no hard feelings on his part for the earlier spectacle. Moreover, such was the nature of the mutually copacetic feelings Kekkonen had established with his unpredictable guest—not to mention the quantity of the liquid refreshments—that by the time the latter's spifflicated party went bobbling into the night, he had managed to obtain Khrushchev's acquiescence for Finland's application to join the newly formed European Trade Association (EFTA), which he, rightly, considered crucial to the country's livelihood.

The entry that evening in the journal which the Finns assiduously kept gives one some notion of the convivial nature of the two leaders' relationship, as well as literally high-spirited manner with which the Finns and Soviets conducted business in those bygone days: "The negotiations lasted until 5 A.M.," the exuberant presidential diarist penned as he sat in his study at Tamminiemi next to the elaborate phone console from which he essentially ran Finland. "We ate three times. A little was drunk [*sic*] and occasionally we sang."

The Soviet premier's decision to allow Finland to join EFTA, a move that his hard-line deputy premier Anastas Mikoyan ardently opposed, was the real coup. My friend the late Max Jakobson, Kekkonen's former press secretary, who later became a renowned historian in his own right, considered it the greatest achievement of his former boss's first term.

As Kekkonen wrote in his journal, "Khrushchev said to me several times 'You are a wizard when it comes to us.'" The CIA agreed. A 1972 historical report by the US intelligence agency said as much. "The Soviet agreement to tolerate Finland's association with EFTA," it concluded, was based "primarily on the good relations between Kekkonen and Khrushchev." Indeed those relations were a mite *too* good for Anastas Mikoyan and the other hard-liners on the Politburo. Khrushchev's partiality toward Kekkonen and Finland is reputed to have been one of the factors that led to his removal five years later.

In any event, Kekkonen was in an ebullient mood when 1961, the sixth and final year of his presidency, and the year of the Note Crisis, dawned. And little wonder. He had proven his command of the Finnish ship of state, gaining Moscow's grudging support for Finnish neutrality and its acquiescence to Finnish membership in EFTA, while securing an economic tow-line to the West.

Now, he felt, it was time to further bolster Europe's odd man out's still tenuous and poorly understood geopolitical position in the greater world by strengthening respect for Finnish neutrality in the West. Of course, there was still the little matter of the upcoming 1962 presidential election, but he was not too worried about that. Nor were Kekkonen's friends in Moscow. That would soon change.

In the meantime, the Cold War had significantly heated up. Indeed, if relations between Helsinki and Moscow were at a high point at the beginning of 1961, relations between Washington and Moscow were as fraught as ever, and getting more so. A brief period of good feeling between the two superpowers, the highlight of which had been Khruschev's 1959 visit to the United States, including to President Dwight D. Eisenhower's Gettysburg farm, had combusted after the U-2 incident of May 1960, leading to the infuriated the Soviet leader's storming out of the Paris summit meeting with his erstwhile American friend.

Far from being disheartened, Kekkonen saw the contretemps as his opportunity to prove Finland's value to both East and West by becoming a "bridge builder" between the two, as he saw his new diplomatic role, a kind of Switzerland of the north. Finland, he roundly declared in his New Year's speech, has a unique border between the East and West, one which has led to it become the setting for considerable bloodshed over the year. Was it not time for Finland to use its special position as a bridge builder between East and West?

Perhaps. To be sure, it took a few days for Kekkonen's friends at Tehtaankatu, as the Soviet embassy in Helsinki was called after the leafy street where it was located, or for the Politburo to process the new look in Finnish foreign policy, but soon enough the word came down that the Kremlin was okay with it. After all, the Soviets trusted him. To be sure, there were limits to the Soviets' trust, as the hopscotching Finnish president learned later that year at the end of his hitherto triumphant visit to the United States, but for now the ambitious Finnish president had the Kremlin's blessing to put Active Neutrality, as the new forward-looking Finnish foreign policy was called, into action.

At any rate, in February 1961, Kekkonen instructed his foreign ministry to lay the groundwork for a tour of the United States, including a meeting with its newly elected president, Kennedy, the first time a Finnish president had visited the US or was even asked to. Whether or not Kekkonen discussed his contemplated sortie with the Kremlin, or whether it would have approved it if he had, is not clear.

More importantly, Kennedy's secretary of state, Dean Rusk, approved the idea and sent a memo to President Kennedy endorsing it. "We have been worried about the Finnish posture towards the USSR since 1958 when Soviet pressure brought down the pro-Western Fagerholm government," Rusk wrote JFK on March 23, 1961. "Consequently," Rusk continued, "an informal visit by President Kekkonen to Washington would demonstrate our interest in Finland and could be used to encourage a firmer Finnish attitude towards the USSR."

As can be seen now, with his request for an "informal visit" to the US—which would ultimately morph into something just short of a full-blown state visit—Kekkonen had inadvertently set in motion one of the vectors that led to the Note Crisis. Meanwhile, as Rusk's memo confirmed, the Acheson/Dulles line on Finland was no longer in force. The "game" for Finland, in John Hickerson's phrase, was now on, more or less. How that game would wind up remained to be seen.

During the interim, the other vectors that eventuated in the Note Crisis, as well as the stakes for the three countries directly involved, Finland, the United States, and the Soviet Union, and their leaders, Kekkonen, Kennedy, and Khrushchev, respectively gained in moment.

Confident in his new self-anointed role as bridge-builder, the Finnish president went ahead with a series of highly publicized visits to London and Norway. Kekkonen's British sortie, in May, which featured a ride in an open carriage with Queen Elizabeth II and a rousing speech at a lunch in his honor at Guildhall, was especially successful.

You need not worry about Finland, Kekkonen told the impressed audience. If you looked at the map of Europe, he continued, you could see that Finland was the only one of the countries that survived World War II with its independence and social system intact. "This has not been without cost," he declared. "Both in war and peace we have had to defend our freedom. In the eyes of many people abroad, we Finns are living in a dangerous place."

"Be that as it may," he declared, "we have no wish to change our role."

"We ourselves, with bold and confident hearts," the Finnish leader closed, with a line that seemed directed as much to Moscow as to London and Washington, "we will continue to work for the preservation of peace and of our freedom." *Hear hear!*

So far so good. Kekkonen's Norwegian sortie, during which he took the opportunity to do the Kremlin's bidding and advise the Norwegian foreign minister and his Danish counterpart who was also on hand, to take the USSR's suggestion about creating a Nordic nuclear-free zone under strong consideration, was less successful. Fortunately the two upset diplomats kept mum about the kerfuffle. Anyway the photos of the robustly athletic Finnish president skiing around Oslo looked good.

In the meantime, to both Kekkonen's and Moscow's surprise, the matter of his reelection the following January no longer looked like a done deal. Although the Social Democrats, as expected, had put up a candidate, in this case an unprepossessing nonparty man by the name of Olavi Honka, who also happened to be chancellor of justice, what neither expected was how quickly the six opposition parties had united behind Honka, or how much support he had.

A poll in May showed Kekkonen leading Honka by 58 percent to 28 percent, a comfortable margin, but close enough to make both Kekkonen and his friends in Moscow agitated. Once again, as during the 1956 election, which he had barely won, this one was shaping up to be a real contest. An article in *The New York Times* captured the surprising turn of events, "The Finnish people, though, accustomed to unusual political maneuvering," it reported, "are now watching with incredulity the unfolding of a David and Goliath contest over the presidency."

So were Urho Kekkonen and Nikita Khrushchev. Clearly, there was more opposition to the Paasikivi-Kekkonen "line" than either expected or realized. This surprising development, in turn, bolstered the importance of the Finnish president's scheduled trip to North America, which Kekkonen saw as a golden opportunity for him to display his diplomatic skills to the Finnish people and the world, while bolstering Finnish neutrality.

In the meantime, relations between Washington and Moscow continued to deteriorate. After a promising start with the inauguration of Kennedy, the forward-looking US president, 1961 wound up being as perilous a year for world peace as fraught 1960. In the event, the spring and summer of that year saw a serious escalation of both the arms race, and the revived Berlin crisis which the tempestuous Soviet premier had ignited three years before.

Hopes for progress on both fronts dissipated after a disastrous meeting between Kennedy and Khrushchev in Vienna in June, which wound up with the Soviet leader browbeating his young and still relatively inexperienced American counterpart. If the US challenged the USSR's position in the divided German city, the Russian hectored, the latter would respond.

"It is up to the U.S. to decide whether there will be war or peace," Khrushchev declared.

"Then, Mr. Chairman," Kennedy responded, giving as good as he got, "there will be war." "It will be a cold winter," the shell-shocked American rued before exiting, even though it was still only spring. Things worsened from there.

In August Khrushchev decided, with the enthusiastic support of the East German leader, Walter Ulbricht, to ratchet up the pressure on the US, shutting down the border between East and West Berlin and erecting a concrete wall topped by barbed wire. Now the East-West conflict had a suitably forbidding symbol, and a killing zone to boot.

The following month, September, the USSR shocked the world—and Kennedy—by resuming nuclear testing, abrogating the moratorium on testing the two countries had signed in 1958. Over the next two months, Moscow conducted an average of one high altitude nuclear test every second day, to which Kennedy reluctantly followed suit. The cold winter which JFK had predicted after his confrontation with his Soviet counterpart in Vienna now bid fair to be the world's first nuclear winter, as panicky Americans began building bomb shelters.

For his part, Kekkonen did not seem too bothered by Moscow's decision to resume testing, on the evidence of his journal. "The Soviets do not want a repeat of the events of 1941," he wrote blandly on September 2nd, after a meeting with his friend, Aleksey Zakharov, the Soviet ambassador, when the matter came up. For the moment, he was more worried about his opponent in the forthcoming presidential election, Olavi Honka.

The issue of the Soviet atomic tests did come up three weeks later when the Finnish president welcomed Zakharov's comrade, Leonid Brezhnev, the Soviet president and future leader of the USSR, to Helsinki. We know that from the transcript of Kekkonen's pivotal October 16 meeting with Kennedy, during which Kekkonen confided that Moscow was planning to test its biggest device ever, as indeed it would in November.

But of course nothing in public was said about this during Brezhnev's visit, as the smiling Finn whisked the burly Soviet potentate around Helsinki. The big kiss that Brezhnev planted on the Finn's cheek when he pulled into Central Station said it all. He still had Moscow's trust. Or did he? Kekkonen and the world would soon find out.

Meanwhile, as the Kremlin was turning up the heat in the stratosphere with the new wave of nuclear tests, it continued its bully tactics over Berlin, pressing Washington to sign a separate peace treaty with its East German satellite, the so-called German Democratic Republic (GDR) and increasing the pressure by pouring thousands of Soviet troops into the Cold War battle zone, to which the frustrated US president responded in kind with American troops, leading to a face-off between Soviet and American forces at Checkpoint Charlie.

What did Khrushchev—or That Man in Moscow, as the US press sometimes called the infuriating Soviet leader—want? Did he really desire war? Kennedy could not figure him out. Apparently the CIA was not particularly helpful in this regard.

On October 15, 1961, the day before the Finnish president flew to Washington, *The New York Times* reported that President Kennedy had specially asked Llewelyn Thomas, the long-time US ambassador to Moscow, and virtually the only US diplomat who could be said to have a good relationship with Khrushchev, to remain at his post in order to help him decipher the combustible Soviet premier's intentions. Doubtless he also hoped that Kekkonen, the Western leader who enjoyed the best relationship with That Man, would help him figure out his impetuous Soviet counterpart as well. And of course he was curious about this "special relationship" between Finland and the Soviet Union which he had heard so much about.

Hence the open arms with which Kennedy and his wife Jacqueline greeted Kekkonen and his wife, Sylvi, when they stepped off the DC-2 at Anderson Air Force base that Kennedy had sent to fetch them from their last stop in Ottawa on the morning of October 16, 1961, as the US Air Force band played the Finnish and American anthems. "We respect you in peace, we respect you in war," Kennedy declared in his rousing welcome speech.

Kekkonen was thrilled to be there, as well. By accident rather than design, the Finnish head of state had arrived in Washington at one of the most explosive moments of the Cold War, and he was determined to make the most of it. And, naturally, he was keen to meet the charismatic young American president he had heard so much about. For his part, Kekkonen was somewhat skeptical of Kennedy. "So this is the Kennedy policy," he harrumphed in his journal in April after the botched Bay of Pigs invasion of Cuba.

And so on that fall afternoon sixty-four years ago the two presidents talked and probed, and jousted and took each other's measure as their respective foreign ministers and aides listened in, and the State Department's stenographer dutifully recorded the two hour long conversation, and Arthur Schlesinger, Jr., Kennedy's special assistant and future biographer took his own notes.

Interestingly, if not surprisingly, I found, when I compared the two transcripts, Schlesinger's record of the historic conclave was somewhat franker than the State Department's. Both are gold mines for anyone interested in either president or the Cold War. It is no accident that the longest chapter of *The Finnish Front Line* is devoted to the two-day powwow.

For the Kennedy scholar, the transcripts of the Finnish-American summit offer a frank look at the thirty-fifth president as he continued to grow into the demanding role of commander-in-chief. And clearly he had grown considerably in a short amount of time. Gone is the flailing Kennedy of April who had endorsed the CIA's disastrous plan for the invasion of Cuba.

The John Kennedy revealed here was not going to let Nikita Khrushchev get the better of him again, as he had in Vienna earlier that year. Here one can see the steel-nerved JFK who would face down exactly a year later during the Cuban Missile Crisis. Clearly the forty-four-year-old president was still in the midst of his learning curve, but he was getting there. And the fact that he was so interested in as well as knowledgeable about the affairs of a small country like Finland is a pleasant surprise.

Memorandum 189, the official title of the transcript, is no less valuable to the Kekkonen scholar, revealing him at both his best and his worst. Learned, articulate, never at a loss for an answer—even on occasion a disingenuous one—the top Finn comes across more or less as Kennedy's equal, as well as his elder, and one his American counterpart took a liking to and respected (as Schlesinger, who was a friend of the author, confirms in his diary).

One sees why Kekkonen put so much stock in personal diplomacy. He was good at it. One can also see why he was the right man for the position of Finnish president, at least at that time, and indeed, arguably, probably the only one. One can also see how he was clearly the democratic leader who knew the Soviets the best, which of course was one of the reasons why Kennedy was so anxious to meet him.

At the same time, one can also see Urho Kaleva Kekkonen's less attractive qualities. His arrogance, his tendency to be less than truthful—including with himself—his willful naivete, especially vis-à-vis Soviet intentions, are also on display in Memorandum 189.

How much Kennedy's understanding of That Man was furthered by the meeting is debatable. He does seem to have gotten a better grasp of Finland's challenging geopolitical situation, however, as well as the delicate balancing act the Finnish president had to play as he steered *Finlandia* between the Charybdis of the West and the Scylla of the East.

Interestingly, at one point of the chat, when the two men were discussing the tense situation in Berlin, Kekkonen mentions Article 2 of the 1948 Fenno-Soviet treaty, also known as the Agreement of Friendship, Cooperation and Mutual Assistance, the same explosive clause that Moscow would invoke two weeks later, triggering the Note Crisis. If one were looking for a smoking gun to prove that the Kremlin was already thinking of employing the clause, or had discussed using it with Kekkonen as an excuse to influence the outcome of the 1962 election, as some allege, there it is. It is hard to say.

In any event, neither Kennedy nor Dean Rusk, who was also sitting in on the meeting, along with Kekkonen's foreign minister and right-hand man, Ahti Karjalainen, seem to know about the trigger clause, or what it entailed. They certainly would get up to speed on it two weeks later, when the crisis broke.

The conversation that Kekkonen had the following day, October 17, with Rusk, Kennedy's hard-headed secretary of state, is equally fascinating, while also containing a portent of how the putative Finnish game would ultimately play out. At one point during the somewhat tetchy talk, which was noticeably less warm than the one Kekkonen had had the day before with JFK, Kekkonen reminds America's top diplomat that Finland "was not selling its neutrality abroad, but was seeking the understanding of the greater powers." "Demonstrative support for the policy," he added cryptically, "would not be helpful." Kennedy and Rusk would shortly know what Kekkonen meant.

Withal, if the two-day Finnish-American conclave was not exactly a meeting of minds, it definitely had been a meeting of friends, as the amiable joint communiqué Kennedy and Kekkonen issued on October 17, 1961—including the explicit recognition of Finnish neutrality, Kekkonen's main objective—underlined.

The two leaders clearly came away with an enhanced respect for each other. "Of all the U.S. presidents Kekkonen met," Jaakko Kalela, who would serve as his chief of staff during the 1970s, told me, "Kekkonen liked Kennedy the best." Schlesinger's comment in his unpublished diary confirms that the feeling was mutual. "A sturdy old man," he writes. "The President enjoyed the meeting very much." As proof he cites the fact that the meeting was considerably longer than the half hour scheduled.

Urho Kekkonen certainly was pleased. A key span of the bridge between East and West had been laid down. The policy of Active Neutrality, his updated version of the Paasikivi line, had now been validated by both Moscow and Washington. The pièce de résistance was the well-received speech Kekkonen gave the following day, October 18, at the National Press Club in which he expounded on the raison d'être for that policy—"The Finnish paradox," he called it.

"It would seem that when in a border country between East and West, the influence of the Western world is on the increase, the influence of the East would correspondingly diminish," the Finnish leader declared to the packed audience of journalists and diplomats. Finland was one of those countries. "But in our case," the distinguished guest from Helsinki continued, "the better we succeed in maintaining the confidence of the Soviet Union in Finland as a peaceful neighbor, the better are our opportunities for cooperation with the Western world." The positive coverage of Kekkonen's visit and speech confirmed that, after a long season in the postwar diplomatic wilderness, poor misunderstood Suomi had found its place, as well as its new role in the tumultuous postwar world, as had its visionary president.

Regarding the health of Finnish democracy, Kekkonen assured the audience at the National Press Club, in his sole reference to the ongoing presidential campaign, "if anyone had doubts of the vitality of our democratic institutions, "let him go to Finland to have a look at the vigorous presidential campaigning taking place there."

One suspects that some of the members of the Finnish press in attendance might have raised their eyes at that remark. The fact is, Kekkonen had studiously avoided campaigning and had yet to deliver a single speech.

Olavi Honka? Never heard of him.

But that was Kekkonen, too. At any rate the ebullient bridge builder certainly did not appear to be a man worried about anything, including his own political future, as he continued his triumphant American tour during the last two weeks of October 1961.

That was then. What a difference a month and one well-timed, explosive diplomatic note, coupled with a Tsar Bomb, can make.

So there Gufler, the US ambassador to Helsinki, was at Tamminiemi, on the evening of November 16, before Kekkonen's scheduled trip to meet Nikita Khrushchev to try to resolve the sudden crisis in Soviet-Finnish relations the aforementioned note had set off, reading the top secret message from his new friend, President Kennedy, offering to do everything he could to support the visibly beleaguered Finnish president short of going to war. The game for Finland, in John Hickerson's memorable phrase, was definitely on now.

In the event, Kekkonen's message was essentially the same one he had given Kennedy two weeks before after Andrei Gromyko had handed the shock note to Eero Wuori, the Finnish ambassador to Moscow, invoking the dread Article 2: thanks but no thanks. *This* time, during *this* crisis, Brave Little Finland, as Finland was known in America during the Winter War, would manage on its own. And so the following day, November 17, 1961, off Kekkonen flew for his appointment in distant Siberia with Chairman Khrushchev.

The rest is well-known. Khrushchev decided that bilateral military discussions were not necessary after all: the sword of Damocles hanging over Finland was withdrawn. The people of Finland, as well as the peoples of the other Nordic countries, especially neighboring Sweden, went to full alert in anticipation of a possible Soviet invasion, breathed a collective sigh of relief.

In the meantime, Olavi Honka, Kekkonen's opponent in the forthcoming election, withdrew his candidacy in the national interest. Moscow also was relieved. No longer did it have to fret about its dear friend, Kekkonen, facing opposition in the 1962 election, nor the one after that. Or the one after that. All told, the lord of Tamminiemi would serve another twenty years as Finnish president, before he was forced to retire in 1981 because of ill health.

The accommodationist Kekkonen line toward the Kremlin that had been forged during the Night Frost, and which the Note Crisis confirmed, would remain essentially intact for another thirty years, through the fall of the Soviet Union, although its vestiges, including Finnish neutrality and Finnish press self-censorship persisted for another thirty years until 2022, when Russia invaded Ukraine, giving Finns a case of bad déjà vu—shades of 1939 and the Winter War. The ghosts of Stalin and imperial Russia were back.

Today, Finland is a full-fledged member of NATO. The Finnish "game" is over. Now Suomi is irrevocably part of the West. And proudly democratic Finland, the NATO member with the longest contiguous border with Vladimir Putin's revanchist Russia, is very much back on the world's geopolitical map. And what, one wonders, would Urho Kekkonen, no less Nikita Khrushchev, have made of that?

Prologue
Mission to Kekkonen

LOCALE: Helsinki, Finland. The road to Tamminiemi, the home of Urho Kekkonen, the eighth president of Finland.

TIME: Late evening, November 1961.

FADE IN: An unmarked car belonging to the motor pool of the United States embassy, Helsinki is speeding out of town, en route to Meilahti, the Helsinki suburb where Tamminiemi, the palatial home and principal residence of Urho Kaleva Kekkonen, the Finnish president, is located.

The car has two passengers, Bernard Gufler, the current American ambassador, and Eric Youngquist, the twenty-three-year-old Finnish-speaking member of the embassy's economic section who served as interpreter. Gufler was posted to Helsinki in March. Previously he had served for two years as ambassador to Ceylon, as Sri Lanka was then known.[1]

Before that Gufler, a career diplomat who joined the US Foreign Service in 1929, had been the de facto ambassador of the US mission to Berlin in East Germany, where he was known for his antagonistic attitude toward the Soviet Union and its East German Communist surrogates on the other side of the recently erected Berlin Wall. Gufler's combativeness reportedly was one of the factors that led to his being posted to Colombo, something of a demotion.

Figure 1. President John F. Kennedy meets with seven of his ambassadors in the Oval Office, April, 1961. Bernard Gufler, the new envoy to Helsinki, is second from the left. Seven months later, at the height of the Note Crisis, Kennedy would entrust Gufler with a confidential letter to the Finnish president Urho Kekkonen offering his assistance.

His posting to Finland, the only democracy bordering the Soviet Union, then engaged in an increasingly tense "cold war" of nerves with the United States, was considered a step up. Thus far the fifty-eight-year-old diplomat had managed to keep his virulent anticommunism, as well as his skepticism about the so-called special relationship between Finland and the USSR—including President Kekkonen, who saw the management of that relationship as his principal job, and his alone—under wraps.

The president and the ambassador had a working relationship. Altogether Gufler had already made the fifteen-minute journey by automobile to Tamminiemi half a dozen times, beginning in April, when he first presented his credentials to the imperious, much-loved, much-despised Finn, then at the beginning of the sixth year of his first term as president.

This visit to Tamminiemi, however, was different from before—quite different, as a matter of fact. This time Gufler was carrying a letter from the US president, John F. Kennedy, addressed to Kekkonen. There was nothing innately extraordinary about that—presidents send letters to each other all the time—however this letter was *not* to be hand delivered. According to the explicit instructions the envoy had received from the US State Department, he was only supposed to read Kennedy's letter verbally.

"Message should be conveyed orally and written communication not left," the terse, top secret memo accompanying Kennedy's teletyped message stated. Also, Gufler's visit was supposed to be strictly *sub rosa*. "Approach should be made inconspicuously," the memo continued. Hence the unmarked car. "We [the US] wish to avoid public knowledge that American ambassador saw President immediately before his departure to meet [Nikita] Khrushchev."[2] No mention of Gufler's visit was supposed to be made to the press.

The precise date is November 21, 1961, day 1,543 of Kekkonen's presidency, day 23 of what would ultimately become known as the Note Crisis, the best known political crisis in Finnish history, and still the most controversial.

Briefly, the crisis began on October 30, while the Finnish president was relaxing with his entourage in Hawaii after what had been a successful tour of Canada and the US. The highlight of Kekkonen's visit, on October 16 and 17, was his stop in Washington, which included an elaborate luncheon at the White House for him and his wife, Sylvi, and two lengthy dialogues with Kennedy and Dean Rusk, JFK's interventionist-minded secretary of state. The extended *kaffie klatsch* was followed by a joint communiqué celebrating American-Finnish friendship and underlining President Kennedy's zealous support for Finnish neutrality.

Then, two weeks later, while Kekkonen and his advisors were still basking in the afterglow of his much-publicized visit, Andrei Gromyko, the po-faced Soviet foreign minister, handed Eero A. Wuori, the long-time Finnish ambassador to Moscow, a demarche invoking Article 2, the dread clause of the 1948 Fenno-Soviet Agreement of Friendship, Cooperation and and Mututal Assistance Treaty.

Said clause entitled either signatory to call for joint military consultations in the event of a serious threat of war by West Germany or its NATO allies via Finnish territory. With the new Berlin crisis, which the impulsive Soviet leader, Nikita Khrushchev, had triggered three years before, still boiling, the Kremlin contended that such a threat by the allegedly "revanchist" West German regime existed. Consequently such consultations between the military staffs of the two countries were a must.

The talks, if the Finns had agreed to participate in them, would unquestionably have damaged Finnish neutrality, while also reducing Suomi to the grand duchy status it held during Russian imperial days. Once again, Moscow had dropped the boom on the pesky Finns, just as it had three years before during the so-called Night Frost, except that this time the boom was accompanied by the very audible and lethal sound produced by the fifty-megaton atomic bomb the Soviets test-dropped in the Arctic several hours before Gromyko's meeting with Wuori (who may or may not have been a Soviet agent himself).[3] Anatoliy Golitsyn, the Helsinki-based KGB agent who later defected to the CIA, claimed that a number of Finnish officials were Soviet assets, among them Wuori. Or, as Halvard Lange, the outspoken Norwegian foreign minister drily put it, the heat-seeking note had been delivered "to the accompaniment of big explosions."[4] Coincidence? The last time anyone checked, Moscow did not traffic in coincidences.

Caught with his swimming trunks down (so to speak), Kekkonen (who happened to be an avid swimmer) initially downplayed the seriousness of The Note, as it came to be called, insisting that nothing about Finland's relationship with the nuclear-armed Neighbor to the East had really changed. He pointed out that the body of the strident-sounding letter had been directed against West Germany and its putatively bellicose Nordic NATO allies, Norway and Denmark. Finland had only been "the mail box" for the Soviet note, Kekkonen rationalized in his journal.

Nevertheless the truth was that it was the *Finnish* government to whom the demarche had been addressed, it was the *Finnish* government that Moscow was insisting on having joint military consultations with, and it was the *Finnish* government that would have to respond to that demand. *Keep calm and carry on* had been Helsinki's motto. And so, more or less, the Finnish public had, while their most cautious Swedish neighbors had begun preparations for evacuating their government, and making other preparations for the worst.

During the three weeks since it had been delivered, while Finland and its neighbors lived "in the shadow of the note," in Kekkonen's phrase, the Finnish president had done every thing he could to assuage Moscow and avoid the fact that his putative Soviet friends really *did* want to have those dreaded consultations, including dissolving the *eduskunta,* the Finnish parliament, in order to expedite the formation of a strong majority party government led by his party, the Agrarian League, as well as one that would be more favorable to the USSR, rather than the current weak minority one.

Meanwhile, the Kremlin continued to emphasize that it really *did* want to have those talks.

Or else.

Or else what? Who knew? A demand to include the Finnish communists in the next coalition government? A new Soviet base on Finnish soil? Who knew? As the foreign correspondents who had once again descended on Helsinki, as they had during the nerve-racking run-up to the Winter War twenty years before, noted, it was beginning to feel a lot like 1939 again. All was in suspense.

Finally, on November 19, day 22 of the crisis, the Finnish cabinet, in a Hail Mary move, had asked the Kremlin whether it would be all right if President Kekkonen might go to Moscow himself to meet with Chairman Khrushchev to try to resolve the situation and somehow put off the dread talks. After all, the two leaders, with their shared chemistry, had been able to resolve the last Fenno-Soviet crisis back in 1958, the so-called Night Frost, when Moscow put a six-month stranglehold on Finnish trade, while Kekkonen and his Soviet patron secretly confabulated in Leningrad.

Of course, the Night Frost had not affected the entire Baltic region, as *this* crisis had—if anything the political stakes (if not the economic ones) were even higher now. And the two men had not met in almost a year. But the Cabinet felt it was worth a shot.

In any event, to everyone's relief, Khrushchev had agreed to meet Kekkonen—not in Moscow, however, but in faraway Novosibirsk in Siberia, while the Soviet leader was on a tour of agricultural communes. Khrushchev would not come to Moscow to meet his Finnish friend. If his Finnish friend wished to see him, the Soviet Foreign Ministry announced, he would have to come to him.

Kekkonen agreed. It was set: the Soviet leader would receive the Finnish president at a cottage on the outskirts of Novosibirsk the following Friday, November 23, 1961. No Finnish or Western reporters would be allowed to attend.

A number of matters hinged on the outcome of the two leaders' secretive Siberian powwow. For one, the relationship between Finland and the USSR—or "the special relationship," as the onerous if mutually beneficial postwar relationship between Moscow and Helsinki was known—did.

So did the future of Finnish neutrality, which Kekkonen had just spent the better part of the year building up credibility for in the West. The Finnish government's much ballyhooed policy of "active neutrality," by which the hop-scotching president sought to have Finland become "a bridge between East and West," as he had put it in his New Year's speech, wouldn't mean very much if the Kremlin managed to force his military staff to "consult" with their Soviet counterparts, no less if it made the Finns accept a Soviet base on their soil, as some feared, would it? By the same token, if Finland's "special" relationship with the Soviet Union hung in the balance, so did its somewhat hazy relationship with the West, particularly the United States.

Ever since the end of the Second World War and the postwar Finnish rapprochement with the USSR, Washington had adhered to a strict hands-off policy vis-a-vis Finland and "the special relationship." Finland was too far away, and Juho Paasikivi and Kekkonen, the two presidents who had overseen Finnish foreign policy since 1946, when Gustaf Mannerheim, the former commander in chief of Finnish armed forces, retired, had been too kindly disposed to Moscow, and the risk of triggering an adverse Soviet reaction too great for the US to offer anything more than muted moral support and low-level economic aid.

As Dean Acheson, then US secretary of state, put it in a memo he wrote President Harry S. Truman in 1950, when Finland was laboring under the political weight of the 1948 Agreement of Friendship, Cooperation and Mutual Assistance, "it would be most dangerous to make any efforts in the direction of Finland that would produce a reaction on the part of the Russians."[5] Put simply, hands off.

Now, on the eve of Urho Kekkonen's fraught pilgrimage to Siberia, President Kennedy, on the strong advice of his activist-minded secretary of state, Rusk, had decided to revamp that policy. "If we continue to maintain a hands-off position [toward Finland]," Rusk warned Kennedy in the urgent memo he sent the president two days before, on November 20, "the Soviets are likely to achieve a good portion of their objectives," including "effective control" of the Finnish government," "weakening the determination of the Scandinavians to stand up to them," and "impairment of free world [*sic*] resolve." Consequently, Rusk declared, it was necessary to "accept a confrontation with the Soviets in Finland, despite all the advantages the USSR possesses in that area."[6]

In the phrase of Gufler's predecessor, Ambassador John D. Hickerson, who was envoy to Helsinki during the Night Frost three years before and had urged much the same thing, it was time to "get into the game" with Moscow over Finland. This "involve[d] a readiness to assist Finland in the political, economic and propaganda spheres," including publicly going to bat for Finland in the United Nations Security Council.[7]

According to the aggressive new American line, the US not only respected Finnish neutrality, it was willing to *fight* for it in every way short of war. Even though the threat of a literal Russian invasion was slim, the threat of Finland being reduced to a Soviet satellite was substantial—substantial enough for the US to become more involved. Finland was *more* than another neutral now, Rusk maintained, it was an *allied* neutral. The northeastern border of the Free World now extended to the Fenno-Soviet border, and Finland was a proxy for Western interests.

The only problem with this new equation, Rusk conceded, was the person to whom the Free World was entrusting as surrogate for its interests—Urho Kaleva Kekkonen. The simple fact was that Rusk did not trust Kekkonen. The Finnish president was too "pliable," the State Department's favorite word to describe him, along with "clever." Still, given the situation, the US did not have much choice *but* to trust Kekkonen. "While [Kekkonen] has shown himself in our view overly pliable in the past in relations with the USSR," Rusk wrote, "there seems to be no alternative but to place reliance in the first instance upon him."[8]

The following day, November 21, JFK hastily endorsed the new US line on Finland and approved the fighting message Rusk had composed for him, which then had been cabled to Ambassador Gufler. Now Gufler was carrying that message to Tamminiemi to impress it on its presidential resident. "On the eve of your departure for Novosibirsk I am sending you this private message," read the key line of the top secret message to Kekkonen, "so that you may not be in doubt of the position of the United States."[9]

"You will appreciate that our concern in this matter derives not alone from our great interest in the welfare of your country. We have placed on ourselves a solemn obligation to respect that neutrality at all times and in all ways." By the same token, Kennedy's letter continued, "In our own national interest we have to expect that in turn Finland will in fact be truly neutral."[10]

In football terms, Rusk had relayed the ball to Kennedy, the metaphorical quarterback for the US team. Kennedy had now had "thrown" it to his man down the field, Gufler, who was about to pass it on to Kekkonen, who was expected to carry the ball for the West. The question was: would he? Would Kekkonen give his putative friend, Nikita Khrushchev, as good as he got when they met in Novosibirsk?

Gufler's unmarked car was approaching Tamminiemi now.

Above all, neither John Kennedy nor Dean Rusk wished to pressure Kekkonen, who himself was something of a combustible quantity, or to be seen as doing so. Three years before, during the Night Frost, the Finnish president had haughtily—and publicly—rejected an offer of American aid.

Three weeks before, at the start of the current crisis, Kennedy had also—publicly—reached out to Kekkonen. This time his rejection was more polite. "Thanks, no thanks," the Finnish president had instructed his military aide-de-camp to reply to a note from JFK, whom he had just met in Washington two weeks before, whether there was anything he could do for his Finnish counterpart, now that Moscow was breathing down again. Later, after returning to Finland from Hawaii, Kekkonen had publicly disclosed Kennedy's note and his polite rebuttal to Washington's distress.[11]

That was then; this was now. Three weeks earlier, the Finnish president had been confident that he was in control of the situation. Now, as JFK's envoy would see by the "desperate" visage of the man who greeted him at Tamminiemi, as he later described it, clearly he was not.

Three weeks earlier, Kekkonen had been confident that the situation would resolve itself. Now he was not.

More important, or just as important, *now* the White House was offering to do much more for Finland. "We would be willing to carry to the United Nations actions seeming to threaten your country's independence," the secret letter Gufler was carrying in his diplomatic pouch read.[12] Put another way, Kennedy was prepared to make the Finnish crisis a test of America's will to stand up to the Kremlin, in effect to the new Berlin.

Now the US was prepared to go to the mat for its sister republic. The question was would President Kekkonen be willing to go to the mat for the US and the West when he met Khrushchev in Siberia? Above all, Ambassador Gufler's visit was supposed to be secret. "Should press learn of your meeting suggest you [should] say only that you called to obtain President Kekkonen's views," the memo accompanying JFK's letter read. "You should agree with Kekkonen beforehand on this line to be followed with press in case of queries or leaks."[13]

Doubtless, if it did leak, there would be an explosion. Who knew how would Nikita Khrushchev or his suspicious comrades react then?

CHAPTER 1

Stormy Weather (2/56–1/57)

> Kekkonen at the present moment is the man who would be the best president after me. But he ought to restrain his ambition so that he does not muddle his ideas. He places too much emphasis on Russian support. Amongst his own people he has no support at present except in his own party, and then not entirely. But the president of Finland is not and must not simply be a Russian governor. Kekkonen ought to seek support amongst his own people.
>
> —Diary of President Juho Paasikivi, 1950

> The Finnish nation stands at the beginning of the new political path determined for it. Broad, ready-built roads are closed to us. We must construct a new national course through marshland and mountains. Fortunately we are a pioneering nation, whose physical endurance and mental perseverance help it to carry through whatever difficulties face it.
>
> —Radio speech that Urho Kekkonen gave after the armistice following the Continuation War, September 1944

> He loved bad weather, the worse the better. He was always happiest when the weather was stormy. I think it appealed to his sense of conflict.
>
> —General Juha Engstrom, former aide-de-camp

(NEWSREEL)

Open to scenes of pitched fighting between striking workers and mounted policemen in Senate Square. It is March 1, 1956, the first day of the first term of the newly elected president, Urho Kaleva Kekkonen. Hours before, the new Finnish president had been ushered into office to the accompaniment of fanfare and the grandest inauguration since 1937. Unfortunately for Kekkonen, his inauguration also coincided

FIGURE 2. A smiling Urho Kekkonen, then Finnish prime minister, with his mentor, President Juho Paasikivi, at an official event, 1954. Paasikivi was fond of his protégé, but feared the latter's eagerness to accommodate the Kremlin.

FIGURE 3. General (formerly colonel) Juha Engstrom, who served as Urho Kekkonen's aide-de-camp during his fifth and last term as president, from 1977 until Kekkonen's retirement in 1981. Photo taken by the author from the interview he conducted with Engstrom in Helsinki in 2014. "He always liked stormy weather," said Engstrom.

with the first general strike since the birth of the Finnish Republic nearly half a century before.

According to historian David Kirby, Kekkonen's "first term of office was particularly difficult."[1] If anything that was an understatement.

Indeed, no peacetime Finnish president started office under such adverse conditions—or with such a heavy cross to bear. The narrow circumstances of Kekkonen's victory, the unstable state of postwar Finnish politics, a long-running prices and incomes crisis that exploded into a general strike by the Trade Workers' Federation, along with the withdrawal of dairy products by the enraged national farmers' organization, among other things, all contributed to a baptism under fire unlike any other of his peacetime predecessors had faced.

Most importantly, Kekkonen had to prove to his countrymen, many if not most of whom still hated the Russians, that not only was his predecessor's policy of going along to get along with Moscow the correct one, indeed the only sensible one to follow—but that *he* was the best person, indeed the only one, who was qualified to execute it; while *also* convincing Kremlin hard-liners that he was the best partner to carry the Paasikivi line, as the accommodationist policy vis-à-vis Moscow confirmed under his predecessor was known, forward.

All of this came at a time of increasing tension between East and West, tensions that would peak five years later in 1961, at the height of the second Berlin Crisis, which Nikita Khrushchev, the Soviet premier, had impulsively triggered in 1958, during the midst of the extended Night Frost drama.

Not that everything the Russians themselves did made total sense. Although favorably disposed to him, Kekkonen's putative Russian partners, particularly the volatile Khrushchev, often did not make his job easier.

And yet, somehow, Kekkonen and Khrushchev *did* become friends, despite the fact that Kekkonen could not speak Russian, a formidable achievement. "There was real affection between the two men," said Sergei Khrushchev, the late son of the Soviet chairman, and his close advisor. "Of course, it took some time for it to develop."[2]

At the same time, the new Finnish president constantly had to fend off criticism both from domestic critics and the West that he was getting too close to his Soviet partners, and was so eager to do their bidding as to make Finland something of a quasi-Russian satellite—charges that would surface again and again during his twenty-five-year-long tenure. Withal, it was quite a tightrope for the new president to walk, one he continued to walk, with varying degrees of ease, for the next quarter century. That said, Kekkonen managed the feat well during his first shaky term, even while his bearish friends in the Politburo made that tightrope as wobbly as possible.

To an American, reading the record of Fenno-Soviet relations in *The New York Times* and the *Times* of London from the first nerve-racking year of Kekkonen's tenure, which coincided with the uprising by the Finns' ethnic cousins, the Hungarians, and Moscow's brutal suppression of same, which horrified Finland, and deeply embarrassed Kekkonen; through the Night Frost crisis of the fall of 1958, when Moscow precipitated the fall of a Finnish government headed by Karl-August Fagerholm, his Social Democratic opponent in the 1956 election, and co-father-in-law, which was not to its liking and suspended trade relations; through the relatively halcyon 1959 to 1961 period, which coincided with the U-2 espionage crisis and the Second Berlin Crisis; through the Note Crisis of the fall of 1961, when, at least to some Finns, a Soviet invasion seemed a real possibility, one is struck by how often, as well as in how many different ways, and how brazenly Moscow intimidated Helsinki.

Of course, this only undermined Kekkonen's domestic and international position, no matter how heavily the clumsy Khrushchev was patting him on the back. Quite a tightrope dance. One wonders, in retrospect, how Kekkonen managed to maintain his personal balance through it all.

In fact, as we shall see, sometimes he did not.

In any event, however one characterizes it, whether the Finnish president gave in to the Russians too much, as his critics contended, and still contend, or just enough, as his supporters counter, Kekkonen's essentially single-handed management of Fenno-Soviet relations, particularly during his fraught first term, certainly qualifies as one of the more impressive one-man balancing acts in the history of international politics. At least he did not fall off—although he came close, particularly during the extended, somewhat farcical, deeply traumatic, now virtually forgotten Night Frost episode.

Another thing that strikes this historian, as he flips through the old microfilmed pages of *The New York Times* and the *Times* of London, both of which maintained offices in Helsinki in the 1950s and 1960s, was how closely reported and analyzed Finnish developments were. Not since the Winter War had the world's spotlight shone as brightly on the world's northernmost country. That was because Finland, living cheek by jowl with its nuclear-armed neighbor, chief benefactor, and trade partner, was situated on the front lines of a still very hot Cold War. And right in the center of that spotlight, his actions and statements pondered, parsed over, and criticized, was Kekkonen.

Did Urho Kaleva Kekkonen thrive on stormy weather? There certainly was plenty of it during his first six years in office.

FIGURE 4. A grim-faced Urho Kekkonen descends the steps of the eduskunta, the Finnish parliament, on March 1, 1956, following his inauguration as eighth president, accompanied by Paasikivi, his predecessor. Kekkonen had reason to be grim: the lavish inaugural coincided with Finland's first general strike since independence.

An editorial that appeared in *The New York Times* on March 2, 1956, the day after Kekkonen was inaugurated, conveyed the combination of hope, puzzlement, and high expectations, both on the part of the Finnish people and observers in the West, which greeted the newly christened Finnish head of state.

> Dr. Urho Kekkonen was inaugurated as Finland's eighth president this week almost simultaneously with the beginning of an economic catastrophe in that country, the beginning of a struggle between organized workers and organized farmers. The general strike ordered by the Finnish Trade Union Federation and the retaliatory stoppage of food deliveries by farmers have posed a problem which will call for statesmanship on the part of the President and other Finnish leaders.

How had the down-to-earth Finns, known for their practicality and common sense and *sisu*, the Finnish word that roughly translates as perseverance, allowed matters to come to such a sorry and chaotic state? the *Times* wondered. "We in this country, whose admiration for the admirable qualities of the Finnish people is of long standing, can only express bewilderment that internal economic tensions were permitted to come to so explosive a result."[3] Hopefully Kekkonen, the former prime minister and long-time Finnish political fixture, still largely an unknown quantity in the West, would be able to knock some sense into his countrymen's heads and get Finland working again.

More importantly, since steering the country's foreign policy was the new president's most important brief—although Kekkonen would ultimately expand his portfolio to incorporate all sectors of Finnish life—the newspaper fervently hoped that on his watch Finland would continue to live in peace with its restive Soviet neighbor, but also with honor. To *The New York Times*, at least, that also meant getting the Kremlin to return or relinquish even more of the former Finnish territories it had acquired or seized as reparations for the Winter War and the Continuation War, the two wars within World War II which Finland had fought against the Soviets, and lost.

Now, remarkably, here was America's most influential newspaper explicitly encouraging such irredentist fantasies:

> Finland's new President has pledged himself to a policy of peace and friendship with the Soviet Union. That the Finnish people wish to live in peace with the Soviet Union is understandable.

"But friendship is a two-way street, and the return of the Porkkala naval base," the editorial continued, referring to the naval base Helsinki had been forced to relinquish to Moscow after the war and which it had now returned, "far from expunges Soviet obligations to Finland. The wounds of Russia's unprovoked aggression in the 'winter war' of more than a decade and a half ago, have still not been healed."

> We of the West know and admire Finland's brave fight for independence from foreign domination. As we wish President Kekkonen well in his heavy new responsibilities, we do so in the hope that he will measure up to the aspirations of his people.[4]

What did *that* mean? Wisely, the paper refrained from saying. But of course anyone who knew anything about Finland knew what *that* meant: it meant *also* recovering the part of historically Finnish Karelia forcibly annexed by the Soviet Union after the Winter War and which it reannexed after the second and final Fenno-Soviet armistice following the Continuation War in 1944.

Wishful thinking? Perhaps not. To be sure, during the wild and wooly 1956 presidential campaign, the Agrarian League had dropped strong hints that if its candidate, Kekkonen, was elected that Moscow would return some or all of the territories it had gained after the war, hints that he himself did nothing to discourage. Now, incredibly, here was America's most prominent newspaper urging the newly inaugurated president to do just that.

Doubtless Kekkonen, who felt strongly about the Karelian question, perhaps even expected his new "friends" in the Kremlin to make his pipe dream come true. Such was the roseate, and wildly unrealistic atmosphere that followed as word of the shock speech that Khrushchev made just the week before to the twentieth Congress of the Communist Party of the Soviet Union (CPSU) denouncing Joseph Stalin's crimes filtered out to the rest of the world. If Nikita Khrushchev was capable of such brave new thinking, many thought, perhaps he could be persuaded to give back Karelia, particularly since Stalin's principal rational excuse for seizing Karelia in the first place—to protect Leningrad from a land invasion from the West—had been rendered moot by the missile age.[5]

Speculation that a Karelian giveback was possible was further fueled the following spring and summer by two portentous announcements: firstly, that the Karelo-Finnish Soviet Republic, the faux Soviet republic, headed by Finland's most infamous turncoat, Otto Wille Kuusinen—would be folded into the USSR proper, along with the subsequent announcement that Stalinist holdover and survivor of the Kremlin wars, Marshal Kliment Voroshilov, chairman of the Supreme Soviet and nominal Soviet head of state, would visit Finland in August.[6]

Perhaps the aging marshal, who oversaw Stalin's original botched invasion of Finland in 1939—the not-so-hidden objective of which was to annex Finland, including Karelia, in the first place—would kick-start the process of returning Karelia when he came, some Finns—including many if not most of the estimated four hundred thousand displaced Finnish Karelians, who had since been resettled in the homeland—hoped—and perhaps his host, President Kekkonen, did as well. Would that not be poetic, as well as historical, justice, as well as a major public relations coup, both for the new "peaceful coexistence"-minded Kremlin, and Kekkonen?

Unfortunately, as things turned out, Marshal Voroshilov did *not* bring a promise to return Karelia with him when he made his "triumphant" return to his old revolutionary stalking grounds on August 19th, 1956. Indeed, it seems, Voroshilov's putative good will visit was something of a bust.[7]

The two brief, barbed dispatches about his visit that ran in *The New York Times*, on the nineteenth, the day the marshal arrived, and another one, on the twenty-fifth, when he departed, tell the story.

Herewith the first:

VOROSHILOV TO FINLAND

Soviet President on Visit Will See Old Hideout Places

HELSINKI, Finland, Aug. 19—Marshal Kliment Y. Voroshilov, Chairman (President) of the Presidium of the Supreme Soviet, is going to revisit some old Bolshevist hideouts in a five-day tour of Finland this week.

In prerevolutionary days, Marshal Voroshilov, now 75, recruited men and weapons in areas of Finland, then a part of Czarist Russia. Stalin, Lenin and Voroshilov frequently hid out in Finnish territory when things got too hot for them in the interior of Russia.

President Urho Kekkonen of Finland has arranged tours of Central Finland, where Marshal Voroshilov can revive old memories. Marshal Voroshilov arrives Tuesday.[8]

The second read:

VOROSHILOV LEAVING FINLAND

HELSINKI, Finland, Aug. 25—Kliment Y. Voroshilov, chairman of the Presidium of the Supreme Soviet, today wound up a week-long goodwill tour of Finland that appeared to have made little impression on the Finnish man in the street. The 75-year-old Russian leader visited an old folks home, dropped in on a farm family and dined with Finnish President Urho Kekkonen today. He will leave for Moscow tomorrow.[9]

Evidently some memories of the brutal winter of 1940 died hard.

So much for returning Karelia. Not for Urho Kekkonen, however. By numerous accounts, including those of several of his closest advisors, he never stopped dreaming of getting Karelia back from Moscow and would often bring it up in his subsequent meetings with Soviet leaders over the next twenty years. "This was always his secret dream—to get Karelia back," said Kauko Sipponen, Kekkonen's chief of staff from 1973 to 1976.[10]

Sergei Khrushchev, the late son and confidante of Nikita, also recalled the Finnish president's Karelia-*nostalgie*, which became something of a wistful leitmotif of his father's relationship with Kekkonen when the author interviewed him in 2016. "Yes, he often spoke about recovering Karelia," said Khrushchev. "My father never exactly said 'no.' But he never said yes."[11] "I used to have to tell him to hold off on it a bit," Khrushchev junior continued. He refused to accept that for Lenin Finnish independence was just a temporary state," Sipponen, Kekkonen's former chief of staff, said. "Actually, he could be quite silly about it," the latter recalled.[12]

Not that there was very much for a realistic observer of world affairs to be silly, or romantic about in the year of 1956, particularly the latter

FIGURE 5. One of the happier moments of Kekkonen's tumultuous first year in office was the visit of United Nations general secretary Dag Hammarskjold in July 1956. Finland became a member of the UN in 1955, after Moscow withdrew its objections.

part, as the Cold War continued to heat up and the limits of the Kremlin's new supposedly reformist era became brutally clear.

Any illusions about the Politburo's liberal tendencies disappeared in November of that year, when the Kremlin dispatched a thousand Soviet tanks to Budapest to suppress the Hungarian Revolution. The revolt, and the brutal Soviet crackdown, which resulted in the deaths of over 2,500 Hungarians and the arrest (and eventual execution) of reformist Hungarian premier Imre Nagy, provided an early test of just how "friendly" Kekkonen could be to Moscow when circumstances dictated. In this case, as well as in other touchy matters involving Soviet behavior and policies, this meant essentially saying nothing.[13]

As the Finnish scholar Vesa Vares has written, "the fears," both domestically, and abroad, about Kekkonen's pliability, seemed to come true, "and the first real evidence seemed to come during the Hungarian uprising." As evidence of Kekkonen's "subservience," as Vares terms it, he cites the Foreign Ministry's subsequent reluctance, doubtless on Kekkonen's orders, to contribute to the report of the UN Special Committee on the Hungarian Uprising, which Moscow opposed, as well as the Finnish president's refusal to denounce Nagy's execution, and his move "to suppress the "moral outcry which the executions [of Nagy and his aides] deserved from every democratic and free man."[14] For Kekkonen, keeping mum about the murderous Soviet crackdown was a matter of painful expediency. Who knew what other imperialistic notions the hard-liners in the Kremlin had, now that the true fist within the deceptive, "reformist" Soviet glove had been revealed?[15]

Just what sort of designs Kremlin hard-liners had vis-à-vis Finland during the fall of 1956 and winter of 1957 were revealed in June 1958 when Arvo Tuominen, the former Finnish communist leader turned Social Democrat, published an explosive letter in *Helsingin Sanomat*, Finland's leading newspaper. In the letter, Tuominen—a one-time candidate member of the Soviet Communist Presidium who had been offered, and rejected, the presidency of the People's Democratic Republic of Finland, the short-lived puppet state that Stalin created to replace the Finnish Republic in 1939—revealed the contents of a secret meeting that took place between Finnish communist leaders and Dmitri Shepilov, the then Soviet foreign minister in Moscow in February 1957.[16]

According to Tuominen, Shepilov, after noting his "astonishment" at the panic that Soviet actions in Hungary had stirred in Finland and left-wing circles elsewhere in Europe, went on to tell his stunned Finnish comrades that the Soviet Army's bloody suppression of the Hungarian uprising was neither "incomprehensible nor unique," and that the Red Army was "not only for Russia but was a liberation army for the whole world's proletariat." No less remarkably, Shepilov added that if the Finnish communists were able, even temporarily, to "create a situation" similar to that which Janos Kadar, the hard-liner who succeeded the murdered Nagy, "when the formalities were in order and there was reason to ask the Russian Army help suppress a bourgeois and Social-Fascist counter-revolution, then the Russian Army was ready to come."[17] Tuominen, the communist-turned-socialist, speculated that his former Russian comrade, Shepilov, who since had been dismissed by Khrushchev, was cashiered in part because of such "wild" talk.[18]

In any event, neither the British nor Washington were really in a position to criticize Helsinki—particularly after their own failure to do anything to succor the beset Hungarians. Moreover, as was evident by the record of the West's actions, or more accurately, lack of action, during the Winter War, when the Allies dithered about assisting Finland, if push came to shove, and the Soviet Army came crashing over the Fenno-Soviet border once again, the Finns were very much on their own. That was the lesson that Kekkonen, who had been bitterly disappointed by the West's failure to succor Finland during the *Talvisota*, as Finns called the Winter War, had taken from the back-to-back Fenno-Soviet wars, including the so-called Continuation War that followed it, during which nearly 100,000 Finnish soldiers and civilians died and over twice as many —including Kekkonen's brother, Jussi, who was blinded—had been wounded.[19]

And that was the bitter and necessary truth that both Paasikivi and now Kekkonen yet more fervently impressed, and would keep on trying to impress on their countrymen. And if this meant keeping mum about the atrocities being committed against the Finns' Hungarian Fenno-Ugric cousins, or otherwise being in selective denial about Moscow's behavior—so be it. This, to Kekkonen, was the price of the heavily circumscribed freedom Moscow had granted Helsinki, as well as his own political survival, even if it meant abasing himself.

In his memoirs, Viktor Vladimirov, the then KGB station chief or *rezident* in Helsinki, describes the difficult position which Moscow's crackdown put their Finnish partner in. "In 1956 the USSR made a military intervention in the uprising in Hungary to suppress an uprising against the current regime," he wrote. "The Hungarian crisis had a very negative impact on the already strained trust towards the USSR in Finland. Also, it was a difficult situation for President Kekkonen, who was forced to go against public opinion, and not condemn the Soviets for Hungary."

Nevertheless, the former Soviet spy maintains, "Kekkonen finally managed to resolve the situation without losing face. For its part, of course, the Kremlin was pleased and relieved. For the Soviets, who had never entirely forgotten Kekkonen's virulent anticommunist past, his silence about the Hungarian bloodbath helped confirm their sense that they had a reliable partner in Kekkonen.[20]

And so he did, for the remainder of his first term, with the exception of a memorable speech he gave during Khrushchev's second visit to Helsinki in September, 1960 (more about that anon). "There was a certain dependence there [on Moscow]," says Jaakko Kalela, who joined Kekkonen's office as chief foreign policy advisor seventeen years later, in 1973, and continued to work for him until the end of his presidency and, some say, is the living person who knew him the best, regarding his still controversial actions and statements vis-à-vis the USSR, especially during his stormy first term. "But," Kalela declares, "he [Kekkonen] played his own game."[21] Did he? That much was not clear yet. To all appearances the Urho Kekkonen of his first term played by Nikita Khrushchev's rules—or at least he did when he was able to understand them.

(NEWSREEL)

Flash forward eight months to June, 1957. Scenes from the British Pathe newsreel, "Bulganin and Khrushchev Visit Finland." Nikolai Bulganin, the kindly looking, goateed Soviet premier and his barrel-chested companion, Nikita Khrushchev, the head of the Soviet Communist Party, exit Helsinki's Central Station clutching bouquets and wave to a crowd of several thousand Soviet and Finnish flag waving "well-wishers" and curiosity seekers (mostly the latter to judge from the newsreel), assembled to greet them. Cut to long distance shot of a motorcade of Cadillac limousines slowly winding its way past the station in the direction of the harbor and the presidential palace.

Cut to the palace, where the broadly smiling Finnish president strides into the room and greets his guests effusively, vigorously pumping Bulganin's hand first, as per protocol, then Khrushchev's, as Andrei Gromyko, the Soviet foreign minister, happily looks on.

This roving two-man performance was called "the B and K Show," and for several years in the mid-1950s it was the biggest spectacle in international diplomacy, as the two Russian potentates flew or sailed around the world accepting bouquets, reviewing honor guards, and immersing themselves as best as they could in the cultures and customs of diverse foreign lands. The two Soviet leaders' forays abroad, particularly their visit to London in June, 1956, when they called on Queen Elizabeth II and visited a factory in Manchester, and an even longer journey "B and K" made to India in November, when they journeyed to the heart of the subcontinent, did much to dispel the Kremlin's gloomy postwar image, notwithstanding Bulganin's tendency to commit verbal gaffes, such as when he compared he compared Gandhi to Lenin during a stop in Calcutta.

Then, several months later, came the Hungarian uprising and the frightening images of Russian tanks speeding through the streets of Budapest and the good feelings engendered by the earlier images of the two chatting up the queen and taking tea in Tamil Nadu just as soon vanished.

Bulganin and Khrushchev's post-Budapest visit to Helsinki in June, 1957 had a threefold objective: to help repair the Kremlin's' problematic public image; to improve the still shaky state of Fenno-Soviet relations, including increasing trade with the USSR, which had declined at the end of 1956; and last but not least, to show the Kremlin's support of its "friend" Kekkonen, and his estimable predecessor, Juho Paasikivi, whose grave the two Soviet magnificoes visited on their first day in Finland.[22]

As such, the visit was a mixed success, although one would never know it from reading the front-page article in *Helsingin Sanomat* describing the lavish dinner at the presidential palace that the Finns threw for their Russian guests, including the effusive speech with which Kekkonen kicked off the fête. In his unabashedly sycophantic remarks, the Finnish president thanked his guests for paying homage to Paasikivi's grave, and their efforts to follow in his predecessor's pacific steps. "There is no reason to hide the fact that at first we were reluctant to go down this road," he declared, referring to the uneasy postwar Fenno-Soviet rapprochement.

"But when it was seen that the Soviet Union consistently respected Finland's freedom and independence, and from this base wished to build a friendly relationship with Finland, all doubts and misunderstandings vanished," he continued as the hundred odd Russian and Finnish guests, seated around a huge horseshoe-shaped table festooned with seven hundred carnations and ninety candles, tucked into their *velout de morilles* and *poussin roti a la Finlandaise*, washed down with a wine list featuring Dry Sack Rupperts Berger Hofs Tuck 1953 and Chateau Cortin Crancey 1952, according to *Sanomat*'s meticulously detailed account.

"Over the years, trust, mutual assistance and understanding have only become stronger," the Finnish head of state affirmed. As was his wont on such occasions, Kekkonen devoted part of his speech to the domestic and foreign critics of the accepted postwar Finnish foreign policy vis-à-vis Moscow now also known as the Paasikivi-Kekkonen line. "I've noticed that when people have criticized the new road that Finland has taken in its foreign policy, they have mentioned that our policy is dictated by necessity."

"But," he proclaimed, "does that necessarily devalue such a policy?"[23]

PRESIDENT KEKKONEN: SUSPICIONS AND MISUNDERSTANDINGS HAVE EVAPORATED

Helsingin Sanomat trumpeted.[24]

To be sure, all was definitely not sweetness and light during the two Soviet officials' week-long Helsinki engagement. According to Drew Middleton, the distinguished, long-time foreign correspondent of *The New York Times*, the efforts of the two Politburo members to sell Soviet friendship to the Finns seemed to have made little headway.[25] According to Middleton, the Finns, who already relied on the USSR for 20 percent of their trade, encountered "amiable pressure" from the Kremlin to buy even more from the Kremlin, and less from the West. This pressure would be renewed with a vengeance later that year, and even more so the following year, 1957, culminating in the Night Frost episode. Despite a helpful nudge from Kekkonen, who was striving to endear himself with the Kremlin, Finnish industry resisted.

Even an offer from the visiting Reds to send the renowned Bolshoi Ballet to Helsinki reportedly drew only "polite interest." The Finnish public, too, was also underwhelmed by the B and K Show, according to Middleton. When the leaders emerged from their talks "looking expectant, the American wrote, "Soviet photographers flashed their bulbs," but "the crowd of Finns stood with blank faces," while others turned their backs.[26] Khrushchev and Bulganin's visit to parliament, which included a flash of Khrushchev's famous temper, evidently went no better. At one point the communist potentates stopped to sign the visitors' book, but not before Bulganin, the Soviet premier, insisted on reading it first. "Bulganin is a banker," cracked Khrushchev. "He never signs anything he doesn't read. I can sign anything!"[27]

At one point, the once and future prime minister, now speaker of parliament Karl-August Fagerholm, tried to make small talk with the two Soviets: mistake. As head of the Communist party, Khrushchev must be an important person, Fagerholm suggested hopefully, unaware that Khrushchev was only appearing officially as a member of the Soviet Presidium—not that the distinction fooled anyone.

Nevertheless Khrushchev seized the opportunity to attack the Finnish Social Democrat. "Did I say the party is important?" Khrushchev lashed out at the hapless Finn. Prescient encounter: eighteen months later Khrushchev, who like the rest of the Politburo despised the Social Democrats, would force Fagerholm, by then prime minister, to resign. Indeed, one gathers from *The New York Times*'s account, the two Soviets' sortie was more or less a flop, both from a public relations and business point of view. At any rate, no new Fenno-Soviet business contracts were announced. *Business Week*, which also sent its correspondent to Helsinki to cover the two Soviets' "historic" trip to Helsinki, saw it the same way:

> The Finnish people were preparing to bid a farewell as cool as their welcome to two formidable visitors from the neighbor to the East—the Soviet Union. For a week, Soviet Premier Nikolai Bulganin and Russian [*sic*] Communist Party boss Nikita Khrushchev have been smiling benignly at the Finns. But the smiles have made little more impression than the hints that if only Finland would accept Soviet friendship and trade, its 4.3 million people would find a comfortable niche in the Soviet bloc.[28]

As it happened, both the Finnish and Western press missed the most significant, and constructive, result of Bulganin's and Khrushchev's visit, one that took place largely away from the public eye—the beginning of Kekkonen's relationship, and authentic, if somewhat quixotic friendship with Khrushchev.

Remarkably, Kekkonen was such an adroit actor that he was able to persuade Khrushchev to take an unscheduled and very unofficial sauna with him before he left. To be sure, a character trait of Kekkonen's that many of his extant close associates still remark on was his chameleon-like quality and preternatural ability to transform himself to suit the occasion and his "audience," irrespective of station, whether he or she be a monarch or a miner, and still come off as sincere. Or as Jaakko Iloniemi, who worked with Kekkonen in various capacities, including undersecretary of state and ambassador to Washington, during the latter decade of the Kekkonen regency put it, "Kekkonen could be a prince with a prince, or a farmer with a farmer."[29]

Khrushchev, of course, was neither. He certainly was no prince. He *was* a former miner; not quite the same thing, but close enough. Indeed, on the surface, the two men could not have been more different, as Vladimirov, the one-time KGB co-station chief remarks in his memoir:

> It wasn't easy for Kekkonen to befriend Khrushchev. After all, they were completely different. Deep down, Kekkonen was a highly educated, intelligent and sophisticated man, while Khrushchev was quite unsophisticated, and not a natural [member] of the intelligentsia.[30] Khrushchev always behaved in the same rough way, but Kekkonen was able to change his behavior to suit Khrushchev's company.

"This," along with the partaking of "immense amounts of cognac," continues Vladimirov, "is the reason [Kekkonen and Khrushchev] got along so well." According to him, Khrushchev unsurprisingly balked at first at Kekkonen's invitation for him to join him in the sauna because he "wasn't sure the head of a great nation should show himself naked in front of the representatives of another country."[31] However, according to the former KGB man, Kekkonen's remarkable sales skills won the day and Khrushchev duly peeled off his clothing and agreed to take his first Finnish sauna, or take sauna, as the Finns say.

To all appearances, the imperious, buttoned-down, book-loving, doctorate-holding Finnish leader could not have been more different from his irrepressible Russian counterpart, who made no pretense about his lack of formal education and indeed flaunted it. On the other hand, perhaps the two men were not such an odd couple, after all.

As the noted American journalist John Gunther wrote, there were two Khrushchevs: Khrushchev the splenetic, fist-banging showman, and Khrushchev the driven political operator and consummate political engineer, and one ought not to mistake one for the other. "One should not pay too much attention to the antics and effervescence. The chief elements in Khrushschev's character are robust common sense, ruthlessness, a drive to get things done, and above all, optimism and confidence."[32] All of these qualities could also just as soon be ascribed to Kekkonen, actually. Indeed, in a way, the two men were kindred spirits, or as the Finns put it, fellow movers and shakers—even though Kekkonen and Khrushchev moved in somewhat different political spheres.

Interestingly, and revealingly, Khrushchev's companion, Bulganin, was not invited to Kekkonen's sauna party. Or perhaps he was. In any case, the premier was not pleased by his comrade's decision to take ablutions with his newfound Finnish capitalist friend. He also decided to make a formal complaint about it after the two returned home. Following the two Soviet leaders' return to Moscow, Bulganin brought up the provocative sauna at a key meeting of the Soviet Presidium, accusing Khrushchev of demeaning the dignity of a Soviet leader by behaving in such a plebian manner.

"You can't be serious," Khrushchev said, looking at Bulganin with a surprised expression. "I didn't go there to wash, but to hold confidential negotiations with the president of Finland—what is more," he joked, "in such heat!"[33] According to the younger Khrushchev, "Father's joke fell flat." "Those present," including Vyacheslav Molotov, the former wartime foreign minister who had presided over the USSR's invasion of Finland twenty years before and Lazar Kaganovich, the venerable Bolshevik and confidante of Stalin, vigorously condemned the visit to the sauna."[34]

The joke, it turned out, was on Molotov and company. At a marathon session of the presidium, Khrushchev, the wily first secretary, was able to outmaneuver the so-called "anti-Party" faction, with the result that Molotov and Kaganovich were forced out and banished to minor or menial posts. The modesty-minded Bulganin lasted a little longer, until March, 1958, when Khrushchev managed to have him removed, as well.[35] Bulganin and Khrushchev's ballyhooed sortie to Helsinki, it turned out, was the last engagement of the B and K Show.

For the next seven years, until he himself fell afoul of the Kremlin's Kafkaesque ways, Soviet foreign policy would essentially be Khrushchev's show to run. In the meantime, the Kekkonen and Khrushchev Show (so to speak) had gotten off to an auspicious start.

Perhaps not *all* the mutual suspicions and misunderstandings overshadowing relations between the two countries had evaporated by the time the two men emerged from Kekkonen's newly christened sauna at his sprawling house, nor even most, but a good start had been made. No doubt about it: He now had a firm friend in the Kremlin.

Or so he thought. The Finnish president would soon be disabused of this notion.

There is an amusing and revealing postscript to the tale of that famous sauna.

In July 1957 after Khrushchev returned to Moscow, and quashed the attempted Stalinist coup by Bulganin and his collaborators, Kekkonen phoned him and asked him whether he would like to have his own, custom-made Finnish sauna, according to Sergei Khrushchev. "He [Kekkonen] said that he would send his specialists and they would assemble it wherever Father wanted."[36] This provoked a somewhat hysterical reaction from the KGB, which objected to the notion of foreigners visiting the first secretary's secret dacha, no less building anything there. Nevertheless the sauna builders, innocent of the controversy they had stirred up, came. The Finns arrived in Moscow with logs, boards, and washbasins—everything right down to the last nail. And with that, things came to a halt. They were not allowed onto the dacha grounds. Kekkonen had to call Father.[37]

Khrushchev Senior promptly "flew into a rage," and called Ivan Serov, the head of the KGB.[38]

"Do you think I roasted in that hothouse in Finland for pleasure?!" he barked at his top spy.

"I was trying to establish good personal relations with the leader of a neighboring country *which may be small, but is very important to us!* [author's italics]. And now you are ruining everything."

"Let the Finns get to work immediately!"

"I will order it," Serov responded.

And so it was done: several weeks later Khrushchev was the proud owner of a brand new Finnish sauna. But there was something which Urho Kekkonen did not know, or which his new friend, Nikita Khrushchev, had failed to tell him, as the latter's son recounts: "Father carefully examined the new sauna, sent Kekkonen his thanks, but never again visited the sauna. When he [Khrushchev] had worked in the mines, he had gone to the *banya*, the Russian equivalent of the sauna, but afterwards had acquired a bath tub. The *banya/sauna* remained to him a symbol of poverty and disorder."[39] Instead, Khrushchev's son and his friends, for whom sauna had no such objectionable associations, confiscated the Finnish-built facility for themselves.

Meanwhile, another crucial piece of Kekkonen's mental and moral armature had fallen into place: Tamminiemi, the newly refurbished presidential residence at Meilahti, the Helsinki neighborhood north of the city proper, itself. Two of Kekkonen's three predecessors, Risto Ryti and Gustaf Mannerheim, had resided at the Jugend-styled turn-of-the-century villa located on a tract of land which once belonged to Fabian

Steinheil, the early nineteenth-century Russian governor general; however it was Kekkonen who truly made it his own.[40]

It was Ryti's tragic predecessor, Kyosti Kallio, who formally took deed of the former Villa Nissen from its prior owner, Amos Anderson, the editor-in-chief of *Hufvudstadsbladet*, the Swedish-language newspaper, in January 1940. The grandfatherly Kallio had looked forward to living out the remainder of his presidency at Villa Kallio, as it had been christened. Unfortunately, in one of the more melodramatic deaths in Finnish history, Kallio died before he could take possession, keeling over into the arms of Mannerheim, the Finnish commander-in-chief and future president, while reviewing a guard of honor in December 1940, midway through the murky 16 month long "interim peace," as the Finns call it, between the end of the Winter War and the Continuation War, when the Finns went back to war against the USSR as co-belligerents with Nazi Germany in June 1941.

Kallio's star-crossed successor, Ryti, the former prime minister, made fairly extensive use of Tamminiemi during the three and a half years of his own truncated presidency. The buttoned-down former banker and his wife, Gerda, spent most of their summers there, as well as part of the winter of 1944, before the final stage of the Continuation War, when the Soviet Air Force regularly bombed Helsinki, rendering the presidential palace unsafe.

Not particularly sports-minded, Ryti liked to take short walks on adjoining Seurasaari Island; however when he was at Tamminiemi he generally preferred to remain indoors and conduct his business there. There was much business to conduct during those long, trying years of 1941, 1942, 1943, and 1944: the most significant addition to Villa Kallio was a map room where Ryti and his advisors could follow the back-and-forth progress of Finland's second war with the USSR after he and Gerda moved there full-time in January 1944. The hard-pressed head of state had neither the time nor the inclination to take advantage of Tamminiemi's natural surroundings during the first half of 1944, as the Continuation War careened to its inevitable end.

Somewhat fittingly, Kekkonen first visited Tamminiemi on June 23, 1944, two weeks after the successful landings at Normandy and the beginning of the final act of World War II, which coincided with a simultaneous, renewed Soviet assault on the battered Finnish line on the Karelian Isthmus as well as the area around Lake Ladoga and Lake Onega. At the time Kekkonen was chairman of a group of parliamentary representatives and "transitioning" Russophobes like himself, who had "seen the light," as he had, and understood the necessity of a fundamental reorientation of Finnish foreign policy and mind set, if the fatherland was to avoid being swallowed again by its massive neighbor, and proposed a separate peace with the USSR and the formation of a peace cabinet.

The day before, June 22, Ryti had received a surprise visit from his harried cobelligerent Joachim von Ribbentrop, the German foreign minister, pleading with him not to agree to such a pact. However, Ryti, too, had seen the writing on the wall. Three days later, the dejected president sat down at his desk in the presidential study at Tamminiemi and wrote a personal letter to Adolf Hitler vowing, somewhat disingenuously, that neither he nor any cabinet named by him would settle for a separate peace of the kind that Kekkonen and his accommodationist allies had urged, but which he now understood was inevitable.

A month later, on August 1, Ryti sat down at his desk again and wrote out his letter of resignation, paving the way for the inevitable. Seven weeks later, on September 19, to Hitler's and Ribbentrop's extreme discomfiture, the fateful armistice was signed by a delegation led by the ailing prime minister, Antti Hackzell, by which time Mannerheim, the weary Finnish commander, had reluctantly accepted Ryti's and the *eduskunta*'s summons to replace Ryti and serve as Finland's sixth president.[41]

All in all, as fond as he was of it, Tamminiemi was not a source of very much happiness for Risto Ryti. Two years, and another era later the crushed president, the former Finnish foreign minister Vainö Tanner, Ryti's two prime ministers, Jukka Rangell and Edwin Linkomies, and two other wartime officials would go on trial in Helsinki during the so-called war responsibility trials, which Finland had agreed to hold in order to appease Moscow's desire that those putatively most responsible for the prosecution of both the Winter War and the Continuation War be held accountable for their putative "crimes"—and which Kekkonen, the former Russophobe, who was now minister of justice, actively helped prepare. Ryti was sentenced to ten years in prison, during which time his health broke, before he was pardoned in 1949.[42]

The seemingly cursed presidential residence was not exactly a source of joy to Gustaf Mannerheim either during the nineteen months of his foreshortened presidential tenure. Continuing in the role of commander-in-chief, Mannerheim spent the late summer and autumn of 1944 at his headquarters in Mikkeli, in eastern Finland, as the defeated nation dutifully complied with the draconian provisions of the Peace of Moscow, which among other things compelled Finland to expel the substantive German forces remaining on Finnish soil in Lapland, which culminated in the third war which Finland fought during World War II, the so-called Lapland War.

When his official duties required him to be in Helsinki, the reluctant president and commander-in-chief divided his time between his customized railroad salon car and Tamminiemi. The "Father of Modern Finland," as Mannerheim was already being called, liked his pastoral residence, and sometimes took walks on Seurasaari, the island adjoining Tamminiemi, as well, like his prison-bound predecessor. However the demanding marshal found the rickety manor left much to be desired for an official residence. He was far more attached to his beloved, trophy-festooned villa in Kaivopuisto, where he had lived during the interwar period.

The septuagenarian soldier-statesman was also too distracted by his combined military and political duties, as well as his own worsening health problems, for which he was forced to leave the country to seek treatment for weeks at a time in 1945 and the first part of 1946, to properly appreciate the venerable manor house. He also was concerned that he would be forced to stand trial, along with his predecessor, as the dread Soviet-ordered "war responsibility" tribunal approached. In the event, he was not, and the ailing Mannerheim, who had five more years to live, was allowed to conclude his four-decade-long service to Finland in peace.

Tamminieimi meant even less to his successor, Juho Paasikivi, who took the reins from Mannerheim in March 1946, after the latter retired to Switzerland. The lifelong city dweller had no special ken for nature or the outdoors and openly declared his preference for the former Imperial Palace, now the *Presidentinlinna*, the presidential palace, overlooking Helsinki harbor. If he wanted to take a walk, the veteran minister and diplomat harrumphed, he could jog along Esplanadi, the long cobblestone street in front of his house. If he desired to look at water, he could look out the window.

The blunt-speaking, cane-wielding Paasikivi did not live at Tamminiemi at all during his decade-long presidency, which paralleled the long, difficult reconstruction period, as the Finnish people put their backs together to pay the crushing reparations bill the Soviets had forced on them and he laid the ground work for "the Paasikivi line," as it came to be called. Instead, the once stately, now tatterdemalion home was loaned out to relatives of Paasikivi's wife, Alli.

Thus Tamminiemi was something of an orphan when Paasikivi's ambitious protégé, Kekkonen, took the reins of office from him in 1956. The new president and avid sportsman quickly decided to do something about *that.* In contradistinction to his sedentary mentor, Paasikivi, Kekkonen openly disliked the austere presidential palace; nor, for that matter did he harbor much love for Helsinki itself, a bias that would influence his actions and statements on urban planning, and even reportedly held back the capital's growth.[43]

With the enthusiastic assent of his nature-loving wife, Sylvi, he immediately decreed that the historic Meilahti estate would be both their home and the principal place for transacting presidential business, and, after an extensive and expensive renovation lasting most of the spring and summer of 1956, so it became.

For five months, during what remained of Kekkonen's short-lived presidential honeymoon, insofar as he could be said to have had one, he and his wife continued to live at their former residence on Kampinkatu

FIGURE 6. Taking charge. Kekkonen sitting at his desk in his study at Tamminiemi, 1957. Behind him is the jewel box gifted to him by Kliment Voroshilov, the president of the Soviet Presidium, who visited him earlier that year. Little did he or his countrymen know that he would remain seated behind that desk for another quarter century.

in the city center, as architects and construction crews labored to transform and resurrect the aging manse according to the first couple's demanding specifications.

In addition to thoroughly repairing the weather-battered exterior, the old Jugend-styled interior was totally gutted and modernized. The closed spaces, dark shades, and ornamental tiled stoves of the former edifice were banished. The claustrophobic drawing room and adjacent rooms on the first floor were melded to form a new large foyer, large enough to convene the occasional governmental conclave. It was here that the twelve prime ministers who ultimately served under Kekkonen would present their revolving door cabinets over the next twenty-five years; of course, no one, including he, had an inkling that there would be so many, or that he would remain in office for so long.

Other aspects of the structure were revamped in order to give it a more modern, open feeling. The creaky old teak staircases were gotten rid of. Oak parquet floors were installed. Large bay windows were built in order to permit more light and a better view of the house's surroundings. Oil heating made its belated arrival, along with a modern kitchen, as well as an electric switchboard with which the Kekkonens could summon their staff.

New, functional tableware and textiles, specially selected by Sylvi, who worked for the Friends of Finnish Handcraft Association in her youth and whose decorative eye was said to be unerring, were brought in. The new, light-hued textiles were made by Liisa Suvanto, the noted Finnish artist, beginning a long tradition of the Kekkonens' sponsorship of the arts, one that would deepen over the years. If the resultant, still austere-feeling residence was not exactly *svelte*, it certainly was a vast improvement.

Last but not least, a large log sauna was constructed. It was here that Kekkonen would relinquish his troubles and convene his weekly Saturday conclaves with the rest of the members of his steamy sauna crew. And it was here that he led the visiting Nikita Khrushchev to the aforementioned historic ablution, against his scornful traveling mate's wishes.

In 1969, the second year of his third term, the presidential sauna, which by then had become the most celebrated such facility in Finland, if not the world, was expanded to include a swimming pool. Ultimately, as Kekkonen customized Tamminiemi—and the Finnish presidency along with it—to his liking, he would add new rooms and features to suit his expansive, brawny tastes, including a svelte "space age" bar right out of *Mad Men*, and an even further off-limits, sports paraphernalia-lined, upstairs "man cave" that one female visitor would call "the most masculine room I have ever been in."[44] But that was still far in the future.

The Kekkonens formally took occupancy of Tamminiemi on October 10, 1956, three weeks before the Hungarian uprising, bringing along their diverse art collection from their apartment in the city, as well as their several thousand volume-large library, which would continue to mushroom as the two devout bibliophiles, prolific authors themselves, acquired yet more books.

Now the couple had an elegant new home and Urho a proper and effective place to transact his business and communicate with government officials, both in Finland and abroad, as well as to entertain his steady stream of official and private guests. But for Kekkonen, and for Finland, Tamminiemi would be much more than an official residence, or even the site of the presidency, for that matter, during the two and a half decades he lived there, including the eight years he spent as an increasingly lonely, heartsick, and physically sick bachelor after his long-ailing wife's death in 1974.

To put it in contemporaneous Western terms, for someone who held office at the same time—or roughly the same time—as Dwight D. Eisenhower and Winston Churchill, his American and British contemporaries, respectively, Tamminiemi was a combination of the White House and Camp David and Eisenhower's Gettysburg farm, in American terms; in British ones, a combination of 10 Downing Street and Chequers, with something of Chartwell, Churchill's country home, thrown in.

But for Urho Kekkonen, Tamminiemi became more than that. Tamminiemi was his Parnassus, the place whence he looked out at the world, and validated his view of the world; the fortress whence he sallied forth to make diplomacy, to tour his country, knock ministerial heads together, and liaise with his various mistresses. It was his citadel and his castle, and his refuge from the storm.

Eventually, during his still controversial fourth and final term, from 1978 to 1981, it would also become his Xanadu, the place where he would indulge his growing megalomania and hubris, an asylum where he devolved into a figurehead, propped up, and to some extent manipulated by his handlers, somewhat like the American president Woodrow Wilson after he suffered a debilitating stroke at the end of his second term of office. It would be the place where he lived out his sad final days, after he was finally forced to retire in 1981, a full quarter century after he first took occupancy of the former Villa Nissen. It would be the place where he would die, but in 1956, all this was still far in the uncharted future.[45]

For the moment, the president of Finland had a new address, all roads led to Tamminiemi, and the new master of the house was in acute control of his faculties. He would need them in the coming months and years, as he steered the Finnish ship of state between the Scylla of the West and the Charybdis of the East and tried to garner respect for Finland's avowed neutrality, while dealing with his still skeptical people and occasionally surly governmental crew.

Also, for Kekkonen, basing himself at Tamminiemi was another way of distinguishing himself from his urbanite predecessor and mentor. Paasikivi, the city dweller, may have scorned Tamminiemi and the rural countryside it represented, but for Kekkonen the converted seaside estate was his true home, and so it would remain, until the bitter end.

> First of all, I must humbly beg forgiveness for writing to you, Mr. President. Before you, Mr. President, ever became president at all, I told my friends that if Prime Minister Kekkonen becomes president I will write him. Now they have asked me many times if I have written. I have told them that I haven't yet. It is probably best to say why I am writing. I am a widow, and my only child died in the [Continuation War on October 27, 1941].
>
> I now must humbly ask Mr. President, why we, the parents of fallen soldiers, are paid a smaller allowance than war widows? If the women of the time, hadn't made sons, where would the women have gotten their husbands from?
>
> —From an unpublished letter to President Kekkonen from Maija Elo, from the northern village of Leppäniemi, May 7, 1956[46]

Another way in which Urho Kekkonen differed from his predecessor was his attitude toward letters, both writing and receiving them. An indifferent writer, Paasikivi had no great love for epistles. For him, like most of his predecessors, letters were a tool of high office.

By contrast, his successor was a prodigious and enthusiastic letter writer who used his personal letters as a means of extending his unofficial and official influence, as well as expressing his dislike for this or that person or policy. Among the recipients of these epistolary barbs were stubborn politicians, journalists, civil servants, and other leading figures in Finnish society. The letters were private, but their tone, and the identities of those who had fallen into disfavor were not state secrets.

At the same time, Kekkonen also for the most part, read and responded to the dozens of letters that poured into Tamminiemi from Finnish citizens. On becoming president, he made the quixotic decision that every halfway rational letter addressed to him would be answered. Correspondence with citizens was his way of keeping in contact with people all over the country while he wrestled with the problems of the world, while also cultivating his image as a man of the people, and the son of a humble master lumberjack from northern Finland.

There is a stereotypical view, particularly amongst his critics, of Urho Kekkonen as the aloof wheeler-dealer, playing one hapless minister or political hack off against another in his quest to remain in power. There is, to be sure, a lot of truth to that picture. But there was another side of Kekkonen, that of the president who cared about his people, particularly the people of the small villages and towns of the north, with whom he seemed to particularly empathize. Reading these letters from his early days as president sheds light on this "softer," sentimental side of his, while also revealing the hardships faced by those who lived on the fringes of a country which was going through a deep recession, and who had fallen through the cracks.

Thus, for example, on October 22, 1956, the heartbreaking epistle from a crestfallen woman from the tiny northern village of Karunki by the name of Toini Harjunpää excerpted below, landed on his desk.

> Revered Mr. President Kekkonen
>
> You have in so many ways worked for us ill-fated people. So I dare you to ask for help for my children, of which I have 8, the ninth [having] died in spring. We have a frontiersman farm on the lands of the Karunki parish. I have got it partly for rent, when my husband was on the frontier, and we have owned it after the war ended.

The forlorn woman's tale of woe continues:

> My husband likes to drink and doesn't care about his family, so I have had to deal with everything myself. First, I could not get a loan, because my husband was drinking in Helsinki, but I managed to get help and a roof over the children's heads. The eldest of the children is in the sanitarium, he has a lung disease and there are two younger ones with the same disease at home. I am falling

> apart. Now the father has been away for two months and I don't know where he is, he has not sent money or anything else for the children. I have bought 2 cows with the child allowance [*sic*], so there would be milk for the children. I received over 8,000 marks, but the municipality took these as my husband's taxes. I asked the commission for 10,000 marks to pay for a second cow, because I haven't been able to [find money] because of all this illness.
>
> They could have had the money from next year's child allowance, but the Municipality official said that they don't have the ability to pay. But they [the township authorities claim] have the right to take the father's taxes from the children.

A municipal official to whom she had discussed her situation had "just laughed and told me to sell my animals and eat them." Such was life in the Finnish provinces in the fall of 1956. "Why do we have the whole social welfare system," the letter writer asked the president, "when it doesn't help a miserable woman?"

The addressee heard Toini's poignant plea. A week later, on October 29, 1956, the president, who had been moved by her predicament to contact the township authorities himself, dictated the following reply:

> On account of your letter I have been in touch with Karunki, and have been told, that the social committee of the municipality has [decided] to supply you with an allowance of 12,500 marks a month. Your unpaid taxes and municipal taxes have been pardoned and ordered to be returned to you.

Kekkonen ended his note by expressing the hope that as a result of this relief, she could return to work. At the same time he hoped that she could see that the township authorities did indeed have a heart, after all and that the woman could "look into the future with peace of mind, and concentrate on raising your children."

"That is your very most important duty, and one in which I wish you courage."[47]

Two decades earlier, after the Winter War and the forced evacuation of Karelia, as head of the Siiurtovaen Huollon Keskus, the organization charged with caring for the 400,000 plus Karelians who lost their homes and land, Kekkonen had proven that he cared for the common man. Here was proof that the eighth president of Finland still cared.

Chapter 2

A Brusque Intervention (6/57–10/58)

> Amongst Finnish-speaking onlookers could be heard comments about the coincidence of a visit by the Russians when their government was trying to form a cabinet.
>
> —*The New York Times*, July 31, 1958

(NEWSREEL)

President Urho Kekkonen of Finland arrives in Moscow, June 1958 for his first state visit to Russia. Large Kremlin-style posters of Kekkonen and Kliment Voroshilov hang on the outside of the terminal of Moscow airport, as the Aero Oy turboprop bearing the Finnish president comes into view. As per protocol, the durable Voroshilov, still the nominal head of state, steps forward to greet the Finnish leader as he disembarks. Voroshilov is followed closely by First Secretary Nikita Khrushchev, who in turn is followed by Soviet deputy prime minister Anastas Mikoyan. The deposed Nikolai Bulganin is nowhere in sight.

Next Kekkonen reviews a Soviet honor guard. We then see him from a distance, standing up in his ZIL limousine, Voroshilov and Khrushchev standing beside him, trailed by a long motorcade of cars, flanked by a double phalanx of uniformed motorcyclists. And now the newsreel camera pans to the crowds of Russians lining the route of the motorcade, including clutches of jovial young men and women perched on lampposts, who wave at Kekkonen's car.

As the fall of 1957 approached, Urho Kekkonen continued to stress about his relationship with his supposed new friend in the Kremlin, Nikita

Khrushchev. Kekkonen and Khrushchev may well have bonded in the sauna at Tamminiemi in June 1957—but that did not mean that Khrushchev and his colleagues did not mind making things difficult for him. Put in familial terms, the Fenno-Soviet relationship during Kekkonen's first term was a little bit like a big burly friend (USSR) who grabs another, newfound smaller friend-cum-former enemy (Finland) affectionately by the neck, while giving the latter an occasional punch in the stomach to remind the latter who was really in charge.

The *Times* of London explained Finland's unique geopolitical predicament this way:

> If the countries of eastern Europe are satellites revolving in more or less tidy orbits around the Soviet Union, then Finland is a comet. For months at a time it appears to be as independent of Soviet influence as any of the other Scandinavian nations. Yet at all times Finns recognize that good relations with Russia are an essential condition of their survival.

"And," the British paper's droll Helsinki correspondent continues, "every now and then a brusque Russian intervention reminds them of this fact."[1]

Generally, these "interventions" or "frosts," as Khrushchev dubbed them, took the form of threats to cease accepting Finnish products, particularly those from Finland's ship and steel manufacturing industries, the very industries which the Finns had built up in order to pay off the massive $300 million *kultadollari* (gold dollars) war reparations bill the Soviets had imposed on them after World War II as the price of peace. These industries, which faced stiff competition from the West, were hardly self-sufficient, however. Put simply, the USSR had Finland over an economic barrel. Of course, most Finns knew this, but that did not mean they had to like it. And they liked it even less when Moscow reminded them of their predicament by bullying them.

Moreover, the long-term benefits of Finland's codependence on the USSR had not yet become evident to the Finnish people. Although conditions had improved since the war, times were still hard, particularly for the elderly. With 80,000 Finns out of work, unemployment was at a ten-year high. Emigration was an increasingly attractive option: five thousand Finns emigrated to Australia, one of the more popular destinations for emigrants, in 1957 and 1958 alone. Conditions were still better than immediately after the war, nevertheless the country was still a pressure cooker, what with the Soviets breathing down the country's neck.

In this context, trade with the USSR and the Soviet bloc was still seen, quite understandably, as a form of necessary tribute or extortion, rather than a harbinger of better times. That is why Finns turned their backs on visiting Soviet officials. Political and economic exigencies notwithstanding, in their hearts, many if not most Finns were still willing to fight the Winter War again.

Occasionally this resentment of the Big Brother in Moscow would manifest itself in public, as it did most dramatically in the summer of 1962, at the start of Kekkonen's second term, when to his chagrin riots broke out in Helsinki to protest the Communist-sponsored World Youth Festival. At the same time, Moscow's penchant for bullying Helsinki raised the question of how much support Kekkonen really had in the Kremlin, regardless of how well the Finnish and Soviet leaders had apparently bonded.

On October 24, 1957, a mere four months after Khrushchev and Kekkonen took sauna, as the Finns say, at Tamminiemi, the first Soviet-administered punch was delivered when the Kremlin, incensed by the news that Kekkonen had—reluctantly—invited the aging but still formidable Väinö Tanner, chairman of the Social Democratic Party, and one of the most outspoken critics of the so-called Paasikivi-Kekkonen line, who Moscow still loathed—because of Tanner's role as Finland's foreign minister during the Winter War, for which he was also tried during the postwar Soviet-enforced "war responsibility" trial and served a prison sentence—to form a government, whereupon the Soviet foreign ministry notified the Finnish government in Helsinki that the negotiations for a new trade pact that had been scheduled to take place in several days would be indefinitely postponed, as *The New York Times* reported:

SOVIET REBUFFS FINLAND

Calls off Trade Talks and Attacks Tanner as Leader

HELSINKI, Finland, Oct. 24—The Soviet Union notified Finland today that commercial negotiations scheduled to start in Helsinki Monday would be postponed until further notice.

No reason was given but the Finns believe it is Soviet reaction to the announcement yesterday that Vaino [*sic*] A. Tanner, Social Democratic leader, had been invited to try to form a government.

Today the Moscow radio said Mr. Tanner was a war criminal and was aiming to achieve power in Finland. Mr. Tanner will report the results of his negotiations to President Urho Kekkonen tomorrow.[2]

Of course, Kekkonen knew how Moscow felt about Tanner. But that did not make his job, including the never-ending job of selling friendship with Moscow to the Finnish people, any easier.

A month later, the harried president instead brought in his most reliable yes man, the colorless V.J. Sukselainen from his own party, the Agrarian League and a new minority government would be formed and life, and the passive-aggressive Fenno–Soviet relationship, would continue.

Still, Kekkonen was shaken by the Soviet broadside.

Obviously, this was hardly the ideal background for cultivating respect for Finnish neutrality, no less the "active" Swiss-type brand of neutrality that the ambitious statesman envisioned. In the meantime, his envisioned Switzerland of the North would have to settle for being something between a neutral and a satellite.

Meanwhile, the lord of Tamminiemi had had another epiphany: that the balance of power in the Cold War had shifted from Washington to Moscow. To be sure this was not an unreasonable conclusion. It may be hard to believe now, but there was a time, in the late 1950s and early 1960s, when many people, including many if not most Finns, believed that the USSR was winning the Cold War, insofar as such an inherently inchoate conflict would be "won." The murderously effective Soviet crackdown of the Hungarian Revolution in 1956, along with the Eisenhower administration's ineffectual response, which impressed Finns, helped reinforce this view.

Then, in the fall of 1957, on October 4th, the USSR shocked the world with the successful launch of the first orbital satellite, Sputnik 1. That was followed less than a month later by the launch of its successor, Sputnik 2, which was "manned" by its celebrated, if doomed, canine passenger, Laika. Americans were particularly stunned by the successful back-to-back missile launches. Along with undermining their belief that the US was number one in everything, especially anything to do with science and technology, the successful Sputnik launches meant, at least theoretically, that Moscow was capable of putting a nuclear warhead in orbit, too.

The space race, a key adjunct of the arms race, was officially on, and, suddenly, shockingly, Moscow seemed to have taken the lead. This impression was reinforced in December, when the first American satellite, Vanguard 1, exploded on the launch pad in Florida in living Technicolor. During the interim, the Soviets continued to produce an unknown number of intercontinental ballistic missiles (ICBMs), leading many Americans and other frightened observers to believe that the USSR had opened a "missile gap," in the famous phrase of senator and future president John F. Kennedy—a belief that was reinforced by Nikita Khrushchev's claim that the USSR had hundreds of ICBMs and was turning out the nuclear-capable missiles "like sausages."

This was hokum. There was no "missile gap." According to later CIA estimates, the Soviets had at most a dozen functional ICBMs at this time, and the US many times more. Khrushchev knew this, and so did President Eisenhower, but Eisenhower was reluctant to reveal that he knew this because it meant he had to reveal *how* he knew this. And JFK, who would later make the "missile gap" a major issue of the 1960 US presidential campaign, probably knew this as well.

One suspects that Kekkonen, with his wide contacts in both Soviet and Western intelligence, knew that whatever lead, or putative lead, which the Russians had in the space race and/or the arms race, was only a temporal thing, and that the putative "missile gap" was a convenient Soviet—and American—fiction, too. Or at least that a part of him did. One thing Kekkonen was not was naïve.

Nevertheless, Kekkonen had made up his mind: the USSR was really winning the Cold War, at least on the technological front, a belief that would evince itself during the pivotal meetings he took with JFK and his secretary of state, Dean Rusk, in October 1961, which likely were a factor which helped trigger the Note Crisis, as we will see later.

Of course, it was convenient for Kekkonen to believe in Soviet supremacy in that it reinforced the of the value of "the Russian card," i.e., access to the Kremlin, and by extension, that he was the only one capable of employing that access for the betterment of the Finnish nation, something which many Finns, including his numerous critics and opponents, were *not* yet convinced of, nor would ever be.

But he genuinely seems to have believed that the Soviets were ahead, and nothing that either they or the Americans did or did not do, for the next decade and a half—until at least 1969 when the United States "won" the space race (or at least the manned space race) by landing a man on the moon, and probably for the remainder of his presidency, would shake it. Nor did his one visit to the US in October 1961, which coincided with the Note Crisis, alter that belief.

More inexplicably, and by way of illustrating how susceptible Kekkonen was to Soviet propaganda, the Finnish leader also believed, at least for a time, that Russian living standards were improving at a greater rate than in the West.

In turn, this belief that the balance of power had in fact shifted to the Soviet side, had led Kekkonen to believe that in order to preserve Finnish sovereignty it was necessary to accommodate Moscow as much as possible.

Thus Kekkonen's handling of the prolonged "brusque intervention" by Moscow that came to be known as the Night Frost, a five-month-long episode that would leave an indelible impact on both Finland, the Kekkonen presidency, as well as the emerging Paasikivi-Kekkonen line.

In point of fact, the well-worn phrase the Paasikivi-Kekkonen line is something of a misnomer insofar as it implies that the Kekkonen "line" on relations with Russia was an extension, or extrapolation of that of his predecessor and political mentor, when it actually was a significant enhancement or broadening of that "line," and one that his predecessor, Juho Paasikivi, chided his ambitious protégé about even before his protégé succeeded him.

For Paasikivi, accommodating Moscow was one thing; placating it as Kekkonen was inclined to do, was another. How far *was* Kekkonen prepared to go to assuage the Kremlin's long list of grievances, which now extended from the composition of the Finnish government to what books and films Finns were allowed to consume?

Quite far—perilously far—as Finns, and the world, would soon find out during the Night Frost.

Too far, as far as the US State Department was concerned. "Kekkonen's excessive accommodation of the USSR, *which goes beyond the Paasikivi line* [author's italics], is extremely risky," according to a declassified telegram the department sent its London and Helsinki embassies on September 2, 1958, at the start of the episode. "Even if he succeeds in cultivating [the] USSR without jeopardizing Finnish sovereignty [Kekkonen] is likely to establish a pattern of relations in which less clever leadership in the future will be compromised."[3]

If the pliable Finnish president was not a Soviet puppet, in Washington's view, he was certainly close to one. His actions and statements during the ensuing "brusque intervention" would only confirm this impression.

The stage for what would mushroom into the most serious crisis in Fenno-Soviet relations since the attempted communist coup of 1948—and nearly provoked a proxy fight over Finland between Washington and Moscow as well—was set in late May 1958, at the start of the third year of Kekkonen's momentous first term. That was when the Finnish president undertook his first state visit to Moscow, the first of twenty-seven official visits, and numerous more "unofficial" ones that he would make during his quarter-century-long tenure as Finnish head of state.

A number of wrinkles in the "special relationship" had arisen during the intervening year, first and foremost being the large ruble deficit Helsinki had accumulated. Bottom line: Finland was buying too few goods from the USSR and too many from the West. This made Khrushchev and his associates, who fretted that Finland was tilting toward the West, unhappy. Also elements of the Finnish press, particularly *Helsingin Sanomat*, and its unapologetically impertinent cartoonist, Kari Suomalainen, continued to be highly critical of Moscow, to the latter's distress. Both of these vexing issues awaited the Finnish president when he arrived by plane at Vnukovo Airport on the afternoon of May 22 to a hero's welcome.

When President Paasikivi traveled to the Russian capital in 1955 on his first state visit as president, the Politburo sent a special plane to pick him up, and the proud, aging president wore a white rose in the lapel of his coat. Paasikivi later called that trip, the highlight of which was his success in persuading the Kremlin to give back the Porkkala peninsula it had forced Finland to cede in 1944—a concession most likely timed in order to ensure the success of his prime minister, Kekkonen, in the pending presidential election—the most enjoyable of the seven state visits that *he* made to the USSR during his presidency, when the template for Finland's postwar relationship with its erstwhile "hereditary enemy" was set.

Paasikivi's successor's first official visit was not quite as enjoyable, nor as successful, but reasonably rewarding to both the Finnish and Soviet sides nonetheless. In the event, Kekkonen decided this time it was more appropriate to fly Aero Oy, the predecessor of Finnair; also he was not wearing a white rose on his coat lapel.

The huge Soviet-style banner bearing the bald-headed, bespectacled Finn's photographic likeness, alongside that of Voroshilov, the Soviet head of state, depending from the drab façade of the international arrival terminal of Vnukovo airport was a nice, if perhaps embarrassing touch for a man who was already accused of crafting his own personality cult.

So was the troupe of cheery Soviet leaders led by Kekkonen's new-found friend, Khrushchev, and deputy prime minister Anastas Mikoyan,

Khrushchev's chief ally in the Politburo, also known as "the Armenian fox," and other members of the apparat pressed forward to greet him as he jauntily descended the ramp from the Convair 580 twin engine turboprop Finnliner.[4]

What was more surprising was the unabashedly enthusiastic reception accorded the Finnish VIP by the thousands of Muscovites, most of whom looked to be in their teens and twenties, as the gleaming limousine bearing him and Khrushchev, accompanied by two columns of stone-faced Red Army motorcyclists, made its way to the Kremlin for the first round of their official talks, a reception that stood in stark contrast to the comparatively muted, even hostile, one, which Helsinkians had given Khrushchev and the conspicuously absent Nikolai Bulganin the year before.

Although stage managed in the best Muscovite manner, real enthusiasm was in evidence here, as can be seen in reviewing the Pathe newsreel of the event. See the jovial young Russians dangling from a police observation tower in order to get a better view of Comrade Kekkonen. And check out that young Fennophile in the distance, who caught up in the emotion of the moment, dashes past the phalanx of policemen lining the route to shake the surprised Finn's hand. If Helsinki had turned its back, literally and figuratively, on the visiting Soviets, Moscow evidently felt quite differently about Kekkonen and *Finlandia.*

Clearly moved, the Finnish president did his best to return the sentiment, cocking his head upward in the direction of the spectators leaning out the windows of the buildings lining the route and clapping his hands together, Soviet-style, a gesture which would most likely have elicited jeers at home.

The reception that awaited Kekkonen within the crenelated walls of the Kremlin itself was decidedly less rapturous. The Soviet leaders, it developed, were genuinely put out by the growing trade imbalance between the two countries which was approaching record proportions, and which in their paranoiac view, they saw as an indication of a drift westward by Finland, and made their feelings about this known to their guest. Khrushchev and his adjutants were also indignant about what they considered as the increasingly anti-Soviet tone of the *Sanomat* and other Finnish newspapers, as the Soviet premier made clear in his remarks at the first official luncheon for Kekkonen on May 22.

Eager, perhaps too eager, to assuage Russian sensitivities on this count, the Finnish president conceded that his hosts had a point, referring to the unnamed offending journals as "scum" on the otherwise robust surface of Fenno-Soviet relations, according to the *Tass* report.

Doubtless the subject of the forthcoming Finnish general elections in July, which presumably would result in a stable Soviet-friendly coalition government to replace the caretaker governments that had replaced the last minority one that had fallen in November 1957 came up, too. However, that does not appear to have been as great a concern to the Soviets, the expectation being that the six political parties, including the SKDL Finnish communist party, which had polled 20 percent in the last election, would be returned with roughly same ratio of seats and that the resultant coalition would maintain the same foreign policy.

Although the Politburo would have obviously preferred that the communists be included in the new government, contrary to myth, there does not seem to have been any special pressure placed on Kekkonen to incorporate the SKDL; that could happen in good time (as in fact it eventually did, in 1966, during Kekkonen's second term). Most importantly, the Soviets did not want to see anyone associated with the despised Väinö Tanner.

Ridding the Finnish media of its anti-Soviet "scum," as Kekkonen had obligingly put it, was fine for the moment. As George Maude has written about the first half of Kekkonen's critical first term, "what is interesting is that throughout this [1956–58] period the Soviet government did not exploit the Kekkonen presidency [more]" as an instrument for shaping the Finnish polity to its liking.[5] From Khrushchev's point of view, this was understandable. For one, as the well-manned KGB station in Helsinki confirmed, the Finnish president did not have full control of his own political party, the Agrarian League. For another, he had to yet prove to the skeptical Soviets that he truly *did* have a grip on Finnish domestic and foreign policy, as well as himself, including his notorious temper and private proclivities, of which Moscow was well aware.

In the event, Khrushchev, Mikoyan and their comrades basically liked what they heard from their Finnish friend and client during his nine-day-long visit to the USSR. Thus, the amiable joint communiqué issued on May 27, 1958, the seventh day of Kekkonen's visit, which noted that the two sides had reached agreement in several key areas of economic concern. First, overcoming its misgivings, the Politburo acquiesced to

Kekkonen's anxious request that the pending negotiations for the bilateral trade agreement, the economic foundation that girded the special relationship, and ultimately Finland's economic security, for the period 1961 to 1965 would go forward without delay.[6]

Second, Moscow agreed to consider a long term, low interest loan of 400 to 500 million rubles to Helsinki in order to bolster the Finnish economy and provide employment and to correct the growing trade imbalance between Finland and Russia, as well as counter the effect of liberalizing imports from the West. The only caveat was that the loan was in the form of Soviet goods. Additionally, Khrushchev and his cohorts also agreed, acting on a proposal that Kekkonen had first made when he was prime minister in 1953, that as a reward for the "good and friendly relations" between the two countries, they were prepared to lease the Saimaa Canal, the century-old waterway connecting Lake Saimaa with the Gulf of Finland near Viipuri that Helsinki had been forced to abandon after it lost Karelia following the *Talvisota*.

At the same time, as the Soviets also made clear, the Kremlin was in no rush to return any part of the Karelian Soviet Socialist Republic proper itself, as Kekkonen wished. Still, he could always hope—as he would for the remainder of his presidency. "Getting Karelia back was Kekkonen's dream," according to Khrushchev's son, Sergey. "My father didn't encourage it. On the other hand, he didn't do anything to discourage it either. He was always respectful of Kekkonen's feelings, or at least tried to be." In the meantime Khrushchev was pleased to let Finnish boats ply the Saimaa again.[7] Perhaps it wasn't Karelia, but it was *something*.

By his own somewhat skewed measure, Kekkonen's first official visit to the USSR had been a great success. In any event, things seemed as chummy as they could be between host and guest when the Finnish Embassy held a farewell gala reception and dinner for Kekkonen on the evening of May 28, 1958, an event that most of the Moscow diplomatic corps attended, according to *New York Times* correspondent William Jorden, one of the Western journalists who was invited to record the bilateral bonhomie.

Today, the notion of the *Times*, or any major English-language newspaper, devoting an entire column to such an affair might seem farfetched. It is well to remember, however, in those high Cold War years that Finland, as one of the USSR's top client states, was news. "America's sweetheart," as she was known during the Winter War, might not be at

FIGURE 7. Soviet embassy, Helsinki. The massive Soviet embassy on Tehtaankatu, Kaivo, the capital's embassy district. During Kekkonen's first term, many felt that Tehtaankatu, as it came it to be called, was the true seat of political power. Kekkonen's actions during the Night Frost and Note Crisis, the two crises that bookended his initial tenure, did little to dispel that notion.

war with the USSR anymore, but as a "friendly neutral" and the only democracy bordering the USSR, many in the West were still rooting for it, as well as worried that it had fallen to a slow-motion Soviet coup, led by her new president.

Jorden's report did little to allay those apprehensions. According to his telling, Khrushchev was in particularly good form at the vodka-fueled soiree, even to the point of making fun of the hapless French ambassador, Maurice Dejean:

> At one point during the reception Maurice Dejean, French ambassador, approached a group gathered about Premier Khrushchev just after the Soviet leader had proposed a toast: "Down with the Russians, up with the Finns!" He kept M. Dejean out of the circle for a moment, then let him join the group only after saying: "We voted to make you a Finn!"
>
> Mr. Khrushchev, Marshal Voroshilov and other Soviet officials displayed great friendliness with President Kekkonen and other Finns. The reception was a gay and friendly occasion and no one gave too much weight to anything that was said about serious matters.[8]

However, as *New York Times* readers would also soon learn, as would Kekkonen, the bilateral bonhomie of that bubbly evening, as well as of the Finnish president's ostensibly successful inaugural visit to Moscow would not last.

Meanwhile, simultaneous with Kekkonen's visit, the *other* Khrushchev, the unsmiling, ruthless Khrushchev, made it clear that he did not suffer diversionists gladly, including and especially ones from the Warsaw Pact states, giving János Kádár and his murderous Hungarian associates approval to give the Imre Nagy, the imprisoned former premier and the face of the abortive 1956 Budapest revolution, a summary court martial.[9] Nagy was executed on June 16, 1958, shortly after Kekkonen returned to Helsinki.

Kekkonen had mixed, if not antithetical feelings about Nagy's execution, as his journal entry for the following day, June 17, reveals. On the one hand, the president, the one with the big heart, writes, "One who is absolutely against [the] death penalty sees the execution of Nagy supposed [as] a truly disgusting and horrific deed." On the other hand, Kekkonen the cold-blooded political operator observes, "Politically it was done [at the same time] as a confused international situation, so the timing was chosen with skill." At the same time, "it also was a warning to the USSR's internal opposition."[10] Here, in the course of several sentences one can see the Manichean nature of Kekkonen's character, as well as his mixed feelings about his ruthless, but "skilled" friends in Moscow.

Most important, at least for him at the moment, his first official visit to Moscow had been a smashing success.

In any event, Kekkonen was in an ebullient mood when he returned to Helsinki, just in time to take the salute at the parade celebrating the fortieth anniversary of the Finnish Army.

There was a distinct difference in this year's procession, as a reporter for United Press International noted.

This time the army's processional down Esplanadi, past the presidential palace, did not include Soviet tanks captured during the *Talvisota*. Nearly two decades had passed since the botched Soviet invasion of its neighbor. Now, for one reason or another, those rumbling relics of Finland's finest hour, and one of Moscow's most inglorious, had conveniently disappeared. The most prominent Soviet vehicles to be seen in Helsinki in 1958 were Moskvitches or Pobedas, or other Soviet-made cars.

Three weeks later, on July 6 and 7, 1958, the eagerly awaited Finnish general election was held. To most Western observers', as well as many Finns' surprise, SKDL, the Finnish communist party, benefiting from the continued depressed economic conditions, including a record rise in unemployment, posted its best effort ever, amassing nearly half a million votes or 23.2 percent of the electorate, a significant increase from its previous showing, giving it fifty seats, in the *eduskunta,* making it the largest party in the parliament. The rival Social Democratic party and Kekkonen's party, the Agrarian League, were tied for second place with 23.1 percent, good enough for forty-eight seats, apiece. Fourth place went to the conservative National Coalition Party, which upped its share of the vote to 15.3 percent, which gave it twenty-nine seats, an increase of five seats.

Such a result, the anxious president knew, particularly the increased tallies for the Social Democrats and the Conservatives, was bound to create a problem both for him and for Finland. And so it would, although it would take another month, and the formation of a government that Moscow most decidedly did not care for, for the problem to manifest itself.

On July 31, Kekkonen went through the motions of calling upon Eino Kilpi, the SKDL's vice chairman, to form a new government. Kilpi dutifully informed Kekkonen that he would try to form a left-wing coalition. No one, including the Soviets, expected him to succeed, especially as the other likely coalition partners, the Agrarians and the Social Democrats, excepting the Social Democrats' Moscow-friendly Skog faction, pledged not to participate in any government which included them.[11]

Next the exasperated top Finn called upon the Conservatives to give it a whirl. That did not succeed either. It was just as well: Kekkonen knew that Moscow would never accede to a coalition that included the party that represented Finland's business interests.

Finally, and inevitably, the baton passed to Kekkonen's and the Kremlin's least favorite party, the Social Democrats. Accepting the nod, his co-father-in-law, three-time former prime minister Karl-August Fagerholm, made the familiar drive to Tamminiemi and told his relative that he would do his best. In the meantime, the Politburo, now suddenly anxious, made its interest in the governmental discussions known in the most obtrusive manner possible, dispatching the cruiser *Ordzhonikidze*, the same, imposing 700-foot, 16,000-ton Sverdlov-class cruiser that had ferried Khrushchev and Nikolay Bulganin to England in 1956, and two Soviet destroyers, on a courtesy call to Helsinki.[12]

Of course, there was nothing courteous about the Soviet warships' visit, as Werner Wiskari reported in his dispatch for *The New York Times* on August 7:

> Many of the onlookers spoke Russian and there was the usual presentation of flowers to Russian sailors by local girls. Among Finnish-speaking onlookers could be heard comments on the coincidence of a visit by the Russians when [their] politicians were trying to form a Government.[13]

Indeed. The mailed fist in the Russian glove was beginning to show its hand.

The Soviet warship's visit, clearly intended to frighten Fagerholm out of forming a coalition government, a message reinforced by a flurry of phone calls from the increasingly frantic president, did not take. Three weeks later, an exhausted but triumphant Fagerholm reported to his unhappy co-father-in-law that, against all odds, he had succeeded in forming a majority center-right government, comprising the Social Democrats, as well as the Agrarian League plus the Swedish People's Party and the People's Party. Only the Skogs, the Social Democrats' left-wing faction, and the Communists were excluded.

The resulting coalition, the resolutely anticommunist US ambassador John Hickerson happily cabled Washington, was the most pro-Western Finnish government since World War II.[14] "Fagerholm is middle-of-the-road Social Democrat twice before Prime Minister," noted Hickerson in his upbeat telegram of August 30, 1958.[15]

The Kremlin was also surprised, and unpleasantly so, by the appointment of Väinö Leskinen, as well as that of Leskinen's fellow right-winger, Olavi Lindblom, who was given the lesser position of deputy transport minister, in "Fagerholm III," as the new government came to be called.[16]

Moscow's response was swift. Although the Kremlin had been vague about exactly what sort of cabinet it wanted, it was quite certain about what sort it did *not* want, and this was it. On September 2, *Izvestia*, the Soviet propaganda daily, angrily characterized the new government as representing the forces of "resurgent reaction" and accused it of planning to alter Finnish foreign policy, a charge that took the new foreign minister, Johannes Virolainen, a member of the centrist faction of the Agrarian League and a protégé of Kekkonen, by surprise—especially since it had been thought that his inclusion would assure the Kremlin that nothing had changed—no less that the government had yet to even make a foreign policy announcement.[17] For his part, Kekkonen, who anticipated that the Kremlin would be displeased by the inclusion of Leskinen and Lindblom, if perhaps not quite *how* displeased, took the formation of Fagerholm III as a personal defeat and promptly went, well, a bit mad.

To be sure, Kekkonen took *everything* personally, as the British author D. S. Connery explained in his 1967 book *The Scandinavians*. According to Connery, a leading Finnish editor told him that "Kekkonen's troubles [are] his very Finnish traits, his inability to forget a hurt or criticism for years back. This keeps him from being a great man. He has a kind of pettiness which keeps coming to the surface. He is so stubborn and convinced he is right that he disparages the views of others."[18]

What was true in 1966, when the headstrong Finn was midway through his second term, was even truer in 1958, when he was approaching the midpoint of his first term and he was faced with the first crisis of his presidency. To those Finns who saw him coming and going from Tamminiemi, the, six-foot-tall president with the ramrod straight posture was his usual self-contained, self-assured self. In truth, however, he was in turmoil.

Just how difficult this extended crisis, which consumed both Kekkonen, as well as Finland, through January of 1959, was for Kekkonen can be seen from the tempestuous and in many cases seriously unbalanced entries from his journal from the latter half of 1958. Thus, revealingly, in his journal entry for July 20, two weeks after the election, Kekkonen approvingly cites an anecdote about his mentor, Paasikivi, relating to a temper tantrum the latter had had at Kultaranta, the presidential summer residence, which Urpo Levo, Kekkonen's first aide-de-camp, had witnessed and relayed to him.[19]

Upset about one thing or another, someone on the premises, evidently Paasikivi's wife, Alli, had told the truculent octogenarian to put a lid on it. "*Fucking hell, I will yell in my house if I want!*" Juho reportedly retorted.[20]

At least on the evidence of his journals, the increasingly distraught head of state certainly seems to have done a lot of his own bellowing at his recalcitrant fellow Agrarians, whom he felt had personally betrayed him by agreeing to join the new majority government which Fagerholm, the new prime minister, had managed to cobble together, particularly by leaving the Communist-friendly Skogists out.

Not that the thin-skinned Kekkonen had much respect for any political figure of his era, Finnish or otherwise. Thus, on June 12, after returning from his voyage to Moscow, he levels his verbal shotgun at Rainer von Fieandt, the penultimate prime minister who had headed the previous stop gap "professional" government, dismissing him as "silly" and "stupid."[21] A little earlier Kekkonen had aimed his fire at Veikko Vennamo, his fellow Agrarian, flatly declaring that the future founder of the Finnish Rural Party and his political opponent, ought to be kicked out of his party altogether.[22]

On and on it went that turbulent year, as the irascible president swung his verbal cane at putative friends and foes alike. Interestingly, in the same passage of August 4, he quotes Harry S. Truman, the former US president, who served from 1945 to 1952—the period that paralleled Kekkonen's remarkable political volte-face, from hardened anti-Soviet parliamentarian to pro-Soviet prime minister—about the stupidity of waiting to make a political decision.

Truman? Franklin D. Roosevelt, the American president with whom Kekkonen is most often compared and was at the time, one can understand. Devious, often two-faced, as well as arguably the greatest president of the 20th century, FDR is the US chief executive who bears the closest resemblance to Urho Kaleva Kekkonen.

Roosevelt? Perhaps. But Truman? Direct, scrupulously honest, a man incapable of and allergic to intrigue, as well as a formidable politician in his own right, Truman was, if anything, the anti-Kekkonen. But here is Kekkonen oddly citing Truman, "the Average Man," as he was sometimes called, as a role model.

In any event, neither Roosevelt nor Truman, nor Paasikivi's ghost could help him now. Nor could Moscow. Although he was still welcome at the impressive Soviet embassy on Tehtaankatu, Kekkonen had to find the best way out of the long freezing fog from the East that was about to settle on Finland on his own.

Speaking of Tehtaankatu, as the Soviet embassy was also called, another striking aspect of Kekkonen's journals for 1958—the first year when he actually decided to keep a journal—alongside the pervasive pettiness and ad hominem remarks these hastily written pages reveal, is just *how* closely involved he was with the Soviets, including how often he met with his Russian contacts—at least once a month if the journal is any reliable measure; and just as important, how clearly awed Kekkonen was by the Kremlin.

That was not something that one could have said about his predecessor, Paasikivi, who reputedly told off Viktor Lebedev, the Soviet ambassador, when the latter visited him prior to the 1956 presidential election.[23]

"Mr. Ambassador," the blunt-speaking president is alleged to have said, "who the Finnish people wish to have as their president is none of your business. Good Day!"[24] Although Kekkonen would wind up ultimately telling off his share of Russians in the later years of his presidency, it is difficult picturing him saying that, or anything like that, especially after reading his diaries from the first part of his first term, when he was doing his utmost to persuade the Soviets that he was, in fact, their man.

If he was not a Russian governor, as Paasikivi had called him, or a KGB agent, as would also be alleged, he arguably was a de facto one during this critical passage of his presidency. Adding to Kekkonen's insecurity vis-à-vis Russian intentions and actions was his genuine confusion about which of the welter of disparate messages he was being bombarded with—including those from Tehtaankatu, including both the ambassador, Lebedev, and the KGB *rezidenta*, Vladimir Zhenikhov and Viktor Vladimirov, as well as Ahti Karjalainen, his principal go-between with the Embassy and emerging right-hand man—he ought to give the most weight and credence to.

Then there were the Russian state media, *Tass*, *Izvestia*, *Pravda*, as well as Radio Moscow, all of which Kekkonen closely read, listened to, or followed, along with the veritable mound of foreign media that Kekkonen, who today would be called a news junkie, consumed. Then, too, there was the SKDL, the Finnish communists, and *its* press, whose opinion often deviated from that of Moscow.

That is a lot of messages. Little wonder that Kekkonen sounds frazzled in his journals. He was.

Ultimately, Kekkonen saw what he wanted to see, or, perhaps more accurately, what he felt compelled to see, and heard what he wanted to hear. In this respect, as the de facto hostage of Soviet policy toward Finland, he seems to have suffered from a sort of Stockholm syndrome or a Finnish variety of the same, during the successive crises of his first term.[25]

But *what* ultimately did Moscow want? And did it still value Kekkonen's services? It was hard to figure. Adding to Kekkonen's consternation and confusion was the information he was receiving from his long-time lover, Associated Press correspondent Anne-Marie Snellman, who may or may not have been a KGB asset. In any case, Snellman, considered the dean of the Helsinki foreign press corps, certainly seems to have had a direct line to Tehtaankatu.

As Vladimirov, the Helsinki KGB station chief notes in his 1991 memoir, he and his colleagues were not particularly happy with the svelte reporter, whom he and his colleagues felt had too big a mouth:

> Kekkonen's relationship with Anne-Marie Snellman worried also KGB to some extent. After the war, when she worked as the Finland correspondent of Associated Press, she held a political saloon, which was visited by the crème de la crème of Finnish society and many foreign diplomats. There were a lot of open-minded conversations about political topics—KGB's anxiety wasn't groundless.[26]

In any case, the Soviets seem to have used the gabby newswoman to get the message, or one of their messages, to Kekkonen. Thus, on August 28, 1958, in a passage of his journal that illustrates both how tentative Kekkonen felt vis-à-vis the Soviets, and vice versa, he writes that Yuri Voronin, another of the several dozen KGB agents among the Russian embassy's two hundred large staff, had asked, after seeing a Russian language book about the Paasikivi line at Snellman's house whether her lover actually had a grip on foreign policy."[27] Voronin evidently concluded that the Paasikivi line was in danger.

A meeting with the Soviet ambassador, Lebedev, on August 11, following the Soviet ships' putative courtesy call, while the negotiations which eventuated in Fagerholm's new government continued, did little to calm Kekkonen's nerves. Two years earlier, Lebedev, one of the more competent envoys Moscow posted to Helsinki, as well as one who had hitherto been kindly disposed to the Finns, had explicitly assured the Finnish government that the Kremlin had no intention of inserting itself into the country's domestic affairs.

Now, as the *Ordzhonikidze* and its escorts bobbed menacingly off Helsinki harbor, there was no such disclaimer. In his meeting with the anxious president, Lebedev, who seems to have been better informed about Kekkonen's party than the president was himself, expressed concern about the Agrarians' evident intention to "abandon" the Soviet-friendly Skogists, and go into coalition with the right-wing Tannerite wing of the Social Democratic party. For the USSR, Lebedev told the alarmed president, as the latter recounts in his journal, forsaking the Moscow-favored Skogists in favor of the "Tannerites," signified an ominous "change of direction" in Fenno-Soviet relations.

Non-plussed, Kekkonen replied that the foreign policy line of the Agrarian League was clear. He professed not to know what Lebedev was talking about.[28]

But of course he did.

By the time Fagerholm sprung his postelection surprise government at the end of the August, the *Ordzhonikidze* and its threatening escorts had returned to Russia.

Then again, they could always could return.

If the president was put out by his conversation with Lebedev, after it was translated for him—somewhat surprisingly, Kekkonen himself had only a poor grasp of Russian, in contrast to the Russian-fluent Paaskivi, nor interestingly, did he evince any serious interest in learning it—as his journal records, he became even more distraught over the next few days as the full dimensions of the billowing political crisis became clear.[29]

To be sure, to say that Kekkonen was upset when Fagerholm III was announced, is to understate the case. He reportedly made no attempt to hide his anger when the newly minted prime minister made the customary drive to Tamminiemi to present his new government, conspicuously refusing to congratulate Fagerholm. The fact that Fagerholm was Kekkonen's co-father-in-law made the situation tenser. There certainly seems to have been no love lost between the two men, despite the fact that they now had a grandson, Timo, in common.

Fagerholm, who was proud of the work he had done putting together the new cabinet, reportedly calling it the best government Finland ever had, certainly was not quitting, no matter how irritated the Soviets were. As prime minister in the 1948–1950 minority government that followed the abortive Soviet coup he had dealt with his share of pressure from Moscow and prevailed, with the aid of President Paasikivi. He was sure he could do the same this time.[30] As he was soon to learn, however, Urho Kekkonen was considerably more pliable than his predecessor. Two subsequent developments made him even more upset.

On September 1, shortly after Kekkonen refused to congratulate his relative for fathering his doomed Cabinet, Tass, the Soviet news agency, angrily announced that the Finnish embassy in Moscow had refused to issue Otto Kuusinen a visa to visit his former homeland. Kuusinen, the president of the Finnish People's Republic, the short-lived puppet government Stalin and Molotov had installed in Karelia in 1939 during the Winter War, as well as its longer-lived postwar successor, the Karelo-Finnish Socialist Republic, now a distinguished member of the Russian Communist Party presidium, had been invited to celebrate the fortieth anniversary of the Finnish Communist Party, now headed by his firebrand daughter Hertta.[31]

The Finnish Foreign Ministry, presumably with the consent of Virolainen, the new foreign minister, had turned him down, however. This was probably just as well for Kuusinen. Twenty years after the *Talvisota*, the aging turncoat remained one of the most hated men in Finland. Rolling out the red carpet for Kliment Voroshilov, who had helped plan the 1939 Soviet invasion, was one thing. The Foreign Ministry could not guarantee the safety of the still widely loathed Kuusinen.

Still, as the terse Tass bulletin made clear, the Kremlin was vexed. So was Urho Kekkonen.

Meanwhile, to his further consternation, the president learned that Klaus Waris, the director general of the Bank of Finland, was about to fly to Washington in order to follow up on a request to the US government for a large loan in order to allay Finland's immediate economic difficulties, as well as to obviate the necessity of accepting the 400 million ruble one from the Soviets that Khrushchev and his comrades had agreed in May.

Evidently Waris, who had been director of the bank for a year and had never hidden his fondness for America, had been planning on making the move for some time. The Caesarian birth of Fagerholm III was his moment to act.

Even worse, as Kekkonen discovered, to add further weight to Waris's provocative—and still secret—mission the trouble-making banker was to be accompanied by his normally reliable and obedient political utility man V.J. Sukselainen, the former prime minister, now speaker of the parliament. Waris had already sent a request for a loan of $30 million to Washington in July. Now he intended to follow up with a personal appeal.

"This is so damn unfortunate," Kekkonen commiserated in his log. "All the time and effort [I have] invested in domestic and foreign policy seems to be melting away!" One envisions the beset president sitting at the desk of his study, downcast and preoccupied, cursing to himself, and to his diary. "Lumberheads!" he writes on August 30, after hearing that Waris and Sukselainen were about to depart for Washington.[32] *Fucking hell!*

Indeed. The following day, the third, Zhenikhov, the friendly local KGB co-*rezidenta* confirmed that the chill was in. The objectionable new government, the Russian told the distressed president, was the first to "change [Finland's] policy" toward Russia since the war. "The next time," Zhenikhov told Kekkonen, "you"—lumping him and his co-father-in-law's troublesome government together, "will go further," whatever that meant. As far as the USSR was concerned, Kekkonen and the new Western-minded cabinet were one and the same. Moscow was already considering withdrawing its ambassador, the KGB man calmly informed the president. "That would be going too far," the president protested, according to his account.

Zhenikhov's reply is not recorded.[33]

It was at this point of this political opéra bouffe that, unbeknownst to Kekkonen, another character, the aforementioned American ambassador, Hickerson, joined the cast. A career diplomat and former assistant secretary of state for UN, Hickerson was arguably one of the most capable and intelligent men Washington ever sent to Finland. A dedicated anticommunist who had a leading role in shaping both NATO and the Marshall Plan, Hickerson had a vivid memory of the Soviets' takeover of Czechoslovakia in 1948, including the defenestration of Jan Masaryk, the democratically elected foreign minister, as well as the abortive Soviet coup in Finland that same year, which had been narrowly averted by the change of heart by Yrjö Leino, the communist minister of interior.[34]

Hickerson's three years of observing the current Finnish political scene, with its interchangeable weak governments rising and falling under Kekkonen's Machiavellian eye had made the American envoy pessimistic about Finland's future as a democracy, including its ability to stave off the Kremlin. He also clearly was no admirer of Urho Kekkonen.

The feeling was reciprocated. The ambassador was a "dolt," Kekkonen wrote in his journal.[35]

Hickerson's concerns about the health of the Finnish commonweal were reflected in a bleak situation report he sent Washington in May, 1958, on the eve of Kekkonen's first state visit to Moscow. "On the negative side," the ambassador wrote, "the political scene continues to be characterized by the instability of policy and leadership. It has become increasingly clear that the real leaders of stature Finland has known in the past," he continued, referring to Kekkonen, and his predecessors, Mannerheim and Paasikivi, "are now lacking in active political life." Consequently, he warned, "there has been a faltering of Finland's position as a really neutral state independent of Soviet pressure." To halt this trend and strengthen Finnish democratic forces, the ambassador recommended various measures, including increasing US investment, as well as recruiting Finnish scientists in "non-military programs," whatever that meant.[36]

Hickerson's proposal went nowhere. Finland was not a priority for the State Department in 1958. Although the Eisenhower administration's foreign policy, as guided by Secretary of State John Foster Dulles, had little use for Finland's self-described neutrality, or its president, the US had other more important ideological and potentially military battlegrounds to monitor: Taiwan, Berlin, and Lebanon. Finland was far down the list. For now the isolated Finns would have to make do on their own.

Three years later, under another US president, John F. Kennedy, that would change, as will be seen.

Nevertheless, with the appointment of the new avowedly pro-Western government, and the daring Waris mission, the American ambassador saw an urgent opportunity to change the geopolitical equation in northeast Europe and strike a resounding blow for the West. "I urge as strongly as I can to give a favorable answer to the Waris mission," Hickerson wrote on September 2, while the Bank of Finland official was en route to Washington.[37]

"It is not too much to say that Finland now stands at the crossroads" the agitated envoy cabled. "The government that is just taking over was organized only after the greatest difficulty. From our standpoint it is a good government bringing together as it does all of the political elements which stand most firmly for preservation of both Finland's real independence and her Western orientation."[38]

Unless Finland's loan application was approved, Hickerson predicted, the new Fagerholm cabinet "will almost certainly fall within a few months." The alternatives, he warned, "would either be a minority government, seeking and dependent upon Communist support," as in fact ultimately occurred, or, worse yet, "a majority government including the Communists." As the American saw it, there was no such thing as a patriotic Finnish communist, no difference between Finnish communists and Russian ones.[39] "Either of these [eventualities] would involve a severe weakening of the solid anti-Communist front maintained in domestic politics since 1948," he continued. "And this might well be but the beginning, with the final result being over a period of years a disastrous instance of a free people voluntarily giving Communists a real voice in their affairs."[40]

Waris, the Bank of Finland director, painted an equally dire picture in his meeting with a group of State Department officials headed by Walter Elbrick, the US assistant secretary of state for European affairs, on September 4. The fate of the new government, and with it of Finnish democracy, the banker underscored, depended on the infusion of American monies and support.

If the Finnish banker expected to return home with a check for $30 million, however, he was disappointed. Moral support was one thing, Waris was told; however Elbrick informed him, because of America's other commitments he "could not be hopeful" that the US would grant Finland a loan, at least as large as the one requested, roughly a third of the amount of the prospective Soviet loan.[41]

However Waris's government's allies at the US State Department along with Ambassador Hickerson, had only begun to fight. Thus, on September 15, while the Finnish loan request was being kicked around through the Washington bureaucracy, General Charles P. Cabell, deputy director of the CIA, sent Christian Herter, the acting secretary of state, then standing in for the ailing Dulles, a memo endorsing the request, which squared with Ambassador Hickerson's dire assessment of the situation.[42] "In our view there are few cases where the timely application of American economic assistance would have more clear-cut prospects of overall benefit to a friendly government, the continued welfare and independence of which is of *high interest to and direct relation to the United States* [author's italics]," Cabell wrote Herter.[43]

Nevertheless the acting head of the department felt that the matter was too portentous to make on his own and decided to wait for his boss to return.

In the meantime, while Washington dithered and dallied, Urho Kekkonen was very clear about where Moscow stood. On September 11, a week after the apparent failure of the Waris mission (which one suspects was known to the Soviets), his lieutenant, Ahti Karjalainen, relayed the essence of a conversation he had had with Viktor Vladimirov. The new government, the KGB man told Karjalainen, had completely lost Moscow's trust.

Henceforth the Kremlin's policy toward Helsinki would be one of "passive resistance."

The Finnish public, for its part, knew nothing of these Byzantine doings. The first indication of a rift between Helsinki and Moscow took place on September 15, 1958, when as Zhenikhov, the KGB co-station chief, had warned earlier, the Kremlin withdrew its ambassador, Lebedev, without informing the Finnish Foreign Ministry, as per standard protocol. The official explanation was that the Soviet diplomat was leaving on a vacation.[44]

In the meantime, the Finnish government announced the members of the delegation it had chosen to send to Moscow to continue the discussions for the vital new Fenno-Soviet trade pact, which had begun during Kekkonen's May visit, while suggesting a date of October 7 for the two teams to meet.

There was no word from the Kremlin. Something was amiss. "SIGNS OF COOLNESS," the *Times* of London's Helsinki correspondent reported.[45]

Cooler signs were to come.

For the distraught Finnish head of state, Moscow's abrupt withdrawal of its ambassador confirmed that things were indeed serious. Now he just had to get that through to his fellow Agrarian League members, particularly his misguided protégé, Johannes Virolainen, who had been foolhardy enough to participate in the new government.

Was one of the expectations of the Finnish presidency that Kekkonen sever his party ties and not get involved in politics? Never mind. There he was on September 17, according to his dyspeptic journal, presiding over an Agrarian League meeting, badgering and belittling Virolainen and his four fellow wayward ministers.

Virolainen already seems to have gotten the general picture. Kekkonen notes that the foreign minister was "almost in a panic" and "didn't think that the new government could handle its affairs or regain [the Soviet's] trust."[46] Now, he wished, if only his foolish colleagues and his dense co-father-in-law, Fagerholm got the message as well.

That, it seems, would still take considerable doing.

On September 27, Kekkonen laments in his journal that "only the Finnish government and its foreign minister are unable to see that relations with the USSR have cooled."[47] Five days later, on October 2, he notes that the Soviets had informed the government that it was no longer possible to discuss the issue of Finland's membership in the Organization for European Economic Co-operation (OEEC), the global organization and predecessor of the European Economic Community (EEC), which Finland was keen to join.[48]

"If relations [had been] as good as before," Kekkonen quoted Virolainen as saying, "there could have been a mutual understanding of the matter. Now it was no longer possible."[49]

That evening, on October 3, the irate president invited the foreign minister and the four other Agrarian ministers to dinner at his house. According to his own account, the Finnish president appears to have spent most of the evening berating his guests. The new government would "end in disaster," he said he told them. "I do not recognize you as members of the same party to which I belong!"

There was more. The party was engaged in "adventure politics," Kekkonen fumed. "Not one of you can point to a time when I have been disloyal to you!"

His guests' reaction is not recorded. At any rate, none of them said they would resign, as he evidently hoped.

More pressure would have to be supplied before Fagerholm and the five Agrarian ministers would retire from the scene.

Moscow was happy to oblige.

Johannes Virolainen seems to have been in denial of the obvious when he appeared in Parliament six days later, on October 8, 1958, according to Werner Wiskari, the Helsinki correspondent of *The New York Times*. "The specter of cooling relations with the Soviet Union haunted today's session of the Finnish Parliament," he wrote.[50] Nevertheless the undaunted foreign minister declared that

> nothing had changed as far as Finland was concerned. He said the foreign policy of the five party coalition under Premier Karl-August Fagerholm continued to be based on assuring "good and dependable relations with all nations, especially with our neighbors."[51]

In the meantime, the *Times*man noted, the Soviet press had continued to criticize the new government, noting an article in *Izvestia* which criticized Helsinki for failing to live up to the terms of the new Fenno-Soviet trade agreement—the same agreement which Moscow now refused to finalize!

In parliament Virolainen insisted that Finland stood ready to negotiate the Soviet loan arranged during President Kekkonen's recent visit to Moscow, however, he added, putting the best face on the Kremlin's stonewalling, "the Soviet Union has not considered itself yet able to begin talks on the matter."[52]

According to Wiskari, the *Times* reporter, Virolainen, who was still respected on both sides of the aisle of the *eduskunta*, was listened to "intently and without heckling."[53] However the budget speech delivered afterward by his prime minister, Fagerholm, was loudly jeered by the sixty-strong Communist-Skog claque. Still, to both Moscow's and Kekkonen's annoyance, the good ship Fagerholm III would not sink.

To eliminate any further doubt where the Kremlin stood vis-à-vis Finland, and Finnish foreign policy in September I. V. Spiridonov, the secretary of the presidium of the Supreme Soviet, the Soviet equivalent of the president of the US Chamber of Commerce, devoted a speech to its rambunctious Finnish client state which *Tass* published in full, according to Kekkonen's journal. Although Spiridonov had no real power, the fact that *Tass* printed his rodomontade gave it weight.[54]

Kekkonen, who included a long summary of the jeremiad, possibly the most anti-Finnish speech delivered by a Soviet official since the war, in his journal, certainly was listening. Among other things, according to Kekkonen's lengthy approbatory synopsis, Spiridonov proclaimed that it was delusory "for a small country to conduct foreign policy which ignores its geographical location and contradicts the interests of the superpower in whose economic area of interest the country is located." Be in no doubt, the Soviet spokesman, a key ally of Nikita Khrushchev declared, "*Finland firmly belongs in the Soviet sphere of influence and Soviet interests and those interests determine Finnish policies* [author's italics]."[55]

Using Moscow's favored phrase for its policy for dealing with the capitalist world, Finland's relationship with the USSR had been a good example of "peaceful coexistence between 2 different systems," the top Soviet pitchman continued, according to Kekkonen, with "the big socialist country assisting the development of [the] small capitalist one."[56] Nevertheless recent developments in Finland, including the formation of the new government, were worrisome. Specifically, the USSR could not overlook the inclusion of the Conservatives in (the new) government and Väinö Tanner, the ever-loathed Social Democrat and his party, in Finnish politics.

In the area of foreign policy, in a passage that worried many Finns in which he menacingly alluded to the clause of the 1948 Friendship Cooperation and Mutual Assistance treaty under which Moscow was allowed to call for mutual military consultations in case of the perceived threat of war by NATO, the same clause that the Kremlin would invoke at the start of the Note Crisis three years later, Spiridonov noted that the "international situation . . . is becoming tense and the Soviets must know that Finland [would] not serve as a springboard for NATO countries at Soviet border." While he was at it, he also took a swipe at "Finnish neutralism" at the United Nations.[57] So much for Finnish neutrality, or Finnish sovereignty for that matter.

Nevertheless, despite the overwrought president's best efforts Virolainen and his fellow ministers, following Karl-August Fagerholm's flinty lead, as well as their consciences, refused to leave the stage and resign.

To be sure, for Kekkonen loyalists, the so-called Great Savior's statements and actions during the Night Frost crisis make for depressing reading. In addition to attacking and undermining the Fagerholm government, including playing its members against each other, the Finnish leader also tried to placate Moscow by suppressing books and other media which the Soviets found objectionable, most notably the memoirs of Yrjö Leino, the postwar communist minister of the interior whose last-minute action may or may not have forestalled a Czech-like coup.[58] Leino's memoirs, which were sure to raise Soviet hackles, had been scheduled to be published that fall by Tammi, the prominent Finnish publisher.

As Kekkonen's journal entry for October 20, 1958, the sixth week of the crisis makes clear, the president played an instrumental role in the halting of the book's publication. At the same time he also underlines how poorly he thinks of his relative, Fagerholm, to whom Tammi, the Finish publisher had sent the galleys for the Leino opus, and saw nothing objectionable in it.

While Kekkonen busied himself with scrubbing the Finnish media for Moscow, the Kremlin announced that it had decided to expel Boris Pasternak, the Nobel Prize-winning author of the novel *Doctor Zhivago,* from the scrolls of the official Soviet literature society. The self-defeating, and seemingly irrational move puzzled the top Finn. "The USSR will suffer a propaganda loss by condemning Pasternak," he wrote on October 30th, "but still maintains its line."

"Well," the bemused diarist wonders aloud, "What do we learn from this?"[59]

What indeed. Kekkonen himself seemed stumped.

Meanwhile the new Finnish government, now approaching its second month in office stood fast, despite the concerted bullying of Urho Kekkonen and his Soviet friends. One cannot escape the suspicion, in retrospect, that one of the reasons why it lasted as long as it did—nearly one hundred days, relatively long by recent standards—despite both Moscow's and Kekkonen's explicit and pronounced opposition, is that it was holding out for a strong expression of Western support. As declassified US documents indicate, Hickerson, the pugnacious American ambassador, was certainly doing his best to obtain that support, including the loan it had requested, and more.

On October 13, the distressed diplomat sent a telegram to Washington enumerating the mounting pressures, which now included denying visas to all Finns excepting government officials, Moscow was exerting on Helsinki, both directly and indirectly, and urging approval of the loan to the Bank of Finland.

"Within the last few days," Hickerson wrote, the US "Embassy has been reliably informed: 1) Soviets have not responded to Finnish proposal that new trade talks begin on October 7, 2) Soviets are currently issuing no visas to Finnish nationals, 3) Soviets broke precedent and did not inform the government that [Viktor] Lebedev would not return as ambassador (Finns learned of his release from a press announcement).

"[It is] now clear," Hickerson concluded, "Soviets are engaged in [a] many-faceted pressure campaign against present Finnish Cabinet."[60]

On October 23, Gerald Smith, the US assistant secretary for policy planning, sent a long memo to his superior, Christian Herter, the acting secretary of state, strongly corroborating Hickerson's concerns and endorsing the Bank of Finland's loan request. As Smith noted, aside from the fact of the loan itself, "the psychological effect of announcement [is] important."[61] Slowly but surely the US government, or elements of it, was rousing itself to do battle for the Finns. "No overall objective of US foreign policy has a higher priority than reducing or preventing the expansion of the area subject to Soviet domination," the aroused American diplomat wrote. "With the exception of Iran, Afghanistan and Turkey," he pointed out, "Finland is the only nation in the world free of foreign domination which possesses a common border with the USSR."[62]

According to Smith, the Fagerholm government's predicament and its request for US assistance was nothing less than a test of US resolve. "The area of most direct confrontation between the free West and Soviet imperialism is in Europe," he reminded his chief, in soaring words which doubtless would have given heart to the embattled Finnish cabinet, and angered Urho Kekkonen:

> *The Finnish situation presents a good case of Western ability in assisting a free nation to withstand Soviet political and economic pressures. It is also a test of [our] ability to move swiftly when the occasion requires. If we and our allies cannot or do not meet these in the psychologically important case of Finland,*

we must recognize that there are serious limitations in our ability to compete with the USSR in the cold war [author's italics].[63]

Finland was off America's map, so to speak, no more. The question was, as Gerald Smith put it, could the US move swiftly enough to bolster its beset government? More to the point, did it desire to do so? Did the US, which hitherto had had an essentially hands-off policy regarding Finland, wish to engage with the USSR in a pitched economic-cum-propaganda fight over it or perhaps even more? On the evidence of the State Department archives, a growing contingent at Foggy Bottom certainly did.

And thus, as the third month of the crisis commences, the remarkable picture emerges of a Western-oriented Finnish government in utter limbo. On the one hand, it was being pressured by its president—who himself was being pressured by Moscow—to resign, while, one the other hand, the resolutely anticommunist US ambassador, Hickerson, and his allies in Washington State were urging *their* superiors to fortify it.

To be sure, the embattled new government did have its domestic supporters, too, including the press. Thus on November 3, as Kekkonen notes annoyedly in his diary, *Hufvudstadsbladet*, the Swedo-Finnish daily, invoking the famous wartime Finnish phrase, exhorted the government to "have ice in its stomach."[64]

Fine words. Ultimately, however, the fate of the Fagerholm government was not in its own hands—or in Urho Kekkonen's, for that matter, but in Moscow's and Washington's: Finland had become a pawn in the Cold War.

Four days later, on November 6, 1958, Ambassador Hickerson, impatient of the State Department's delay, sent his strongest call for action yet. The Kremlin was tired of playing around, he cabled Washington. Based on his best information, he warned, Nikita Khrushchev was about to ratchet up the pressure on Helsinki and launch a "systemic Soviet economic boycott with serious economic consequences for Finland."[65]

Anticipating such a move, the American minister considered it essential that the department determine urgently whether emergency aid, probably in the form of loans, could be offered to Finland over the transitional period between the possible cut-off or sharp decline Soviet trade and the time when displaced Finnish trade could be reoriented to the west.

Thirty million dollars would no longer be enough, according to the dismayed American ambassador; at least twice as much would be needed to tide the Finns over during the pending blockade, he felt. As far as the government itself was concerned, Hickerson signaled, it was standing tough, with certain prominent exceptions, most notably President Kekkonen: "The main elements [of the] Cabinet appear resolved [to] resist firmly Soviet pressure. Certain other non-Communist elements, especially within the Agrarian League and reportedly *including President Kekkonen* [author's italics] actively seeking overthrow Cabinet [to] satisfy Soviets. Aim of my proposal is to strengthen hand of first named and to stiffen backs of wavering groups in between."

For the moment, however, Hickerson cautioned, stealth was required. Obviously the American rescue operation would become public knowledge soon enough. In the meantime, he advised, "assurance [of American aid] would have to be *on a secret basis to selected leaders* [author's italics]."[66] And Urho Kekkonen was definitely not one of those leaders.

Not wishing to sound overly alarmist, the envoy closes his remarkable cable with a caveat. "It remains possible of course that Soviets will abandon their pressure. [It is] important [to] note they so far have avoided any positive actions, having limited themselves to dragging feet in various areas. . . . Nevertheless discreet assurance regarding our position if worse comes to worse highly desirable *if we are not to risk loss of game* [author's italics] by default."[67]

Quite a "game" this was turning out to be, in Hickerson's phrase.

The question was: who would win? Kekkonen or Fagerholm? The East or the West?

At the moment the answer to that question was in doubt.

Chapter 3

The Boom Drops (11/58–1/59)

> Suddenly the attitude of our hosts, which had been friendly, turned frosty.
>
> —Eino Uuistitalo, Finnish member of parliament, describing the sudden change of temperature during his visit to Moscow at the start of the Night Frost

In the event, John Hickerson's intelligence about Soviet intention was accurate. "Passive resistance" was not working for the Politburo anymore. Nor, unfortunately, were the ministrations of Urho Kekkonen. The time for back-room manipulation and dinner party tantrums was over. Nikita Khrushchev decided that stronger, "positive" action was now required to resolve the "Finnish question." As Hickerson predicted, a "systemic economic boycott" and complete freeze-up of Finnish-Soviet relations was now enjoined.

Thus, on November 6, 1958, the same day that he sent the above all points bulletin to Washington, according to the CIA after action report: "The first positive statement by the Soviet government that discriminatory economic action was to be taken was made . . . when the Soviet government reportedly told a Finnish delegation, which was in Moscow to discuss stockpiling arrangements that the USSR could not supply the stockpiling items which Finland was willing to take to reduce the ruble balance and that unless Finland [was] willing to take the 'regular items' under the trade agreement the USSR would have to reduce immediately its purchases from Finland."[1]

Eino Uusitalo, an Agrarian member of parliament who belonged to the snubbed group, remembers his Moscow hosts' change of heart well. "Suddenly the attitude of our hosts, which had been friendly, turned frosty, including the service"—including drinks. No more vodka for the Finns![2] "I didn't mind that so much because I wasn't much of a drinker," Uuistalo recalled years later. The MP, who was due to return to Helsinki the next day, was more put out when he was suddenly told that he would not be able to board his scheduled train the next morning.[3] In the event, Uusitalo, who would go on to achieve notoriety as Kekkonen's Soviet-friendly minister of interior during the 1970s, was able to board his train after explaining with some difficulty that he was legally bound to return to the *eduskunta* the following afternoon.

Meanwhile, Khrushchev was preparing to instigate another more portentous crisis with the West, and one that, inevitably, would have a knock-on effect on both Kekkonen and Finland. Four days later, on November 10, 1958, the Soviet leader stunned observers by opening, or rather, reopening, a major new front in the Cold War: Berlin. In a shock Moscow speech, Khrushchev issued an ultimatum to the United States, Great Britain, and France demanding that the Allies withdraw their forces from Berlin, warning that otherwise the USSR would turn over access to West Berlin to its East German satellite.

Two and a half weeks later, on November 27, Khrushchev transposed the essence of his speech into demarches to Washington, London and Paris declaring the original 1945 Four Power agreement dividing the occupied former German capital null and void and demanding that Berlin be turned into a "demilitarized free city." If no agreement was reached within six months, he threatened, Moscow would sign a peace treaty with the German Democratic Republic (GDR) and the Allies would have to settle matters with its East German comrades.

And so, just as it had during the first postwar Berlin crisis of 1948, which culminated with the Berlin airlift and to a lesser extent the East-led Berlin uprising of 1953, the spotlight of the world turned to the troublesome German capital, and so it would remain, more or less, for the next three years, as the rekindled Berlin Crisis mushroomed, culminating in August 1961 with the building of the infamous wall. Inevitably, too, the new Berlin crisis altered the way both East and West viewed the smaller, parallel crisis forming over Finland. Khrushchev's decision to force a solution to the Berlin question made him more impatient to resolve the Finnish one. At the same time, the renewed focus on Berlin made Washington less reluctant to engage with Moscow on what was now a secondary front. Yet it would take another month of Soviet frostiness for the "Finnish question" to resolve itself and for the beleaguered third government of Karl-August Fagerholm to fall.

During the interim, both the Soviet and Finnish Red press poured it on, falsely lambasting Helsinki for its putative failure "to deal successfully with the USSR" (i.e., its refusal to ditch its democratically elected government), while Kekkonen kept up the pressure on his own, particularly on his luckless protégé, Virolainen, the foreign minister. On November 6, Kekkonen demanded outright that the embattled Virolainen resign to clear the way for a new government acceptable to Moscow, however the obstinate foreign minister refused. Over the next ten days Kekkonen continued to put the pressure on his beset foreign minister. Moscow was so upset, learned Virolainen, who was then in Oslo, that according to Kekkonen, there were rumors that Khrushchev was considering invoking the 1948 Fenno-Soviet "mutual assistance" treaty—well-founded rumors, in light of Spiridonov's speech. That certainly got Virolainen's attention. "If this is your stand," the worried diplomat wrote back, "the possibility has to be immediately rejected!"[4]

The stubborn foreign minister finally got the message. Six days later, on November 17, 1958, the self-satisfied Finnish president records, Virolainen informed Kekkonen that he and the four other Agrarian ministers had reluctantly decided to resign by the end of the month, on the grounds of their differences on "foreign policy."

No, Kekkonen instantly replied: that would not do. "Then everyone would think that the USSR had pressured [you] into resigning!"[5]

Meanwhile, the fast-accelerating crisis continued. Two days later, on November 19, according to Kekkonen, Virolainen dutifully announced that he would be resigning from the Cabinet putatively because he could not properly manage Finland's relationship with the USSR. For Kekkonen that was a start.

Nevertheless things were not moving quickly enough for Moscow. Now it was time for Ahti Karjalainen, Kekkonen's hard-nosed, hard-drinking adjutant, who would later become his foreign minister, to administer a push. "Time for conclusions," Karjalainen wrote the next day in *Maakansa,* the Agrarian League flack sheet.[6] Still, Virolainen had yet to get the message and tender his resignation.

Now, Khrushchev decided, it was finally time to drop the boom. Consequently, on November 22, the Soviet trade representative in Helsinki sent formal letters to three top Finnish metallurgical and ship-building firms cancelling all orders "not boxed for delivery" (whatever that meant) for the remainder of the year, and informing them that there would be a delay in payments of 1.9 billion finnmarks, or approximately 5 percent of total Finnish exports to the USSR that year. Things were definitely getting frosty now.

And yet from the point of view of the average Finnish man or woman on the street, there was no crisis, nor even a hint of one. Stockmann's famous department store still opened in the morning. Water still sprouted from the mouth of Havis Amanda, the landmark sculpture facing the Helsinki water front. Excepting the small number of Finns wishing to travel to Russia who had been denied visas, nothing had untoward happened.

Newspaper readers were dimly aware that all was not well with the government, and that it might fall, but what of it? The Finnish people had already seen three cabinets come and go over the last year, including the short-lived 1957 V. J. Sukselainen one, and the two "professional" ones headed by . . . by . . . *what were their names again?* What difference would it make if another one fell? Except for a handful of Finnish, Russian and American—officials and diplomats, and a few savvy journalists, no one was aware that behind the scenes a great "game," as John Hickerson put it, was being played out behind the scenes, one that would the shape the tenor of Finnish democracy and government, including the presidency, for decades to come, as well as Finland's relations with both East and West. Finland was indeed at a "crossroads," as the US ambassador had cabled.

Nevertheless one could have fooled the average Finn. As Kekkonen, the principal beneficiary of the Night Frost, remarked in his notorious December 10 broadcast to the Finnish nation about the now all-but-forgotten affair, and prelude to the better-known Note Crisis: "There are many peaceful citizens who have not noticed anything unusual, let alone a crisis in foreign policy, because it has not yet greatly affected the course of their everyday lives."[7]

Nevertheless a crisis there certainly was. If one doubts it, all one needs to do is to read Kekkonen's traumatized journal entries from the fall of 1958, as well as the frenetic cable traffic between the State Department and the US embassy.

Three days later, on November 25, 1958, two weeks after Khrushchev issued his new Berlin ultimatum, John Foster Dulles, the US secretary of state, and chief architect of American foreign policy during the Eisenhower administration, cabled Ambassador Hickerson, who still was hoping that Washington would throw the sinking government of Karl-August Fagerholm a life preserver, what the US was prepared to do: essentially nothing.

The message from the ailing Cold Warrior, suffering from the cancer that would kill him six months later, briefly taking the helm back from his acting secretary, Christian Herter, was short and to the point:

> For Ambassador. Careful consideration has been given to steps which might be taken in light prospects [Hickerson had previously outlined]. While we share your hope that assurances US sympathy and desire help may bolster Finnish will to resist Soviet pressure, *we do not wish any US offer to create situation in which US and USSR would appear engaged in economic struggle over Finland. Such situation in our view would not be in best interest US or Finland* [author's italics].[8]

Dulles did authorize Hickerson to extend "limited economic assistance" in case of a full Soviet blockade, including the sale of petroleum; however he did not sound very enthusiastic about it. This was certainly not the full-throated statement of support which either Hickerson, or the teetering Finnish cabinet, or its ally at the Bank of Finland, Klaus Waris, had hoped for.

The message was clear: Washington did not wish to engage in an "economic struggle," as Secretary Dulles put it, over Finland—or a political one, for that matter. As such, Dulles was reaffirming the policy line toward Finland which had been established eight years before, in 1950, during the administration of Kekkonen's supposed idol, Harry Truman, by Truman's influential secretary of state, Dean Acheson. Its essence can be found in a memo Acheson sent to Truman after a meeting with the president in which the subject of US policy toward Scandinavia, specifically Finland, had come up.[9]

Acheson's advice to Truman: hands off. His memo, dated February 9, 1950, two short years following the abortive 1948 communist coup, is worth quoting at length:

> The President had on his desk a copy of a long telegram from Stockholm which raised some question [regarding] Scandinavia.
>
> The President thought it was desirable for me to see this telegram . . . because he wondered whether it would be desirable for the National Security Council to review our policy towards the

> Scandinavian countries looking towards a closer alignment [with] the West.
>
> I replied that it was always desirable to keep our policies under review. It seemed to me, however, that it would be most dangerous at the present time to make any efforts in the direction of Finland since that would produce a reaction on the part of the Russians that would be most dangerous to the Finns.[10]

In rebuffing Hickerson, the ailing Dulles had now revalidated Truman's and Acheson's line on Finland. With Berlin now back on the front burner, Washington now had more important fish to fry with Moscow. Just as in the winter of 1940, when Suomi looked in vain to Washington for succor from the invading Russians, the Finns would have to find a way of dealing with the Soviets on their own.

That policy would continue to remain the basis of American policy toward Finland for the next three years until the Note Crisis of October, 1961, when Dulles's intervention-minded successor, Dean Rusk, decided to change it with the approval of President John F. Kennedy and finally get into the Finnish "game" himself.[11]

While we are on the subject of John Foster Dulles, a brief aside about that quintessential Cold Warrior is perhaps apropos here. In his memoirs, secretly smuggled out of the USSR six years after he was deposed, Khrushchev makes no secret of his dislike for the hardcore anticommunist, who oversaw American foreign policy at the start of the Cold War.

Dulles, who Khrushchev calls "a vicious cur," was "obsessed" with encircling the USSR, Khrushchev recalled, as indeed Eisenhower's secretary of state had been. "Not even Soviet tourists and chess players were permitted to visit the United States," Khrushchev wrote. "I remember, too, that when the US sponsored some sort of international convention of chefs, our own delegation wasn't allowed to attend."

Perish the thought: America denied the best of Soviet cuisine! At the same time, Khrushchev conceded, his American nemesis knew where to pick his spots, as well as how much he could push the other side, a lesson which the Soviet chieftain would learn for himself to his regret three years later when he decided to push Eisenhower's successor, Kennedy, and the United States in Cuba.

"Dulles knew how far he could push us," Khruschev wrote. "For instance, when the forces of our two countries confronted each other in the Near East during the events in Syria and Lebanon in 1958, Dulles stepped back from the brink of war."[12]

Dulles might have been a "cur," according to Khrushchev, but he was a "prudent" one. Overruling his subordinates, he decided that Finland was not a good place to confront the Kremlin. If that meant losing the "game" in northeastern Europe, as Hickerson had warned, so be it.[13]

And yet, despite the vitriol and fustian being thrown its way from both Moscow and Kekkonen, the Fagerholm government continued to stand. As the Finnish president himself peevishly noted, in his entry for November 21, his co-father-in-law's cabinet still commanded a considerable amount of support, particularly within the Finnish business community.

Meanwhile, in anticipation of the Fagerholm government's fall, the coauthor of its collapse was already on the defensive. Thus, on November 22, Kekkonen, back to his "normal" petulant self, disingenuously complains that some, particularly "those in Swedish-speaking circles," alluding to the country's Swedish speaking minority with whom he had mixed relations, especially Nils Meinander, the prominent Swedish-speaking MP, claimed that he was responsible for the government's difficulties, "even though I was the one who warned about such a government forming at its start."[14]

Thus, on November 25, the same day that Secretary Dulles instructed John Hickerson to disengage from his pro-Fagerholm efforts, at a closed meeting of the foreign relations committee of the parliament, at which Kekkonen was present, Virolainen, who likely had been informed of the US stand down, wearily announced that he would resign as foreign minister.

And yet the drama was not over, as the *Times* of London, one of the Western newspapers which had been maintaining a death watch on the government, reported: "To-day he [Virolainen] seems to have spoken only for himself," the paper's correspondent noted. "However he has not yet handed to the Prime Minister his formal resignation."[15] When would *that* happen, Zhenikhov, Vladimirov, and their colleagues at KGB's sizable station, who effectively were now representing the USSR in Helsinki in the absence of the "vacationing" ambassador, Lebedev, kept asking Kekkonen's faithful go-betweens, Karjalainen, and Arvo Korsimo, the Agrarian League secretary.[16]

Meanwhile, the effects of the Soviet trade freeze were beginning to kick in. On November 30, the Finnish shipbuilding companies affected by the embargo announced that they would have to shut down for several weeks, resulting in the off of nearly 3,000 workers, adding to the 82,000 Finns who lost their jobs because of the crisis. On December 2, Kekkonen records the sense of a conversation he had that day with Korsimo following the latter's latest huddle at the Soviet embassy with Zhenikhov. "Must hurry—Moscow is very restless, asks about the matter every day," he wrote. Once an acceptable government was formed, the KGB man had assured Korsimo, "relations would improve immediately."[17]

Unsurprisingly, the Helsinki KGB co-*rezident* had some clear ideas about what constituted an acceptable government. Russia was no longer pretending that it would not interfere in Finnish affairs. For one, Zhenikhov stipulated, the next cabinet could not include the Social Democrats. A "clean sweep" was necessary: none of the current ministers could reenlist. And yes, it would be good, Zhenikhov implied, if the SKDL, Finnish communists, were included.

For his part, Fagerholm, the prime minister and captain of the doomed government was still refusing to jump ship, according to Ambassador Hickerson. The sympathetic envoy continued to offer the beleaguered prime minister qualified support, despite the discouraging instructions received from Secretary Dulles. "I did say that although available funds are limited, US Government might consider seeking further funds from Congress, if required, and that Finland's excellent reputation in US should facilitate favorable action," according to a telegram he sent Washington on the evening of December 3, 1958. Hickerson's cable illustrates the unrelenting pressure Fagerholm was under from various sides, including president Kekkonen, during the waning hours of his star-crossed third government. According to his telegram, the stressed politician "expressed deep appreciation [of US] proposals." Despite this, "he said that he had reluctantly decided that 'minor' changes in government should be made, but that he would not be a party to major change in [its] alignment."[18]

Of course, he promised the loyal US ambassador, he would not abide incorporating the communists into the kind of disingenuous "popular front" government which had preceded the fall of Czechoslovakia under Edvard Beneš, the war-time prime minister, ten years before.[19] Beyond that, he could promise nothing. Although the isolated and angry politician refrained from naming names, Fagerholm made it clear which one of "them" bore the greatest responsibility for the unfolding debacle—Urho Kekkonen.

The next day, December 4, Fagerholm III finally fell, with the Agrarian League contingent leading the walk-out, and the disconsolate prime minister reluctantly following suit. "Virolainen left official notice of resignation, other Agrarian League members did the same," Kekkonen notes without emotion in his journal. "Fagerholm left notice of: resignation for entire government."[20] To be sure, there still was the matter of forming a new government to replace it. In the meantime the cabinet that Moscow had just caused to be removed, with the connivance of Kekkonen, would continue in a caretaker capacity. RIP, Fagerholm III.

Did Kekkonen sign away Finland's freedom in 1958 and 1959, when he was under maximum Soviet pressure? James Ford Cooper, the deputy chief of mission at the US embassy in Helsinki in the late 1980s and early 90s, and the author of *On the Finland Watch: An American Diplomat in Finland during the Cold War*, feels it did. "It is possible to believe that workable relations might have continued under the Fagerholm III government had President Kekkonen been willing to make clear to the Soviet Union that it was in fact the duly constituted government of Finland," writes Cooper. "And that he would permit no significant change in Finland's foreign policy."[21] So, Cooper continues in one of the more damning passages of his book, "he [Kekkonen] allowed the Soviets into the Finnish process, redrawing the line that had been set by Paasikivi and Mannerheim."[22]

Cooper possibly may be judging Kekkonen's motives too harshly. Although he was the ultimate survivor, his actions, including the devious ones he took during both the Night Frost crisis and the subsequent Note Crisis three years later, were rarely dictated solely by his desire to survive, as his former ambassador to Washington, Jaakko Iloniemi, and long-time observer reflected in an interview with the author in 2015. "Kekkonen never, or at least rarely acted solely for himself," said Iloniemi. "All his important actions, including the most seemingly selfish ones, were, at some level, motivated by his desire for Finland to survive." "Of course," Iloniemi added, "in his mind these were the same things. He was Finland, and Finland was he. And the Finnish people had to trust that he knew the way."[23]

Now that the cabinet had resigned, Kekkonen had his "Russian card," his chief political weapon back. As we can see today, however, it had been a close thing—probably closer than even Kekkonen realized.

On December 6, 1958, two days following the government's fall, the chief of state hosted his third Independence Day celebration at the presidential mansion. Paavo Laitinen, a foreign ministry official who had the role of serving as an usher at the affair, recalled the event in an interview with Cooper.[24]

One gathers from Laitinen's account that the tensions between his father and his father-in-law had driven the thirty-year-old Taneli, then on the cusp of a long and distinguished diplomatic career, to drink, something of an occupational hazard amongst high-flying Finns in those bibulous days.

"I was then in the commercial department of the Foreign Ministry, and Taneli Kekkonen, the son of the president was sitting in the same room as I," Laitenen recalled. "He was a very intelligent and analytic person. He was drinking too much. Nevertheless he was one of the best diplomats we ever had."

"When the government was formed, he was telling me every day about the problems he had. After all his father-in-law was Fagerholm! Taneli was married to Fagerholm's daughter, Brita. He told me [that] Kekkonen was constantly telephoning Fagerholm. And Fagerholm always told him that everything is all right, you don't need to worry, and put the receiver down. So he kept Kekkonen at a distance during the time when he forming his government."

Laitinen recalled Kekkonen's mounting dismay at the billowing tensions between Helsinki and Moscow, which culminated in Moscow's refusal to participate in the discussions for renewing the Fenno-Soviet trade pact in mid-September:

"Then the Russians informed [us] that they were not coming for the negotiations. So Kekkonen telephoned Fagerholm and asked what was happening, and Fagerholm said they were [still coming] and hung up the receiver."

But of course, as we know, the Russians were not coming.

Flash forward to the intense scene at the Finnish presidential mansion on December 6th, in Laitinen's recollection: ". . . Then on the 6th of December, I was at the Independence Day party, as a kind of usher. [President] Kekkonen came to me, and told me Taneli [was] drunk, and could I please take him upstairs to our private rooms. [So] we went up there, and he went directly to his father's bedroom. There was a small cabinet there, and he took out a cognac bottle. He was just pouring a big glass when his father walked in."

Apparently there had been similar scenes between father and son before. Thereupon followed a strange charade involving the two Kekkonens and their captive guest, Paavo Laitinen, according to the latter:

"Taneli got a little scared and said that, 'I am just pouring this for Paavo Laitinen.' Kekkonen said, 'Let me help you, your hands are trembling.' [So] Kekkonen poured a whole glass of some thirty centimeters in the glass and said to me in Finnish 'bottoms up.' And I drank that, and he watched me very carefully."

Unsurprisingly, Laitinen, not one to disobey his president, finished the whole glass. Taneli's reaction to this intimidating display of his father's displaced pique is not recorded. Occasionally, it seems, Kekkonen, who relished making his ministers squirm also did the same with his son.

To be sure, the president had other things on his mind, besides his son's tippling, as well, most notably the political tempest which had just felled his unfortunate relative's government.[25]

"I say only one thing," Laitinen recalls that Kekkonen declared at the time. "I am determined to make sure that they in Moscow believe that I am in charge here in Helsinki."

"To me," Laitenen says, "that was kind of a clear-cut statement [on the president's part] that this was . . . his political will and he was determined to act on it, he wanted to show them [the Kremlin] who is the boss in Finland."[26]

Was he? Many Finns wondered about that, and his craven actions during the Night Frost did little to quell their doubts on that score.

On December 10, 1958, six days after the fourteen ministers of the Fagerholm cabinet tendered their resignations under duress, Urho Kekkonen took to the airwaves to speak to his people about what had happened.

Although Kekkonen's speech, which was broadcast over radio and TV, was directed at the Finnish public, it was also aimed at Moscow. What had occurred, the president explained, in his carefully worded and considerably misleading tour d'horizon, was that after a period of "trustful collaboration" between the two neighboring countries over the past decade things had suddenly gone sour. Excepting a "brief period of coolness," which presumably included the abortive '48 Soviet coup, everything had basically been hunky-dory since the end of the war.

Trade has increased from year to year, the president asserted. Cultural relations had flourished, mutual trust and understanding had been enhanced, and so forth.

Meanwhile, in a nod to his predecessor, Paasikivi, as well as himself, although "the world [had] experienced many threatening crises, Finland, thanks to her foreign policy" had managed to steer clear of trouble while garnering respect for her "special position" from near and far. This was a hopeful way of putting things, however if you ignored such matters as the curt reception that Khrushchev and Bulganin had received the previous year and the prior, shorter trade freeze of 1957, it was basically true. The fact was, relations between Helsinki and Moscow *had* improved during the 1950s.

So what had happened? Suddenly the USSR had "lost trust"—a big word in Kekkonen's lexicon—in Finland. One proof of this was Moscow's decision to withdraw its ambassador, Viktor Lebedev, in September. Obviously the new trade freeze was another, although Kekkonen did not mention it. In any case, the president asserted, the blame for the latest crisis was entirely Finland's, particularly that of its hypercritical and irresponsible press, as Nikita Khrushchev had helpfully pointed out during Kekkonen's visit to Moscow the prior May.

"The Soviet leaders spoke of this [criticism of the USSR by the Finnish press] during my visit last summer and wished to emphasize the regret that they felt because of Finnish publications," Kekkonen continued. "We got a clear picture of how important this matter was regarded in the Soviet Union. The observation that Prime Minister Khrushchev made in his speech on this matter expressed a view to which serious consideration must be given."

The president then recalled how he had responded to this criticism. "In my reply I defended us by saying that it was unfortunate that such publications" acted in this manner—presumably he was referring to the same publications, the same ones which he had derided as "scum"—"but [this] was something superficial that the strengthening of friendly relations would remove." The president said that this criticism by The Neighbor to the East had continued, notwithstanding the Soviet press's friendly attitude toward its small neighbor.

Or as Kekkonen said, in the closest thing in the hour-long address to a blatant lie, "[*what*] *we cannot ignore is that articles and books hostile to Finland have not appeared in the Soviet Union in recent years* [author's italics]"—this despite the "menacing flood of abuse [which] poured from the Soviet press and radio in which [putatively anti-Soviet members of the government] were singled out by name."

This had never happened, according to Kekkonen, nor had the Soviet minion I. V. Spiridonov's attack on the Finnish party October. In fact, there was virtually no mention of the purged government at all, or its presumptive contribution to the rupture in Fenno-Soviet relations. Indeed, Kekkonen said, the just departed cabinet had not specifically made any changes in foreign policy: "I realize that the Government that has just resigned has not made any decisions to produce changes in our foreign policy."

Now he approached the heart of the matter, while simultaneously avoiding it. "But," Kekkonen continued, in the same murky vein, "the fact that our neighbor, *possibly on account of other things, some of which I've already mentioned* [author's italics], no longer has full confidence in our sincerity and furthermore our official assurances have not helped matters."

What were these dread "other things" which had caused Moscow to lose "confidence" in the "sincerity" of the Finnish government? The disingenuous speaker did not say. "Concealing or denying [that the USSR had lost confidence in Finland] will not alter it," he declared. "It is up to us to decide what conclusions to draw."

There was more tendentiousness on the subject of "outside interference" (i.e., interference from the West in Finland's affairs). By now, Kekkonen had learned of Ambassador Hickerson's vigorous if unsuccessful exertions, in concert with his Finnish allies, including Waris of the Bank of Finland, to get Washington to come to Finland's aid, and he wanted to guarantee that these efforts would not recur.

The last passage of Kekkonen's speech, in which the prickly president implicitly rebuked Hickerson and his friends and sympathizers for such "interference" left little doubt of where his true loyalties lay. "We have been given in the press of many Western countries and also in other ways *good advice* [author's italics] as to what we should do," he continued, turning sarcastic. In this case, he was also referring to the unwanted ministrations of a certain Western government. "Of course," he continued, "we need all the sympathy and economic aid we can get, and we shall pay back our loans to the very last penny. But politically our position is fixed. Any outside interference—however well intended—will be rejected, because it would harm us.[27]

Message to Washington: *hands off!* The Eisenhower administration certainly got the message. So did the irate American ambassador, Hickerson, who was angry at having his hard, if unsuccessful, and supposedly confidential, efforts on behalf of democratic Finland exposed. "It goes without saying that I feel that there is an element of dirty pool based on partisan considerations in the President's publicly airing aid issue, particularly [his] overtones on 'intervention,'" he cabled the next day.[28]

For his part, the Finnish head of state was pleased with his speech. So was his dutiful wife, Sylvi, who watched and listened eagerly, he records.

So had Moscow, which was also pleased. The next day, Kekkonen's speech was printed in Tass in full.

The next order of business for the harried president was to put together a new government to replace the forcibly collapsed one, whose ministers still remained in office, in an embarrassing placeholding capacity, unable to transact significant business. So the wheels of government, which had only been running at half-speed anyway, completely stopped. And the now four-month-long crisis continued.

Meanwhile, the exasperated Kekkonen and his crony Kauno Kleemola, the secretary of the Agrarian League, endeavored to find "a good government," as Zhenikhov, the KGB co-*rezident* had stipulated, i.e., one that would pass muster with Khrushchev.[29] As the president understood it, this also meant bringing the SKDL, the communists, into government. Thus, on December 13, three days after his speech to the nation, Kekkonen records that Zhenikhov, the KGB *co-rezident*, had stressed to Korsimo that SKDL should be in the new government.

Soviet threats were still flying fast and loose. Nor were those threats empty. After all, the *Ordzhonikidze*, the menacing Soviet cruiser, and her escorts could always still make a surprise courtesy call, as they had done in August. And those laid off Finnish shipbuilding workers were still very much laid off.

And so over the next two weeks of December, while the Finnish nation did its best to prepare for the holidays, Kekkonen worked the phones and Kleemola and his other adjutants worked the corridors of the *eduskunta* doing their best to placate Moscow, and get Finland working again.

Meanwhile, a clear political line had been crossed. Ten years before, when Moscow was exerting pressure on the first Fagerholm government, Paasikivi had stated: "Above everything else, we must hold tight to this [line], that is we the Parliament and the President, not Moscow decide which people will become members of government. If we surrender in this we are finished."[30]

Of course Kekkonen, his protégé and successor knew this. He also knew that by his statements and actions, including his blatantly mendacious speech of December 10th rebuking the Finnish press, he was confirming the worst suspicions about him both at home and in the West. Damage, possibly irreversible, was being done to the Finnish presidency, as well as to Finland.

That was all right, too. Because Kekkonen was confident that he knew what he was doing. This was the essence of Kekkonen's hubris, as well as the seed of what would ultimately become his megalomania.

In the meantime, the president, his confidence restored, felt that he could shrug off the criticism of the West, including putative "dolts" like the American ambassador Hickerson.[31] For his part, the nettlesome envoy, foiled in his effort to prop up the vanquished Fagerholm cabinet, refused to fade away. On December 13, 1958, Kekkonen notes that "every time [I run] into Hickerson's view that [if they let] Communists into the government they would be difficult to get rid of."[32]

To be sure, some educated Finns already believed in Kekkonen's greatness. One of these was Erik Tawaststjerna. One of the most intriguing Finnish figures of his time as well as prolific, Tawaststjerna was the most prominent musicologist of his generation, among other things. He also was a pianist, pedagogue, and critic. He also was a government official: from 1948 to 1960 he held various posts in the Department for Press and Culture of the Foreign Ministry.[33]

In November 1958, when Kekkonen was preoccupied with the Note Crisis, the forty-two-year-old pianist-cum-government official, then toiling on his doctoral thesis about the piano works of the great Finnish composer, Jean Sibelius, was moved to share his thoughts on the nature of "national art." Tawaststjerna, who ultimately would become well known for his biography of Sibelius, discerned a bona fide connection between Sibelius's musical genius and what he considered Kekkonen's political one.

Kekkonen had already struck up an acquaintance with Tawaststjerna when the latter wrote him on November 25: "I am currently writing a doctoral thesis on Jean Sibelius's works," his admirer's letter begins. "In connection with my work I have pondered the question of 'national art.'"

Tawaststjerna goes on to explain how he found that national art, including the works of Sibelius, also have their own strong persona.

> Certain of Sibelius's works are typically called national. Partly this is, of course, because they contain stylistic devices relating to Finnish folk music. But most importantly, they contain the personality of the composer. We usually believe his music depicts Finnish nature . . . even when they are expressions of Sibelius's personality.

They are described as "national," when in reality they express the individual views of a genius.[34]

Now the musicologist got to the part concerning Kekkonen's supposed Sibelius-like political genius. In his view, he went on, "the above principle also holds in the acts of statesmen. A great political design, the culmination of patriotism, is [also] created by an individual." Tawaststjerna claimed to have been reminded of this "great principle" reading Paasikivi's book about his dealings with the Russians during the Winter War and the shadowy period that followed it, also known as the Interim Peace.

"Allow me to tell you that in the same vein I also thought of You," the unabashed fan continued, deliberately capitalizing "you." "You are also a personality who creates political lines and gives content and meaning to the concept of patriotism. In your acts the people of Finland will find themselves." He continued, "While leading our country's *kohtalonsinfonia*," a Finnish word that roughly translates as "symphony of fate," "you have already often transmuted a threatening minor note into a triumphant major one."

"In closing," the president's acolyte wrote, "I say to you that a president such as yourself is an inspirational and fortifying example for the nation, including intellectuals [like himself]."[35]

Evidently Urho Kekkonen was not the only one who believed that he had a rendezvous with destiny.

If Erik Tawaststjerna understood the epic national symphony that Kekkonen was composing, members on both sides of the aisle of parliament had more difficulty learning the notes, particularly the discordant one regarding Kekkonen's insistence—or Moscow's insistence—that Finland's next government include the SKDL, the Finnish communist party, or else.

The result: continued political stalemate. The exasperated president and his cronies could huff and puff and play all the piccolos they wanted, while Russian kettle drums sounded ominously in the distance, but no one it seemed wished to serve with the Finnish Reds.

And so Finland's political paralysis continued.

The next day, December 20, 1958, there was a break in the clouds. According to Karjalainen, who had met with Vladimirov, the Soviet KGB co-*rezident*, who was effectively running the Soviet embassy in the absence of a proper ambassador, the Kremlin was withdrawing its demand on including the Communists in the next government.

"A center-dominated government would be acceptable to USSR, even if it was a minority government," Karjalainen told his boss. [36]

This gave Kekkonen and his fallback man of choice, Vieno Sukselainen, who now had the task of putting "a good government" together, a little more room to move. Thereupon followed three more weeks of agonizing negotiations, with the irascible president butting heads with the sad sack future prime minister, Sukselainen, as the latter skidded around snowbound Helsinki meeting with prospective ministers.

The opéra bouffe reached its height the second week of January 1958, as memorialized in Kekkonen's journal. Reading the lunatic, backbiting entries for those days over half a century later, one understands why the Finnish government, including its foreign service, had difficulty attracting talented people in the 1950s, as well as why foreign observers like John Hickerson felt there was a vacuum of character in Finnish politics. There was.

To be sure, the character of the president also left something to be desired, if these mad, sad entries, which resemble the script for a slapstick 1920s silent movie comedy constitute evidence. A digest will suffice:

January 9: Emil Skog, head of the Soviet-friendly Skog faction of the Social Democratic party, informs Kekkonen that his group would not participate in a government with the rest of the party. He also tells him that such a government would fail on grounds of "foreign policy." Kekkonen conveys sense of talk with Skog to Sukselainen, who had already lined up a new government "without telling [him]." The new line-up included six Agrarians, six Social Democrats, two Swedish People's Party, and one Communist. Kekkonen warns him that such a government, including the Social Democrats, who Moscow had specifically blacklisted, would fail. Vladimirov, the Helsinki KGB man, agrees. Exit Sukselainen.[37]

January 10: Sukselainen visits UKK in the morning. UKK castigates the man slated to be Finland's next prime minister for his "blundering." Sukselainen swears "he didn't do anything behind my back."

Calls Sukselainen "pathetic creature!"[38]

Another official who found himself in the choleric president's crosshairs during this strange interlude was the Finnish ambassador to the Soviet Union, Eero A. Wuori. Witness the entry for the following day, January 11, 1961, in which Wuori features. Like so many other Finnish officials including and especially those who transacted business with the Russians, Wuori, who would continue in his post until

1963 despite his boss's manifest contempt for him, was well on his way toward becoming an alcoholic.

To be sure, the ability to trade vodka shots with one's Russian counterparts until reduced to something approaching a fetal state, while also keeping a compartment of one's brain open for business was a virtual requirement for any Finnish diplomat or businessman who spent time in the USSR during the Kekkonen era. Apparently Wuori did not have it. Also, the tipsy envoy had also allegedly tried to involve himself in the formation of the new government, another no-no in the suspicious Kekkonen's book.

January 11: Wuori had said that the crisis with the Soviet Union had been exaggerated. Kekkonen reprimands him for getting involved in domestic politics, including trying to help form the new government, blames him for the Swedish People's Party rejection of "the government agenda," i.e., refusal to serve with the SKDL. The mistrustful president suspected that his dipsomaniac ambassador was angling to become the next prime or foreign minister. No way, he told Wuori, after the latter's abject mea culpa.[39]

A strange picture indeed. Looking back, one wonders why Sukselainen, Wuori, and other Finnish officials of that day put up with this sort of abuse. Were they not fans of Kekkonen's "symphony of destiny?"

It certainly does not sound like it. Nevertheless the fact remains that they were loyal, or mostly loyal, to Kekkonen, despite themselves, and he to them.

And so it went in the backrooms and corridors of Helsinki, and the office of the president of the Finnish republic, in the murky winter of 1959 at the top of the world.

Finally on January 13, 1959, the Agrarian League delegation to the *eduskunta* agreed to form a new cabinet, with the anodyne Sukselainen as prime minister and the reliably inoffensive Ralf Törngren of the Swedish People's Party replacing the banished Virolainen in the thankless post of Finnish foreign minister.

At last, Finland had a functioning government, albeit one with narrow parliamentary support, as well as one which had the Kremlin's seal of approval.[40]

Or did it?

Kekkonen had received so many mixed and conflicting messages from the Soviet camp during the half year long crisis—from the Soviet embassy, from the Soviet press, the Finnish communist press—as well as from his chief courier-cum-enforcer, Karjalainen, who put his own spin on those messages, that he could not be sure. Just as importantly, after letting him twist in the wind all that time, so to speak, the Finnish leader naturally wanted confirmation that in fact he did have the Central Committee's approval. After all, with wild man Nikita Khrushchev, who had just stunned the world with his Berlin gambit, one never knew.

So, seizing the initiative Kekkonen decided to go to Russia again—not to Moscow, that would be too obtrusive, but to Leningrad, and learn for himself how Khrushchev felt—not on an official visit, which would take weeks to arrange, but on a short "private visit" with Sylvi, in person.

Fearing adverse press reaction, arrangements for the trip, which lasted from January 21 to 25, were kept secret from all but a few government officials. As far as whom he would like to meet, Kekkonen only said that "the higher the better," according to his journal.[41] Presumably, he wanted to meet with Khrushchev, who had instigated the crisis in the first place, however he did not want to force the issue, since he was essentially inviting himself. In retrospect, a brave move: in effect, Kekkonen was challenging the Soviet leader to revalidate their friendship, and Moscow's confidence in him. To help smooth the way, the Finnish president left word with his Foreign Ministry that it could announce that Finland agreed with Khrushchev's extortionate "solution" for resolving the Berlin crisis.

FINNS MOVING CLOSER TO RUSSIA

read the headline of a dispatch by the *Times* of London's well-informed correspondent, the day that the president and his small party, comprised of himself and his wife, his aide-de-camp, Major Urpo Levo, and security staff, unobtrusively boarded the train to Leningrad outside Helsinki.

> President Kekkonen and his wife left to-day by rail for a short private visit to Leningrad. In some political quarters here the visit is seen as a good omen, and it is thought possible that it will prove to be an opening move towards better relations between Russia and Finland.
>
> It is believed that President Kekkonen will meet some of the Soviet leaders, even if officials negotiations are out of the question.[42]

The following day, January 22, Nikita Khrushchev, who had quickly agreed to meet his Finnish friend, flew to Leningrad along with his foreign minister, Andrei Gromyko, along with his wife Nina and daughter Raisa, to greet Kekkonen's party.

FIGURE 8. Väinö Tanner, the long-time chairman of the Finnish Social Democrats and Moscow's bête noire. One of the Finnish officials who was tried during the so-called war responsibility trials following the Continuation War and who subsequently served prison time before returning to political life; the Kremlin never forgave him.

The Soviet premier's decision to go to Leningrad to meet Kekkonen was reportedly a complete surprise to local Soviet officials, who scrambled to make the necessary arrangements for the impromptu summit. The 21st Communist Party Congress, the preeminent event of the year, was scheduled for the following week. It was thought that Khrushchev would have been too busy preparing his Seven Year plan, his great design for the Soviet future. The plan, the end objective of which was to overtake the US as the world's leading industrial power, was an ambitious one.

It also was not *that* delusory. In point of fact, the Soviet Union had already taken the lead in the space race, much to Washington's chagrin. Moscow had already logged another first in that sector of the Cold War days before, with the launch of the Lunik I satellite that ended up orbiting the sun. It was gaining in steel production, another key power gradient. Of course, the USSR was still seriously lagging behind in the arms race, especially vis-à-vis its production of intercontinental ballistic missiles and long-range bombers, but that was not known yet, nor would it be for some time, and Khrushchev certainly was not telling; nor was the CIA.

Little wonder that Kekkonen thought that the Soviet Union was winning the Cold War, a belief he would continue to hold for some time. In outer space, it actually was triumphing.

Indeed Nikita Khrushchev had a lot on his plate at the beginning of 1959. But having good relations with Finland, a prime showcase for peaceful coexistence, was important, too. Also, Khrushchev was aware of the West's sentimental attachment to Finland dating from the Winter War. Having Finland survive and thrive while under the Soviet sphere of influence, while retaining its capitalist system and bourgeois ways—freedom of the press excepted—was another way of sticking it to the West.

The Soviet leader also had to have been impressed by how hard Kekkonen had exerted himself in undermining the government of his co-father-in-law. The fact that Kekkonen was also acting in his own political interest was beside the point. The Finnish leader had certainly outdone himself, including lying, as he did in his grossly disingenuous speech of December 10 following the forced resignation of the Fagerholm cabinet. This, Khrushchev no doubt felt, merited rewarding.

Moreover, Khrushchev genuinely liked Kekkonen. The two "shared a radical temperament and a robust sense of humor," writes Max Jakobson, who would soon become the Finnish president's press secretary. Now he liked him even more, even if he was a capitalist![43]

So yes, the Soviet premier signaled, he would be pleased to meet with Kekkonen. Mind, he *would* have to speak his mind, and whatever was on it. After all, Khrushchev was Khrushchev.

Among other things it was decided that one of the sites for the Fenno-Soviet powwow would be the Smolny Institute, the historic building dating from the czarist era which housed a school for women, before converting to the headquarters of the Bolsheviks during the October revolution. That was also here where Lenin, the revolutionary Soviet leader, signed the document authorizing Finnish independence in 1917. Kekkonen, who was an unabashed admirer of Lenin, would doubtless appreciate *that!*

The meeting between the two sides, which took place over two days, January 22 and 23, and included a luncheon and several hours of private talks, went as smoothly as could be expected under the frosty circumstances. Unsurprisingly, mostly Khrushchev and Andrei Gromyko talked, and Kekkonen listened.

First off, Khrushchev confirmed his approval of the new look of the government in Helsinki. By the by, the Soviet leader also confirmed that the unofficial freeze in trade relations was officially over. Payment for goods contracted, boxed or otherwise, would be made. The Finnish shipworkers who had been laid off could return to the shipyards and get back to work.

The Soviet kingpin made no bones about why Soviet-Finnish relations had "undergone a night frost," in Khrushchev's memorable phrase. Foreign policy, per se, had nothing to do with it, regardless of what his emissaries had said. The moment the Fagerholm government entered office, with its Social Democratic contingent, he said that there would be trouble.

Unsurprisingly, the combative Soviet premier used the occasion to take several gratuitous pot shots at the United States, including the ongoing American trade embargo. "America does not trade with us and is conducting a discriminatory policy," he exclaimed, as his Finnish guests were forced to listen, "but this does not worry us." The American policy was a "fiasco," he continued.

"The United States ruling circles thought by their trade restrictions to retard the development of our economy, [and] the development of our science and technology. And what came of it? Sputnik, that is what came out of it," Khrushchev continued, listing the various Soviet missile and technological feats of the past year. "And Lutnik too!"

"I think the Americans too will develop rockets and launch them," he boasted, "but the difference is that they will launch and we have already done that!" This would not be the last time when Khrushchev would use a meeting with Kekkonen to make a propaganda point.

Returning to news of the neighborhood, Khrushchev was even more forthright in his private talk with Kekkonen and Karjalainen, calling out the man he considered the real villain of the affair, Väinö Tanner, the Social Democratic leader. He had nothing particular against Fagerholm, the deposed former prime minister, whom he basically considered harmless, he said. "But behind Fagerholm is a broad back," the Soviet leader continued. It was Tanner, the man who stood behind Fagerholm, who was at fault, Tanner the war criminal, Tanner the troublemaker.

Andrei Gromyko was eager to chip in. "When Khrushchev mentioned Tanner, Gromyko reminded him of Leskinen, too," Kekkonen noted in his diary, referring to the deposed minister, somewhat taken aback by the two Soviets' readiness to call out the offending Finns by name.[44]

Once again, as he had during his visit to Moscow in May, the Finnish leader had to listen to a lecture about the evil ways of the Finnish press. Even though he had already admonished the indigenous press for its criticism of Moscow in his speech of December 10, a number of newspapers evidently had not gotten the message, according to Khrushchev and his foreign minister. As proof, the latter had helpfully brought along a collection of recent articles containing anti-Soviet comments. The vehement manner with which Khrushchev and Gromyko made these points made Kekkonen realize that the crisis was more serious than he thought, he later said.

Perhaps so. In any event, *now* Kekkonen understood. He resolved to continue to do his best to muzzle the Finnish press. Or better yet the Finnish press would have to learn to muzzle itself. Message received!

Most important, at least far as Kekkonen was concerned, the gamble he took in taking the secretive meeting with his Soviet counterpart, including asking for it in the first place, had paid off. Khrushchev, for his part, seemed to be pleased as well. By way of underlining the success of the Leningrad conclave and the continued bonhomie that existed between the two leaders and their governments, the two men even exchanged hats.

As far as Kekkonen was concerned, his principal "official" objectives, to secure Khrushchev's approval of the new government, and to get the vital Finnish-Soviet trade moving again, had been achieved. At the same time, this third and by far most important meeting between the two leaders, reconfirmed Kekkonen's access to the Kremlin. The prior two had been warm-ups. This spontaneously and secretly arranged one was the real thing, further vindicating the Finnish leader's belief in the magic of personal diplomacy. As historian David Kirby writes, the 1959 Leningrad meeting was "the first major initiative along the path of personal diplomacy that Kekkonen was to use with great effect to boost his status and authority at home and abroad."[45]

Chapter 4

A Clever Man (1/59–7/59)

> Mr. Kekkonen is known for his sense of humor. His favorite book, he says, is *Don Quixote*, because "I see myself in it."
>
> —*The New York Times*, January 1959

Finally, the long strange crisis was over. The "night" that had hovered over the special relationship was over. The "frost" had melted.

Once again the Kremlin could point to Finland as a display case for its policy of peaceful co-existence. What was the price of that peace? What exactly had Kekkonen lost by ceding the Kremlin veto power over the composition of the Finnish government? What had been gained? Time would tell.

In the meantime, the grateful Finnish president had a few words of appreciation to say about his hero, Vladimir Lenin. Actually more than a few. On January 24, his last day in Leningrad, by way of underscoring his appreciation for his Soviet hosts, as well as his admiration for the original Bolshevik leader, the Finnish leader delivered himself of a long encomium for Lenin and his comrades. "The great October Revolution plays a significant role in the history of the Finnish people as well as the Russian people," Kekkonen declared.

"This role was in fact decisive, as the great October Revolution created the preconditions for the independence of Finland. For that reason, we Finns feel a genuine gratitude for [it] and the great man who led it. Why would Finns not have granted Lenin sanctuary?" he exclaimed. "After all, we were fighting a common battle against the czarist regime.

Decades before the decisive events of 1917, Lenin had clearly declared that the rights of the Finnish people had to be safeguarded against the threat posed by the czar. As leader of the revolution, he also highly valued the support that the Finnish people had given the revolution by fighting for their rights against the czar."[1]

Izvestia could not have done a better job. To commemorate the occasion Kekkonen had commissioned a special plaque of gratitude from the Finnish people, to be hung on the wall of Lenin's former office in the Lenin Museum at the Smolny Institute. And then after a final dinner topped with speeches of mutual admiration on the evening of January 24, Urho and Sylvi returned to Finland Station the following morning to begin the voyage home to Helsinki and Tamminiemi.

There is no plaque to commemorate Kekkonen's January 1959 meeting with Nikita Khrushchev at the Smolny Institute. Perhaps there should be. If there was it might say something to the effect that in that room the foundation for Finlandization, the pejorative term for the "special relationship," was formally laid.

Among other things, Kekkonen's sortie to Leningrad also confirmed his status as a rising statesman, witness the generally laudatory profile of him which *The New York Times* published on January 24, the last day of his pilgrimage. "President Urho Kaleva Kekkonen of Finland, who is in Leningrad to negotiate better relations with the Soviet Union is a practical statesman with a pliable policy," the paper noted. There was that word again: pliable.

"Mr. Kekkonen is bald-headed and hard-headed," the article went on to say. "But," it continued, recalling his wartime volte-face from staunch foe of the Soviet, as the USSR used to be called, to friend, as well as his savvy in appointing his former presidential opponent, Karl-August Fagerholm, to head his first government, "he has swayed with the political winds to remain upright in his career."[2]

Indeed. In addition to Kekkonen's celebrated malleability, *The New York Times* noted the Finnish president's sense of humor, especially his attachment to a certain famous seventeenth-century novel. "Mr. Kekkonen is known for his sense of humor. His favorite book, he says, is *Don Quixote*, because "I see myself in it, sometimes as Don Quixote and sometimes as Sancho Panza."[3] Who did he see as himself now, now that he had weathered his first major crisis with the Kremlin, one might have wondered. The paper did not say. One suspects that Don Kekkonen—or was it Sancho?—was simply pleased to have managed to remain upright and not fall from his saddle.

Following his return to Helsinki on January 25, when a small crowd of appreciative officials greeted him and his wife, the president gave another radio speech about his successful peacemaking sortie. The speech was also televised: Kekkonen was getting comfortable with the still novel medium (at least in Finland). Essentially the address was a replica of his December 10 talk following the fall of Fagerholm III to the political winds.

Once again, the Finnish paterfamilias gave himself credit for resolving the crisis just passed; once again he read the riot act to the Finnish press; once again, he underlined the importance of mutual trust and confidence as the sine qua non of successful Fenno-Soviet relations and Finnish foreign policy. As was his wont, and would continue to be so for the next two decades, Kekkonen deliberately used the specter of Soviet displeasure as a means of frightening his subjects.

This time, however, Urho Kekkonen was not crying wolf. The bellicose manner with which Khrushchev and his foreign minister, Andrei Gromyko, had denounced the alleged Tannerite "mob" in Leningrad had convinced him that this time the Soviets were not bluffing. Whether or not the Kremlin actually intended to go to war over the composition of the next Finnish cabinet, no less the sarcastic musings of a Finnish cartoonist—Khrushchev had also included Kari Suomalainen, the muckraking Finnish caricaturist in the enemies list which he gave to Kekkonen during his trip—was questionable. However Kekkonen did not wish to find out. The Soviet premier, he knew, liked surprises.

The domestic reaction to Kekkonen's speech, like the reaction to his surprise rendezvous with Khrushchev was divided. Those who, in the words of Erik Tawaststjerna, understood his "grand design" saw their faith vindicated. For its part the right-wing opposition and other nonbelievers saw it as more evidence of Kekkonen's hubris and contempt for democratic tradition. Perhaps Kekkonen had not agreed to allow the Kremlin to build an air force base in the Åland Islands, as one conservative newspaper had alleged. Still, to them, Kekkonen had dangerously exceeded his remit.

One outspoken dissident was Bruno Salmiala, a conservative professor of law, who wrote an outraged letter to the president on January 30, 1959. An alumnus of the former radical right-wing party, the Isänmaallinen kansanliike (IKL), Salmiala was angered by what he considered the toadying tone of the speech Kekkonen had delivered at the Smolny Institute.

"In your speech of reply," the irate professor wrote in his formal-sounding, but outraged note, "You Mr. President of the republic . . . said amongst other things, Your [Khrushchev's] speech, was as you noted, generous and direct. We Finns appreciate direct and honest talk. . . . Upon reading the above words, have you Mr. President accepted Mr. Khrushchev's view, which if put into practice would be in starkest conflict with the basic principles of our democratic rule of law and our nation's independence?"

"These words," the correspondent continued, in the formal language of the academy, "imply that you Mr. President have thought it possible to admit to the Russians that part of the Finnish population, a small number of thick-headed individuals, does not want good relations with the USSR. I think this is very dangerous.[4]

In his letter the professor went on to criticize what he felt was the disingenuousness of Kekkonen's speech, how the president had deliberately obscured the main reason for the recent crisis, i.e., the Kremlin's anger at the makeup of the Fagerholm government and how he instead had focused on the supposedly critical attitude of the Finnish press.

> I know that countless Finns have hoped that You Mr. President of the Republic would have in your radio speech would [have clarified this] but instead you did not . . . refer at all to the aforementioned [actual] factors which Khrushchev gave as the primary reasons for the "night frost," a repeat of which he clearly threatened. The press and the printed word, which you Mr. President of the Republic focused on as the main cause of the "night frost" was only a secondary cause [of the crisis according to Khrushchev].[5]

Kekkonen's response to his academic critic was dismissive: "I am content to say that you are wrong," he barked back, "in all of your accusations and suspicions."[6]

But was he? Many patriotic, and not unreasonable Finns, besides dyed-in-the-wool conservatives like Salmiala, were not so sure.

In the event, Kekkonen's secret meeting with the Soviet premier also had the effect of redoubling the efforts of the political opposition, such as it was, to find a suitable opponent to run against Kekkonen in the 1962 presidential election. Although the contest was three years off, the country was already focusing on it. So was Kekkonen, now that he had his access card to the Kremlin back and could begin to see his way through to reelection.

Now that the crisis was over and the shipyards were busy again, the "hard-headed, bald-headed president," as *The New York Times* described him, could return to the things that kept him going: his long daily walks in the woods around Tamminiemi, sometimes stretching for ten or twenty miles; his favorite recreation, skiing; his voracious reading; his weekly conclaves with his sauna crew buddies; playing with his new grandson, Timo; and spending time with his wife.

Which brings us to the subject of Sylvi Kekkonen. A half a century after her death in 1974 at age seventy-four, Sylvi is one of the forgotten women of Finnish history. Much, arguably too much in the author's view, has been made in recent years of the "other women" in Kekkonen's life. That there were other women in Kekkonen's life, there is no doubt. The reason for that is no great mystery.

According to Jouko Loikkanen, Kekkonen's former secretary and long-time friend, after giving birth to the twins and an ectopic pregnancy later on, Sylvi had difficulties having relations with her husband.[7] The fact is, Kekkonen also happened to have a strong sex drive. Ergo, there were other women.

The aforementioned Anne-Marie Snellman, who had been Kekkonen's mistress since the early 1950s, when he was prime minister, and who may or may not have been a Soviet agent, was certainly one of these women, and perhaps the one who had the most real influence on him, insofar as any did.

Anita Hallama, the wife of Jaakko Hallama, the foreign ministry official who served as Kekkonen's ambassador to Moscow during the latter part of his presidency, with whom the president became involved during the 1960s, was another. Maarit Tyrkkö, the young journalist who the president met in the early 1970s, his companion after Sylvi's death in 1974, was yet another. Doubtless there were others.

This is not, or ought not be, earth-shaking news, in light of her infirmity, as well as the length of the Kekkonen presidency.

Moreover, by the late 1950s, Sylvi, who suffered from rheumatism, *was* visibly infirm, while her sporting, weight-obsessed husband was still very much in his prime and would be for at least another decade. The contrast between the Kekkonen's physiques and health, even though they were both the same age, is evident in photos of the two, as the tall president with ramrod posture towers over the slight form of the not quite five-foot-tall first lady. The fact is, there was only so much that the two *could* do together, apart from sex, at least physically; they no longer skied together, as they did when the Kekkonens were young, nor did they take many long walks together. Moreover, this former pastor's daughter was not a physical person, nor, apparently, one who encouraged physical affection.

"I do not recall that there was much visible affection around in the Kekkonen family," Timo Kekkonen later told the author. "No kissing, hugging or even holding hands."[8] "This does not mean that the atmosphere [at Tamminiemi] could not be very nice, cozy and friendly, but nothing which I would describe as affectionate," he said, somewhat clinically. This was in contrast to the Fagerholm household, which the president's grandson recalled as being much more boisterous and outgoing.[9] If the expansive, full-blooded athletic Kekkonen needed more affection—as well as sex—he would have to go outside his marriage, something that, one infers, Sylvi was well aware of if not necessarily approving of.

Husband and wife slept in separate bedrooms at Tamminiemi. Sylvi's was full of handicrafts, a wistful souvenir of the time she spent working at the Finnish Handicrafts Association in the 1920s, as well as her beloved books. Kekkonen's study, as one can see today when one visits the former presidential mansion, now a national museum, was also lined with books. However, he also had his own top floor weapon- and trophy-lined sportsman's retreat, as Gordon Shepherd, author of *The Scandinavians*, who visited the presidential residence in 1964, describes—"his holy of holies, where he [Kekkonen] can relax in what one woman visitor described as 'the most masculine room I have ever seen.'"[10]

FIGURE 9. Kekkonen and his wife, Sylvi, at Tamminiemi, 1957. Although Kekkonen was known to have other lovers, he remained devoted to her. An accomplished writer in her own right, she was his principal advisor.

Obviously, the Kekkonens had an "arrangement," admittedly an unusual one for a European head of state, no less a Finnish one, but certainly not one unheard of in twentieth-century annals. Francois Mitterand, the president of France in the 1980s and early 90s, had such an arrangement. So did Kekkonen's contemporary, Georges Pompidou. Charles de Gaulle was monogamous (so far as is known)—one thing he did *not* have in common with Kekkonen, with whom he is sometimes compared.

So was Nikita Khrushchev (so as far as known). So was Dwight Eisenhower (excepting his alleged wartime affair with his driver, Kay Summersby, when he was the Allied commander-in-chief). So was Kekkonen's elderly but still fierce, cane-wielding predecessor, Juho Kusti Paasikivi. Gustaf Mannerheim was a lifelong bachelor (unless one believes the rumors that he was gay).

In this case one could say Kekkonen devised his own "line," as far as his sex life was concerned. In any event, his "other life" does not seem to have affected his presidency in any serious way, at least insofar as any of his mistresses having an influence over his decisions—as Hélène de Portes, the mistress of Paul Reynaud, notoriously did with the French prime minister at the time of the fall of France, and whose disastrous meddling in her weak-willed consort's affairs expedited that fall.[11]

Nor, unlike John F. Kennedy, Kekkonen's reckless American contemporary, whose dozens of liaisons included the girlfriend of a mafia don, and would have caused a public scandal if they had been known, did Kekkonen's nocturnal adventures put either the Finnish presidency or the republic in appreciable danger (at least as far as is known).

In any event, despite her self-effacing nature, Sylvi Kekkonen was no typical cuckolded wife, nor a token one, but a formidable figure in her own right, as well as the moral and spiritual bulwark of the Kekkonen household, as a profile of her published in the *Times* of London in May 1961 on the occasion of the Kekkonens' state visit to Great Britain, observed. "Since 1956 Madame Kekkonen has also proved that small and frail though she may appear to be," the paper noted, "this seemingly fragile façade hides not only gentleness and modesty, but considerable energy, and the ability to carry successfully the heavy burden of responsibility devolving on the President's wife, qualities which have endeared her to the Finnish people."[12]

In addition to handicrafts, and doting on her husband of three decades, this country woman born and bred had several lifelong passions. One of them was horses; Sylvi was a frequent visitor to horse shows, which she often visited with her husband. The other passion, which she also shared with him, was a love of books. To be sure, Timo Kekkonen points out, the couple's mutual love of literature was one of the fundaments of their relationship. Before the war, one of the favorite pastimes of the Kekkonens was to shop for books and peruse them together. There was less time to do that now that Urho was president, but, according to their friends, their conversations, when they had them, were often about the arts, including and especially literature.

In addition, Madame Kekkonen was a prolific author herself. Over the previous decade she had produced four books of her own: *Kiteitä* (Crystals), a book of aphorisms; two novels, *Kotikaivolla* (At the home well) and *Käytävä* (The corridor), both set in hospitals; as well as *Amalia*, her most recent tome, the story of a simple peasant woman's life. The latter, published in April 1958, came as a pleasant surprise to her husband, who was traveling at the time. "Sylvi's new book *Amalia* has just appeared and I read it during my train journey," he writes on April 2. Evidently Kekkonen underestimated his wife's literary prowess. "An impressive and surprisingly well-made, realistic book," he continues, approvingly (if stiffly). "A rural woman has gotten a beautiful portrait."[13]

As Timo points out, his grandfather may have been slightly jealous of Sylvi's way with words. "I believe Sylvi was more of a writer than Urho," he says. "Urho was good at writing speeches, columns and so forth, but he was not in the same league as an artist and he knew it."[14] "Her style is clear and concise," notes the *Times* of London, "but not without humor. One feels that here the author is revealing herself."[15] So did Sylvi's compatriots and readers, most of whom still lived in the countryside in rapidly urbanizing Finland, and still felt a strong tie to the farm and who made her paean to rural life a best-seller.

Of course, the fact that the author also happened was the wife of the president might also have had a little to do with it, too. Not that Sylvi traded on her status as first lady of the land. Quite the opposite, as the *Times* noted, "It is not all unusual in Helsinki to see her [Sylvi] in a bus or a tram, instead of journeying in a presidential car," the admiring correspondent notes, "or shopping quietly alongside less exalted customers. That few turn to stare on such occasions is more a sign of respect than indifference."[16]

A proud woman, she was without hauteur. She had no qualms about being in her husband's shadow. At the same time, this compact, emotionally self-sufficient pastor's daughter cast not a small shadow of her own. Nor was Sylvi a shrinking violet. Although she was her husband's strongest defender, she also could be his fiercest critic.

For his part, Kekkonen was always attentive to his wife in public. One of the most famous photos of them together, from the 1960s, shows him literally bowing to the seated Sylvi, who proffers her hand with a knowing and grateful smile. The photo is not staged: he truly revered his wife. Physically, they may no longer have been close, but spiritually and psychologically they remained married until death parted them. The best proof of this is how unhinged the desolate president became after Sylvi died in 1974, even though they had long settled into a relationship with another woman, Hallama, the wife of his ambassador to Moscow.

As Loikkanen, Kekkonen's former secretary, put it, "Sylvi was his best friend and closest advisor."[17] She was more: she was his pillar. If, for Urho Kekkonen, all roads led to Tamminiemi, they also led to Sylvi, and would for some time to come.

One Finn who did *not* get the president's message about exhibiting due respect, either to him or the Friend to the East, was Kari Suomalainen, the cartoonist for *Helsingin Sanomat.* In October 1958, at the height of the Night Frost crisis, Suomalainen, whose pictorial talents, as well as his penchant for speaking truth to power, or drawing it, had begun to attract international attention, had been invited to mount an exhibit in London. For the well-publicized show, the famous caricaturist drew a cartoon depicting Khrushchev as a Volga boatman, shouting "Shame on you imperialists!" to Western leaders, as an anxious crew of oarsmen, representing the Soviet satellite states, labored to transport his vessel upstream.[18]

The cartoon, which reportedly was the star of the London show and had since been published both abroad and in Finland, drew a formal protest from the Kremlin. Its irritated subject, Khrushchev, doubtless had mentioned it to Kekkonen during their comradely huddle in Leningrad. Although Kekkonen did not mention the cartoonist by name in his speech to the nation of January 28, one presumed that he had Suomalainen in mind with his renewed rejoinder to the press—*including* cartoonists—to exercise "restraint and responsibility."[19]

If so, the caricaturist in question was paying no or little heed. Several days later, Suomalainen published his retort in the form of a cartoon depicting a cartoonist drawing a dove of peace in a room in which the visage of a bald-headed, bespectacled man menacingly glaring down from a framed picture on the wall. At the bottom of the frame the words

"BIG BROTHER IS WATCHING YOU" were emblazoned. "What possible cartoonist could the President have been talking about?" read the caption.[20]

Predictably, the president was not amused. "There is a tall, thin, irreverent Finn who has infuriated the Russians, irritated President Kekkonen and delighted most of his admiring countrymen," noted *The New York Times* in a feature about Finland's best-known gadfly published several weeks later. "A cartoonist," Suomalainen told the paper, "must be fearless. A second part of his credo is that a cartoonist's art can serve as a safety valve in times of tension."

And tense times they continued to be, as Big Brother Urho continued to watch over Finland, and Kekkonen's Big Brother in Moscow continued to glare down on *him*.

Kekkonen, for his part, continued to have difficulty discerning *who* actually spoke for his Soviet friends. His difficulty was compounded by the tension between the KGB *rezidentura* and the new Soviet ambassador, Aleksey Zakharov, who had replaced the departed Lebedev.[21] One of the reasons why Kekkonen liked to meet with Khrushchev as often as possible, apart from the fact that he genuinely liked the latter, was that their meetings allowed him to speak to him directly, rather than via channels.

"Vladimirov and Zhenikhov badmouth Zakharov," Kekkonen writes on June 7, 1959.[22] The tensions between the two KGB men and Zakharov would continue for years, along with the two parties' differing interpretations of Moscow's wishes, particularly on the emerging issue of Finland's desire to join EFTA, the newborn European Free Trade Association, the predecessor of the European Union finally freed of the long arm of the Kremlin, which Finland joined thirty-five years later.

This could only portend trouble: which messenger to believe? Meanwhile, the hard-pressed Finnish head of state soldiered on as best as he could, as he continued to steer Finland between the Scylla of the West and the Charybdis of the East. If some of his critics thought that he was tacking too close to the latter, that was their problem. Most importantly, he, the Great Savior, was certain that knew what he was doing. And so, he was equally certain, did the Finnish people.

In late February and early March of 1959, Kekkonen, still flush from the success of his sortie to Leningrad, gave interviews with two inquiring Western reporters, Tom Ready of the Associated Press and Werner Wiskari of *The New York Times*. The interview with Ready, who took a critical tone with his subject, was somewhat combative. What price had the president paid at Leningrad for Nikita Khrushchev's blessing, the correspondent impertinently asked?

"I don't pay prices," huffed the incensed president, according to his own account. If the Soviets had demanded a "price," he shot back, he would have sent for his ministers. Regardless of what anyone in the West thought, or wrote, he said, democracy would survive in Finland as long as Finns wished. However, he warned, loud enough for both Moscow and his domestic opponents to hear, if "the Tanner-Leskinen line," as he put it seethingly, raised its head again, "then the direction [the country would take] would be very different."[23]

So Väinö Tanner and Väinö Leskinen, the villainous Social Democratic duo, now had their own "line." Kekkonen was learning Soviet-speak well.

Several days later, on March 4, the prickly president sat down for an on-the-record interview, his first since taking office, on political subjects, with Wiskari. The Finnish-American journalist, with whom Kekkonen had an agonistic relationship, decided to play the part of friendly listener on this occasion. Kekkonen, keenly aware of how closely the interview would be read on both sides of the Atlantic, chose his words carefully. "Mr. Kekkonen spoke in his study at his seaside residence on the outskirts of Helsinki shortly after having come in from his favorite recreation, skiing," the reporter wrote, striking a Kekkonesque, sportsmanlike note.

Unsurprisingly, Kekkonen's foreign policy balancing act was the main topic. "[President] Kekkonen declared that Finland's relations with the West depended on how well she handled her relations with the East."[24]

Contrary to what some critics supposed, the president continued, "Finland, can do what she likes but "naturally we must take into account the fact that our vital interests require that our neighbor trusts us." At the same time, in case anyone was wondering, Kekkonen disingenuously pointed out, "the Soviet Union has not attempted to "dictate to Finland what course it she should take either in internal or in external affairs."[25]

Wiskari, who had just spent the past half year reporting the Night Frost crisis, was too polite to demur. He also conveyed without comment his subject's apparently sincere belief that the preservation of the Finnish commonweal depended in the long run on maintaining a standard of living that was competitive with the putatively rising Soviet one. Was the Soviet living standard and its clunky consumerist accoutrements actually rising vis-à-vis that of the West?

Khrushchev, who would get into a heated television debate about this with US vice president Richard Nixon that summer in the model kitchen of the American National Exhibit in Moscow—the so-called Kitchen Debate—certainly thought so. So did the head of the friendly capitalist neighbor who was tending the Finnish shop window of "Peaceful Coexistence."

Striking a blow for Finnish neutrality, which Moscow pointedly had not yet formally acknowledged, the Finnish president asserted Finland's "right to remain outside big power conflicts." Finland's censor-in-chief insisted that he respected the right of freedom of the press. "But this right," he told Wiskari, "imposes an obligation on the nation's press as well—to match the neutrality of the government by being *objective* [author's italics] in handling foreign news."[26]

As it happened apparently, unbeknownst to Wiskari, the thin-skinned Finn had a personal bone to pick with the press, particularly *Helsingin Sanomat*, the closest thing that Finland had to a newspaper of record at the time, which was not particularly close. Except for Suomalainen's satirical cartoons and the occasional critical article, the *Helsingin Sanomat* of the 1950s and 1960s, with its endless, virtually interchangeable, and uncritical accounts of the president's pronunciamentos and comings and goings, was little more than a house organ of the state.

Nevertheless, Eljas Erkko, the puckish managing director of Sanoma Osakeyhtio, the corporation that owned the *Sanomat*, enjoyed getting Kekkonen's goat. Several weeks before, the paper had run an article alleging that certain university students had held parties or "sauna evenings" in the paper's description, at Tamminiemi, with Kekkonen's blessing.

In fact, the president had invited one group university students to visit the presidential mansion, with his and Sylvi's blessing, though one would be hard put to describe the rather tame event as a "party." The author of the article had strongly implied otherwise and the president-cum-host took umbrage, firing off a letter to Erkko taking issue with both the article about the gathering, a tradition which he would defiantly continue, the origin of Kekkonen's so-called "children's parties" and the other "many personal attacks" on him the paper had allegedly made.[27]

"The Finnish government does not prevent the free flow of news," Kekkonen blithely continued. "Nor has ideological debate been precluded."[28] One doubts that many *New York Times* readers were reassured. However the Kremlin apparently liked what it read. A month later, Kekkonen noted that the newly arrived Soviet envoy had toasted him at an embassy function, praising him for his role in enhancing Soviet-Finnish relations. Best of all, the self-satisfied diarist writes, the Soviet official spoke about the "Paasikivi-Kekkonen line the whole time."[29] As far as all the Soviet officials on the premises were concerned—including both of the embassy's feuding factions—Kekkonen was Moscow's man. Perhaps it was a little early for the Kremlin to signal that he was also its choice for the next presidential election, in three years, but that could come in time. What more could he ask for?

Well, Kekkonen, ever eager for positive reinforcement, as well as clarity, from the man on top, signaled, another meeting with Comrade Khrushchev would be nice.

Done. As it happened, as part of the Soviet premier's so-called "peace offensive"—or, really, his anti-NATO offensive—the Soviet Foreign Ministry was just now sketching out Khrushchev's schedule for an ice-breaking trip to Norway and Denmark he was planning for the summer. Among other things, Khrushchev hoped to persuade Norway and Denmark to agree to his idea for a nuclear-free Baltic zone, a concept that Kekkonen was initially skeptical of but would ultimately sign up for and fervently promote and press his skeptical Nordic neighbors to join.

Would it be all right, the foreign ministry signaled Helsinki, if the premier stopped off for breakfast with his friend, the president, on the return trip? To be sure, it was summer; Finland would effectively be closed, as it is during the summer. However Kekkonen responded enthusiastically that he would be pleased to have his friend, the premier, as his personal guest at the presidential summer residence at Kultaranta, in Naantali, on Finland's southwestern coast.

And so the preparations for Khrushchev's second visit to Finland, and his first since his and the since banished Bulganin's sortie two years before, went forward, becoming more elaborate as time went on. Originally the idea was for the Soviet leader to stop for an "unofficial" breakfast on his way back to the Kremlin. Soon, however, the projected trip morphed into something considerably grander, with the Soviet bigwig first alighting in Naantali for a private brunch with the president, followed by a public reception in nearby Turku.

Then, according to a somewhat breathless dispatch in *The New York Times* the Soviet leader's party would continue on to Helsinki by cruiser (the *Ordzhonikidze* one presumes), for an "official" three-day visit. Altogether Khrushchev was slated to spend nearly a full week in Finland.

Also, the premier's advance people, perhaps recalling the somewhat mixed reception which Khrushchev and his sidekick had received from the Finnish public two years prior, asked the Finnish president for tips on how to break ice with his frosty Nordic neighbors, the Danes and the Norwegians. "The representatives of Soviet Union here are worried about Khrushchev's visit to Sweden etc. countries" he wrote in his diary. Could Finland perhaps explain its measures of safety and organization to Scandinavian countries?[30]

Now, *that* was certainly a change. A mere six months before, during the Night Frost, Khrushchev had been content to let Kekkonen twist in the wind, in the memorable phrase of Spiro Agnew, the future US vice president. Now he, or at least his people, were asking *him*, Kekkonen, how the Soviet leader ought to behave on his next trip to the neighborhood, as well as how to make sure those pesky Danes and Norwegians behaved properly.[31]

In the event, Kekkonen could have told his apprehensive Russian friends that Copenhagen was not Moscow. The Danish and Norwegian authorities presumably had different ideas about crowd control than the Soviet police. Perhaps it was best, he may have told them, to let their chief do his own thing (so to speak) and see how the Danes and Norwegians took to him.

Also, he could have added, if he dared, it was not only the Danes' and the Norwegians' behavior that Moscow ought to be worried about. What about Khrushchev? As anyone who knew the combustible Ukrainian well, particularly the long-suffering members of his entourage, one never really knew what to expect from him. A revealing entry from Kekkonen's diary for July 28, 1960, following the visit of a Soviet Foreign Ministry official, during which the latter evidently confided in Kekkonen, reads, "Foreign ministry in Moscow *is always scared when Khrushchev opens his mouth: anything can come out of it as he deviates from his speeches ex tempore* [author's italics]."[32]

More importantly, on the subject of the Soviet premier's Nordic peace offensive, the ostensible purpose of which was to persuade the Danes and the Norwegians not to allow American or British nuclear weapons to be stored on their soil, what, realistically, did Moscow expect this quixotic excursion to achieve? "Pacifying Baltic sea [getting Denmark and Norway] to quit NATO," Kekkonen told Zhenikhov, the Helsinki KGB station co-chief, in early July, in response to his query, "and atomic arms are not practical politics. Scandinavian countries are prepared to strictly resist."[33]

Kekkonen was right. The Danes and Norwegians did not like being told what to do any more than Finns did, although they were in a somewhat better position to resist Moscow's blandishments. Despite their skittishness, officials in the three countries, including Finland, which was supposed to be the high point of Khrushchev's Baltic tour, went forward with their preparations.

Then, suddenly, on July 20, 1959, a month before Khrushchev was supposed to set off, the Kremlin announced that it had canceled the visit, citing the reportedly anti-Soviet atmosphere in the three Nordic countries, including Sweden. The communiqué assailed the three Nordic countries for not having halted "insulting" attacks against the USSR by newspapers and opposition leaders. According to *The New York Times*, news of the cancelation produced "a feeling of relief amongst officials and the public in all three capitals," including Helsinki.

One suspects that Russians security officials were relieved, too.[34] As for the Finns, who had gone to so much trouble for the visit, Moscow merely sent a short note of regret.

To be sure, of all the Nordic leaders whom Khrushchev had been scheduled to meet, Urho Kekkonen was the only one who had cause to be disappointed. Among other things, he had hoped to discuss his eagerness for Finland to join the newly christened EFTA, which he, rightly, considered crucial for his country's economic future.

A confidential 1972 report by the CIA analyzing the history of Finnish–Soviet relations explained why this was so, as well as why Moscow was so hostile to Finnish membership in the trade pact. "Because the Soviets view with near-paranoia any move which they think might constitute a turn towards the West by Finland," the report noted, "they are intrinsically distrustful of Finland's participation in any cooperative economic efforts with the West.

> Fearing that these might evolve into political ties, the USSR has opposed Finland joining its Nordic neighbors or other Western nations in economic unions and associations.
>
> With the birth of the European Economic Community (EEEC in 1957, and more importantly for Finland, the European Free Trade Area (EFTA) in 1959, Helsinki faced a serious dilemma. Finland's economy is dependent on exports, and West Europe constitutes her major market. Finland's forest industry accounts for over 50 per cent of its total exports, and both its largest customer for these products (Great Britain) and its main competitors (Sweden, Norway and Austria) were included in EFTA.[35]

"Finnish exports faced a severe handicap," the CIA history continues, "if they [are] continued subject to British customs duties while competitive products could enter Britain free of duty. Finland's difficult dual objective with respect to EFTA was to acquire the economic benefits of membership without incurring Soviet wrath," the report observes. "This involved overcoming the basic Soviet hostility—on political grounds—to Finnish association with any such organization."[36] This was the formidable challenge facing President Kekkonen and the Finnish government as the so-called Outer Seven nations—Great Britain, Denmark, Norway, Sweden, Switzerland, Austria, and Portugal—formed EFTA that year.

Doubtless the Finnish president, with his faith in the value of personal negotiations, and his blossoming relationship with Khrushchev, had hoped to discuss the sensitive matter with the latter during his visit and perhaps grant Finland some corresponding latitude.

Hence Kekkonen's disappointment when Moscow canceled. Now the Finnish leader would have to lobby Khrushchev and the Politiburo at a long distance, via third parties, as best he could. Now he would have to do his best to understand what his maddening friend and sponsor in Moscow really wanted and triangulate the conflicting messages he continued to receive from both the Soviet embassy, including its KGB station, as well as the Kremlin itself, as best he could, until the two leaders which would not be for another year, actually had a chance to meet again.

How much the Finnish public, which was still having trouble warming up to the Soviets, rued Khrushchev's cancelation was arguable. However as Kekkonen's journal makes clear, he was quite put out when he actually received word that his Russian friend was not coming after all. One can be reasonably sure that there was some private yelling at Tamminiemi when he got that phone call.

Not that Khrushchev had forgotten about Kekkonen or Finland, or his perceived Social Democratic "enemies."

The Soviet leader left absolutely no doubt about how he felt about Kekkonen's—as well as his—political adversaries, particularly his principal Finnish bête noire, Tanner, the aging but still formidable Social Democratic party head, and vice versa, in a blazing agitprop shootout in the spring of 1959.

Tanner fired the first shot, along with Kaarlo Pitsinki, the choleric party secretary, in a pair of provocative May Day speeches. Tanner angered Khrushchev by declaring himself in favor of new elections because, he said, the thirteen Social Democrats in the parliament who had defected to the Soviet-friendly Skog faction had rendered an incorrect picture of the people's will. This, of course, was true, insofar as none of the perfidious parliamentarians had consulted their constituents before joining the Skogists, whose tacit support the precarious minority Agrarian-led government depended on.[37]

Pitsinki, whose political career had begun as Karl-August Fagerholm's secretary, went further, describing "Communist imperialism as the biggest danger to world peace, democracy and freedom," according to the *Times* of London. "Communism," he declared to the vocal approval of the party faithful in Helsinki, was "based on ruthless dictatorship in the communist countries" as well as "merciless aspiration for domination in other countries."[38]

The blunt politician also took a shot at President Kekkonen, who he clearly reviled, without explicitly naming him, alluding to the latter's still controversial role in the Night Frost coup, noting that "a very high responsible source has sought a verdict on the Socialist party from a neighboring country" and that the Finnish democratic workers' movement had continuously been the subject of excessive interference—"pinpricking," Pitsinki called it—"from outside."[39]

Unsurprisingly, the two Finnish politicians succeeded in getting the Soviet leader's attention. Several days later, a furious Nikita Khrushchev fired back via *Pravda*, the Kremlin mouthpiece, accusing the faithless Finns of "slandering" the USSR and denying that Moscow had *ever* interfered in Finnish domestic affairs.

Clearly, memories of the Night Frost died hard.

Kekkonen, that avatar of principled pliability, did not seem to mind. But, he knew, many of his countrymen did. To put his frazzled countrymen's minds at ease, the president appeared in a special video broadcast on July 17, 1959, on the fortieth anniversary of the Finnish republic's first government. In that broadcast, as reported in the *Times* of London, the president:

> discussed the question of whether or not Finland can [could] preserve her independence and national freedom. He [admitted] frankly that the question, which was understandable in the light of past historical events, in light of recent events, was whether [Finland's] their eastern neighbour respected [Finns'] their freedom.[40]

Once again, as he often did, Kekkonen invoked the name of his still revered predecessor, Juho Paasikivi, and his foreign policy, which he professed to be faithfully following.

> His own personal view, he said, [Kekkonen said] was that in continuing honestly and consistently the foreign policy which Paasikivi defined and realized, Finland would not only preserve the freedom of the State but strengthen it, and at the same time strengthen international respect for Finland.[41]

Thus spoke Kekkonen.

Nevertheless many foreign observers, including from the Western diplomatic corps, remained deeply suspicious of the Finnish strongman and the risky game they felt he was playing. Prominent among them was the US ambassador, John Hickerson. Hickerson's doubts about the murky course that the Finnish head of state had set for his country, as well as his real agenda, were manifest in his dispatch to Washington of June 4, 1959.

Events over the past year had strengthened his forebodings, he cabled. The envoy proceeded to list a number of discouraging developments on the Finnish front which involved the Finnish president, either directly or indirectly, among them:

> (1) The objective of who can best maintain friendship with the Soviet Union as a central issue of the election campaign of the summer of 1958

through:

> (6) Machinations of the extremist (Kekkonen) wing of the Agrarians and the Skogists (Social Democrats) to secure SKDL representation in the post-election cabinet.
> (7) The flat rejection by Finnish authorities (read Kekkonen) of US offers to lend assistance if needed to withstand Soviet economic pressure
> (8) The fall of the Fagerholm government.
> (9) Kekkonen's meeting with Khrushchev in Leningrad.[42]

All of these developments, said Hickerson, added up to the progressive atrophying of Finnish democracy, as well as the country's claim to independent and neutral status. The principal fault for this, he felt, however, lay not with Soviet pressure, but with the Finns and their feckless leaders themselves. After four years at his relatively thankless diplomatic post, Hickerson's view of Finnish politics and politicians, including and particularly the head of state, was as grim as ever. According to the envoy, the devious Finnish president's principal motivation was to "further his own ambitions and personal spites."[43]

The immediate and perhaps most important question, according to Hickerson, was how Finland would react to the Kremlin's as yet unknown but probably negative reaction to her desire to join EFTA. The Soviet response, the envoy feared, could comprise "direct diplomatic action, economic actions [and/or] press attacks," he messaged. In short, a reprise of the Night Frost, or even worse.[44]

Here, during the expected smash-up over Finland's desire to join or associate with EFTA, Hickerson, still disappointed by America's hands-off policy toward Finland felt, was America's best chance to get back "into the game" in northeastern Europe. To do that, the ambassador recommended a "quiet readiness," as he put it, to provide "emergency assistance" on the order what he had earlier recommended, $60 to $70 million, and which his boss, the ailing John Foster Dulles, had rejected to his dismay.[45]

For John Hickerson, who had as little faith in the minority Suskelainen government as he did in the expanding Kekkonen presidency, the issue of Finland's viability as a full-fledged democracy was still very much in doubt and it was time for the United States to put some fight in the pusillanimous Finns.

CHAPTER 5

Scylla and Charybdis (7/59–12/59)

> Even if he succeeds in cultivating the Soviet leadership without compromising Finnish sovereignty, he is likely to establish a pattern in which less clever leadership is compromised.
>
> —US National Security Council memo about Finland, August, 1959

John Hickerson's apprehensions about the state of the Finnish commonweal, as well as the character and agenda of its "clever" president, were not allayed by a breakfast talk he had with Urho Kekkonen at Tamminiemi which he described to Washington two days later, on July 15. Hickerson's recollection of the talk, in which he came as close to challenging Kekkonen as he dared, shows just how duplicitous, as well as self-deluding the Finnish leader could be.

The envoy started off by asking his host whether he would like to comment on the fraught state of Finnish domestic politics. "I added that my inquiry was made out of [*sic*] friendly conversation and not desire to interfere, "an example," he suggestively added "that I wished would be followed by Finland's neighbor." Kekkonen replied that "he understood my wish but found the situation very discouraging, and saw no realistic prospect of broadening the government lest it suffer the same fate as Fagerholm III."[1]

Next Hickerson broached the even more controversial subject of Kekkonen's pilgrimage to Leningrad six months earlier. His account continues: "Kekkonen said that the atmosphere in Fenno-Soviet relations had improved for [a] time after [the] Leningrad visit, and then it had deteriorated again with the Soviets and Social Democrats exchanging charges. He felt that the May Day speeches of the Social Democrats were particularly unfortunate."

The ambassador persisted. "In this connection I asked again as a friendly observer whether he thought it reasonable to expect 'good Finns' to take abuse from Khrushchev without replying." Kekkonen's response showed him at his most disingenuous—or his most artfully diplomatic, depending on how one looked at it. "Kekkonen replied that he did not know, but that answers always complicated matters and that they could have been simpler." *Simpler?* "He made no comment on my warning that no one could ever know whom the Soviet Union might criticize next."

Continuing in this testing mode the American ambassador made clear his admiration for the same politicians whom Khrushchev had criticized, with Kekkonen's tacit blessing, including Väinö Tanner. "[Hickerson] said that this was an affair in which [he] could not take sides [with] Finns, but had to say that [he] held Tanner and [the] other Social Democrats condemned by Khrushchev in the highest regard." Kekkonen's response was typically two-faced:

> He agreed that Tanner [is] one of the great men of Finland, but also one of the stubbornest he had ever known.
>
> As a parting thought Kekkonen said that he knew we understood Finland's difficult position [but that] despite [that] he had every confidence [the] country [could] handle its relations with [the] Soviets and remain free, although this would time to time require "adjustments."[2]

Interestingly, and revealingly, Kekkonen's recollection of what he said was somewhat different: "[I] I told him Tanner is a great man, but in foreign politics he always makes not small but big mistakes. He is unhappily in love with foreign politics, which does not reciprocate."[3]

Why, one asks, in retrospect, the discrepancy? Hickerson had no interest in fudging his account. Evidently this is what Kekkonen had *hoped* to say, but had not: just as Kekkonen, the Finnish president, tended to see and hear what he wanted, sometimes he remembered what he chose to.

Here is but one instance, of which there would be more in the years to come, where Kekkonen's recollection of an event or a conversation does not square with the record. As such this requires one to take his journals with a corresponding grain of salt, and view them more as a record of his mind set rather than of what actually transpired or was said.

Not that this makes his journals any less important. Indeed, if anything, the opposite. Here, in Kekkonen's skewed remembrance of an intense exchange with a Western diplomat who did not defer to him and strongly questioned his behavior and policies one sees the seed of the megalomania which would ultimately consume him later during the quarter century when he essentially ruled Finland.

The true test of Finland's fiber, and its president, Hickerson felt, would be how firmly Helsinki would press for membership in the European Free Trade Association (EFTA), or the Outer Seven, as the newfangled trade pact had come to be called, and how the country, as well as Kekkonen would respond to Moscow's anticipated resistance.

The worried envoy underlined the essentiality of the nebulously understood issue to Finnish democracy, as did the aforementioned 1959 CIA report. "As we have noted," the diplomat declared in his cable to Washington, "there is a compelling reason for Finland to persist" in joining EFTA. "Finland cannot afford to stay out [of EFTA] because of the competitive disadvantage to her exports," he wrote. "On the other hand, an adverse Soviet reaction seems likely at some point in direct proportion to the degree of success accompanying Finland's desire to affiliate."[4] Here, again, in a nutshell, was Kekkonen's dilemma: how to maintain and enhance his nation's economic as well as spiritual ties to the West, without alienating its powerful neighbor to the East on which it also was dependent: Scylla and Charybdis.

Hickerson also made it clear that he expected a negative outcome from Finland's EFTA campaign, and consequently Washington should be prepared to throw Finland a lifeline. "Under the circumstances, and with the critical period very near at hand," he continued, "I urge the earliest possible authorization for the necessary assurances should appropriate circumstances."[5]

In the event, the envoy's fears about Moscow's intentions were soon realized. In late July, after Nikita Khrushchev's trip to the Baltic region was canceled, the Kremlin broke its silence about how it felt about the matter in the form of a *Pravda* editorial strongly advising Finland against joining EFTA. Ralf Törngren, the Finnish foreign minister, hastily replied for his government stressing that Finland would do nothing to prejudice its economic and other relations with the Neighbor to the East.

Kekkonen, who hitherto had been reluctant to state his position on the explosive issue, partly out of caution, partly because Nikita Khrushchev himself had not said anything about it, remained mum. Both his domestic and foreign critics drew the same conclusion: that Kekkonen did not support Finnish membership in EFTA.

However actually he *did*. The Finnish head of state just did not feel comfortable, or consider it necessary to publicly announce his position. The issue, he felt—quite rightly, as it turned out—was really between him and Khrushchev.

Meanwhile, Kekkonen's numerous critics in the West who were not in sympathetic vibration with the epic national symphony he was conducting continued to watch the increasingly self-assured Finnish leader's balancing act with trepidation. In August, the US State Department learned that Great Britain, Finland's most important Western trading partner, as well as the one with which it had the longest-standing relationship, had also expressed concern about Finland's course, according to a cable from London. The department subsequently sent a cable to its minions in London and Helsinki providing guidance regarding US views on Finland.

The memo, which went out on September 2, 1959, makes clear that Hickerson's superiors shared his pessimism about Finland's future as a democracy. "Kekkonen's excessive accommodation of the USSR, which goes beyond the Paasikivi line is extremely risky in the U.S. view," the aide-mémoire stated. "Even if he succeeds in cultivating the USSR without jeopardizing Finnish sovereignty," it predicted, "he is likely to establish a pattern of relations in which less clever Finnish leadership in [the] future will be compromised."[6]

Clever. If nothing else, American officials were agreed, Kekkonen was a clever man. That double-edged compliment would recur in official American communications for some time. All right—but was he clever enough to save Finland from falling under complete Soviet control? As far as Washington was concerned, as Kekkonen approached the end of his fourth year in office, the answer to that question was still very much in doubt.[7]

Although Finland was only a pawn in the global-wide contest between the US and the USSR it was still an important one in Washington's view. The National Security Council's report of October 14, 1959 enunciating US policy toward Finland underscores just how important it was, as well as how worried Washington was about losing it to Moscow's wiles, as to those of its slippery president. "Finland," the report noted, "is one of the few countries which has a common border with the USSR, but still has managed to remain free from Soviet domination."

"It stands as an example of democracy on the Communist threshold," the NSC continues, "and a buffer state against further Soviet encroachment in an area of direct confrontation between the West and Soviet imperialism."[8]

Further the report stated, the stakes involved in keeping Finland out of the clutches of the Russian bear were as high if not higher than they had been twenty years before, during the Winter War. "Complete Soviet domination of Finland," which the Council evidently thought was a strong possibility, "would be a heavy blow to Western morale and could weaken the resistance of some other small Free World nations to Soviet bloc pressures."

What "small Free World nations" was it referring to? Denmark? The Netherlands? Were those countries not members of NATO? Or neutrals Austria and Sweden? The worried planners did not say.

"In addition," the report's authors continued, raising the hue and cry, Soviet domination or occupation of its democratic neighbor "would put the USSR in control of advance air defense warning positions and additional naval bases in the Baltic [Sea region]." Furthermore, they continued, "if Finland [was] able to preserve its present neutral status—that of a nation able to maintain its independence, despite heavy pressure—it could serve as an example of what the US might like to see achieved by the Soviet-dominated nations of Eastern Europe."

Not that its current president was much help. "Finland's policy toward the USSR is significantly affected by President Kekkonen, the country's leading political figure," the NSC noted. Although Kekkonen was not a communist, he "believes that Finland's best interests are served by greater accommodation to Soviet wishes than many of his countrymen consider necessary."

Just for the record, the paper added, "in case of an East-West armed conflict in Europe or Soviet pressures for military concessions, the Finns would do what they could to preserve their independence and neutrality and avoid assisting the USSR." Translation: the Finnish president might lack spine, but his people did not. "A Soviet attack on Finland"—which the authors seemed to think was possible, they added, invoking memories of the Winter War and the remorseless ski soldiers who descended on the Russian myrmidons from the snow-covered northern fells, "would probably meet armed resistance and Soviet occupying forces would be subjected to intensive guerilla warfare."

For all their respect and concern for Finland, the writers were deliberately vague about just how proactive US policy toward their faraway sister republic ought to be should the USSR decide to invade their small neighbor once again. "[In] the event of a serious crisis endangering

Finland's continued independence," they advised, the US government should "be prepared to take all necessary and appropriate measures to increase the will, strength, and ability of Finland to maintain its independence." What measures were those?[9]

Little wonder that Edson Sessions, who succeeded John Hickerson as American ambassador the following month, wrote in a subsequent dispatch, "Like many other Finns he [Kekkonen] believes that Finland would be abandoned by the United States in time of war."[10] It certainly sounded like it. Once again Brave Little Finland, as it was hailed during the *Talvisota*, had America's full moral support, along with its limited financial support, but that was it.

US hopes for pulling Finland out of the Soviet orbit were further dampened later that month when Anastas Mikoyan, the sharp-tongued Soviet deputy prime minister, alighted in Helsinki on October 22 to inaugurate the fourth annual Russian Trade Fair, and sign the new five-year Fenno-Soviet trade agreement. As was its wont in those post-Night Frost days, when the Finnish press was doing its best to follow Kekkonen's dictum not to rock the boat, the tone of the article in the *Helsingin Sanomat* reporting Mikoyan's arrival at Helsinki's still smallish, one terminal airport, where he was greeted by a phalanx of tightly smiling Finnish officials led by Prime Minister Sukselainen, could just as easily have appeared in *Pravda*.

Excerpt: "Prime Minister, ministers, friends, gentlemen, I bring you greetings from [Chairman] Khrushchev, [President] Voroshilov and the whole Soviet nation, Mikoyan joyously declared upon his arrival from Moscow."[11]

Western observers were also alarmed by Mikoyan's speech following the signing, in which the hoary old Bolshevik, the only senior Soviet official to have survived the murderous caprices of Vladimir Lenin, Joseph Stalin, and now Nikita Khrushchev, referred to Finland as a Russian protectorate, if not an outright satellite.

Did Moscow respect Finnish independence? It certainly did not sound like it. "The Soviet Union with its military power will guarantee the security of Finland," asserted Mikoyan, "and Finns can live without fear for their destiny."[12]

For his part, President Kekkonen was relieved by the agreement that followed, which called for Finland to import oil and fuel and sundry other items, including 5,000 Soviet automobiles for the car-hungry Finnish public in return for 122 ships, including two 22,000 horsepower ice breakers. This treaty increased the amount of Finnish trade with the USSR up to 17 percent, a modest increase. Among other things, it confirmed that Fenno-Soviet relations were back to normal, at least in an economic sense, if normal meant that the USSR still had a virtual stranglehold on the Finnish economy.

That was par for the course by now. However the Finnish president could not have been happy with Mikoyan's manifest disrespect for Finnish sovereignty. And he must have been even unhappier when Mikoyan made it clear during his discussions with the anxious Finns that his country strongly objected to their country's participation in EFTA. Clearly, a lot of bilateral arm wrestling and triangulating messages was in store before his Soviet friends would agree to *that*. It must have been with mixed emotions that the rattled Finnish president saw the Soviet hard-liner off to Moscow after the latter's sortie.

What *is* clear is that the Finnish president was torn over the direction of Finnish foreign policy.

As was his odd wont, the vain Finnish magnifico used his body weight to measure his success or lack thereof in the diplomatic sphere, equating his own health with that of Finland. "I now weigh 78.0 kg or a lot more," he confided to his journal on September 26, "but it looks like this fall I will drop, as I did in the fall of 1958 to around 73–74 kg. That's how bad a direction foreign relations seem to be headed."[13] Apparently seventy-eight kilograms was Kekkonen's, and Finland's, beau ideal: his well-being and the Finnish nation's were interchangeable.

One suspects that Kekkonen dropped at least a few hundred grams (if not more) after Comrade Mikoyan's visit.

As it happened, the visit of Khrushchev's number two man, Mikoyan, to Helsinki coincided with one by Kekkonen's number two man—insofar as Kekkonen, who disliked delegating as much as Khrushchev could be said to have one—Ralf Törngren, the Finnish foreign minister, to the United States.

The overt purpose of the Swedish-speaking minister's visit was to represent Finland at the United Nations General Assembly. However his actual objective seems to have been to sound out the US government on how much it was prepared to do, or not to do, at this hinge point of Fenno-Soviet relations. Toward that end Törngren met with US officials at the State Department in Washington. Presiding over the October 23, 1959, meeting was Törngren's counterpart, Christian Herter, who had succeeded John Foster Dulles as secretary of state, following Dulles's death in May. Also present, according to State Department records, was Edson Sessions, the American ambassador to designate, who was destined to take the place of the dyspeptic John Hickerson, who had been posted to the Philippines.

If the new Secretary of State was as worried about Finland as his subordinates were, he certainly didn't sound like it. According to the official memorandum of the conversation, the genial Törngren expressed his appreciation of the "understanding and helpful" attitude which the US had shown Finland. Herter responded "that there [was] a very good reason for our attitude, namely the great respect the U.S. has for Finland's courageous and skillful handling of its very difficult situation."[14]

Interestingly, and not surprisingly, the sensitive topic of Finland's desire to attach itself to EFTA, which Mikoyan had just scotched, came up. According to the memo, Törngren seemed to be feeling Herter out on the subject. Unsurprisingly, American's top diplomat sounds conflicted.

> Mr. Törngren commented on the potential importance of the Outer Seven Free Trade Area to the Finnish economy. He noted the negative Soviet attitude toward the Outer Seven and the possible political difficulties for Finland, if it joined EFTA if some form of agreement is reached between EFTA and the EEC [the Common Market].[15]

Herter's noncommittal response regarding this potentially explosive matter followed the line which Dulles, his bilious, if careful predecessor had drawn during the Night Frost: "The Secretary responded that the Soviet Union appeared to oppose the formation of any kind of bloc, military or economic."

Torngren replied that "he"—and presumably Kekkonen—"[were] thinking in terms of associate membership in the Seven."[16]

No response from Herter.

Something else extraordinary took place during Törngren's American sortie: the Finnish government daringly invited President Dwight Eisenhower to visit Finland on his way to Moscow during his tentatively scheduled visit to Russia the following spring.

Interestingly, if not necessarily surprisingly, Kekkonen does not mention the invitation in his diary. Nor is there any mention of the remarkable overture in the State Department aide-mémoire of the Törngren and Herter meeting.

The only thing that *is* clear is that the invitation was extended. Proof of this—and as far as the writer can discern the *only* proof—appeared three months later in Ambassador Sessions's telegram to the State Department February 2, 1960, in which the excited diplomat urges Washington to take Helsinki up on the extraordinary offer. "Some indication of how [important] the visit is regarded by the Finns can be seen from the fact that Foreign Minister Törngren, when he offered the invitation, said that it was 'of the highest political importance.'"[17]

The unassuming Törngren, a member of the Swedish People's Party, the party which represented Finland's Swedish-speaking minority, who had briefly served as prime minister in 1954, was hardly one to make this sort of thing up.[18] Whether or not the invitation to "Ike" was his idea is not clear. In any event, Kekkonen undoubtedly was aware of the invitation and gave it the blessing of his government.[19]

Which leads to the obvious question: why?

In order to answer that, one must pull the cameras back to take in the somewhat fluid international scene as it appeared to the Finnish president as he stared pensively out the window of his study at Tamminiemi that autumn. To be sure, it is important to keep in mind, when analyzing or trying to analyze Kekkonen's often seemingly inscrutable moves, as he labored to keep the storm-tossed Finnish ship of state from running aground during his turbulent first term, that, in addition to monitoring—as well to some extent, controlling—Fenno-Soviet relations, he also, perforce, was constantly monitoring US-Soviet relations in order to calculate how much room he had to navigate in his quadrant of the Cold War.

And the fact is, there had just been a significant thaw in *that* larger war, witness the Soviet premier's more or less successful visit to the US the previous September. To be sure, Khrushchev's trip was not without its bumps, including a rocky visit to Los Angeles, when he was refused entry to Disneyland, leading him to throw a fit, as well as a testy meeting with President Eisenhower at Camp David, which he originally thought was an American gulag.

The visitation ended on a happy enough note, however, after Ike invited Khrushchev to his Gettysburg, Pennsylvania, farm, which the latter enjoyed immensely—which in turn led his impulsive guest to invite Eisenhower to visit Russia the following spring, after the disarmament conference in Paris scheduled for the following May, an invitation Ike accepted.

Put another way, if Fenno-Soviet relations were still tense in late 1959, there had been a break in the geopolitical clouds at a higher level and the politically adroit Finnish president, ever eager to bolster Finland's international position as well as his own, had decided to take advantage of the new warming to invite his Russian friend's newest friend to make a side trip to Finland on his way to Khrushchev's dacha. For a sitting US president, no less Eisenhower, the former Supreme Allied commander and leader of the Free World, to set foot in Finland would have been startling, especially if it included a visit to the presidential mansion.

Of course, as we know, was not to be. Six months later, an American U-2 spy plane piloted by Gary Powers was shot down over Russia, causing an enraged Khrushchev to torpedo his highly anticipated tête-à-tête with Eisenhower in Paris and withdraw the invitation to the famously golf-loving president—for whom he had actually built a golf course!—and US-Soviet relations froze up again, nixing the notion of a stopover in Finland.

Aside from Ambassador's Sessions's memo on February 2, 1960, there is no official, or even unofficial, record of the invitation to President Eisenhower, either when it was extended in the fall of 1959, or when it fell through after the U-2 debacle the following spring. There is nothing about it in the Finnish president's journal.

Oddly, too, the matter did not come up in November, when the departing US ambassador and Kekkonen's one-time bête noire, Hickerson, stopped by the president's mansion in order to pay his final respects. One has to assume that if Hickerson's successor, Sessions, knew about the invite so did he. And yet—at least according to Kekkonen's admittedly subjective and incomplete journal—it was not mentioned. According to the diary, the departing envoy's main concern was whether the Finnish communist party, the SKDL, would manage to finagle its way into a future coalition government (as it indeed eventually did in 1966). The president assured the skittish American that he did not think that would happen.

Apparently Kekkonen's estimate of Hickerson, whose eventful tour of duty had paralleled his presidency and whom he had once dismissed as a "dolt," had improved somewhat by now.[20] Thus when the US ambassador advised him to "invite Finnish politicians one by one and tell them not to talk about foreign policy," his reaction was "interesting thought."[21]

To be sure, if word of Kekkonen's invitation to Dwight Eisenhower *had* gotten out, it would have changed his—and Finland's—image in the US, which continued to be problematic.

In the event, the predominant picture of Finland in the American press at the end of the first decade of the Cold War was a grim one. In September 1959, *Reader's Digest* published a downbeat portrait of Suomi by Leland Stowe, the noted foreign correspondent.[22] Entitled "The Finns Still Fight for Freedom," the feature depicted a country besieged by Communist forces within and without. A veteran of the Winter War, when the *Chicago Daily News* writer first gained renown, the unabashed Fennophile saw a direct connection between the real war the Finns had fought with the Neighbor to the East twenty years before and the war of nerves they were currently fighting with the Soviets and their home-grown fifth column.[23]

Recalling the shocking day in March 1940 when the government's decision to sign the Treaty of Moscow which brought the *Talvisota* to a close, Stowe wrote:

> On that tragic March day of surrender women wept uncontrollably and stunned anguish swamped every face. Yet within 24 hours Finns repeatedly declared to me with flaming intensity, "We have been through this before." This is not the end, they asserted.[24]

"They spoke truly," Stowe continued, "for today the Finns still battle for their independence every day of their lives."

"Finland remains free," the veteran correspondent wrote, "but her hold on freedom is precarious." Invoking the still bitter memory of the Night Frost, he warned, "the Soviets' squeeze and freeze play can [still] be applied at any time." Kekkonen himself is not mentioned in the piece; however the writer makes it clear that he is no friend of the current government.[25]

The author of an article in *Reporter* magazine in October, 1959 had no such qualms. Had Kekkonen signed away Finland's freedom? he wondered, leaving the reader in little doubt about the answer. The *US News & World Report* was even more critical, accusing Kekkonen of pursuing a pro-Soviet policy, leading Ahti Karjalainen, the then minister of trade and industry, who was warming to his role as enforcer for his querulous chief, to send a formal note of protest to Washington.

Privately, Kekkonen's moods continued to oscillate from high to low that fall. Thus on November 17, 1959, he vented to his journal about the seemingly hapless Sukselainen. "O dear lord! Sukselainen is deceiving everyone, his friends and his opposition," he laments of his unloved prime minister, who would somehow stagger on in office for another twenty months. "I am tired of this worthless game," he laments. "If only

I could get rid of the whole garbage. Being a babysitter is no fun and it is impossible to succeed if one is faced by total mistrust."

Two days later, on the nineteenth, the presidential diarist is in high spirits again: "I immensely enjoy the passion of crowds, whether it is for or stormily against."[26] To be sure, by this point of his tenure, most Finns were either avowedly for or against their eighth president, a fact that the fifty-nine-year-old seems to have accepted with equanimity.

The polarized character of Finnish politics as well as Kekkonen's own polarizing qualities were the theme of an illuminating series of articles that Werner Wiskari published in *The New York Times* at year's end. "Growing bitterness in Finland's splintered political life intruded into the observance of Independence Day in this southern factory town today," Wiskari began his first dispatch from the small southern town of Riihimäki, on December 6. Relieved as they were by the resolution of the Night Frost, the residents there were still conflicted about Kekkonen's stewardship including the monopoly he exercised over foreign policy:

> For the first time in memory, the high-flown oratory that usually commemorates Finland's declaration of independence from Russia in 1917 was abandoned for a sharp political attack.[27]

The author of said attack, Mauno Peltonen, the editor of the Social Democratic newspaper in the nearby town of Hämeenlinna, clearly was not conflicted about his feelings about the creaky minority government and the officious, Russia-friendly president who presided over it.

> Denouncing the Agrarian League's contention that only it could get along with Moscow, he said that the preservation of Finland's freedom could not be a one party monopoly and accused the Agrarians of using foreign policy to stay in power.[28]

"Adding to the bitterness of the Finnish political scene is the controversy over the role of President Kekkonen, one of the most loved and most disliked men in Finland," observed the sharp-eyed *Times*man. Ten years before, when he was still prime minister, Juho Paasikivi, Kekkonen's predecessor, had bemoaned his protégé's utter lack of support among the Finnish people.

By now, Kekkonen had remedied that glaring deficiency. Now he had the staunch support of the Finnish people, according to Wiskari, but only half of them. The rest evidently loathed him. "He is accused of abandoning the traditional Presidential position of being above politics and directing Agrarian moves to retain political control"—a charge which Kekkonen would not have denied.[29]

The Finnish nation's mixed feelings about its increasingly powerful president were also the main theme of a largely sympathetic, if not uncritical profile of him published in the *Times* the next day, the eighth.

To be sure, Wiskari's exclusive report, which was at once more sympathetic and more critical than the one he had filed earlier in the year following the Night Frost, provided ample grist for both his critics and his admirers. His Manichean subject is described as "a cynical politician who plays a dangerous game with the Soviet Union," wrote Wiskari. "And he is said to have surrounded himself with a palace guard of young stalwarts, who by definition must be suspect." "Against these," the reporter continued, "are Kekkonen's supporters who speak of him as 'that great, kind man' who time and again has been 'the savior of Finland.'"[30]

For US readers Wiskari draws an analogy that probably would have flattered the skittish Finnish president: "The division of Finland into two groups of people—those fiercely for Kekkonen and those against is strongly reminiscent of Franklin D. Roosevelt." The reporter also seems to be taken in by the self-possessed Finn, against his better sentiments:

> Mr. Kekkonen's bearing as he extends his hand in greeting seems to reflect a continual awareness that mantle of the Presidency is upon his tall, trim figure. At no point is the President impassive. He seeks to argue a point, to convince, to answer with questions of his own.[31]

Wiskari also gives Kekkonen a chance to laugh at himself: "He is good-humored and laughs easily when told of an old Agrarian League woman who said she believed in her party, President and God—in that order," he pens.

At the same time, the writer chides Kekkonen for his imperious ways, particularly his tendency to cut himself off from the domestic press, and withdraw to his house. "When he was Premier [*sic*] Kekkonen was easily accessible to the press," he writes. That was then. This is now. Now Wiskari notes, "as President he is aloof. He holds no press conferences. He has granted only one on the record interview," Wiskari writes, alluding to the one the reclusive president had given to him.

Doubtless Kekkonen saw Wiskari's article the following day. One suspects that he was pleased.[32]

Ten days later, liverish Kekkonen was back. This time the source of the president's agita was his faint-hearted countrymen, particularly the considerable number of Finns who recently had decided that they had had enough of life in the Finnish pressure cooker and had left the country and moved to Australia. "If a Finn here [thinks] that the USSR will swallow us up and put an end to our independence"—as many Finns apparently did at the close of 1959, Kekkonen griped to his journal on December 17, "his life will be so gloomy that he is better off moving to Australia," he huffed. "If one trusts that we will take care of [Finland's] independence," he continued, "then this country's soil will provide enough work for us all."[33]

True enough. There certainly was enough work in the country to go around. Unemployment stood at a mere 1.4 percent and would remain at roughly that level for the next five years. Perhaps Finland's living standard was not quite as high as that of its other Nordic neighbors, but Finns were doing well enough. The recession of 1958, which had halted Finland's steady growth of industrial output, and which the Night Frost had exacerbated, was over. Suomi was working again. If some Finns could not take the heat, as Kekkonen's putative hero Harry Truman was fond of saying, they should get out!

Of course the EFTA Gordian knot still loomed over the horizon, but, emboldened by the spirit of Camp David, the Finnish president was sure he could find a way to untie that vexing problem. Thus, when on December 23, the Soviet ambassador, Aleksey Zakharov, remarked to Kekkonen that "the year has gone well."

"I agreed," the Finn replied.[34]

Chapter 6

Seventy-Seven Kilograms (1/60–5/60)

This clever politician has great influence.

—Memo from Edson O. Sessions, the new US ambassador to Helsinki, February 1960

Had 1959 actually been a very good year for Urho Kekkonen? Perhaps okay would be a more accurate way of putting it. For one the weak Agrarian League–led minority government still stood. Kekkonen still had Moscow's trust, although some of his countrymen, as well as most Western governments, continued to have strong doubts about how much Kekkonen had forfeited in return for that trust.

Meanwhile, several formidable challenges awaited the president as he looked ahead to the last two years of his first six-year term of office, challenges that he would have to overcome if the Finnish ship of state wasn't going to wind up on the rocks, and his presidency along with it. Somehow Urho Kekkonen had to overcome Moscow's opposition to Finland affiliating itself with the European Free Trade Association (EFTA).

At the same time he also had to squelch the still widespread view in the West that his country was a de facto Soviet satellite. Otherwise, Finland's value to Nikita Khrushchev as a shop window for "Peaceful Coexistence" would be nullified and Finland might indeed become a real Soviet satellite, as some of Khrushchev's hard-line comrades, like Ivan Spiridonov and Anastas Mikoyan, evidently wished.

And of course Kekkonen still had to win reelection, and that is something he ardently wanted. As much as he disliked some aspects of his position—or, rather the way he had interpreted it, particularly "babysitting" the members of his own, fractious party—the fact remained that Kekkonen loved being president of Finland. And more than ever he was convinced he was the only man for the job.

Remarkably, thanks to his own formidable political talents and instincts, as well as a number of serendipitous events, including the May 1960 Soviet shootdown of the American U-2 spy plane over Russia, Kekkonen was able to accomplish all of these objectives—the Kremlin's clearance for Finland to join EFTA, renewed respect for Finnish neutrality, as well as his own reelection, while also managing to survive the greatest crisis of this presidency, the Note Crisis.

Indeed, in retrospect, the last two years of Kekkonen's first term were the most pivotal ones of his entire presidency, essentially ensuring that he would remain president for as long as he and the Finnish people wished. At the same he also ensured Finland's survival as a democracy for the remainder of the Cold War, albeit one with certain Kremlin-mandated caveats, the most important being that only he, Urho Kaleva Kekkonen, continue as president.

The first of those years, 1960, began on an auspicious enough note for the weight-conscious president. On January first he weighed a robust 77.3 kilograms, the same that he had weighed before the Night Frost. So that was good.

The Finnish president also seemed to be in a sufficiently robust mood when he made his New Year's speech. In contrast to previous such addresses, which were devoted mostly to foreign policy, this time he devoted his annual pep talk entirely to economic and cultural matters. Finland's economy was strong, he asserted in the nationally broadcast address, noting the steady rise in Finnish GDP (gross domestic product) since 1957, as well as the growth in the chemical, metal and mine industries.

Next the president listed a number of noteworthy developments in the educational and cultural spheres, particularly the expansion of Finland's higher education sector including the opening of the University of Oulu, "the biggest cultural event of last year," as well as the completion of the University of Turku's and Jyväskylä College of Education's "up-to-date and architecturally significant main buildings." "I have limited my New Year's review to economic and educational questions," the boosterish speech closes. "It is important to draw more attention to such matters so that Finland can maintain her place at the forefront of civilized countries."[1]

"I spoke on television," Kekkonen noted with satisfaction in his journal that evening. "Not a word about foreign policy."[2]

Of course, foreign policy was still very much on the head of state's mind. How could it not be? On January 4, the seven members of Europe's newest trading bloc, EFTA, including three of Finland's fellow nonaligned nations, Austria, Sweden, and Switzerland, plus Denmark, Norway, Portugal, and the United Kingdom, met in Stockholm to sign the treaty formalizing their remarkable new union, underlining the urgency of finding a way for Finland to attach itself to the "anti-EEC" that both its seven members and the Kremlin could approve.[3] At the time that appeared well-nigh impossible.

Nevertheless aside from Kekkonen's paranoia about what the right-wing members of his party might be up to, particularly the alliance he feared they might form with Väinö Tanner's Social Democrats, and the complications that would inevitably cause, he seems to have begun the year and the decade on a relaxed note, skiing and reading. No doubt he was further relieved when on February 2, the aging Tanner told *Hufvudstadsbladet* that he would not run for reelection as head of his party.

Next, an unexpected medical event, a gallstone attack, sent the president to the hospital for two weeks. However, Kekkonen does not seemed to have minded. On the evidence of the numerous newspaper clips he pasted in his journal during this period, the medical holiday gave him a lot of time to read.[4]

There was a lot to read about.

On February 3, the day before Kekkonen entered hospital, the French Senate voted to allow president Charles de Gaulle, then in the midst of the escalating Algerian civil war, to rule by decree in order to dismantle the power of the rebellious French settlers in French Algeria. Ten days later, France once again dominated the front pages when it became the world's fourth nuclear power after it successfully exploded an atomic bomb in Algeria. The following day, February 4, 1960, the USSR's support of Cuba was confirmed when the peripatetic Anastas Mikoyan was welcomed with open arms by the Cuban communist leader, Fidel Castro, confirming the alliance between the Caribbean island and its powerful new patron.

Ominously, before he departed Mikoyan told Castro that if he wanted the USSR would be willing to sell him "military aircraft," presaging the crisis which two years later would bring the world to the cusp of nuclear war.

While Mikoyan was linking arms with his new Cuban comrades and spreading Soviet largesse, his high-flying boss, Nikita Khrushchev, was also flying the hammer and sickle, so to speak, embarking on a lengthy three and a half week tour of India and South Asia, concluding agreements on economic, cultural and technical cooperation with Moscow's new friends in the Eastern hemisphere. The highlight of his trip was a communiqué issued at the end of the Soviet magnifico's visit to India, affirming India's policy of neutrality, as well as Indian prime minster Jawarharlal Nehru's support for Khrushchev's proposal for nuclear disarmament, the same one he expected to discuss with US president Dwight D. Eisenhower at their forthcoming summit in Paris that spring.

As always the prickly Kekkonen was alert to what was being said about him in the foreign press, positive or negative. Thus, on February 12, 1960, while he was still recovering from surgery, he was pleased when an aide brought him a clip from a West German newspaper in which noted Soviet expert Wolfgang Leonhard—a one-time comrade of East German communist head Walter Ulbricht, who had fled to the West—praised Finland's "skillful" foreign policy.[5]

While he was in the hospital, as the newsprint-devouring Finnish president was doubtless also aware, the on and off again Berlin crisis, which had become Khrushchev's major obsession, had boiled up when the Soviet commander-in-chief of Moscow's East German protectorate, the so-called German Democratic Republic (GDR) issued new passes to members of the US, British, and French military missions that permitted them to travel in the GDR Zone rather than the Soviet Zone, which implied that the Allies had recognized the East German regime, something they most decidedly did not wish to do, triggering protests from the Allied commanders.[6]

On February 19, Kekkonen was discharged from the hospital, sans gallstones. Unsuprisingly, one of the first things he did when he got back to his house was to weigh himself. According to his journal he had lost four kilograms (8.8 pounds). Other than that he was none the worse for wear.

It was the remarkably robust Finnish grandee's last visit to the hospital for ten years.

The Finnish president would have been more put out if he had read the dispatch that Edson Sessions, the US ambassador, had sent Washington two weeks before. If anything, Sessions's view of Finland and its president was even more downbeat than that of his choleric predecessor, John Hickerson.

The US ambassador's lengthy cable began on a positive enough note. "Finland is rapidly emerging from an existence as a small isolated nation devastated by two major wars in a decade into a technically competent, industrialized, viable country," the envoy observed. Unfortunately, Sessions believed, Finland's improving economic health was not matched by that of its commonweal. "The country's political situation should be improving in view of Russia's seeming determination to use Finland as a shop window for co-existence," he continued. In fact, he declared, Finnish neutrality was a fraud—"spurious" is the word the envoy used—and if one looked closely at that shop window one would find a country that was only independent in name, with a president who was close to being a Soviet puppet.[7]

As proof of the USSR's increasing political, economic and military stranglehold on its small neighbor, Sessions cited the following: the ominously increasing number of exchange visits between lower-level officials of both countries; Anastas Mikoyan's recent bellicose speech at the Soviet Trade Fair declaring Finland Moscow's protectorate; the new Soviet-Finnish trade agreement, which gave Moscow a virtual monopoly on Finnish oil imports and thus made it vulnerable to another Night Frost; the fact that the roster of the gargantuan Soviet embassy on Tehtaankatu had ballooned to nearly 200, or four times that of the much smaller, nearby US legation; the increased activity of communist front groups throughout Finland; and Soviet sales of military equipment to the Finnish military, along with the arrival of concommitant Russian personnel.

All in all, a fairly frightening picture—as well as one that, one suspects, would have been endorsed by the other Western ambassadors.

As to who or what was to blame for the Kremlin's tightening grip on its small neighbor Sessions cited, firstly, "Soviet effectiveness." Next was "internal political dissension," particularly among the noncommunist opposition parties. The third cause for this gloomy picture, Sessions noted, as well as one which was directly related to the second, was Kekkonen himself, whose re-election he seems resigned to. "This clever"—there was that word again—"politician has great influence. His term as President does not expire until 1962. He may be re-elected, and he is leading Finland into a type of cooperation which goes considerably beyond the bounds of pure neutrality."[8]

To fix this dire picture, as well as to counter Kekkonen's accommodationist impulses, the alarmed envoy listed a number of suggested palliative measures. Unsurprisingly, first and foremost of these was President

Eisenhower's acceptance of Kekkonen's astonishing invitation to him to visit Finland later that year en route to his prospective rendezvous with Khrushchev in Russia. The importance of the American chief executive's prospective Finnish sortie could not be overestimated, cabled Sessions. If the US was serious about pulling Finland back from the Kremlin's increasingly powerful gravitational field, this was the ideal time to do so. "Such a visit would be an ideal time for President Eisenhower to give a brief statement which could include assurances of our interest in Finland," he declared. Even a refueling stop would be wonderful, the American enthused. "We believe it would be a propaganda victory if President Eisenhower could at least make a refueling stop to greet the President and other government leaders," he added.[9]

In any case, if for some reason the US president could not stop in Finland, the ex-deputy US postmaster had another strong recommendation—invite the Finnish president to visit the United States: "If President Eisenhower cannot stop in Finland, then it becomes even more important to invite Kekkonen to the United States. The invitation, however, should be extended if possible before March 15 of this year, in order to plan his visit before President Eisenhower leaves for Moscow."[10] It is not known exactly when the latter invitation was extended. Kekkonen himself does not mention in his journal.[11]

The earnest diplomat made twenty-two other more or less well-founded recommendations for countering Soviet influence and bucking up the Finns, most of which never were not followed through on for one reason or another, such as a bilateral treaty formalizing the "neutralization" of Finland; and removing the standing restriction on Finnish purchases of American military equipment.

One of the more sensible, if notional, of Sessions's recommendations related to tourism. One of the greatest problems facing Finland, he felt, quite rightly, was its sense of isolation. To help remedy that, he recommended that "the Finns should be encouraged to plan a worldwide 'Visit Finland in 1961' (or 1962) campaign. Finland's sense of isolationism can be lessened by such a project, and the stage is set by the increasing amount of tourist travel to the USSR."[12]

Interestingly, Sessions seems to have had mixed feelings about the quality of Finnish design. The Finns seemed to know what they were doing when it came to the plastic arts, but in other areas, he felt they needed help: "Although designers and manufacturers in some fields such as architecture, furniture, glass and china have an ability to create satisfactory styles, designers in many other fields such as textiles and appliances, require more training in order to be competent in designing for the high style Western market."[13]

Evidently the American ambassador was not yet aware of Marimekko, the celebrated Finnish firm. Jackie Kennedy, the wife of Senator John Kennedy, the future Democratic presidential candidate, would soon take care of that.

Ambassador Sessions's first extended meeting with the Finnish president in April 1960 appears to have been amicable enough, at least on the evidence of the latter's diary, although neither party seems to have been particularly forthright with each other. According to the journal, the US envoy told Kekkonen how much he admired how he had proceeded with Finland's EFTA membership campaign. Nevertheless, he did not think that Finland's terms for joining the trade union would be accepted, to which—oddly—the president responded that he "agreed," even though obviously he hoped otherwise.[14]

Sessions's opinion of Kekkonen seems to have risen somewhat higher, at least according to the latter, who noted how the ambassador told him how much the US government "has a great appreciation personally towards me in the difficult job I have."[15]

In any case, the State Department's opinion of Urho Kekkonen and the general outlook for Finland was still grim. According to the dire assessment of the department's coordinating board, "While the possibility of Soviet aggression against Finland cannot be ruled out, the more likely danger is that Finland will slide gradually into a position of political subordination, economic dependence or military tutelage vis-à-vis the USSR.

"The trend of events in Finland indicates that Finland's determination to resist becoming a Soviet satellite is deteriorating," the report's pessimistic authors concluded.[16] They also were resigned to Kekkonen's reelection, which, clearly, they didn't think was a good thing for either Finland or the West:

> The Finns' marked sense of isolation and consciousness of the rapid rise of Soviet power have implanted a growing tendency towards accommodation to the USSR. Although found in all parties, this tendency is perhaps most marked amongst certain Agrarians, including President Kekkonen who will probably remain in positions of power for some time to come.[17]

Interestingly, there is no mention of the invitation to President Eisenhower to visit Finland during his forthcoming trip to Russia (possibly because it already may have been declined). The board did, however, endorse the idea of inviting Kekkonen to the US. Such a visit, it agreed, might be helpful in order "to gain his confidence and to bring him to realize the full measure of the strength Finland derives from Western power and unity."[18]

The body also endorsed the idea of increasing contact between the Pentagon and Finnish Defence Forces, which Sessions had also favored. The overall message from State to the embassy in its guidance regarding how to proceed was to "tread lightly," more or less as it had been doing for the past two years: "By discreet means continue to develop close relations with the Finnish military establishment in order to sustain their morale and anti-Communist posture, being careful however not to provoke Soviet pressure for further Finnish concessions."[19]

The downbeat if more or less accurate account ended with this gloomy analysis of the Finnish political scene, as presided over by its increasingly powerful head of state:

> Finland's effectiveness in attempting to maintain its independence is hampered by dissension amongst democratic elements—particularly between Social Democratic and Agrarian League parties. A firm stance vis-a-vis the USSR is rendered extremely difficult because governments are unstable, splinter parties acquire disportionate influence, policies are often temporary compromises [and] power tends to concentrate in the hands of President Kekkonen.[20]

Was Finland lost to the West? It basically looked that way to Foggy Bottom.

Meanwhile, as had been the case since Khrushchev had thrown down the gauntlet two years before, the chief point of friction between East and West and focus of diplomatic attention continued to be Berlin. What was the Finnish president's opinion on the matter? France's most prominent journalist, Hubert Beuve-Méry, the long-time editor of *Le Monde*, the prominent French daily, who Kekkonen cordially received at Tamminiemi on April 5, 1960, wanted to know.[21]

No surprise there, Kekkonen told the inquiring reporter. Once again Kekkonen endorsed the Kremlin's position: "recognizing two Germanys and maintaining political and social of the people of West Berlin."[22]

Any lingering mystery about Urho Kekkonen's or his political party's plans for the next election was removed two weeks later, on April 22, when the Agrarian League's parliamentary delegation voted unanimously to make him its candidate in the next election. In point of fact, the presidential poll was nearly two years away. Given the tumultuous state of Finnish politics, no less the world, anything could happen between then and January two years hence. Nevertheless as far as his party was concerned, Finland's eighth president was still the only man for the job.

Although some time would elapse before he formally announced his candidacy for reelection, the latter obviously agreed. Unlike his predecessor and mentor, Juho Paasikivi, who had to be persuaded to run for a second term, Kekkonen had no qualms about throwing his hat into the circle again. Then again, Paasikivi was already seventy-nine and in questionable health when he reluctantly decided to run again in 1950; his protege, Kekkonen, was twenty years younger. He certainly was good for another six-year term.

Who could possibly know that he would be good (more or less) for another four?

Four days later, as if to rebuff Kekkonen, as well as Moscow, the Social Democrats reelected the Kremlin's most despised Finnish politician, Väinö Tanner, who supposedly had retired, as the leader of the party. Even though he, too, was was already seventy-nine, Tanner decided that his fractious party still needed him, and so did his country. The Social Democrats had yet to nominate a candidate for president, nor would they for another year.

In any case, if the lord of Tamminiemi was worried, he did not show it. Nevertheless, with Tanner back as the head of the leading opposition party, he knew that the path to his re-election would be a rocky one.

Kekkonen certainly did not help his cause with the defeatist sounding May Day speech he delivered a week later. In the televised speech, which mystified opponents and supporters alike, he told his four and a half million countrymen that independence should be "lived and experienced with gentleness."[23]

If Kekkonen wanted to unite the nation behind him, this seemed an odd way to go about it. Predictably the delphic address triggered a torrent of criticism from the press. What exactly did the president mean, *Kauppalehti*, the Finnish business weekly, asked in its editorial, that Finland should bargain with its independence?[24]

Actually, as was sometimes the case with Kekkonen's more obscure presidential sermons, what he meant was *not* clear. Most likely the speech was part of the complicated game he was playing with Moscow in his effort to secure the Kremlin's permission for Finland to join EFTA, which remained his overarching goal and virtual obsession that year. If so, it seems to have worked on Aleksey Zakharov, the Soviet ambassador. Several days later, the envoy, who had replaced Viktor Lebedev, the envoy who was recalled during the Night Frost, assured him that Moscow trusted him completely, according to Kekkonen's diary.[25] He also told Kekkonen that he had given Ahti Karjalainen, who had taken on the additional role of the president's chief EFTA point man, a note to take to Moscow that would clear the way for the president to present his case about the matter personally to Khrushchev, as he had hoped to do the prior summer before the latter canceled his Scandinavian tour.

Once again, as in the case of his odd May Day speech, as Kekkonen's aide and confidante Jaakko Kalela put it, Kekkonen was playing his own game, even if some of his own supporters had trouble making out just what his game was.

Still, as anyone who truly knew Kekkonen could attest—and as he would later prove on numerous occasions, including the surprising speech that he would give in the visiting Soviet primier's presence that September—he wanted no one to doubt his love of his country, or his willingness to fight for it if necessary. That much was clear, or ought have been clear again, on June 4, when the towering equestrian statue of Gustaf Mannerheim, the revered former president and World War II commander-in-chief that had been erected at the entrance to the Helsinki peninsula, was unveiled. To commemorate the occasion, the Finnish army staged its biggest parade since the war.

As a result of the restrictions placed on the force by the 1947 Treaty of Paris between Finland and the Soviet Union, the regular army now only numbered 42,000, one-tenth of its prewar size. Nevertheless no one who looked into the eyes of the men proudly marching past the reviewing stand next to forty-foot-high statue of "The Father of Finland," as Mannerheim was popularly known, astride his favorite mount could have any doubt that either those soldiers, whose ranks included veterans of Finland's wars, were just as willing to fight and die for the fatherland, as they and their kinsmen had done between 1939 and 1945, or the grim-faced president who reviewed them.

Joining Kekkonen on the stand, along with the current commander of the Finnish Defense Forces, Sakari Simelius, who had fought in both the glorious 105-day-long Winter War and the less glorious three-year-long Continuation War that followed it, were members of the Helsinki diplomatic corps. However, as the correspondent of the London *Times* pointedly noted, "the Soviet ambassador, Mr. Zakharov, did not attend."[26]

Meanwhile, in Moscow, Nikita Khrushchev was on the warpath again, thanks to the shootdown of Gary Powers's U-2 spy plane over Russia on May 1, and the capture of the pilot along with his ill-gotten photographic lucre and modified silver dollar compleat with (unused) saxitoxin suicide needle.

Kekkonen recorded the extraordinary incident, which sent the improving American-Soviet relationship into a tailspin and shocked the world, in his journal. "Khrushschev," he writes on May 7, as the shock waves from the incident-cum-scandal were beginning to be felt, "revealed that the Soviet Union has shot down a US spy plane near Sverdlovsk."[27]

The diarist himself does not seem particularly concerned by the matter, even though he knew that it would throw a curve—at the least—into his own diplomatic ministrations. Perhaps he believed, as Khrushchev naively did at first, that the aerial incursion was the fault of rogue militarists within the US military, and that Eisenhower would apologize for outrage.

There was no apology from the US president, however, who, after recovering from his own initial shock and embarrassment, declared that he had indeed authorized the spy flight, pulling the rug out from under the livid Soviet leader.[28]

The only thing that was clear at the moment was that Nikita Sergeyevich Khrushchev was furious, and that the short-lived era of good feeling between the United States and the Soviet Union was definitely over. That much was manifest two weeks later when the still enraged Khrushchev arrived in Paris for his scheduled summit with President Eisenhower and two other Western leaders, President de Gaulle of France and Prime Minister Harold Macmillan of Great Britain. The sputtering, apoplectic man who now faced the French president was "a character so changed in identity as to belong to the realm of Russian fiction," the latter averred.[29]

The next day, May 16, 1960, the first day of the summit, that same phantasmorgical character, hand trembling, eyebrow twitching, laced into the red-faced US president with his prepared marks. Since Eisenhower had not only failed to condemn the Powers flight, but also had stated that such flights would continue, the USSR, in its righteous indignation, proposed to postpone the summit for six to eight months, Khrushchev announced—by which time, of course, Eisenhower, then coming to the end of his second term, would be a lame duck. Moscow preferred to deal with his successor, whomever that might turn out to be.

Likewise, Khrushchev huffed, Eisenhower's much-ballyhooed visit to the USSR would be indefinitely postponed. Clearly, the Soviet leader was stricken by what he regarded as the American's bad faith. "I don't know whether I should use this expression," he blurted at the next and last session of the doomed assembly, "but we don't understand what the devil pushed you into this provocative act just before the conference. If there had been no incident we would have come here with clean hands and a pure soul."[30]

Ike's assurance that the high altitude reconnaissance flights would only be suspended was not enough to mollify Khrushchev, whose sortie to the City of Light ended with a riotous press conference at which he angrily reminded the 2,000 Western journalists in attendance that "I am a representative of the great Soviet people, who under the leadership of Lenin and the Communist party brought about the Great October Socialist Revolution!"[31] And then the angry and disappointed Russian, who had hoped to resolve the Berlin crisis which he had initiated two years before at the meeting, and possibly usher in a new era of nuclear disarmament, stormed back to Moscow.

So much for the so-called Spirit of Camp David.

So the Great Golfer, as the links-loving thirty-fourth president was also known, was not going to be calling "Fore" in Moscow anytime soon—which also meant that Ike would not be visiting Finland either.

So much for Kekkonen's hoped-for conclave with the US leader, and the boost to Finnish neutrality and prestige he had hoped to gain thereof.

Instead of being disappointed by the sudden turn of events, however, Kekkonen, ever the gamesman, saw in the summit wreckage an opportunity to further his main objective: to persuade Moscow to allow Finland to join the European Trade Federation Association, as well as to rebond with the chagrinned Soviet leader. "The failure of [the] Paris top level conference," he penned on May 19, 1960, siding with the aggrieved Russian, "which has been blamed on Khrushchev [wrongly, he feels, one infers] provides a good opportunity for Finland."

Khrushchev, the president wrote, "might wish to profit from the situation" by showing that:

(1) the state visits are useful
(2) negotiations on top level are beneficial
(3) Soviet line is still one of peaceful co-existence.

"All this can be proved," insisted the Finnish president, "by inviting me to Moscow and agreeing on 'Finland-USSR-EFTA.'"

"We'll see if my conjecture is right," Kekkonen confided to his journal that night before retiring.[32]

Chapter 7

A Party to Remember (5/60–9/60)

> I am convinced that even if the whole of Europe turns communist, that Finland will remain traditionally democratic.
>
> —Urho Kekkonen, speaking at a luncheon at the Soviet embassy at which Nikita Khrushchev was present, during Khrushchev's visit to help celebrate his sixtieth birthday, September 4, 1960

Actually, somewhat to the Finnish leader's surprise, his guess was right. How much Finland could benefit from the debacle in Paris via Kekkonen's proposed diplomatic bank shot was not clear. Nevertheless, by the end of 1960, after two more face-to-face meetings between Nikita Khrushchev and himself, one in Helsinki, another in Moscow, the resolute Finn got his way.

First, as had become the maddening norm, Kekkonen had to separate out the conflicted and garbled messages he was receiving about the impetuous Soviet leader's true views regarding EFTA from Aleksey Zakharov, the Soviet ambassador, Viktor Vladimirov, and Vladimir Zhenikhov, the KGB *rezidentura* and his deputy, as well as those which Ahti Karjalainen, his own trade envoy to Moscow and right-hand man, was bringing back from Moscow. A year before, when Kekkonen's poorly concealed campaign to latch onto EFTA was underway, the then US ambassador, John D. Hickerson had posited that the true test of the strength of Finland's character as a democracy could be measured by how determined Kekkonen was in overcoming Moscow's anticipated objections to Finnish membership in EFTA.

If that was true, one imagines that Hickerson would have been impressed by the storm of Soviet static the Finnish president had to endure before he finally got his way. Indeed, reviewing Kekkonen's diary

FIGURE 10. Good friends. Urho Kekkonen greets Nikita Khrushchev at the Soviet embassy, Helsinki, after the Soviet premier invited himself to the celebration of the Finnish president's sixtieth birthday. All was sweetness and light until Khrushchev embarrassed him by using the occasion to denounce NATO. But things ended up well enough.

entries from the spring and summer of 1960, as he records the wildly mixed messages he was receiving from his Russian friends, as well as some of the other slings and arrows of outrageous Finnish politicial fortune he had to endure, the wonder is that he did not lose his wits altogether.

Finally, on August 20, 1960, the static lifted and a clear message came through. Zakharov, the Soviet ambassador, who evidently had overcome the opposition to Finland joining EFTA both within his own embassy, as well as from the Central Committee, was pleased to report that Kekkonen was welcome to travel to Moscow on September 9 and 10 and talk about EFTA. And by the way, the (presumably) pleased envoy asked the (presumably) equally pleased Finnish president, would it be okay if Chairman Khrushchev joined the Finnish president in Helsinki on September 3 to help him celebrate his sixtieth birthday?

Would that be all right?

Would it! "I answered Yes" Kekkonen wrote in his diary.[1] Of course, it would okay! Kekkonen's long, sub-rosa quest to persuade Moscow to allow Finland to affiliate with EFTA was nearly over. Hopefully, the birthday package the Russian would be bringing to Helsinki would include the elusive green light for Finland to join the trade pact.

It did, although the Soviet yellow light is probably the more accurate way of putting it. In any case, the riotous affair that ensued certainly turned out to be a party to remember. Both Kekkonen and his surprise featured guest made sure of that.

So, to the Finnish president's astonishment and relief, there Khrushchev was at Helsinki's Central Station on the afternoon of Friday, September 2, the day prior to his own actual birthday, eager and anxious to join in the fun, "grinning broadly" and "vigorously pumping," as *The New York Times* described it, the birthday boy's hand, as a gaggle of Finnish officials, including Rolf Törngren, the Finnish foreign minister and Ahti Karjalainen, Kekkonen's right-hand man, happily looked on.[2]

In contrast to his first sortie to Finland three years before, when he was accompanied by the exiled and by now all but forgotten Nikolai Bulganin and a large group of apparatchiks, as if to downplay the signifiance of his visit this time, Khrushchev was accompanied by a relatively small entourage comprised of four officials, including Nikolai Lunkov, the head of the Scandinavian Department of the Soviet Foreign Ministry. Earlier, the Soviet leader told a group of curious newsmen who met his train at the Finnish border that, contrary to rumor, he had no intention of visiting the other Scandinavian countries, as he had planned to do the prior summer, before he cancelled his projected Baltic sweep.

So why Finland? Some observers were puzzled by the reason for the sortie. Apparently Kekkonen's birthday was not a good enough reason.

But it was good enough for Nikita Khrushchev.

Upon arriving in Helsinki the Soviet leader took out his bifocals and read from prepared remarks as a crowd of two thousand curious Finns looked on. Nearby, according to a front page dispatch in *The New York Times*—these were still the days when Finland was front page news in the US—were 3,500 members of a communist children's organization who "shouted greetings and waved Finnish and Soviet paper flags."[3]

The description of the correspondent for the London *Times* was drier: "There were about 2,000 people at the station," the underwhelmed reporter cabled. "Some faint cheers were raised and a number of small red flags were waved in the crowd."[4] The distinguished visitor declared that he wanted to say at once that there was no secret or mysterious purpose behind his trip. He just wanted to "greet a good neighbor on his special day."[5] And yes, if the Soviet leader's presence bolstered the case for Peaceful Coexistence and underlined the fact that their beset president had Moscow's full support, so much the better.

To be sure, although Urho Kekkonen's domestic political position was stronger than it had been during the Night Frost crisis, he was still beset. Just a few weeks before, Werner Wiskari had written in *The New*

York Times about the continuing difficulties he had experienced in trying to expand support for his party's minority government: "The hatreds that paralyze Finland's political life have once again dealt President Kekkonen a major defeat."[6]

So yes, Khrushchev had also come to help, and in his inimitably rambunctious way, he did.

First his Finnish friend had something important to say to him. The next day, Saturday, September 3, the actual day of Kekkonen's birthday, the festive program began in earnest when Khrushchev arrived at the presidential manse for a private luncheon.

The last time the two leaders met in Leningrad, twenty months before, following the Night Frost, the speech Kekkonen gave had—rightly—been criticized for being sycophantic as well as disingenuous. The Soviet leader probably expected Kekkonen's remarks this time to be in a similar vein.

They were not. First Khrushchev had a gift for his friend, a resplendent golden vase, which the Finn graciously accepted. Then the man of the hour delivered his remarks, which evidently were intended for both his Soviet guests, as well his own political opposition. "There are those who say that living in a peaceful way as a neighbor to the great Soviet Union will change Finland into a communist state," Kekkonen began.

"I am convinced," he continued, evenly, "that even if the whole of Europe turns communist, [that] Finland will remain traditionally democratic, if this is the will of the people, and I believe it is." There was more: "The leaders of the Soviet Union know that we will defend our own system in all circumstances, because," Kekkonen paused, "we think it is better for us."[7]

If the man to whom Kekkonen addressed his frank remarks was taken aback, he did not show it. The Soviet premier's response was tempered. "I can on behalf of the people of the Soviet Union and the Government, say that we feel full confidence and respect for Finland, the people of Finland and the Government of Finland, and personally for you, Mr. President," Khrushchev responded. He believed that Finland and Russia could continue to be useful to each other, he continued. Also, "we understand that there can be different opinions about the Soviet Union in different Finnish circles. Perhaps there are grudging and guarded feelings. I do not deny this is so."[8]

Nikita Khrushchev being Nikita Khrushchev, he could not resist taking a jab at those nameless Finns who did not favor friendly relations with Moscow: "Try to understand that we, too, in these circumstances may have reason for being on our guard. You have some political party representatives who do not like friendly relations [with] the Soviet Union."[9]

And that was that.

The Finnish president had made his point. After years of being criticized for being overly accommodating to Moscow, he had made it clear that, regardless of what anyone thought, he was no one's stooge. Despite his clear (and growing) affection for Soviet counterpart, he had no ken for the political system he represented, nor did the Finnish people.

Clearly this was not the same Urho Kekkonen who had met Khrushchev in Leningrad the year before and sang the praises of the Soviet Union and its supposedly Fennophile founder, Vladimir Lenin. Here was Urho Kekkonen, the man who twenty years before had opposed signing the armistice that ended the *Talvisota*, the man who had wanted to keep on fighting Soviet Union, the man who was *still* willing to fight for Finland.

Then things began to go even more off-script. During an arranged tour of the Strömberg electric turbine factory outside Helsinki the Soviet premier asked one of the workmen who had been selected for his ability to speak Russian how much he was paid. "Well enough," the Finn replied matter-of-factly, not exactly answering the question, according to *The New York Times*.[10]

"And how are Russian workers doing?" the worker asked with a smile. (Whether the smile was sarcastic is not recorded.) Whereupon the combative Russian replied, "Very well!" Then, in something of a non sequitur Khrushchev loudly announced for the benefit of the pack of curious newsmen who had followed him, "soon we are going to send up a sixty ton satellite!" This was something of an exaggeration: three months later, the USSR did in fact launch a satellite, Sputnik 6, along with its doomed canine passengers Pcholka and Mushka; however it weighed less than five tons not sixty, but who was counting?

Afterward the impulsive Soviet leader shook hands with several of the taller workers clustered around. "I like to talk to big men!"[11] he declared, cryptically, before returning to his limousine with his handlers amid a cloud of curious stares from the assembled Strömberg factory men.

Another distinctly unpleasant surprise, at least for Kekkonen, was in store that evening at the special celebration for his birthday at the

Finnish National Theatre, where the *Times* noted, the unpredictable Russian's presence "threw the proceedings out of focus from the beginning." First the celebratory program was held up several minutes in order to give news photographers a chance to take photos of Khrushchev, who ostentatiously took his place in a box to the right of the stage of the historic eighty-eight-year-old theater.

"In a speech this evening," a winking Werner Wiskari reported, "Mr. Khrushchev, who invited himself to attend today's celebration of the sixtieth birthday of Finland's president paid extensive tribute to Kekkonen."

> Speaking off the cuff, Khrushchev stressed the necessity of continuing the policy of mutual friendship and cooperation with the USSR that had been initiated by Kekkonen's predecessor, Juho Paasikivi, also known as the "Paasikivi line."

Evidently, the audience at the old theater, which dated back to Russian imperial days, was not the only one he had in mind. Then, the *Times*-man continued, "Khrushchev," in a preview of the obstreperous style he would soon display in his now infamous shoe-thumping performance at the following month's General Assembly meeting at the United Nations in New York, "the Russian began his attack."

"It isn't very pleasant to have to say that the international atmosphere has worsened recently," Khrushchev said, by way of prologue. "But," he continued, "we aren't to blame." Who was to blame? The United States for one. "We have not sent airplanes for the purpose of espionage." the Soviet leader bellowed returning to the U-2 affair. "We are not for the continuance of the armaments race."[12]

Hurricane Nikita was just getting started.

Next he attacked Konrad Adenauer, the West German chancellor, because, he claimed, the Germans were keen on acquiring nuclear weapons.[13] In a nod to his hosts, Khrushchev cited Finnish neutrality as a key factor in perserving the peace in the Nordic region. That was something—technically the first time a Soviet official had publicly acknowledged Finnish neutrality.

Another factor Khrushchev cited in a gesture to Finland's western neighbor, Sweden, whose neutrality dated to the end of the Napoleonic Wars, was "Sweden's neutrality and the Swedish Government's refusal to manufacture or acquire atomic weapons."[14] Whatever fleeting satisfaction Kekkonen and the other Finnish officials present might have taken from what amounted to the first official recognition of Finnish neutrality evaporated as their tempestuous guest turned his blunderbuss on Finland's other western and southern Nordic neighbors, Norway and Denmark, blasting them for joining NATO. Now Nikita Khrushchev's other agenda, besides supporting his Finnish friend—blowing up NATO—was coming into view. The fact that his attack was a little late in the day—Norway and Denmark were, after all, two of NATO's charter members, having joined the treaty organization in 1949—was beside the point. As far as the bellicose Soviet premier was concerned, the two countries should not have joined the loathsome organization at all.

Khrushchev qualified his attack by claiming that he did not wish to interfere in either Norway's or Denmark's affairs. But, he warned ominously, if somewhat obscurely, "it depended on them how the cause of world peace would develop." Did he expect the two countries to resign from NATO, just like that? It was not clear.

It did not matter. Khrushchev was putting the West on notice. *The New York Times* duly reported his Finnish hosts' shocked reaction, especially that of the crestfallen guest of honor whose official birthday celebration the event at the National Theatre was supposed to be. "As the Russian spoke, Mr. Kekkonen's head sank to his chest," Wiskari wrote. Perhaps he recalled that Russian diplomat who had earlier complained that when Khrushchev started speaking no one knew what came out of his mouth. *So this is what he meant!* "Other Finnish leaders who had gathered to honor the President seemed stunned by the speech."[15]

"I remain an optimist," Khrushchev declared to the staggered captive audience, while a Finnish-speaking aide did his best to translate—and soften—the Soviet guest's explosive remarks. "The state of things can be repaired, if others will also strive toward this goal. The Soviet Union is for the improvement of relations amongst all nations."[16]

Perhaps so. Still, to judge from the stupefied look on the face of his putative Finnish friend, Urho Kekkonen, the Soviet leader apparently had not considered the effect his barrage would have on Finnish-Soviet relations.

The West certainly took notice. So did *The New York Times.*

KHRUSHCHEV PRODS WEST ON SUMMIT AT U.N. ON ARMS

read the top headline on the front page article about Khrushchev's impromptu rodomontade the following day. And beneath that:

> PREMIER STUNS FINNISH HOSTS WITH ATTACKS ON WEST—HITS NORDIC NATO ROLE[17]

One can only imagine the astonished Finnish president's thoughts that evening as he was driven home. With friends like that, who needed enemies?

On the face of it, Nikita Khrushchev's second visit to Finland had been a debacle. And it was not turning out to be much of a birthday party either.

However, as it turned out, the opera was not over. Evidently the Finnish president rebounded from the shock and embarrassment soon enough, because later that evening he invited his combustible guest to his house. Moreover, as his diary faithfully notes, a boffo time was had by all: "My birthday . . . A celebration at National Theatre during the evening. Negotiation in Tamminiemi after that. Khrushchev, Lunjkov, Zakharov . . . and Ahti Karjalainen. I gave K 'Some points of view.'"[18]

Apparently one of those "points of view" concerned EFTA. Another was about the Saimaa Canal, the venerable nineteenth-century canal connecting Lake Saimaa, the large lake in southeastern Finland with the Gulf of Finland near Vyborg, in what was now Russian Karelia, which had been one of Kekkonen's pet projects. The Kremlin had indicated its willingness to lease the facility during Khrushchev and Nikolai Bulganin's visit to the Kremlin in 1957, but nothing had been formalized. After the Peace of Moscow of 1940 following the *Talvisota* ceded Karelia to the USSR, splitting the waterway in two, the once vital shipping lane had fallen into desuetude. The Finnish president wished to revive it by persuading his Soviet counterpart to finally lease it to Finland so that the canal could be restored and put back to use.

The impetus behind the idea was more romantic than practical. Kekkonen seems not to have considered the massive investment required to make the ancient, thirty-five-mile-long canal economically feasible again. No matter. He was determined to finally get the Saimaa back for Finland, or at least to get Khrushchev to discuss the matter.

And so they did. In a way, the conclave was a reprise of the Soviet leader's memorable visit three years before. The only difference is that this time the two friends did not take sauna.

Otherwise things went swimmingly, by the upbeat host's account: "The negotiation lasted until 5 A.M. No sauna." The kitchen staff at the presidential mansion cenrtainly seems to have been busy. "We ate three times. A little was drunk, and occasionally we sang."[19]

How little is "little?" one wonders.

What was sung? Does it matter? Any hard feelings left over from the party crasher's excruciating performance at the National Theatre earlier that day had evidently disappeared by the time the sated and satisfied Soviet party sped off in the wee hours of that convivial September night. The special relationship between the two countries had been reconfirmed, and so had the one between their two leaders.

If anything, the two men liked and respected each other now even more than before. Khrushchev in particular seems to have been impressed anew with his Finnish friend's political finesse, as the latter happily recorded. "Khrushchev said to me several times: you are a wizard when it comes to your relations with us."[20]

Most important, Urho Kekkonen had gotten what he wanted from Nikita Khrushchev—the Kremlin's acquiescence to Finnish membership in EFTA. And yes, it developed, the Russian was open to discussing Saimaa Canal, too. "An excellent result about EFTA," the presidential diarist enthused, "and later on with Saimaa Canal too."[21]

There was one more item on the two leaders' itinerary—a luncheon later that same day, September 4, 1960, the last day of Khrushchev's visit, at the Soviet embassy, hosted by Ambassador Zakharov and his wife, at which Kekkonen was joined by his wife. One would have thought that that would have been one meal too far, so to speak, in light of the long evening and morning the two men had just put in, but that, too, was a success, on the evidence of a photograph of the occasion showing Khrushchev walking arm in arm with the president's wife, with Kekkonen following behind, accompanied by Zakharov's wife, with everyone smiling. Even Sylvi, who generally is pictured wearing a dutiful, if not exactly sour expression on such occasions, looks bursting with joy. Unsurprisingly, Kekkonen looks happiest of all.

Quite a change from the evening before, when the two were sitting in shock at the National Theatre listening to their Russian guest's tirade. And then, a little more than forty-eight hours after he had welcomed Khrushchev and his entourage at Central Station, there the Finnish president was again happily thanking the chairman of the Soviet Council of Ministers for joining his birthday party, heartily wishing him adieu and telling him how much he looked forward to seeing him in ten weeks' time. And then he was gone.

The happy result of Khrushchev's whirlwind visit, particularly regarding the EFTA situation, was confirmed by the expansive joint communiqué issued as the Soviet leader chugged back to Moscow. In response to those who had accused Kekkonen of procrastinating on EFTA, Khrushchev's statement made clear that it was he who had brought the sensitive matter up: "The President of Finland initiated a thorough exchange of opinion on Soviet-Finnish trade relations. In so doing the President set forth the consideration of the Finnish side in connection with the setting up of EFTA."[22]

To be sure, nothing had actually been agreed yet. The two leaders had agreed to agree to discuss both the question of Finnish membership in EFTA and Saimaa Canal in November, after the upcoming UN General Assembly, when Kekkonen was cordially invited to pay his second visit to the Kremlin and work out the details.

"The invitation was accepted with pleasure," the statement ended.[23] So there it was. Mission accomplished—or nearly accomplished. Of course, the Finns still had to persuade the EFTA members to sign on, but that ought not to be too difficult.

The EFTA Gordian knot had been untied, or at least had loosened. The bet that Kekkonen had made after things had gone bad again between East and West after the collapse of the Paris summit—that Khrushchev would subsequently be even more eager to point to Finland as proof of the success of Peaceful Coexistence, and give it more diplomatic leeway, and perhaps other gifts, had proven correct.

The weeks immediately following Kekkonen's sixtieth birthday party were a happy time, as he received praise from all sides for the masterful way with which he had handled the impulsive Soviet leader, including, and especially the way he had set the latter to rights at the speech he had delivered at the Soviet embassy. As an article in the *Times* of London two months later put it, "It is sometimes said that Kekkonen gained more by the few words he said that day than by anything else as President," and that "it is only lately that his opponents have accepted him with better grace than on the day he was elected."[24]

That turned out to be an exaggeration. In the event, the opposition's "grace" turned out to be short-lived. In the spiteful world of Finnish parliamentary politics at the end of Kekkonen's first, fraught presidential term grace, as such, was an ephemeral quantity.

But it certainly was nice while it lasted, and so was the stream of congratulatory and commendatory calls and telegrams from all over the world, including the US that flowed into Tamminiemi during the days that followed Kekkonen's triumphant rendezvous with Wild Man

Nikita. No less welcome were the hosannas from the temporarily mollified political opposition, including an article from *Uusi Suomi*, the Finnish daily, commending the president for his performance and denying as some sticks-in-the-mud contended, that he had compromised Finnish neutrality.

Perhaps most thrilling was a conversation he had with Rolf Törngren, his compliant foreign minister, in which the latter excitedly told him that his fellow Swedish speaker, Erik von Frenckell, the noted parliamentarian and member of the International Olympic Committee, had told him that "after last Sunday there is no use looking for an opponent to Kekkonen," and that his re-election as president was assured.[25] That was something of an overstatement, as Kekkonen must have known. Nevertheless, that must have been very nice to hear as well, ditto the paeans that flowed from the Soviet side. Thus on September 12 an enthused Kekkonen writes how Zakharov, the Soviet ambassador, had had nothing but positive things to say about his boss Khrushchev's visit.

To be sure, there still were some surprises and discordant notes in the grand symphony the Finnish president was purportedly composing in the weeks leading up to his eagerly awaited second state visit to Moscow. Despite the nearly universal acclaim, particularly from abroad, for the way he had managed the Soviet leader's surprise sortie, and the fruits from same, certain ungracious elements of the opposition, particularly the Social Democrats, continued to cause him aggravation.

The entry in Kekkonen's diary from September 23, 1960, provides a good picture of the author's fraught state of mind at this intense juncture of his presidency, as well as the varying shades of his personal character. Thus, on the one hand, the vain Finnish politician was in an equable enough mood to note how pleased he was by a portrait of himself that his friend, the artist Michel Werboff, had wrought, of which he pasted a copy in his diary.[26]

On the other hand, he couldn't resist taking a shot at his old bête noire, Väinö Tanner, the confounded and confounding octogenarian who still led the Social Democrats, along with his outspokenly anti-Soviet deputy, Väinö Leskinen. Kekkonen's ire at his durable opponent also manifests itself in the diary entry for September 25, in which he describes his reaction to the televised debates for the local elections. "[Kauno] Kleemola performed skillfully," he penned to himself, referring to his the Agrarian

League politician who later became speaker of the parliament, but "poor old Tanner just repeated general slogans against Agrarian and Left-Wing cooperation and the current system. No conciliation."[27]

But that was nothing new, was it?

To be sure, the biggest surprise that took place during the "happy" fall of 1960 came from none other than Nikita Khrushchev himself, particularly the blusterous performance the Soviet premier staged at the UN General Assembly in New York in late September and early October. As it turned out, the wild act Khrushchev unveiled at Kekkonen's birthday party at the National Theatre was just a dress rehearsal, except that the latest version before a global audience was much worse, more chaotic and more damaging to the cause of peace, as well as to himself.

Khrushchev set the tone for his unruly running performance on September 23 when, to the shock and surprise of many (including, apparently, some members of the Soviet delegation), he launched a scathing attack on Dag Hammarskjöld, the respected Swedish secretary general of the UN. Angry at the UN's involvement in the civil war in the Congo, which had thwarted the USSR's ambitions in Africa, the volatile Soviet leader denounced the well-liked and respected diplomat as a "tool of colonialists" and called for him to be replaced by a three man troika, a move that prompted Hammarskjöld to offer to resign, which was loudly rejected.[28]

Things went downhill from there, culminating in the infamous incident on October 12, 1960, when, in response to a speech by the delegate from the Philippines decrying the Soviet suppression of civil liberties in Eastern Europe, Khrushchev removed his shoe and began banging it on the table.

Once again, the impulsive Russian succeeded in making himself a spectacle.

But to what end? It did not make sense, for someone who was presenting himself as a peacemaker. "Khrushchev's behavior in New York was not just extravagant and exotic," observes his biographer, William Taubman. "It was erratic."[29]

One of those who was surprised by Khrushchev's outlandish behavior was Urho Kekkonen. "Khrushchev's performance at the U.N. General Assembly was so merciless in its tone and uncompromising," he wrote on October 1, "that it seems impossible that he intended his U.N. trip to be conciliatory in any way."

"In the West people rejoice that Khrushchev has suffered a crushing defeat," the baffled diarist continued, referring to the shock, anger and incomprehension which had greeted the latter's antics. Nevertheless, Kekkonen maintained, there was more to his Russian friend's rowdiness than necessarily met the eye. "It might [not] look like it," he continued, "but Khrushchev surely knew what would happen if he attacked Secretary General [Hammarskjöld] before he did."[30] Perhaps Khrushchev was deliberately making "the [world] situation" more difficult, Kekkonen mused.

Perhaps Khrushchev felt that it was not the right time to reconcile with the West. Maybe, Kekkonen guessed, Khrushchev felt that this was not the most propitious time to extend the olive branch and that it would be better to wait until the USSR had actually attained parity with the US, or was even stronger.

Of course, this ran counter to Kekkonen's apparent conviction that the USSR was *already* winning the Cold War.

Never mind: as we have seen, the Finnish president was able to rationalize virtually anything if it suited his political purposes, and pretending that there was some sort of strategy to Khrushchev's strange, self-immolating performance suited his own purposes, for now. Maybe, the Finn further speculated, Khrushchev had indeed decided to "postpone" reconciling with the West for five years until such time that he could negotiate from a position of true strength.

Of course, this was assuming that his sometime sauna partner would still be in power in five years—which in fact he would not—but there was no reason to think otherwise at the time.[31]

Perhaps the truth really was that Kekkonen did not know his Russian friend as well as he thought he did.

Come think of it, the more Kekkonen meditated on the situation, as the captain of *Finlandiia* peered into the mist, the better things looked for Finland. Just as he had correctly foreseen the positive effect America's U-2 debacle would have on Finnish-Soviet relations by underlining Finland's value to Moscow as a showcase for Peaceful Coexistence, which Khrushchev had then bolstered by acquiescing to Finnish affiliation with EFTA, so, Kekkonen the opportunist guessed, Suomi might now further benefit from Khrushchev's UN debacle by gaining even more from the Kremlin if he played his cards right. Perhaps, he surmised, he could turn this new turn in the Cold War to Finland's advantage too!

"Finland will reap the benefits," he confided to his diary. "[The] Karelia business will," if his guess was right, "probably be at least partially solved in the near future," he went on.[32]

There it was again—Karelia! So that was the next apple to drop from the joint Soviet-Finnish tree.

Well, one could always dream. . . .

And for Urho Kekkonen, as he reveled in the praise from both home and abroad for the deft way he had managed Khrushchev at his birthday party, the fall of 1960 was a good time to dream. Thus on October 11 he writes that Torsten Steinby, the editor of *Hufvudstadsbladet*, assured him that since Khrushchev's visit many groups representing industry and business have seriously come to believe that they should support Kekkonen in the next elections.[33]

Four days later on October 15 an enthused Kekkonen records the latest hosanna from Karl Overbeck, West Germany's consul general and chief commercial representative in Helsinki.[34] "People in West Germany," Overbeck boasted, "say Finland"—meaning Kekkonen, of course—"has again managed a difficult situation in an exemplary manner and that [my] speeches and statements gained respectful attention."[35]

Ten days later, on October 17, in the same self-congratulatory vein, Kekkonen writes about the excellent meeting he had with Toivo Rapeli, the noted Finnish evangelist, who had just returned from the US, where apparently Kekkonen was the talk of the town.[36] Or at least some American towns. After all, Kekkonen's birthday powwow was front-page news. According to Rapeli, whereas once Americans had asked him whether Kekkonen's Agrarian League "was communist now everywhere there is respect for Finnish politics and Kekkonen."

Even the American people were signing on to Kekkonen's grand design, it seems. Little wonder that Kekkonen was dreaming of recovering Karelia again. Thus on October 17, Kekkonen told a meeting of the Union of Karelian People, the Finnish organization dedicated to the preservation of Karelian language and culture, that although "the international situation has never been as tense as it is now," witness the fireworks Khrushchev set off in New York, the time was ripe for Finland to take advantage of the situation and that regarding the Karelian question "bad times for us were better than good ones."[37]

Was Kekkonen dreaming? Was there a Karelian question? He would find out soon enough.

To be sure, there still was some work to do. At the moment the Finnish president's greatest and abiding frustation continued to be his inability to expand his minority Agrarian-led government.

He had a solution for that too: dissolve the parliament, order new elections, and if the results did not allow for the formation of a majority government that could support him, offer his resignation.

Of course Kekkonen did not directly issue this Gaullist threat himself. Instead, as he sometimes did when he wished to float a sensitive or provocative idea, he conveyed it anonymously, or semi-anonymously in *Maakansa*, the Agrarian League newspaper. Thus, on October 9, while his Russian patron's bizarre political cabaret act was about to reach its shoe-thumping climax on the other side of the Atlantic, Kekkonen, writing under the political nom de guerre of "a lawyer well-versed in theory," published an editorial suggesting that whereas the president had sought to form a government that did not interfere with foreign policy, "parliamentary rules" gave him the right to dissolve the *eduskunta* to allow him to form one that did, and that, after the subsequent election for a new parliament, if he was still not able to do so he should simply resign.[38]

That certainly got a lot of people's attention, including that of his erstwhile friend and booster, Zakharov, the Soviet ambassador. Unsurprisingly, the *Maakansa* article came up at a luncheon he hosted for the Soviet diplomat the following day, October 10. Yes, of course he was bluffing, Kekkonen assured his guest, according to his journal. He actually had no intention of resigning. His real objective was to scare Väinö Tanner and his recalcitrant party members into overcoming their loathing for the left-wing, pro-Kekkonen, pro-Soviet Skogists—as well as of him—and help him form a majority government.

Well, one could always dream. Here again, in the murky world of mid-twentieth-century Finnish politics, Kekkonen's reach extended his grasp. That much was confirmed in a telephone call the president received from Arvo Korsimo, the Agrarian League's party secretary, in which his loyal lieutenant told him that he had heard from Zhenikhov, the Soviet deputy *rezidentura*, who had learned from one of the attendees at the Social Democrats' latest organizational meeting—sometimes information about the president's domestic "enemies" reached Tamminiemi in a very roundabout way—that the party housecleaning, i.e., the purge that both Kekkonen and the Soviets had hoped for, specficially the removal of the key figure who stood in the way of the party realigning itself as per above, Väinö Leskinen, had, sadly, not taken place and that "the general [anti-Soviet] line of the party had been confirmed and indeed was even "harder" than before.[39] "Contact [with Social Democrats] not worth the bother," the angry president penned in disgust.[40]

Shrugging off his disappointment, Kekkonen put his shoulder to the wheel of the Finnish ship of state and sailed on.

Next stop Moscow!

Chapter 8

The Gordian Knot (11/60–12/60)

Kekkonen was able to convince the Soviet leader to trust him.

—1972 CIA report on Finland describing Urho Kekkonen's success in persuading Nikita Khrushchev to acquiesce to Finland joining EFTA

A meeting which Urho Kekkonen took with Aleksey Zakharov, the Soviet ambassador, on October 27, 1960, about the Saimaa Canal, as his next pilgrimage to Moscow approached also took a little wind out of his sails. According to his diary, which always must be taken with a considerable grain of salt, the somewhat stunted repartee went something like the following.

First, the Soviet envoy said that Moscow was willing to discuss leasing Finland the canal, as well as both sides of the president's cherished waterway, for twenty-five to fifty years. Kekkonen responded, somewhat obsequiously, by thanking his Russian friend for his generosity, but that if *he*, Kekkonen, had his druthers, the area leased would include "everything from the canal to the Finnish-Soviet border."[1] Besides, he brashly continued, had not Vyascheslav Molotov, the Soviet foreign minister who had presided over the Peace of Moscow following the Winter War under which the Soviet Union annexed Karelia, including the Saimaa Canal, said at the time that corridors were not a good rule?

That was not a good move.

As Kekkonen knew, or ought to have known, Joseph Stalin's foreign minister was now decidedly out of favor with the Kremlin. As an outspoken opponent of Nikita Khrushchev and his de-Stalinization campaign, the diehard Bolshevik had been banished to Mongolia, where he served as ambassador, something of a demotion.

No, invoking Molotov as an authority to a Soviet ambassador was definitely not a smart thing for someone doing business with Moscow in the fall of 1960, as Kekkonen quickly realized. Of course, the former deputy foreign minister told him, he was familiar with the negotiations that took place between Molotov and the Finnish peace delegation headed by Juho Paasikivi at the end of the *Talvisota* which culminated in the armistice that ended the war. The Kremlin was not proposing to lease Finland a corridor, however.

Moreover, he pointedly reminded his Finnish friend, "our countries' relations are different than they were in 1940."[2] What exactly did Zakharov, his hitherto stalwart backer, mean by that? Did he mean that Moscow was not as accommodating—if that is the word—as twenty years before, when a supine Finland had no choice but to accept Moscow's terms? Zakharov did not elaborate.

He did not have to. Kekkonen had made a faux pax and, as his account makes clear, he knew it. Message to Kekkonen: don't push it. Message received. As best one can tell, Kekkonen never mentioned his Karelian dream again, at least within listening distance of the Kremlin.

While Kekkonen was dickering with Zakharov about the Saimaa Canal, which Moscow was offering Helsinki as a kind of dessert, his adjutant, Ahti Karjalainen, was laying the groundwork for the main course, membership in the European Free Trade Association (EFTA), including persuading the British and the other reluctant EFTA members to accede. Thus the laudatory profile of Karjalainen that the *Times* of London published on October 30, when Kekkonen's aide was in London, titled "A Rising Star in Finnish Politics."

Not that the tight-lipped minister of trade and industry was seeking the limelight. Quite the opposite. As the article noted, "Mr. Karjalainen is a politician who prefers to be reticent and it isn't often that he makes a comment to the press other than 'No comment.'" "This," the British paper mordantly added, "has not added to his popularity." Nevertheless his importance to the Cabinet, and to Kekkonen, "can not be questioned."[3]

The profile went on to recall how Kekkonen's former secretary's star had been on the rise since the Finnish president took the self-effacing politician along with him to Leningrad in 1959 for his "accidental" meeting with Khrushchev following the Night Frost, and even more so since Kekkonen had made him his point man for solving the EFTA imbroglio. As a politician, the piece by the *Times*'s Helsinki correspondent, continued, "Karjalainen belongs to the Agrarian Party [*sic*] inner circle better known in Finland as the K Men group (the letter K comes from such names as Karjalainen, Korsimo, Kleemola, and Matti Kekkonen, son of the President)." Nevertheless, despite his unquestioned loyalty to Kekkonen, in contrast to the other members of the president's inner circle, the article implied, Karjalainen was still his own man. All in all, the laudatory dispatch continued, "[Karjalainen] is without doubt one of the most promising young politicians in the Agrarian League and can be considered a possible future candidate for the premiership."[4]

Whatever pleasure either Karjalainen or his chief derived from the London *Times* piece was offset by the difficulty the latter encountered in persuading the British and their other friends in EFTA to go along with the deal he had made with Khrushchev that would allow the Finns to join their exclusive club. The aforementioned 1972 CIA report summed up the recalcitrant EFTA members' position: "The EFTA members could not countenance granting trade with the USSR equally favorable status as this would violate the principle of exclusivity essential to a free trade area."[5]

"Not so fast," the members were saying now. "It's fine that you have a deal with Moscow, but you still have to deal with us!" Thus, on November 1, two days after the adulatory London *Times* profile of Karjalainen, the latter cabled his boss from London and told him that there was "strong opposition" against Finnish favoritism with the USSR.[6] Two weeks later came official confirmation: "England and Switzerland issued a statement saying they would not accept the Finnish favorable nation clause with the USSR."[7]

Clearly, the captain of the *Finlandia* still had some tacking and jibing to do before the EFTA members would consent to throw his storm-tossed ship a line. Nevertheless, Urho Kaleva Kekkonen was not deterred. He knew that if the EFTA members rebuffed Finland after he reached an accord with Moscow, it would only push Finland closer to the Soviet side of Scylla and Charybdis, as well as alienate the Finnish public from the West, and that is something they definitely did not want. As far as he was concerned, all eyes remained on Moscow, where, the self-confident Finnish head of state was certain, he would seal the deal with the Politburo regarding EFTA and the Saimaa Canal, and who knew what else. The rest, he was sure, would be easy.

FIGURE 11. Urho Kekkonen carousing with Nikita Khrushchev. By the end of 1960, Kekkonen was familiar enough with the Soviet premier to be able to kid around with him—too familiar for some of Khrushchev's hard-line comrades. Khrushchev's fondness for him was said to be one of the factors that led to his eventual downfall.

The sticky EFTA situation aside, Kekkonen's star in the West certainly seemed to be rising. Thus, on November 4, 1960, Douglas Busk, the British ambassador to Helsinki, paid an upbeat farewell visit to Tamminiemi. Along with the usual felicitations, Busk, one of the senior members of the Western diplomatic corps, brought a gift with him: an invitation from his government for him and his wife to make a state visit to Great Britain the following May.

"The Queen will offer a dinner," he cheerfully penned. "A surprise," Kekkonen confided to his journal, "but a pleasant one. I will discuss it with parliament. Personally I rejoice at the invitation."[8]

Ten days later, on the November 15, Busk's American colleague, Edson Sessions, who had evidently enjoyed his Helsinki sojourn and also was departing, stopped by Tamminiemi, too, to say his reluctant farewells to Kekkonen, as well as Sylvi, who had just returned from her own private trip to Rome. Just ten months before, it will be recalled, the newly arrived American ambassador's view of Kekkonen had been even more pejorative than that of his distrustful predecessor, John Hickerson, alleging that the Finnish president was the principal reason why Finland was veering, perhaps irretrievably towards Moscow.

However a year of observing Kekkonen up close, including his deft and determined maneuvering on the EFTA matter, had led the American envoy to modify his opinion. Whereas before the American diplomat had despaired of Kekkonen's "probable" reelection, now he gushed to his pleasantly surprised host, Finland could take care of its own affairs. Now Sessions was actually worried that there would not be anyone to take his place behind the presidential wheel.

To be sure, there was some still some grumbling at home to contend with. Thus in the journal entry for November 14, 1960, Kekkonen includes a clip from *Suomen Sosiaalidemokraati*, the journal of the Social Democratic Party, which states that although the Finnish people were unanimous in their view of what their country's foreign policy should be, the current head of state was ignoring their will.

Never mind, Kekkonen could tell himself. The Social Democrats had yet to name a candidate to oppose him in the 1962 election. Perhaps as his acolyte, Erik Tawaststjerna, had suggested, they would not choose a candidate at all, leaving the field open, or relatively open.

On November 20, 1960, the Finnish president confidently entrained for Moscow. Wisely, Kekkonen, aware of the long arm of the KGB, did not bring his journal with him: the notations for the five days that he was away are blank.

By all reports, including those of the foreign press, as well as the file of the upbeat speeches he made while he was in the USSR (which the presidential diarist faithfully appended to his journal), both Kekkonen and Khrushchev were in a triumphant mood by the end. Both men had gotten what they wanted, more or less.

The New York Times summed up the mutually satisfactory results in its dispatch of November 24, 1960, the last day of Kekkonen's visit:

> **MOSCOW APPROVES FINNS' TRADE PLAN**
>
> The Soviet Union and Finland agreed on a formula to permit Finnish association with a Western European economic bloc without upsetting trade between the two neighbors. The terms will not be made public until Finland has completed negotiations for her association with the seven-nation European Free Trade Association, otherwise known as the Outer Seven.[9]

So there it was: the elusive green light for the Finns to join EFTA. Kekkonen's Gordian knot had been untied. And so, as *The New York Times* reported, had been his dessert, so to speak: a fifty-year lease for the

Saimaa Canal. The calculated bet that Kekkonen had made following the downturn in East-West relations over the past year, that he could work that development to Finland's advantage, as well as his, had been proven good.

Of course that wager *had* been premised on the continued good relations between Khrushchev and Kekkonen themselves. As the 1972 CIA analysis accurately affirmed:

> Finland's handling of the delicate problem [regarding EFTA] had been adept, but Helsinki had also been fortunate. The Soviet agreement to tolerate Finland's association with EFTA seems to have been based partly on the Soviet victory on the Most Favored Nations clause, *but primarily on the good relations existing* [between] *Kekkonen and Khrushschev* [author's italics].

"Kekkonen," the report concluded, "was able to convince the Soviet leader that Finland was to be trusted."[10]

Meanwhile, the good relations between Khruschev and Kekkonen on which the latter had posited his bet continued to be positively copacetic.

The affection between the two leaders was manifest at a boisterous luncheon the Finnish president hosted for the Soviet premier at the Finnish embassy in Moscow on the afternoon of November 23. The latter was on his best behavior this time. No more outbursts this time from the volatile Russian, nor anti-American or anti-NATO diatribes. Even the pesky Chinese Communists, with whom he was then skirmishing, whose president, Liu Shaoqi, was just then attacking him at the international Communist party meeting then taking place elsewhere in the Soviet capital did not seem to bother Khrushchev. Indeed, the two men hit it off so well that the Finnish host felt sufficiently comfortable to mock his guest's recent performance by taking off his own shoe and banging it!

For some reason the extraordinary incident escaped the attention of the Finnish press at the time. However, the irrepressible Werner Wiskari of *The New York Times* could not resist using that memorable moment as the lead for a profile of Kekkonen he published the following October, on the cusp of his first visit to the United States (more about which later). Apparently, Wiskari wrote, the Finnish president, who presided over the lively affair, had difficulty getting his guest's attention. "So the Finn took his shoe and grasping it firmly, pounded the table."[11]

Unsurprisingly, the immediate reaction to Kekkonen's unabashedly sardonic gesture was general shock: "This emulation of Mr. Khruschev's United Nations' performance cast a sudden frozen silence over the luncheon party."

In its own way, the Finn's humorous gesture was just as courageous as the much-talked-about speech he had given at the Soviet embassy two months before.

As it turned out, Nikita Khrushchev also had a sense of humor. Yes, he got the joke, too—albeit after something of a heart-stopping pause: "The Soviet chief shook and roared with laughter," he wrote with a knowing smile, "and Mr. Kekkonen, long adept at getting along with the Russians, had scored again."[12]

All well and good. However, as one other member of the Finnish president's entourage also later recalled, not everyone was amused. Anastas Mikoyan, the Soviet deputy prime minister and Khrushchev's right-hand man, certainly was not, according to Max Jakobson, the deputy director of press affairs of the foreign ministry, who was serving in the dual role of spokesperson and speech writer, a role he would reprise the following year during Kekkonen's trips to Great Britain and the United States. "Kekkonen was a firm believer in the magic of personal diplomacy," recalled Jakobson in his 1998 book *Finland in the New Europe*, one of several books by the diplomat and future historian (and the author's friend) featuring Kekkonen. "He got on specially well with Nikita Khrushchev, with whom he shared a radical temperament and a robust sense of humor."[13]

"There is no doubt," adds Jakobson, who admired Kekkonen but at the same time could also be appalled by his antics, "that he [Kekkonen] persuaded Khrushchev to make concessions that other members of the Soviet leadership considered excessive.[14] One of those dissidents, Jakobson notes, was Mikoyan. For the most part, the fiery Armenian went along with his impetuous chief. His support for Khrushchev had been crucial in resisting the attempted 1957 Politburo coup against him. Mikoyan had continued to support Khrushchev afterward, including the latter's initial resistance to the notion of allowing Finland to join EFTA, which he heartily agreed with and had expressed with gusto a year before at the Helsinki Trade Fair.

It is not that Mikoyan disliked Kekkonen, or the Finns, for that matter. He just did not like him, or them, as much as Khrushchev did. And he definitely did not like the deal the latter had just made with

Kekkonen about joining EFTA to boot. In fact, Mikoyan was outraged. Just a year before he had denounced EFTA as a relic of the Cold War. Now his unpredictable chief had told the Finns it was okay if they joined.

This is how Jacobson, still agog at the memory of the Soviet deputy prime minister's eruption recalls it: "At the end of the complex negotiations in Moscow, Kekkonen invited Khrushchev and the other Soviet leaders, including Anastas Mikoyan, the Politburo member in charge of foreign trade policy, to a luncheon at the Finnish embassy."[15]

Things started off well enough, says Jakobson: "Khrushchev praised the agreement reached between the two countries as an example of the readiness of the Soviet government to take into consideration the interests of a small neighbor." Then all hell broke loose. "Suddenly he [Khrushchev] was interrupted by Mikoyan who shouted, 'Even if the small neighbor demands the impossible?'"[16]

Another stunned silence. "After a few further exchanges," Jakobson records, "Khrushchev told his colleague to shut up."

So much for Mikoyan's "rebellion." Nikita Khrushchev still held the floor—for now. Still, Jakobson wrote, the moment still etched in his memory nearly forty years later, "the incident revealed a glimpse of the inner tensions that a few years later led to Khrushchev's downfall."[17]

Anastas Mikoyan, it turns out, was not the only one who thought that Khrushchev was too generous with Finland. "At a later meeting with Kekkonen," Jakobson adds, the Soviet leader "admitted he had been criticized by more orthodox members of the Politburo for being too friendly with 'a leader of a capitalist country.'"[18]

To be sure, between Kekkonen's banging his shoe and Mikoyan's outburst, it had been quite a trip.

For his part, Kekkonen could not have been happier. At long last, he could see daylight on the EFTA issue. And the lease for the Saimaa Canal the Kremlin had thrown in was nothing to sneeze at either. A buoyant Kekkonen boarded the overnight train back to Helsinki on the evening on November 24, 1960, eager to share the fruits of his triumphant trip with the grateful Finnish nation.

In the event, the Finnish nation was not as grateful as the president expected. Indeed, many if not most Finns, it seemed, were downright ungrateful or at least skeptical of the putative fruits of Urho Kaleva Kekkonen's second official trip to Moscow.

The headline of Werner Wiskari's front-page dispatch in *The New York Times* the following day, November 25, said it all:

> **FINNS SKEPTICAL ON MOSCOW PACT**
>
> President Urho Kekkonen returned today from his negotiations in Moscow. The results of the talks were welcomed here with many reservations.[19]

Getting the Kremlin's assent for linking up with EFTA was well and good, most Finns seemed to agree, however would the new agreement pass muster with the members of EFTA? After all, both Switzerland and Great Britain had publicly stated that it would most decidedly not. Perhaps Kekkonen was confident that he could overcome the EFTA members' resistance, but many Finns evidently were not.

That was understandable. But what really stung the Finnish president was the storm of criticism that greeted the second part of the deal he made with Moscow regarding his cherished Saimaa Canal, as well as the relish with which some foreign reporters, particularly Wiskari, conveyed that criticism. To wit:

> Opinions expressed today in the corridors of the Parliament indicated that Mr. Kekkonen faced a sharp fight over implementing Soviet concessions toward reopening the Saimaa Canal[20]

wrote the *Times*man. The fact was, many if not most Finns were not as nostalgic for the old run-down waterway as the president. Nor did they think that investing the billions of finnmarks that would be needed to restore it was worth it either, particularly in the modern logistical age. Even some members of the Agrarian League attacked the decision to go ahead and lease the canal from Moscow, and they did not mind saying so either, as Wiskari reported.

That evening, November 25, by way of illustrating how closely he followed the foreign press's coverage of him, including *The New York Times*, in his journal Kekkonen mentioned the report by the correspondent of *Le Monde* praising him for achieving the agreement for the Saimaa "in record time" and praised him as "dynamic."[21]

In the meantime, anger as well as skepticism about the results of the latest Moscow pilgrimage, including the point of it all, continued to mount. So did Kekkonen's own anger, which he vented at a meeting of the Paasikivi Society, the society founded in 1958 in order to promote

Finnish foreign policy, on his late predecessor and mentor's ninetieth birthday, as Wiskari also reported:[22]

> President Urho Kekkonen angrily defended today the results of his recent negotiations in Moscow and called for the formation of a coalition Government to implement them.[23]

Clearly the criticism of the agreement regarding the Saimaa Canal had touched a nerve. In response to his "surly" critics, as he branded them, Kekkonen called the deal he had made to revive the venerable canal "an exceedingly important achievement, especially for the economic development of eastern Finland." He also let his anger show:

> He interpolated into his prepared text a sarcastic reference to the "dear" representatives of the foreign press who had sent abroad reports of opposition to the project.[24]

(In the event, the actual lease for the canal was not signed until two years later, in August 1962, after further negotiations. The reconstruction of the canal began the following year. Moscow granted Helsinki another fifty-year lease in 2010.)

In Kekkonen's cantankerous speech, which was carried live over television and radio, the indignant president also went on to defend his weak minority government. Regarding the most important dividend of his trip, the green light from the Kremlin for Finland to join EFTA, Kekkonen, swiveling his blunderbuss toward the domestic press, recalled that the previous summer Finnish newspapers had falsely accused him of "doing nothing about helping Finland join EFTA."

Regarding those who questioned whether the deal he made with Moscow would pass muster with the members of the Outer Seven, particularly after several said it would not, the angry Finn huffed that the "final formula reached regarding safeguarding Finnish-Soviet trade was based *on the assumption* that it would also satisfy the Outer Seven [author's italics]." Consequently, he hectored on, it was all the more important for the parliament to form a broadly based government that could enact such an agreement and safeguard Finland's economic interests particularly "at this time of frightening international tension."[25]

For the moment, happily, the northeastern quadrant of Europe was immune to that tension, but one never knew, he darkly implied, when the Neighbor to the East might cause some of it to blow in the direction of Suomi. "I would be greatly surprised," Kekkonen ominously declared, "if an agreement could not be signed with the Outer Seven before the end of the year."[26]

As it turns out, the self-confident president's prediction was only two months off. In the meantime he still had some choppy waters to steer.

His imperious style certainly did not help matters.

It certainly did not go over well with the political opposition, as Kekkonen discovered on November 28, following his cranky Sermon from the Mount, when he summoned two members of the National Coalition (Kokoomus) Party and told them that it was the "patriotic duty of the bourgeois opposition" to fall in line and form a majority government.

The result, as he annoyedly recorded that night, was not a happy one: "I ended the discussion briefly and said it's useless to talk about, [I] regret I've bothered."[27]

The press, including the usually loyal *Helsingin Sanomat*, was not happy either, as the editors made clear in an editorial the next day which characterized the president's speech as "a schoolmarmish shaking of the finger" and accused the Great Man of setting forth his own interpretation of the Paasikivi line—which, of course, was true.[28]

Clearly, Kekkonen was not happy. Where was the gratitude for the hard work he had put into persuading Khrushchev to change his mind about EFTA?

Evidently the top Finn had some work to do in winning over some members of the Western diplomatic corps, as well.

One of those nonbelievers was William G. Miller, the economic counselor of the US embassy, who was acting as charge d'affaires until the arrival of Ambassador Sessions's replacement. Unlike Sessions, who had overcome his dislike for Kekkonen, Miller was definitely *not* a fan of the president. As far as he was concerned, Kekkonen's latest pilgrimage to the Kremlin was a hollow repeat of his 1958 visit. "President Kekkonen returned from his four day visit to Moscow on November 25 with a series of economic "agreements" reminiscent of his 1958 visit," Miller cabled the State Department in his scathing communiqué of December 3, 1961.[29]

In Miller's view, the Finnish leader's latest outing had been so much shadow play. "Again, on this occasion, it appears that substantially nothing has been accomplished and again worthless 'concessions' are glowingly received," the diplomat sniped.[30] He also agreed wholeheartedly with those Finns who were skeptical of the value of the deal Kekkonen had made for the Saimaa Canal. Miller's disdain for Kekkonen—and, one infers, the residents of eastern Finland who supposedly stood to benefit the most from the restoration of the Saimaa—seeps through the following passage of his surly dispatch: "*Much as the notion of using the Saimaa* [Canal] *may appeal to the uninformed in eastern Finland*, it appears unlikely that Finland will elect to make the large investment needed for the canal so long as it runs through alien territory [author's italics]."[31]

It seems that the Soviet embassy was not the only one where opinions about Kekkonen were divided. Clearly Miller definitely did not share Edson Sessions's admiration for the Finnish president—or Finland for that matter.

Neither, it seems, did the Eisenhower White House. The final report of the Eisenhower administration's National Security Council (NSC) on December 30, 1960, in its official statement of US policy towards Finland, took as dim a view of the Finnish president as ever. To wit:

> All significant Finnish moves are calculated in terms of their effect upon the ever present danger of absorption into the Soviet orbit.... Finland's policy towards the USSR is to a great extent determined by President Urho Kekkonen, the country's leading political figure, who believes that Finland's best interests are served by greater accommodation to Soviet pressures than a number of his countrymen feel necessary.[32]

Deliberately or not, there was no mention in the report of the speech Kekkonen had given on September 4 during Khrushchev's visit to Finland asserting Finnish independence. Kekkonen, the scathing memo continued, "acknowledged an implicit Soviet veto over participation in the cabinet by persons unacceptable to Moscow and has endeavored to increase Soviet confidence in Finland's posture as an example of peaceful co-existence."[33]

One thing was certain. Anastas Mikoyan notwithstanding, Urho Kekkonen still had Moscow's support, including that of its ambassador, Zakharov.

That much was evident on December 23, 1960, when Kekkonen and Ahti Karjalainen hosted a convivial party, including a sauna, for a group of their Soviet friends at the presidential mansion. In addition to Zakharov, the guests again included the head of the Scandinavian department of the Soviet foreign ministry, Nikolai Lunjkov, then just returning from his own tour of the region, during which he had met with the Danish and Norwegian foreign ministers, among others, both of whom, Lunjkov claimed, only had splendid things to say about Kekkonen and his trip to Moscow.[34]

In an interview with the Soviet news agency, *Tass*, Andrei Gromyko, the Soviet foreign minister, confirmed that at least from Moscow's point of view, the Finnish president's visit had been a triumph.

To be sure, according to Kekkonen, his trip had been such a success and he had gotten *so* much for Finland, that at least some of the Communist bloc countries were actually jealous! Take the Poles, for instance. On December 13, the Finnish president enthuses about a letter Ahti Karjalainen had received from Pekka Malinen, the Finnish consul in Gdynia, Poland, which his aide had shared with him. In his journal Kekkonen writes that "the Poles are very jealous of Finland after my trip to Moscow, when the USSR gave everything to bourgeois Finland."[35]

The captain of Finland's storm-tossed ship of state also knew that he still had plenty of backers at home. Runar Bäckström, a businessman and an

FIGURE 12. A pensive Kekkonen looks out the window of Tamminiemi.

Army colonel engineer, for instance, definitely *was* a fan. According to Kekkonen's journal, the former officer, who had once been a close aide to Gustaf Mannerheim during the war, and was now the chief executive of a major lumber company, was moved to write his hero a congratulatory note after his controversial address to the Paasikivi Society that fall, "expressing his highest admiration for [Kekkonen's] fantastic speech." His admirer added that "many people have come around to supporting" Kekkonen."[36]

As far as the knotty EFTA matter was concerned, which had perhaps been the greatest challenge facing him, the Finnish leader was convinced that he had solved the problem, and that the Outer Seven would come around as well.

He was right. The British, the Swiss, and the others would indeed come around and see that they had no choice but to accept the agreement Kekkonen had made allowing Moscow to retain its Most Favored Nation status. They had no choice, really, if they did not want to push Finland further towards the Charybdis side of the treacherous straits between East and West.

In his speech of November 25 he had declared that he was certain that he could persuade the Outer Seven to see the light and allow the Finns to join their club, at least as an associate member, by the end of the year.

In the event, it took until February of the following year, 1961, for the members to open their doors to the Finns. Kekkonen's persistence, along with his continuing rapport with Nikita Khrushchev, had paid off. Perhaps what Kekkonen had accomplished may not have meant that much to the man on the street in Helsinki or Rovaniemi, the capital of Finnish Lapland, but the fact is, by securing Finnish membership in EFTA he had saved Finland's economic future, as Max Jakobson writes in *Finland in the New Europe.* "I am probably to some extent still under the spell of Kekkonen's personality, while repelled by the underhanded methods he used to maintain and exercise power," his conflicted former aide wrote in 1998, a decade after his former boss's demise. "I cannot claim to be a detached historian of his time."

Nevertheless, Jakobson goes on to state unequivocally that "Kekkonen's most important achievement during his first term was to bring Finland into the European Free Trade Area while preserving the profitable bilateral trade with the Soviet Union."[37]

Even America's National Security Council, which took such a dim view of Kekkonen, implicitly acknowledged the success of the difficult political balancing act he had performed in maintaining economic relations with both East and West. "The Finns," the White House conceded, "have thus far maintained, and in some measure, strengthened their economic ties with the West," the NSC's December 1960 report concluded.[38] While apparently reluctant to give Kekkonen credit for what he had achieved, or was about to achieve, in smoothing the way with both Moscow and the Outer Seven to join forces with EFTA, the Council's report underscored just how vital to Finland's livelihood that now all-but-forgotten accomplishment was: "The ability of Finland to associate in one way or another with European Trade Association is of such far-reaching importance," the report stated, "that it may be a major determinant of Finland's fate as an independent country oriented towards the Free World."[39] An achievement was an achievement.

The question of whether that achievement *also* enabled Kekkonen's reelection two years hence was, well, a little less certain as his children and grandchildren gathered around the Christmas tree at Tamminiemi.

Kekkonen evinced his anxiety about his reelection that December by appearing to support a proposal by Arvo Korsimo, the sometime Agrarian League secretary, to revise the presidential voting system by replacing the electoral system with a direct referendum (as would ultimately take place after Kekkonen's death in 1986).

Perhaps he was concerned about his election prospects, but he really was not worried—at least not yet. After all, the election was still two years away. Moreover, he felt, who could possibly take his place at the helm of the Finnish ship of state? Väinö Tanner? Perhaps. "I've thought that Tanner could be a possible opponent for me for president," Kekkonen confided to his diary on December 11, 1960. But, he added, that Tanner was "the candidate of the past."[40] He was sure that he, Urho Kaleva Kekkonen was the man, the only man, who was capable of steering the *Finlandia* through the choppy waters ahead.

Anyway, as the temperamental Finnish chief executive was pleased to see when he stepped on the scale on January 1, 1961, his weight was back up to 78.5 kilos. He had not weighed that much since September 1958, at the start of the Night Frost.

As he and his countrymen would soon find out, the waters through which Urho Kekkonen was steering the *Finlandia* were about to get considerably choppier.

CHAPTER 9

The Bridge Builder (1/61–3/61)

Isn't it time for Finland to use its special position in the world as a bridge-builder between East and West? Perhaps there is a new role for us in this world of need of peace and understanding.

—Kekkonen's New Year speech, January 1, 1961

KEKKONEN CAMPAIGN STARTED IN FINLAND

HELSINKI, Finland, Feb. 11—Supporters of President Urho Kekkonen are pressing his campaign for re-election although the election is a year away.

President Kekkonen, an Agrarian, is the only person to have announced his candidacy publicly. His supporters hope that the vote will be more clear-cut than in 1956, when Karl August Fagerholm, a Socialist, received 149 votes in the electoral college to the President's 151.

—*The New York Times*, February 11, 1961

PRESIDENT OF FINLAND BEGINS TOUR OF CANADA AND U.S.

HELSINKI, Finland, Oct. 10—President Urho K. Kekkonen began today a three week tour of Canada and the United States. The trip, the first to the New World by any Finnish chief of state, was widely hailed here as a new demonstration that Finland was not restricted to her close relations to the East.

Accompanied by his wife and four aides, the President took off this morning aboard a DC-8C jet plane for Montreal and Ottawa. He will confer with Prime Minister Diefenbaker and in Washington Monday with President Kennedy.

—*The New York Times*, October 11, 1961

There are two photographs of Urho Kekkonen taken in 1961, one in January, at the start of the year, and the other, nine months later, in October. Taken together they tell the story of that roller-coaster, final year of Kekkonen's first term, at least as much as can be decrypted from photos of Kekkonen, never the most transparent subject.

In the first shot, taken in January in Kekkonen's study at Tamminiemi, the sixty-year-old president looks out the window in the direction of his celebrated gazebo atop a nearby hillock. He looks pensive, but not unhappy.

The second photo, taken by Kalle Kultala, a well-known Finnish press photographer, while Kekkonen was visiting the United States as part of his campaign to bolster Finnish neutrality, shows a very different Kekkonen. Taken in Hawaii when he was taking a break from his well-publicized trip to the US, his first in thirty years, the photo shows Kekkonen surrounded by his traveling entourage, including Ahti Karjalainen, who was now the Finnish foreign minister; Max Jakobson, who continued to serve in his dual role as press spokesman and ghostwriter, as well as political aide; and Rafael Seppälä, the Finnish ambassador to Washington.[1]

The four bespectacled Finns, each of whom looks more uncomfortable than the other, are wearing shorts and sandals. Kekkonen and Karjalainen are adorned in flowery Hawaiian summer shirts, and have papier-mâché leis around their necks. The effect would be comical except for the group's evident consternation, as Jakobson reads aloud from a document he is holding. The document is the summary of the shock phone conversation he had just had with the Foreign Ministry conveying the essence of the note Soviet foreign minister Andrei Gromyko had handed the no less shocked Finnish ambassador to Moscow, Eero Wuori, that morning invoking Article 2 of the 1948 Fenno-Soviet Treaty calling for joint consultations between the military staffs of both countries in light of the allegedly enhanced threat of armed aggression by West Germany and its NATO allies.

Was the photo, which would become one of the most famous—as well as analyzed—photos in Finnish history, staged as has been alleged? If so, the four men gathered on that bench on Maui on that long-ago October day are excellent actors. Seppälä, in particular, his hand pressed to his cheek, does an excellent impression of the Distressed Diplomat, as does the clearly perturbed Karjalainen.

As far as Kekkonen is concerned, his expression, hidden by sunglasses, is a little harder to discern. Although, from the look of his pursed lips, he certainly is not happy. Was he acting? Perhaps. In any event there certainly is a long gap between the self-assured man in the first pane of our Kekkonen diptych and the seemingly discombobulated one in the second.

Now let us go back to the first photo, and start over. To be sure, whatever one makes of the Hawaii photo, the self-assured look on Kekkonen's face in the January 1961 Tamminiemi photo was most definitely not an act. When that photo was taken, the Finnish president had every reason to feel good about himself. Already, as we have seen, he had achieved one of his main goals, obtaining Moscow's agreement to allow Finland to join EFTA. The fact that he had not received adequate credit either domestically or abroad, for this accomplishment, which even a skeptical White House termed "of far-reaching importance" naturally irked him.

The people who loved him still loved him. And quite a few Finns did. According to a January poll by the Finnish daily *Viikkosanomat*, Kekkonen was the most popular Finn, with 14,617 votes, while Veikko Hakulinen, the famed Olympic cross-country skier, came in second with 7,598 votes.[2]

Certainly the first five years of Kekkonen's presidency, particularly the grueling Night Frost and aftermath of 1958–59, had been no bed of roses, but he still wanted the job—if perhaps not for another twenty years, a prospect that doubtless would have startled even *him* at that point—then certainly for at least another six, or at least as many as his robust mental and physical health allowed. Not only did Kekkonen still *want* the presidency, he *was* the president, and his mien reflected that, as Werner Wiskari describes in a profile of him he penned for *The New York Times* later that year:

> No one could look more a man of command than Mr. Kekkonen as he strides into a Finnish gathering, his heels biting the floor, and his trim posture ramrod-straight.
>
> His manner of speech is hard-hitting, and his language when directed at opponents of his Agrarian party, can be withering.[3]

This was not a man who was worried about being reelected.

Although, according to historian David Kirby, the subject of his reelection came up during his friend Nikita Khrushchev's harum-scarum visit to Helsinki several months before, he was not too worried about it, at least at the start of 1961. Kekkonen's confidence about his reelection is buttressed by a scathing, if grudgingly admiring State Department report prepared that same month for the incoming Kennedy administration.

> Due to his own skill and the division of his opponents, President Kekkonen has used his constitutionally strong position to

> dominate the political scene. Abandoning the theory of a nonpartisan President after his election in 1956, he has unhesitatingly used his office to advance his own concepts and interests and those of his Agrarian Party adherents.
>
> While he has sacrificed some of his prestige and unifying authority, the division and confusion of his opponents—to which he has contributed—*has thus far precluded a challenge* [author's italics].

"The President's election and re-election are closely bound to the EFTA question," the classified memo adds. Kekkonen "will gain markedly and perhaps beyond the possibility of challenge—if Finland is able to associate with EFTA in the near future."[4]

"In the case of failure," the memo continues, "his position would be damaged." That did not appear likely at that point, at the start of 1961. As far as Washington could see, Kekkonen's reelection was a fait accompli.

Not that the State Department felt that that was necessarily a good thing for Finland. Aside from vague statements regarding Finnish independence," the report continued, Kekkonen "has interpreted the Paasikivi line as an accommodation. In return he has not received any substantial benefit from the USSR except lip service for good feeling."[5]

"Like a photographic print whose features become clearer with time," the sharply written document continues, "outlines are emerging which with time would bear a resemblance to the country's unique status of independence under Czarist Russia as a grand duchy."

One imagines that Urho Kekkonen would have been outraged if he could have read that report. At the same time, if he had, one suspects that only would have stiffened his determination to do something dramatic to gain, or regain, the West's respect.

To be sure, as he sat in his study at Tamminiemi over the Christmas holiday, the self-assured steward of *Finlandia* had come to a decision. Now that he no longer had to worry about EFTA or his reelection, he was free to focus on what he felt was the remaining challenge of his first term: restoring the credibility of Finnish neutrality. The resistance he had encountered in the West during his campaign to join EFTA, along with the lack of understanding for Finland's unique geopolitical position had convinced him of that.

Now, in his New Year's speech, he decided to share his epiphany with the Finnish people and the world. "Finland," he declared, "has a unique border between the East and West, one which has led to it becoming the setting for considerable bloodshed over the years," alluding to the three not-so-long-ago wars—the Winter War, the Continuation War, and the Lapland War, as well as the Finnish Civil War—which still hung heavily on the nation's soul. "Isn't it time," he continued, "for Finland to use its special position as a bridge-builder between East and West? Perhaps there is a new role for us in this world in need of peace and understanding."[6] Active Neutrality, he called it.

The reaction of the Finnish press to Kekkonen's "new look" for foreign policy was mixed. According to *Ilta-Sanomat*, the Helsinki daily, the president's novel idea was dangerous. The political opposition was not happy about it, either. "The evident failure of the foreign policy of the past years," declared parliamentarian Tuure Junnila of the conservative National Coalition Party, in a scathing speech on January 17, "cannot be disguised by exciting the nation [with his] future great foreign political role as a bridge builder between East and West."[7]

That was okay by Kekkonen. He did not expect everyone to understand or appreciate the dynamic new course he envisioned for the Finnish ship of state. In the event, and more worryingly, Kekkonen's friend and sponsor, Aleksey Zakharov, the Soviet ambassador, who had just considerably extended himself on his behalf, also found his rebranding of Finnish foreign policy hard to comprehend, as did his superiors in the Kremlin. So what was this "bridge-building" business about the Kremlin's man wanted to know? This was a problem Urho Kekkonen could not ignore, whereupon Kekkonen the wheeler-dealer went into his best doubletalk mode.

The bridge-building metaphor for Finnish neutrality could be seen in three ways, the president assured the anxious Russian, according to his journal. Either Finland could be the eastern part of the Western bridge, or the western part of the Eastern bridge (whatever that meant). Or, Kekkonen told the envoy, Finland could be *the* neutral bridge between East and West, as he suggested in his New Year's speech, helping to increase understanding between the sides.

The protean politician then immediately pulled the metaphorical rug out from under himself. "I don't believe in the practical possibility of the third model," he continued—in other words, the very same model he was proposing!—"but ideologically . . . [it] will gain the support of many of those searching for a new direction who have opposed our current foreign policy." In the new policy, Kekkonen assured the diplomat, opponents of the Paasikvi-Kekkonen line "will find the basis for a new ideology."[8]

Evidently the Soviet ambassador was satisfied with Kekkonen's convoluted exegesis.

In any case, the Finnish head of state felt sufficiently comfortable with Zakharov's response to set in motion his plan to promote the new brand by visiting the United States and Canada. According to Jukka Tarkka, Max Jakobson's biographer, the idea for visiting the United States originated with Jakobson, who saw the transatlantic sortie as a way of repairing the damage to Finland's image from the Night Frost.

Regardless how the idea originated, it is not difficult to understand why it appealed to Kekkonen. For one, the Finnish president retained fond memories of America from the time when he led the Finnish track and field team at the 1932 Los Angeles Olympics.[9] Too, he was well aware that despite the lingering bitterness toward the US as a result of America's failure to come to Finland's aid during the Winter War, as well as Washington's standoffish policy towards his country since then, there remained a deep reservoir of affection for the US among the Finnish people. A visit there, he could see, would undoubtedly be a popular move in both countries, as well as a politically expedient one, in Finland, particularly in the year preceding a presidential election, while promoting the case for Finnish neutrality. And, of course, America did have a newly inaugurated president, John F. Kennedy. It certainly would not hurt to have the Finnish president's photo taken with him.

It is not clear whether Kekkonen discussed the idea of meeting Kennedy with the Soviet embassy. Nor is it clear what the Soviet reaction would have been if he had. Khrushchev, who favored Kennedy over Richard Nixon, Kennedy's opponent in the 1960 presidential election, whom he viewed as an unreconstructed Cold Warrior, still had hopes of forging a good relationship with Kennedy in February 1961. That would change, particularly after JFK showed his Cold Warrior colors during the Bay of Pigs invasion of Cuba that April, and even more so in June after Kennedy and Khruschev's disastrous meeting in Vienna. But that was still in the future. Although Moscow might not have necessarily liked the idea of its favorite capitalistic "client," Kekkonen, visiting the White House, it is not clear whether Khrushchev or the Central Committee would have disapproved of it either, at least at that time.

In any event, Kekkonen instructed the Foreign Ministry to set up the trip. According to State Department records, Seppälä, the Finnish ambassador to Washington, met Dean Rusk, the US secretary of state on February 22, 1961, and told him that his government would welcome an invitation to Kekkonen to visit the US sometime that year.

It took Rusk and his new colleagues at the State Department a while to discuss the idea, but a month later the new secretary of state sent a memo to President Kennedy saying that he thought "an informal visit" by the Finns would be wise. "We have been concerned by the weakening of the Finnish posture toward the USSR since 1958 when Soviet pressure brought down the pro-Western Fagerholm government," Rusk wrote on March 23. Consequently, "an informal visit by President Kekkonen to Washington would demonstrate our interest in Finland and could be used to encourage a firmer Finnish attitude towards the USSR."[10]

As can be seen now, with his request for an "informal visit" to Washington, the Finnish president also set in motion one of the vectors that led to the Note Crisis. As it turns out, Kekkonen's new activistic foreign policy was a diplomatic bridge too far for Moscow to swallow when he journeyed too far over to the western side of his metaphorical bridge.

But he did not know that then.

February 1961 was the month when Kekkonen's self-confidence started getting shaky. On February 15 the welcome word came down from EFTA that despite some of the members' reservations about the deal Kekkonen had made with Moscow allowing the USSR to retain its most favored nation status, which Moscow had insisted on as a condition for acquiescing to Finland's membership application the seven members had decided to allow the Finns into their exclusive economic club. Kekkonen's long, twisty, Sisyphean quest to attach Finland to EFTA and safeguard the Finnish economy was finally over.

Or was it? That same day, the fifteenth, the seven EFTA members announced that they were also applying for membership in the European Common Market (EEC), threatening to scotch Kekkonen's achievement. Joining EFTA was bad enough—Moscow was bound to dislike an economic coalition whose membership overlapped that of the military coalition of NATO—but joining the Common Market, which Moscow also considered an extension of the despised treaty alliance was worse.

That, the Finnish president knew, Moscow would never allow. Sure enough, a worried ambassador Zakharov immediately put in a call to

Tamminiemi to convey his alarm at the latest development. No, of course not, Kekkonen assured the Soviet envoy, Finland would never join EEC.

Nevertheless, suddenly, there was a cloud over Finland's economic future again.

Now, as the long winter of 1961 continued, the domestic front began to look cloudy too.

Thus, on February 19, Kekkonen notes in his journal that the National Coalition Party was trying to agree on a candidate for next year's presidential election.

Easier said than done apparently. According to the journal, Klaus Waris of the Bank of Finland; Waris's predecessor, Sakari Tuomioja; Martti Simojoki, the theologian and bishop of Helsinki; and Edwin Linkomies, the wartime prime minister and one of the seven Finnish politicians, along with Väinö Tanner, who were tried and convicted after the Soviet-mandated postwar trials, which then minister of justice Kekkonen, had supervised, had all been sounded out on whether they were interested in taking on the job of opposing him. All said no.[11]

Two days later, on the twenty-first, Kekkonen notes matter-of-factly that the principal opposition party, the Social Democrats, had decided to ask Olavi Honka, the outgoing chancellor of justice, the country's top judge, to be its candidate.

It does not sound like he was worried. If anything, Kekkonen sounds mildly surprised.

So, actually, was Olavi Honka.

To be sure, Honka was, to say the least, an odd choice for presidential candidate. Something of a political nullity, the sixty-four-year-old jurist, whose post as ombudsman required him to oversee the constitutionality of the standing government's actions, was perhaps best known as the instigator of the ongoing investigation of the directors of Kela, the state social insurance agency, on charges that they had allowed their friends to receive inexpensive loans which enabled them to obtain accommodations in Kela-owned buildings.

Among the officials ensnared in the mess, one of the highest-ever profile corruption cases in supposedly square-dealing Finland, was the low-profile prime minister, V. J. Sukselainen, who also was director-general of Kela, and ultimately would be forced to resign that summer.

Although the Kela scandal had raised the profile of Honka, the self-effacing jurist could hardly be called a public figure. *The New York Times* understated the case, when it noted that "there had been no public clamor for Honka when the Social Democrats named him as their candidate [for president]. In fact, if political lightning had not struck him then just a few weeks before his retirement," the US newspaper noted, few Finns would have noticed his pending disappearance from the scene.[12]

Honka himself admits in his memoir that he was thunderstruck when Väinö Tanner's right-hand man, Olavi Lindblom, approached him that winter and asked him whether he would consider running against Kekkonen. As far as the latter was concerned, he appears to have barely given Honka much thought up until that time, at least on the evidence of his journal.

As someone who saw the Finnish constitution as an advisory document at best, Kekkonen was bound to dislike anyone who had Honka's job. But no, Urho Kekkonen did not care much for Honka, any more than he did for the vast run of Finnish public servants. He made that clear at the reception at his house on New Year's Day when the leading government officials formed the traditional conga line to shake the president's hand and exchange the usual felicitations, and he pointedly snubbed Honka when the embarrassed jurist's turn came.

In point of fact, why Olavi Honka agreed to run for president remains something of a mystery to this day. He certainly had no passion for power. The chancellor's only known passion was his country cottage, where he spent the weekend proudly tending his grove of seventy apple trees. If Honka had a weakness, according to a profile of him in *The New York Times* later in the year, it was his garrulousness:

> He nervously fingers his deeply-lined face and as he talks a torrent of words pour forth. Eager to converse with all he meets, he is known as a man who is likely to unburden his heart to strangers.[13]

In the terminology of American politics Honka was a dark horse, certainly one of the stranger dark horses Finland had ever seen.

In any case Honka did not say yes right away. Being the candidate of only one party would be "against my principles," he told Olavi Lindblom.[14] First the Social Democrats would have to put together the support of the other opposition parties before he said yes.[15]

He also did not say no. For the moment, Honka was only a prospective candidate for president.

This helps explain why Kekkonen did not take much note of Honka's nomination, at least on the evidence of his journal—or perhaps, more accurately, pretended *not* to take note, something that the shape-shifting president was also good at. As we have seen, Kekkonen was quite adept at ignoring things he did not wish to acknowledge or validate.

At any rate, the Kremlin certainly took note of the Honka nomination, and the dark forces it perceived behind the surprise move. As David Kirby writes, "Moscow immediately and correctly detected the hand of the Tannerites."[16] Thus on February 24, 1961, *Tass* declared that by selecting Honka the Social Democrats were "trying to disparage the line of Finnish foreign policy and that sensible Finnish politicians find the Socialist move one which can irreparably harm Finnish interests."

The warning shot had been fired. What neither Kekkonen and his supporters, nor Moscow anticipated, at least at that point, was how quickly this dark horse candidate would draw support from the other opposition parties, as well as how broad and deep the antipathy toward Kekkonen, as well as *toward* the USSR, still truly was.

Ad interim, while Zakharov's superiors in Moscow were digesting the news of Olavi Honka's candidacy, on March 7, the Soviet ambassador had good news for Kekkonen on the foreign policy front, along with a questionable assignment for him to take on. After considered thought the Politburo decided that it indeed liked the new look in Finnish neutrality Kekkonen had promulgated in his horizon-shifting New Year's address, and that his revised, Active Neutrality model comported with "the spirit of the times as the importance of neutral countries has grown," as Zakharov put it, as well as Moscow's plans.[17]

Which other neutral countries was he referring to? India? Yugoslavia? Switzerland? Who knows? The key thing was that Moscow was okay with its Finnish friend's new brand of neutrality. Consequently, Khrushchev's envoy continued, the Kremlin was wondering if its esteemed friend would consider employing his new policy in the cause of world peace and convey the USSR's concern about the increasing cooperation between Norway and Denmark, the two Nordic members of NATO, and their despised fellow NATO member, revanchist West Germany.

As it happened Kekkonen was due to fly to visit Oslo the following day, March 8, where he was supposed to meet the Norwegian prime minister, Einar Gerhardsen, and his foreign minister, Halvard Lange. Before he left the Kremlin conveyed to Kekkonen that it would appreciate it if the president warned his Nordic brethren to stop cooperating with the Soviets' bête noire, the West Germans. Among other things, Moscow was exercised about the recent talk about the joint military command between the two Nordic members of NATO, Norway and Denmark, which Oslo and Copenhagen were talking about forming under the larger NATO umbrella. Additionally, the Kremlin was not happy about the possibility of NATO placing nuclear missiles in Norway.

In Moscow's view, "all the Scandinavian countries" should form a situation where they could remain neutral and outside the superpower politics according to the Soviet envoy. Put another way, Moscow wanted its friend in Helsinki to use his new bridge-building foreign policy to deactivate NATO's northern wing. Would the Finnish president mind?

Six months earlier, as we have seen, Zakharov's boss, Khrushchev, had used the occasion of the latter's birthday celebration at the Finnish National Theatre to convey a similar message to the two Nordic NATO members, to the ashen Finn's intense embarrassment.

What was Kekkonen's reaction to Moscow's request that he personally convey the same message to his Norwegian colleagues now? That was then, this was now.

Now he had no problem with doing the Kremlin's bidding.

And so he did when he met the two Nordic officials on March 8 in Oslo.

In the event, the Norwegian prime minister and foreign minister were not as pliable as the Finnish president or Moscow would have liked. By Kekkonen's own account the push back was immediate. Gerhardsen and Lange said no such agreements would be made without the agreement of their NATO partners. In what must have been a particularly mortifying moment for their Finnish guest, the resistant Norwegians told him that they wanted "good relations with the USSR," but, invoking the memory of the Night Frost, they were "afraid that Soviets would interfere with Norwegian internal affairs as they did in Finland in 1958," according to Kekkonen's journal.[18]

The contentious conversation then moved on to the rumors that Norway was considering allowing NATO both to store nuclear weapons, including nuclear missiles, on its soil, a subject that alarmed both Moscow and Helsinki. According to Kekkonen, the Norwegians again pushed back, with Gerdhardsen, the Norwegian prime minister, insisting that "they [the nuclear weapons] might be required if the political situation" changed. "A counter-weapon to the atomic missile will be invented at some point and then," he told Kekkonen, and "reaction speed will be important."[19]

Now, by his own account, the Finnish president took off his gloves. "Your starting point is that the West will not start [a] war, but the Soviets will" their guest said. "If the Soviets start it," he told his hosts—which evidently Kekkonen considered a possibility—"then the counter-weapon will be destroyed first [and] Norway will be the first target."

Pivoting back to the putative threat posed by West Germany, which Kekkonen also believed he continued in the same bellicose vein, "[in order to fight] West Germany [only] 20 nuclear bombs are needed. . . . *And you can be sure they're ready and waiting in place* [author's italics]."[20]

Message delivered. The two presumably mortified Norwegian officials' response to this thinly veined threat is not recorded. Apparently Kekkonen and his hosts decided to keep the kerfuffle to themselves.[21] On the evidence of the Finnish color newsreel of the Norwegian state visit, all was sweetness and light, at least for the cameras. . . .

(NEWSREEL)

Open on a shot of King Olav V, the jovial Norwegian monarch greeting his fellow sovereign at Oslo Central Station, while being serenaded by a Norwegian Army hand. Here Olav and Kekkonen, who seems to be enjoying himself, are waving to the friendly, flag-waving crowd as they ride in the king's limousine.

And here, in the ultimate sign of Nordic comity, Olav and Kekkonen, both wearing caps, ski up to the reviewing stand of a Norwegian-Finnish skiing competition. Kekkonen, the veteran skier, seems to be in particularly good form, quickly skiing up to the stand, before shaking hands with some of the veteran skiers gathered to meet him, as the sun continues to shine on this picture of Nordic togetherness.

Meanwhile, on March 9, the day following Kekkonen's loaded conclave with the Norwegian prime minister and foreign minister, while he was still in Oslo he spoke by phone with his top Soviet contact, Aleksey Zakharov. Presumably Kekkonen told the Soviet ambassador about the conversation he had had with Gerhardsen and Lange.

But that was not what the worried envoy was calling about, according to his journal. Zakharov had learned that the Kremlin was worried about EFTA and EEC, particularly the former's eagerness to meld with the latter. Now the Russian wanted to talk about that.

Kekkonen dutifully told the Soviet ambassador, as he had also had done during his last visit to Moscow that "if this happens, it will be impossible for Finland to join EFTA. . . . Moscow hope[d] that the word of the P[resident] of [Finland, Kekkonen's, promise] is sufficient guarantee that Finland will not join this alliance [of] leading countries [*sic*] of NATO."[22]

Once again Kekkonen found himself between a rock and a hard place.

Clearly, clouds were gathering on both the domestic and foreign fronts for the Finnish president. And yet as he shook hands with his fellow former Olympian skiers on that sunny day in Oslo before the whirring newsreel cameras, all, seemingly, was sweetness and light.

Chapter 10

The Perfect Storm (3/61–9/61)

> The Finnish people, though long accustomed to unusual political maneuvering, are now watching with incredulity the unfolding of a David and Goliath bout over the Presidency.
>
> —*The New York Times*, April 9, 1961

> The Soviet Union will not allow a repeat of the events of the year 1941. Therefore the [nuclear] tests.
>
> —Urho Kekkonen's journal, September 2, 1961

It was not long following his return from his private set-to with his contentious Norwegian colleagues, Einar Gerhardsen and Halvard Lange, that Urho Kekkonen began obsessing about domestic politics again. Thus on March 13, 1961, he writes in his journal about a visit his friend Kustaa Vilkuna had paid to Edwin Linkomies, one of those who may have been tapped by the Social Democrats to run against him in 1962 and had declined the honor, during which the former prime minister denigrated Olavi Honka, to Kekkonen's evident delight:

> Kuttura visited me. Had met Linkomies. He has not been asked [to run as] a candidate. Vennamo only accepted Honka. That's why it was decided.
>
> Linkomies himself [said that] Honka will not be able to handle the presidency. Linkomies supports Kekkonen.[1]

And so on and so forth, the entry continues in this childish and unflattering vein.

Kekkonen's friends at the Soviet embassy, particularly Aleksey Zakharov, the ambassador, were only too happy to join in the fun. Thus on April 6, Kekkonen gleefully reports that "Zahkarov [recounted] with amusement how Honka kept trying to greet him [at a] reception, but he [Zahkarov] always turned his back to him."[2]

Meanwhile no matter how much Kekkonen and his coterie continued to disparage the putatively hapless chancellor, Olavi Honka and his various sponsors must have been doing something right because on March 17, he was able to announce that he had accepted the ad hoc anti-Kekkonen coalition's nomination as candidate for the presidency after meeting with representatives of the Conservative, Small Peasant, Liberal, Swedish People's and Finnish People's parties, as well as the Social Democrats. The London *Times* deemed the development significant enough to report the surprise announcement on its front page:

> **FINNISH CANDIDATE FOR PRESIDENT SOCIALIST NOMINEE TO OPPOSE DR. KEKKONEN**
>
> Mr. Olavi Honka, the Chancellor of Justice, a non-party man, has announced that he has accepted the nomination as a candidate for the Presidency of Finland in next year's election.[3]

As the broadsheet noted, it was not yet clear how much support Honka actually had:

> The extent of the support for Mr. Honka will not be clear, however, before the party meetings in the spring and summer.[4]

Still, Kekkonen's party, the Agrarian League, was already worried, witness the coercive wording of the invitation *it* had sent to the Conservatives and the Swedish and Finnish People's Parties for *their* support.

> Considerable surprise has been caused by the wording of the invitation which states that the broadest possible unity behind the renomination of Dr. Kekkonen would be the best way to "safeguard peace at our borders and the continuance of the successful and proved neutrality line."[5]

Once again, as in 1956 when he was first elected, Kekkonen's backers were using "the Russian card" as a cudgel to intimidate the opposition.

Now, as the long Finnish winter slowly turned to spring, and Kekkonen realized that his reelection was no longer a done deal, he began to panic. Thus, on March 27, he is distressed to report that Jussi Saukkonen, the chairman of the Coalition party, which represented the business community, had sent him a message confirming that at the party's meeting "the general mood" was to support Honka and only a few supported him.

Even more surprisingly Kekkonen also confides how Reino Kuuskoski, the jurist who served for a short time as prime minister in 1958, before the Night Frost, and was still Kekkonen's ally, told him that Finnish industry would give little or no support to him during the presidential campaign.[6] Clearly angered, Kekkonen told Kuuskoski that he had a message for him to take back to his friends "You make me run around the world chasing after EFTA membership," he snorted, "and then slap me on the behind with a stick!"[7] Lèse-majesté!

Over the next half year the Finnish leader continued to fret about the 1962 election. Most knowledgeable observers, including the staff of the US embassy, continued to doubt Olavi Honka's chances. But now, with a number of leading newspapers backing Honka, and Kekkonen losing support in the business community, the election certainly did not look like a walkover anymore. Once again, as during the 1956 election, which Kekkonen had barely won, difficult as it was for him to believe, the next presidential contest was again shaping up to be a real fight.

Meanwhile, the months between April and September 1961 saw another precipitous decline in relations between Moscow and Washington, along with an escalation of the arms race between the two, as well as a parallel escalation of the Berlin crisis as Nikita Khrushchev, having given up hope on coming to terms with the new US president, John F. Kennedy, decided to turn up the heat. Indeed, after a promising start, 1961 wound up being just as perilous for world peace, if not more so, than the previous year. Among the flashing lights on the road to the abyss were the invasion of Cuba by an anticommunist force of 1,500 ersatz commandos organized and equipped by the CIA, a wrongheaded operation that the young American president had inherited from the Eisenhower administration, and thoughtlessly approved.

In addition to a marked loss of prestige for Washington, the invasion, which was ruthlessly put down by Cuban leader Fidel Castro, now a full-blooded Soviet surrogate, caused Khrushchev to mistakenly write off JFK as a bumbling amateur, dimming hopes for a détente between the United States and the Soviet Union.

Hopes for progress on both the disarmament and Berlin fronts further dimmed after a disastrous meeting between the two leaders in

Paris in June, which culminated with a bellicose Khrushchev lecturing and threatening the US president, who seemed out of his depth. "Worst thing in my life," Kennedy later told a *New York Times* reporter.

> According to a State Department memo, Khrushchev said that if the U.S. challenged the Soviet position in divided Berlin, the U.S.S.R. "must respond and it will respond."
>
> "It is up to the U.S. to decide whether there will be war or peace," Khrushchev declared. Kennedy responded: "Then, Mr. Chairman," Kennedy responded, giving as good as he got, "there will be war."

"It will be a cold winter," Kennedy rued before he exited, even though it was still only spring.[8]

Things soon got even chillier on the Berlin front, as Khrushchev decided to ratchet up the pressure there, with the enthusiastic backing of Walter Ulbricht, Moscow's vassal East German leader, and decided to close the border between East and West Berlin to stop the embarrassing exodus of East Germans by erecting a concrete wall topped with barbed wire along most of the border with West Berlin.[9]

Now the East-West conflict had a wall for a symbol, The Berlin Wall, and, soon, too, a killing zone, as a number of desperate East Berliners died trying to cross it, shot down by the East German police.

Then, at the beginnning of September, just when it looked as if things could not possibly get any worse, Moscow decided to resume atmospheric nuclear testing, breaching the unofficial testing ban that both superpowers had thus far adhered to. Over the next three days the USSR detonated three more atomic bombs in Siberia, each bigger than the other, further unnerving the civilized world. In his journal, Arthur Schlesinger, Jr., the noted Harvard historian who had joined Kennedy's staff as a special assistant, summed up how perilous things appeared to a thoughtful, sober-minded American on September 4, three days after the Soviets resumed testing. "For the first time," wrote the normally optimistic intellectual that day, "I feel gloomy about the state of the world."[10]

"The Soviet decision to resume testing," continued Schlesinger—who would meet the Finnish president along with Kennedy, as well as Dean Rusk, his secretary of state, six weeks later at the White House when the former visited Washington—"on top of recent events convinces me that Khrushchev has decided on a very risky power play over Berlin. This is brinksmanship with a vengeance, and it may get us very close indeed to war."[11] Such was the view of the avowedly peace-loving professor-in-residence (and the author's late friend) at the White House as the world seemed to be sliding toward Armaggedon.

Suffice to say that Schlesinger's melancholy view did not square with that of the professedly peace-loving resident of Tamminiemi. To be sure, reviewing Kekkonen's diary from the spring, summer, and fall of 1961, one notes that the aforementioned international events are only mentioned in passing, and when they are his perspective is more or less interchangeable with that of the head of a communist bloc country—unthinking, loyal to Moscow, and only mildly critical, if at all. Nor is there any indication that the gathering political storm clouds, enhanced by the quite authentic mushroom clouds his friend in the Kremlin started setting off that fall, might affect either his own country or his quixotic mission to become a bridge builder between East and West.

Thus on May 11, three weeks after the American debacle in Cuba, the Finnish president writes: "Kennedy after the fiasco of Cuba: 'If nations of this hemisphere mistreat their duties to reject the communism pushing in outside, I want to make it completely clear that US government doesn't hesitate to fill its primary duty, which is to take care of our own nation's safety.' [Thus] Kennedy's doctrine."[12] It does not sound as if Kekkonen was very impressed with his American counterpart, at least at that point.

The Berlin crisis itself rates only the following, desultory mention on August 14, 1961, after the shock East German move to build The Wall, as the execrable structure dividing the two Germanys would soon become known: "Border between West and East Germany had been closed on August 13th. Stream of immigrants to the West turned into a flood," Kekkonen continues, dispassionately.[13]

When it comes to West Germany Kekkonen appears to have swallowed the Soviet line on Bonn's supposed military ambitions whole. "I have for years said that the greatest danger to world peace is arming West Germany," the Finnish president declares on August 16th. "If there is unrest in East Germany [as there was in 1953 in East Berlin] and they [*sic*] appeal to West Germany for help, no force in the world will stop the *Bundeswehr* [West German army] from crossing the border and giving aid. War!" "The old Nazi spirit has never died," continues Kekkonen, in the same righteous vein, "and these days it is raising its head up high." How exactly "the old Nazi spirit" was raising its head up again in West Germany the writer does not say. "Blind are the Western statesmen who armed West Germany."[14]

The Finnish leader's reaction to Moscow's decision to resume nuclear testing is equally uncritical. "Soviets do not want a repeat of the events of 1941," the one-time diehard anticommunist writes blandly on September 2, after a meeting with Zakharov, in which the Soviet ambassador refers to the 1941 German invasion of the USSR, as if that explained everything.[15]

Kekkonen's overarching concern during this time period, perhaps not unnaturally, is with his surging presidential opponent, Olavi Honka. On May 26, he records the results of a *Helsingin Sanomat* poll that showed him leading Honka by 58 percent to 28 percent, a comfortable enough margin under normal circumstances, one might think, but not for Urho Kekkonen. Nor for the Soviet embassy for that matter.

To be sure, Kekkonen's greatest joy during this period, aside from his voracious reading, along with his occasional forays into town to liaise with Anita Snellman and his other distaff friends, seems to be hearing, either directly, or indirectly, how much the Soviet ambassador dislikes Honka, and enjoys humiliating him. Thus on April 8, after meeting with Zakharov, Kekkonen eagerly shares this: "Moscow [is] very concerned about developments in Finland . . . will retaliate if Honka is chosen as President. His reign will not last many days."[16]

On and on Kekkonen bloviates as he fixates about his opponent, and the possibility of his election, along with the equally worried, seemingly ubiquitous "Z." Thus on May 25 he writes:

> [Matti] Valtasaari [businessmen and long-time Kekkonen friend] visited me. Told me he had breakfast [on May 18] with Zakharov who had talked all the time about the election. Why Honka? [Zakharov had asked.] UKK [Kekkonen] had skillfully taken care of foreign policy. . . . USSR had only accepted UKK's proposal about [Finnish EFTA membership] because it trusts him. So the issue is whether or not to change Finnish foreign policy, as it has been ever since Honka's nomination.[17]

Three months later, Kekkonen is still happily relating Tehtaankatu's latest attack on the opposition candidate. Thus on September 6, he revels in Vladimir Zhenikhov's, the KGB man, latest threat against Honka, which Zhenikhov had passed on to Kekkonen's friend Matti Valtasaari, who in turn had passed it on to him. "If Honka is elected," something that Moscow—and evidently he, too—feels, and fears, is possible at that late point of the campaign, "relations with be cut [with Finland]," Kekkonen writes, quoting what Zhenikhov told Valtasaari.

Again, from the same entry, paraphrasing Zhenikhov: "If one is so stupid as to become Tanner's candidate, one cannot be but stupid. [Honka] will not get a visa to USSR."[18] Evidently this was music to the Finnish president's ears.

In the meantime, Kekkonen forged ahead with his campaign to garner respect for Finnish neutrality in the West and promote his country as a "bridge builder" between East and West and become the new Switzerland of the North.

The high point of the first half of 1961 for him was his and his wife's state visit to Great Britain in May. The visit, including the speeches he expected to make, both during his British foray and his upcoming trip to North America, were sufficiently important for Kekkonen to hire an English tutor to help bring his rudimentary English skills up to royal par. The four-day visit, which came with the ruffles and flourishes that the British are good at, including a luncheon party given by Queen Elizabeth and the Duke of Edinburgh, received extensive coverage in the British press, most of it positive.

An article in the *Economist* was particularly kind to Kekkonen. "President Kekkonen of Finland, who has been visiting Britain this week, is often treated in the West as slightly suspect, on the ground, first, that he is excessively effusive towards the Russians and, second, that he plays party politics with the presidency," the piece began. "Since Mr Kekkonen became president in 1956," the magazine continued, "Finnish politics have been complicated by a split within the Social Democrats—the chief rival, among the democratic groups, of Mr Kekkonen's Agrarian party; one faction of Social Democrats, being vehemently anti-communist, has briskly criticised the president's handling of foreign affairs. Thus the political controversy surrounding Mr Kekkonen cannot be laid solely at his door."[19]

"Mr Kekkonen's foreign policy is, in fact, a continuation of 'the Paasikivi line' laid down by his predecessor," the magazine continued. "This is based on the hardly challengeable maxim that Finland, to survive, must avoid giving offense to Russia . . . to maximise its liberty, it [Finland] must exploit the amused and slightly sentimental affection the Russians feel for their tough little neighbour," the anonymous writer explained, "rather like the feeling the English have for the Irish." That was certainly an interesting way of describing the relationship between the two historic foes.

> When Mr Kekkonen is accused of carrying deference to extremes—as he was last year when he went to Moscow to ask, apparently, if Finland could join the European Free Trade Association—he can reply that his deference is justified by results. Finland has been allowed to attach itself to Efta; and over the last four years the Russians have let the Finns gradually reduce the proportion of their trade they conduct with the communist bloc.[20]

Continuing in the same sympathetic vein, the influential organ then discussed the new quandary facing Kekkonen and Finland, as a result of Britain's desire to join the Common Market, or the EEC: "The Finns now face the possibility that, if Britain joins the Common Market, the buyer of a quarter of their exports will vanish behind the common market's tariff wall." "The best hope," the *Economist* concluded, "would then be that the Russians, having permitted Finland to associate itself with Efta, might decide to go the whole hog and let the Finns link themselves with the common market as well."[21]

"If that were to happen," the anonymous writer continued hopefully, "Mr Kekkonen's policy of sailing eastward while edging westward would have been triumphantly vindicated."[22] Well, one could always hope.

In any event, it was nice to have friends! And the insignia of the Knight Grand Cross of the Order of St. Michael and St. George that Queen Elizabeth invested the Finnish president at the luncheon party she threw for the Finnish couple at Buckingham Palace was also very nice.

Most importantly, in addition to providing a welcome distraction from his reelection worries, the British sortie gave Kekkonen an opportunity to correct the pejorative view of his country and its foreign policy which he felt many Britons and other Westerners still had, while expounding upon his new, "activistic" definition of Finnish neutrality before a sympathetic and interested audience, as he did in the speech he gave in his newly fluent English at Guildhall, in London, on his last evening in the British capital, on May 10, 1961.

You need not feel sorry for Finland, Kekkonen told his listeners. She was one of the small European countries that emerged as independent nations from the chaos of the First World War, the tall, bald man in the tuxedo told his rapt listeners. If one looked at the map of Europe today, he continued, as Sylvi, sitting next to him, offered silent encouragement, "you will see that Finland was the only one of those countries that survived World War II with its independence and social system intact."[23]

"This has not been without cost," he reminded his audience. "Both in war and peace we have had to defend our freedom." "In the eyes of many people abroad, we Finns," the tall, bald Finn declared, "are living in a dangerous place." Be that as it may, he continued, "we have no wish to change our role. After many difficulties and many misfortunes, we believe that we have found the right road: the road of good neighborly relations, and mutual confidence between neighbors."

"We ourselves, with bold and confident hearts," the Finnish leader closed, with a line that seemed directed as much to Moscow as to London or Washington (if not more), "will continue to work for the preservation of peace and of our freedom."

And so, in the words of *Economist*, the aspiring diplomatic bridge builder continued to sail eastward, while carefully edging to the West.

Was the captain of the *Finlandia* edging too far to the West for the Kremlin's taste? He and the Finnish nation would find out five months later when the Note Crisis hit.

Kekkonen played host to several foreign leaders in 1961. Several weeks after he returned from Great Britain, he was pleased to return the hospitality of King Olav V, welcoming the Norwegian sovereign to Helsinki for a short visit. The weather was too warm to go skiing again, as the two leaders had done during Kekkonen's visit to Oslo four months earlier; however on the evidence of their smiling visages in *Helsingin Sanomat* the visit was a success, as well.

It also inspired a memorable cartoon by Kekkonen's reliable thorn in the side, *Sanomat* cartoonist Kari Suomalainen, who used Olav's visitation to make fun of the Finnish leader's incipient megalomania. In the first pane of Suomalainen's cartoon, Kekkonen greets Olav, who is decked out in full royal regalia, including his towering, regal hat. In the next pane, the Norwegian king leaves his hat on a table, and walks outside, leaving it behind. In the third and last panel, Finland's would-be king is standing in front of a mirror trying out Olav's helmet for size.

Less than three worrisome months later, as he was preparing for his own forthcoming visit to Canada and the United States, Kekkonen also played host to an extended visit by Soviet president and future strongman, Leonid Brezhnev. If anyone had any doubts about how Moscow felt about Kekkonen the warm kiss he planted on Kekkonen's cheek as his train pulled into Helsinki's Central Station, as depicted in the British

Pathé News's newsreel of the visit, put to rest any doubts about that. Even Khrushchev never did *that*, at least on camera.

On the evidence of the short newsreel, which begins with a panoramic view of Helsinki before cutting to the scene at Helsinki's Central Station as a phalanx of Finnish officers in dress uniform dutifully stand by, things went swimmingly enough. Here Brezhnev and Kekkonen jointly receive bouquets from two Finnish schoolgirls. There, bouquets in hand, the broadly smiling Soviet president is greeted by a large and apparently enthusiastic crowd of several thousand well-wishers, no doubt bused in by the SKDL, the Finnish Communist Party.

Next Brezhnev, accompanied by Kekkonen and an extremely attentive group of Finnish and Soviet officials, can be seen on a tour of the Nokia cable factory, where he is greeted by a knot of attractive female workers adorned in native dress, with whom he exchanges flirtatious salutations, while other male workers, waving small Finnish and Soviet flags, smilingly look on.

In the event, as we know from the transcript of Kekkonen's pivotal meeting with President Kennedy the following month, the Finnish leader took the occasion to ask his Soviet VIP guest some questions about matters in the news, including the recent aggressive moves by Moscow in Berlin, as well as the Kremlin's decision to resume atmospheric nuclear testing—questions to which Kekkonen received some surprising and concerning answers, as he later revealed to Kennedy.

But that discussion took place behind closed doors. Nor was there any mention of the actual dialogue or what the two men actually talked about in the Finnish press. The main message Khrushchev's deputy was interested in conveying was how highly Moscow regarded its Finnish friend, a message that was underscored by both the Soviet and Finnish, as well as British newsreels of the event, as well as the length of the Soviet president's several day-long visit itself.

So far as is known, the forthcoming presidential election was not mentioned.

CHAPTER 11

The View from Tapiola (10/61)

> [Before the Note Crisis] Finns had good reason to view 1961 not only as the best year since the war but perhaps the best year since indepedence. The President had almost completed a series of successful official visits. Relations with the Soviet Union had been relaxed; the visit of President Brezhnev had passed off in an atmosphere of general amiabilty, and Finland had been able to associate with EFTA.
>
> Life in Finland goes on with enjoyment and intensity, in what observers from afar, but never the Finns themselves call "the shadow of Russia."
>
> —Wendy Hall, in her feature about Finland in the London *Times*, November 3, 1961

The Finnish political landscape had certainly changed as Urho Kekkonen prepared to embark for his much-anticipated historic trip to the United States, the first ever by a Finnish head of state, on October 10, 1961. Eight months had passed since the new Kennedy administration had first invited Kekkonen to visit the United States. It will be recalled that Edson Sessions, the then US ambassador, had first formally suggested the idea of a visit by the Finnish president in his long memo of February 1960. The notion had then fallen between the diplomatic cracks after the U-2 debacle the following spring and the subsequent refreeze between Washington and Moscow.

Now, a year later, at the behest of Secretary of State Dean Rusk the new administration had formally revived the idea of inviting Kekkonen to the White House for the same reason that had moved Sessions to suggest it, to give the Finns a more positive view of the US and American power. At the same time a trip to Washington comported with the new bridge-building role Kekkonen had set for himself.

In February, the Canadian government, acting in concert with Washington, had also invited the Finnish president to visit Ottawa so he could connect with the Canadian-Finnish diaspora in the western provinces. So it was set.

At the time, in February, Kekkonen had no formal opponent in the forthcoming 1962 presidential election. Although the Social Democrats had nominated Olavi Honka as its candidate, Honka had not yet accepted the nomination, refusing to do so unless the other opposition parties formed a coaliton to support him, as the Coalition Party and four other parties ultimately did, a prospect which had seemed unlikely at the time. In any event, in February Kekkonen was not particularly bothered by the bowtie-wearing ex-chancellor.

Now, in the fall, Honka was the active and—as best as could be judged from the turnout at his well-attended campaign appearances—increasingly popular candidate of a formidable, five-party anti-Kekkonen coalition. Now Kekkonen *was* worried. So was Moscow, as the headline on a story that Werner Wiskari of *The New York Times* filed on October 7 read:

FINNISH ELECTION WORRYING SOVIET

Russian Afraid Opposition May Topple Kekkonen

"The Russians are concerned over the possibility that President Urho Kekkonen might not win a second six-year term in the coming Presidential election," wrote Wiskari.[1]

Evidently Moscow still had difficulty understanding the workings of Finnish democracy, no less why Honka, the unlikely opposition candidate, who was also the candidate of their bête noire, Väinö Tanner, had garnered so much support.

> Russian concern is expressed in private conversations. At virtually every opportunity Soviet diplomats here were reported to be asking Finnish officials and prominent Finns why there is such a wide-scale attempt to topple the President.
>
> As one Soviet diplomat put it, they [the Soviets] have nothing personally against Dr. Kekkonen's rival, Olavi Honka, the 67 year old retired civil servant now in politics for the first time.
>
> But they look upon Honka as only a front. They are vehemently opposed to some of his sponsors—especially to Väinö Tanner, the 80 year old Social Democratic leader. The Russians regard Mr. Tanner as their arch-foe in Finland.
>
> [The] President's own Agrarian Party [*sic*] also seems to be somewhat concerned over his prospects. Dr. Kekkonen has not been campaigning personally. It is not customary for a [Finnish] President to stump the country, but some of his supporters have suggested that Finnish independence may be endangered if Mr. Honka wins.

> This has infuriated the Honka backers who accuse the President of having used foreign policy to keep his party in power.[2]

Wiskari himself hedged his bets about the election, now but five months away:

> Most political observers here think that there is little cause to doubt Kekkonen's re-election, besides the backing of his Agrarians, the [implicit] backing of the Finnish [Communists] and the extreme Left-wing Socialists, the President is expected to draw enough vote from within the other parties to win.
>
> Nevertheless, one prominent Finn seemed today to share Soviet and Agrarian doubts when he said, "I think Honka will lose, but I would not bet on it."[3]

If the domestic Kekkonen-centered Finnish political landscape had dramatically altered since the top Finn had set the wheels for his epochal visit to the US in motion eight months earlier, so had the larger, geopolitical one. The fuse to conventional or nuclear war, or both, between the US and the USSR, which had basically been tamped down since the 1960 U-2 incident, had been relit as the two sides stumbled towards Armageddon again.

Whether or not one believes that the Note Crisis, which coincided with Kekkonen's trip to the US, was partly or completely staged, a question that will be examined later, it is doubtful that the cunning Finnish president knew that the Russians would drop the boom on him when he was at the tail end of that trip. Or when John Kennedy, Kekkonen's perplexed American counterpart, was most in need of someone to help him peer across the chasm between Washington and Moscow and help him penetrate the mysteries of the mind of That Man on the other side.

By chance Finland's eighth president was due to visit the US at one of the most explosive points of the Cold War.

It would be a cold winter, a disheartened John Kennedy had predicted after the disastrous failure of his Paris summit meeting with Nikita Khrushchev in June 1961. That winter could be said to have begun three months early on September first when the USSR resumed nuclear testing, unilaterally abrogating the moratorium on testing the two countries had signed in 1958.

Several days later, on September 5, Kennedy and his dismayed ally, Harold Macmillan, the British prime minister, issued a joint appeal to Moscow to renew the nuclear test ban, while dropping their previous insistence on joint inspections. For naught: over the next two months the Soviets conducted an average of one high-altitude nuclear test every two days for a total of forty-five tests, making a mockery of Khrushchev's prior call for mutual disarmament. On September 15, the US reluctantly followed suit, conducting an underground nuclear test at its Nevada test site. He had no choice but to do so, the American president said. The long winter JFK had predicted now bid fair to be the world's first nuclear winter, as panicky Americans began considering building atomic bomb shelters.

Finns were not building bomb shelters yet, but they were were beginning to get the jitters, too.

Meanwhile, 700 miles away, in Berlin, where the East Germans had just built the hideous Wall with Moscow's blessing after a short pause following Kennedy's reluctant decision not to contest the shock move, tensions continued to rise as Moscow continued to press Washington to sign a separate peace treaty with its satellite state. Otherwise the Kremlin threatened that the US and its allies would lose access to West Berlin.

A glance at the headlines and the lead paragraphs from some of the articles in *The New York Times* during the ten days prior to the Kekkonens' visit shows just how explosive things had become.

10/7 KENNEDY AND GROMYKO EXCHANGE BLUNT VIEWS; SCANT PROGRESS

President Kennedy and Andrei Gromyko, the Soviet Foreign Minister exchanged blunt views on Germany and Laos but made virtually no progress on either issue.[4]

Mr. Kennedy stated the West's position with great care, stressing his determination to defend West Berlin and access to it. Mr. Gromyko offered little more than the Soviet position of recent months: the Soviet insistence on a peace treaty with East Germany that would establish its sovereignty over Berlin and its conversion into a free city.[5]

10/8 KENNEDY-GROMYKO TALKS SAID TO HAVE GONE BADLY

Mr. Kennedy is said to have conveyed to Premier Khrushchev once more the West's determination to protect the freedom of West Berlin in the hope that Moscow will agree to negotiate on something other than its own terms. But Mr. Gromyko is reported to have offered little hope for the future.

Mr. Kennedy is said to be somewhat disturbed by the Russians' tendency to speak one way with visitors to Moscow and in public speeches, [and differently] in direct confrontations.[6]

10/10 BRANDT MAY ASK NEW BERLIN ARMS

Mayor Willy Brandt said today he would discuss with Western Allied authorities whether the West Berlin police were armed well enough to cope with the East Berlin guards.[7]

10/11 SOVIET BUILDING UP FORCES IN GERMANY FOR MANEUVERS

50,000 Soviet combat troops and 10,000 Polish troops have arrived in Communist East Germany to take part in Warsaw Pact maneuvers near the West German border.[8]

Thus the pressures building on Kennedy during the run-up to his meeting with Kekkonen.

That same day, October 10, 1961, the day the Kekkonens left for Ottawa, the first stop on their North American trip, *The New York Times* also carried the following dispatch about fellow European Free Trade Association (EFTA) member Great Britain's eagerness to join the Common Market.

BRITAIN PROMISES FULL MARKET ROLE

Britain announced today her readiness to "fully subscribe to the aims and objectives of the European Common Market.[9]

Of course there was nothing Kekkonen could do about that. If Britain and its fellow EFTA members joined the Common Market, as they apparently were eager to do, Finland would be left high and dry, as the Finnish president later pointed out to Kennedy. "This is our Berlin," he would put it later, referring to the perpetual EFTA miasma.[10] In any event, the president of Finland also had a lot on his mind, as he continued with his good will tour of Canada, while preparing for his rendezvous at the White House.

It is worth pointing out here that, despite the housing scandal that led to the resignation of V. J. Sukselainen, the unfortunate Finnish prime minister and his cabinet and his replacement by fellow Agrarian Martti Miettunennen in July, and the continued static on the political front,

1961 had otherwise thus far been a pleasant year for most Finns.[11] Indeed, as Wendy Hall, correspondent for the London *Times* pointed out several weeks later, "the Finns had good reason to view 1961 not only as the best year since the war but perhaps the best year since [they] declared their independence in 1917."[12]

If Urho Kekkonen had worries about the state of Finnish politics, as he obviously did, as did the Soviets, both parties had managed to keep them to themselves, as Kekkonen continued with his campaign to promote Finnish neurtrality, as well as his drive to be reelected president, as Hall recounts:

> Relations with the Soviet Union had been relaxed: the visit of President Brezhnev had passed off in an atmosphere of general amiability, and Finland had been able to associate with EFTA.[13]

Indeed, in almost every way, things were looking up for Finland on the eve of the Note Crisis. "Above all," Hall blithely observed, "1961 had been a year of economic prosperity, industrial peace, and a full employment previously unknown." To be sure, she added, Finns were all too aware of the shaky basis for the boom, especially given Finland's unclear future status vis-à-vis EFTA and the Moscow-verboten Common Market.

> For a boom year it has been, the Finns know too well the inherent weakness of their economy to uncross their fingers for too long. They are too dependent on a single industry, [forestry] and too much at the mercy of economic decisions made by the Soviet Union on the one hand, and the shifting balance between EFTA and the Common Market.[14]

All the more reason for the Finns to enjoy their boom while they can. And so the consumer-mad populace had been doing. "But the Finns, with their gift for living for the day," Hall wrote, continuing her upbeat tour d'horizon, "have been enjoying their boom." Some Finns had even been splurging on deep-freeze refrigerators, the Briton reported. "They have bought more cars, television sets, and washing machines: they have even imported deep-freezes into a land where cellars and long frosts have done the work of a deep freeze."[15]

And that was not all. According to Hall the once dour Finnish capital was actually becoming a "hot" tourist attraction, or at least a more welcoming one: "[The Finns] have opened more restaurants and coffee bars,

FIGURE 13. John F. Kennedy and Urho Kekkonen standing at attention after Kekkonen's arrival at Andrews Air Force Base, Washington, DC, October 16, 1961.

and built more modern and elegant hotels to lodge tourists and congress delegates for whom Helsinki has become a frequent rendezvous."[16]

Meanwhile, greater Helsinki with its growing population of 455,000—or 10 percent more than in 1956, the first year of the Kekkonen presidency—had continued to expand and grow stylish new towns and suburbs, like the already famed "garden suburb" of Tapiola, the architectural jewel of Espoo, Helsinki's adjoining borough. The Fennophile correspondent even managed to get in a dig at the Swedes, while describing the capital region's revivified landscape.

> Tapiola in the forest a few miles away from Helsinki, typifies [the Finnish] approach. Here several architects have been given a free hand and the result is a splendid and stimulating variety in style and type of dwelling.
>
> In Finland there is space to experiment and diversity can be unified by the natural setting. The Finns, unlike the Swedes across the Baltic, do not annihilate every green thought when they build a

> new town or suburb. The forest remains and not a tree more than necessary is cut down.
>
> They are building, too, many churches of a boldness and conception that strips away all burden of tradition.[17]

Perhaps most surprising—and doubtless alarming to the Soviet embassy—there had been a boom in Anglophilia, doubtless helped by Kekkonen's much-publicized state visit to Great Britain in May.

Unfortunately the boom also had a dark side. "There has been a rise in crime and violence amongst the young," Hall wrote. Drunkenness was also on the rise, and so was drunken driving, although the Finns had developed a robust solution to that problem which seemed to having an effect, she drily reported:

> The automatic consignment of drunken drivers, whoever they may be to labor camps where they spend a few months making roads or building, seems to be having an effect. A glance at the empty glasses at a party leaves no doubt that the Finns prefer tomato juice to road-building.[18]

As elsewhere in the capitalistic world, there also had been a boom in motorcycles, and the *pärinäpojat* (blaring noise boys), as the Finns called them, who came with them. The Finns, it seems, were beginning to develop their love of racing both motorcycles and cars. Still, they also had developed a means of keeping that in check, too:

> In a Helsinki suburb church and commune to provide a racing drivers' club, presided over by a champion with a racing speed track. The club administers a sharp reprimand to anyone driving noisily or dangerously, and the surroundings have regained the quiet which even today distinguishes Finland from noisier countries further west.[19]

In the event, Finland's rising Anglophilia also included the appearance of a number of self-styled "teddy boys," as the British teen rebels were called, according to Hall.

> There are teddy boys, too, but they have not yet become as troublesome as elsewhere, partly because police have been quick to move them off the streets, and partly because active sport provide an outlet for so high a proportion of Finnish youth.[20]

In short, Hall reported, all was basically well in Kekkonen's booming, green-minded, essentially well-behaved, forward-looking Finland of

1961. If anything, according to the upbeat correspondent, living in Moscow's shadow had enhanced Finns' zest for life.

To be sure, as per their president's lead, most Finns were at once aware of, and in denial of The Bear:

> Life in Finland goes on with enjoyment and intensity, in what observers from afar, but never the Finns themselves call "the shadow of Russia."[21]

"The Finns are an optimistic people," Hall concludes her elegy to Suomi:

> and they have their own defences: in laughter, for they have an immediate sense of the ridiculousness of pomp and power . . . in the peace and spacious tranquility of their endless and beautiful lakes and forests . . . and in the world of creative imagination and activity which is proof against despair.[22]

To be sure, Wendy Hall's report probably erred a bit on the Polyannaistic side. Nevertheless, at least at that point, in most respects, 1961 did look to be the most prosperous and trouble-free year for Finland since World War II, and perhaps even since independence. Perhaps the superpowers might be edging toward war again, however in their tree-covered corner of the Baltic region, most Finns had it pretty good. Of course, that could all change in a stroke if the British and their fellow EFTA members were able

Meanwhile, in the untidy world beyond the garden suburb of Tapiola, the real Berlin crisis continued to worsen, as the retrospective ticker tape from *The New York Times* confirms:

> **10/12 PRESIDENT KENNEDY NOT HOPEFUL OF BERLIN SOLUTION**
>
> President Kennedy said today that a month of quiet talks between the United States and the Russians had given him no hope of an easy solution in Berlin and Germany.[23]

> **10/13 PRESIDENT WARNS OF LONG STRUGGLE WITH COMMUNISM**

The prior day, in one of the most despairing speeches of his presidency, at a convocation at the University of North Carolina, President Kennedy warned his listeners that it was delusory to think that communism would ever be defeated. "If we can do our duty undeterred by fanatics or frenzy at home or abroad," he told the subdued crowd,

FIGURE 14. President Kennedy and his wife, Jackie, with President Kekkonen and his wife, Sylvi, accompanied by presidential guard, at the entrance to the official luncheon for the Kekkonens at the White House on the afternoon of October 16.

"then surely peace and freedom will prevail [and] we shall be neither Red nor dead."[24]

> **10/14 REDS AGAIN FIRE OVER BERLIN LINE AS 9 YOUTHS FLEE**[25]
>
> **10/15 SOVIET AIM SEEN TO HUMILIATE US ON BERLIN ISSUES**
>
> Until last week's visit of Andrei Gromyko there was some hope amongst [Kennedy] advisors that the Soviet Union might be brought to negotiate arrangements that would ease the points of friction around Berlin. Now they assume that Khrushchev's maneuvering is meant to break the ties between West Berlin and West Germany and let West Berlin "wither on the vine" . . . and divide West Germany from her allies and break the power of NATO.[26]

On the same day, October 15, *The New York Times* carried an report about how Kennedy had asked Lewellyn Thompson, the long-serving US ambassador to Moscow, who was supposed to leave his post, to remain on duty a bit longer in order to help the White House decipher Soviet intentions vis-à-vis in Berlin and Germany. The White House needed as much help breaking Moscow's "code" as it could get.[27]

10/16 US CANADA TEST OF AIR DEFENSE RATED A SUCCESS[28]

The previous day, October 15, in a test of readiness for possible nuclear war, all commercial flights in the United States and Canada were canceled for twelve hours, something that had never occurred before—and would not recur for forty years until the September 11, 2001, attacks, while US and Canadian air forces patrolled the skies over North America in a mock drill.

That could have been a problem for the Kekkonens, who were just then wrapping up their tour of Canada prior to their much-anticipated visit to Washington. Fortunately, the Finnish couple were only due to arrive on October 16. The Canadian part of their tour, which gave the Kekkonens a chance to connect with the Canadian Finnish diaspora population, was pleasant. There was not much news to report, however, which is why Max Jakobson, Kekkonen's press aide, was able to leave for the US capital several days before to help prepare for the American segment of the trip.

CHAPTER 12

Two Days in Washington (10/16–10/17/61)

We respect you in war, we respect you in peace.

—President John F. Kennedy, welcoming remarks upon Kekkonen's arrival in Washington

Finally, on October 16, 1961, the Kekkonens landed at Andrews Air Force Base, where they were greeted by President John F. Kennedy and his wife Jackie. Kennedy looked happy in the photo on the front page of *The New York Times* as he stretched his hand out to his Finnish guest. So did Urho Kekkonen.

On the recommendation of Secretary of State Dean Rusk, a new category of presidential visitation had been created for Kekkonen's visit: the presidential guest. Essentially this was the equivalent of a state visit, except that the new category did not require a reciprocal visit from Kennedy, which might have put Kekkonen on the spot with his Moscow friends. In every other way, however, Kekkonen's visit would be a state visit.[1]

So it was agreed: President Kekkonen was to be accorded the full VIP treatment. After all, he, Kennedy's first presidential guest, was very important, and so, as one of the briefing papers in the Finland file in the Kennedy archives underlined, was Finland. "Although the Finnish problem is not as urgent as others," the paper stated, "it deserves our prompt attention. The prestige of the US and the future of Eastern Europe are deeply involved. Independent and prosperous, scorning the need for communism Finland can be a beacon of hope in Eastern Europe. Drifting toward communism, it is a symbol of democratic failure and American weakness."[2]

To assist with the honor of welcoming the presidential guests, JFK, as he was popularly known, brought along his glamorous wife, Jacqueline. Already a style icon, Jackie, as she was known by the adoring American public, wore a fashionable pillbox hat. She also had a a bouquet of roses for Sylvi. There is a photo of the two couples standing in front of the US Air Force Military Air Transport plane that the US president had dispatched to convey the Kekkonens to Washington. In the photo Jackie is beaming while the diminutive Finnish first lady clutches the flowers, looking a bit abashed, as does her husband.

A moment later the famed US Air Force Band played the two countries's anthems, as the Kennedys and Kekkonens stood at attention. "We respect you in war, and we respect you in peace," the American chief executive declared in his welcoming remarks, after the last notes of "The Star-Spangled Banner" wafted into the brisk fall air, as his first official presidential guest and his wife listened attentively.[3]

And then Kennedy ushered the Kekkonens and Jackie into the Marine helicopter waiting to fly them for the short hop to the White House for the lavish, bilateral lunch the presidential staff had prepared for the Kekkonens, complete with crossed Finnish and American flags at every table. When Kekkonen exited the American helicopter he was wearing a top hat, something of a novelty for him. This was a big deal for him, too. Then again, Kekkonen, who also fashioned himself something of a style maven, did like his hats!

As any historian, or archaeologist knows—for history after all is a form of archaeology—sometimes the richest historiographical finds are hiding in plain sight (as it were). This is the case with the transcript for the extended conversation that took place in the second floor living room of the White House between 3:30 p.m. and 5:45 p.m. on October 16, 1961, between President Kennedy of the United States and President Kekkonen of Finland, as well as to a lesser extent the transcript of the conversation between Kekkonen and Dean Rusk, the US secretary of state, which took place the following afternoon, October 17, which are available in the State Department archives and Kennedy Library archives, respectively.

In this author's opinion, document 189, Memorandum of Conversation, as per the State Department title for it, is one of the most fascinating and revealing documents to emerge from the mid-Cold War years. For the historian, for one, the memo vividly illustrates just how fraught things were in the larger world on that mid-October afternoon in 1961.

At several points during the two and a quarter hour long colloquy, at which eight ranking American and Finnish officials—four Americans, four Finns—were in attendance, the exasperated US president indicates his willingness to go to war with Moscow. Not that John Kennedy was looking to lock horns with the Soviet Union; however it did not seem to him that Moscow was giving him much choice, not if the USSR stuck to its guns and continued to threaten to abrogate American right of access to Berlin unless the US agreed to sign a separate peace treaty with East Germany.[4] This was something that Kennedy would not, and could not do if the US was to remain leader of the Free World.

No, Kennedy was not about to write off Berlin. Nor would he permit the US to be humiliated, as Nikita Khrushchev seemed intent on doing. As best as he could tell, the volatile Soviet premier wanted to go to war, or at least wanted the West to know that he *was* willing to go to war in order to protect the rights of the USSR's vassal states, and Soviet prestige.

At one tense juncture of the presidential parley, the Finnish leader notes that the Soviets were no less prepared to shoot it out. If US aircraft entered Berlin's airspace, as they had during the Berlin Airlift of 1948, Kekkonen told Kennedy that Leonid Brezhnev, the chairman of the Presidium of the Supreme Soviet and Khrushchev's chief deputy, told him during their recent meeting in Helsinki that the Russians would shoot them down. "That [would] mean war," Kennedy immediately responded.[5] "That was a difficult moment," Arthur M. Schlesinger Jr., the historian who was serving as special assistant to Kennedy at the time, and one of the attendees at the meeting, later told the author.[6]

The fuse to war had definitely been lit. One can literally hear it sizzling in Memo 189 (let's call it), as well as in Schlesinger's own transcript of the meeting. A skilled stenographer, the historian decided to record the meeting on his own as a memo for himself: his record of the talk takes up a full twenty double-spaced typed pages of his own daily journal. Schlesinger, the author of *A Thousand Days*, his Pulitzer Prize–winning history of Kennedy's presidency, which he published in 1965, considerably earlier than he expected two years following Kennedy's assassination, did not do that sort of thing very often in his journal. He knew at the time that this would be an important meeting. Schlesinger also highlighted the meeting in *A Thousand Days*, both because he recalled it as an occasion when the late president presented "the American case in Berlin with particular cogency," as he writes, and because it coincided with the conclusion of the renewed crisis over the city.[7]

For the biographer of Kennedy, Memo 189 offers a frank look at the American chief executive as he struggles to get a rational handle on his mercurial Soviet counterpart, as he continued to grow into the demanding role of commander-of-chief and head of the Free World. Gone is the flailing Kennedy of April who approved the half-baked CIA plan for the invasion of Cuba, the same one who Kekkonen contemptuously dismissed, or the hapless one who Khrushchev berated and "savaged" (as Kennedy put it).[8]

The John Kennedy revealed here was not going to let Nikita Khrushchev humiliate him, or the United States, or the West again. Here, in JFK's resolve not to take any more nonsense from Khrushchev one can begin to see the steel-nerved Kennedy who a year later would face down his unpredictable Soviet counterpart during the Cuban Missile Crisis. In that sense, Memo 189 presages the famous so-called 1962 Ex Comm tapes, so named after the Executive Committee of the National Security Council, the political-military executive committee that convened after the discovery that Moscow had placed nuclear missiles in Cuba the following year. The memo also shows how well-briefed Kennedy was on Finnish affairs, and the trouble he had gone to acquaint himself with them before meeting Kekkonen, which clearly flattered the latter. One wonders how much Kennedy's predecessor, Dwight Eisenhower, knew about Finnish affairs, or history, or cared. Finland is barely mentioned in Eisenhower's two-volume presidential memoirs.

In any case, Eisenhower's successor, John F. Kennedy, certainly cared. JFK, who had headed the Help Finland student aid organization during the Winter War when he was an undergraduate at Harvard in 1939, was surprisingly conversant with Finnish affairs and history. Max Jakobson, Kekkonen's press secretary, who had gone ahead to Washington to help lay the groundwork for Kekkonen's visit, saw this several days before, when his counterpart, Pierre Salinger, the US press secretary, invited him to join him on Air Force One as it ferried Kennedy and Salinger to Boston, whence they planned to spend the weekend at the Kennedy compound at Hyannis Port.

On the plane Jakobson was ushered in for a brief audience with the president, who, he could see was studying up for the conclave with his Finnish counterpart. During their conversation Jakobson saw that

Kennedy was up to speed on Kekkonen's effort to attach Finland to the European Free Trade Association (EFTA). The Winter War came up. So did the Night Frost. Above all, Kennedy wanted to know why the Soviet Union had allowed Finland to remain independent.

Jakobson's biographer, Jukka Tarkka, describes how Jakobson responded. It was a question that the press aide and future Finnish ambassador to the United Nations had heard before. "Jakobson began his standard answer by challenging his interrogator," writes Tarkka. "It was a leading question," he told Kennedy, as the president patiently listened as the turbo-prop plane headed toward Massachusetts. The question contained the premise that Finland's independence rested only on the good will of the Soviet Union. It completely overlooked the [responsibility] of the Finns for [their own] independence. With this bias, Jakobson told the president, the destruction of Finnish independence looked logical and its survival was so odd that it was probably part of a Soviet plot to outfox the West. Jakobson was just getting into the heart of the matter when the president's plane began its descent after the short hop to Boston. "You seem to have run out of time," Kennedy smiled.[9]

The same question, as well as the qualities that would endear Kennedy to both Jakobson and Kekkonen would emerge three days later when JFK met Kekkonen, along with Jakobson at the White House on October 16. They also can be seen in Memo 189. Curious, articulate, intensely conscious of his responsibilities towards both the US and the Free World, resolved not to take any more nonsense from Moscow, the John Kennedy of Memo 189 shows him at his best. And the fact that he was clearly so interested in as well as knowledgeable about the affairs of a small country like Finland is an added bonus.

And what about Urho Kekkonen? What is the value of Memo 189 to the biographer of the Finnish president? For him Memo 189 is as valuable and revealing of his protean subject as it is of his American counterpart, if not more so.

For one thing, the transcript, recorded by a State Department stenographer, combined with Schlesinger's own unofficial transcript, which basically confirmed the accuracy of the latter, while adding a few key lines of dialogue which the official stenographer decided to omit or word more diplomatically, is that rarest of things, a reliable and objective record of a Kekkonen meeting with a democratic head of state, no less the leader of the Free World.

Presumably there are records of the meetings that Kekkonen took with Presidents Richard Nixon and Gerald Ford during his subsequent terms, but one doubts that they are as long or as wide-ranging, or as revealing as the single-spaced, eight page document that emerged from the Kennedy-Kekkonen parley of October 16, 1961. As such, Memo 189, along with Arthur Schlesinger's parallel transcript, comprises perhaps the best record of how Kekkonen deported himself, as well, as to some degree, his thought process, during these encounters, which he supposedly thrived on.[10]

The timing of the presidential conclave, in the midst of the Berlin crisis, just when the American president was struggling to gain some clarity into Moscow's motives and thinking, while his guest was simultaneously seeking to gain respect for Finnish neutrality, makes Memo 189 even more valuable. Regarding the Note Crisis, which took place two weeks following the Kennedy-Kekkonen meeting—and may well have helped trigger it—the transcript contains a strong hint that Moscow was indeed thinking of invoking Article 2 of the 1948 Fenno-Soviet Treaty.

At one point in the middle of the extended conversation, when the two presidents are discussing Berlin, Kekkonen told Kennedy that Finland "has a special position with regard to the Berlin problem," whereupon he went into a rote recitation of Article 2 of the 1948 Fenno-Soviet Treaty, which contains a clause whereby Finland was committed to accept Soviet aid if necessary in order to repel any attack directed against the Soviet Union across Finnish territory, from Germany, or from any powers allied with Germany. Which of course is not exactly true. In point of fact said clause states that Finland is *only* obliged to call for military consultations with the Soviet, *not* necessarily to accept aid. Freudian slip—and a revealing one. Thus the Stockholm syndrome (see earlier).

The reference to the treaty, which JFK does not seem to be familiar with, seems to rub him the wrong way. Annoyed, he dismisses it. "It is not relevant to the situation in Berlin," he snaps. The shape-shifting Finn, who at that point of the dialogue seems to be trying to get back into his host's good graces, does not contest the point. In any case, if one were looking for some sort of smoking gun to show that Moscow was thinking of invoking Article 2, or had discussed the possibility of invoking it with Kekkonen, there it is in Memo 189. It is hard to say, as Tarkka writes in *Max Jakobson*: "With hindsight [the reference to Article 2] can be seen as relying on the knowledge of the impending note or a hunch about it," he observes. On the other hand, "of course it is equally possible that Kekkonen was thinking about some other unspecified matter."[11]

As far as serving as a window onto Kekkonen's character, the document has value, too, if perhaps somewhat less so than its does into Kennedy's because he is not as forthright as his host. Which of course itself reveals something about *his* pliable character. Put another way, the transcript of the conversation also shows Kekkonen at his best, as well as, one has to say, his worst. Learned, articulate, and never at a loss for an answer, even if at times a disingenuous one, the Finnish president comes across in these pages more or less as John Kennedy's equal, as well as his elder and one whom Kennedy took a liking to and respected, as Schlesinger confirms in his diary.

One sees why Urho Kekkonen put so much stock in personal diplomacy. He was good at it. One can also see why he was the right man for the position of Finnish president, at least at that juncture of history, and quite likely the only one. It certainly is difficult to imagine Olavi Honka managing as well as Kekkonen did at the White House. Also, one can say, as he also proves here, that Kekkonen was clearly the democratic leader who knew the Russians best, which also was the principal reason why JFK was so anxious to meet him.

Whether Kekkonen actually succeeds in his role as ad hoc Kreminologist is arguable. Kennedy seems just as mystified by Khrushchev at the end of their meeting as he was at the start. But at least Kekkonen tries, as much as he can within the constraints of his relationship with Moscow. Aware of the long arm of the KGB, he also may have pulled his punches somewhat, at least at first, however he soon opens up to a surprising degree about the Russians and what he knows about them. As we will see, Kekkonen even confides—or pretends to confide—some "inside" information about Russia's plans for its nuclear test program, which Leonid Brezhnev may or may not have told told him on a confidential basis during his visit to Helsinki the prior month, but doubtless expected Kekkonen to pass on.

How sincere or up front the crafty former intelligence officer was in this respect is unclear. What *is* clear, however, and what does come through, upon reading the transcript a half a century later, is Kekkonen's sincere wish to build a bridge between the White House and the Kremlin, which of course was the objective, or one of the objectives, of his new outward-looking foreign policy. Above all, Kekkonen succeeded in breaking through the sterotypical view of Finland as a glorified Soviet satellite—bolstering the US president's appreciation for Finland's precarious position as the only democracy on the Russian border.

At the same time, we can see, Kekkonen also helped Kennedy understand and empathize with Finland's—and his—excruciating geopolitical predicament. In one of the more poignant moments of the conversation, after Kekkonen explains to his curious host why Soviet policy toward Finland was animated by security rather than ideology, Kekkonen confesses that sometimes even Finns do not entirely comprehend their precarious position. His host seems to accept that.

In that respect, the meeting, which actually comprised two meetings over two days, including one that was not officially recorded, was a success both for Kekkonen and for the cause of Finnish neutrality.[12] The fact that that success was almost immediately nullified, or partly nullified, by Moscow's decision to invoke Article 2, the explosive clause of the 1948 Fenno-Soviet treaty, two weeks later, setting off the Note Crisis—which Kekkonen may or may not have expected—does not detract from that accomplishment.

At the same time, Memo 189 also shows Urho Kekkonen at his most elusive, and mendacious. At several points during the conversation, particularly on the subject of the Soviets and the pressures they had exerted on Finland as well as him, he plays coy for the sake of playing coy. Here writ large is Slippery Urho, the devious Kekkonen of lore.

Weirdly enough, the Kekkonen who emerges from Memo 189 sounds quite like the shifty Nixon of the Nixon White House tapes, minus the expletives. Perhaps most damningly, as well as sadly, we also see how readily Kekkonen lied to himself about the actual state of affairs on the other side of the Fenno-Soviet border. Thus his somewhat pathetic reference in the interview to the effort the Russians made to prove how much nicer their homes were then they were depicted in the West—or his apparently sincere belief which he reiterated in his subsequent conversation the following day with Secretary Rusk that the Russians were actually winning the "lifestyle" war with the West. Here, for all to see, is Kekkonen the hostage president, the victim of the Stockholm syndrome, the national leader who claimed to be the one who knew the Russians the best, yet did not really know them that well.

And that is a sad and damning thing to see. Perhaps Urho Kekkonen *was* a great politician. However it is difficult to call the blinkered, fearful person revealed here a great man, or for that matter, a great president.

In that respect, although the Kekkonen of Memo 189 does come off, more or less, as Kennedy's equal, *as a politician*, he comes off somewhat his inferior as a man.

Also, it is well to remember that Kekkonen would be president of Finland for another twenty years, and he still had quite a few surprises—including ones for Moscow—up his sleeve. His character would also grow insofar as that was possible for someone who was already in his sixties, to some degree. And ultimately he would have a more clear-eyed view of the Soviets, especially after his friend, Nikita Khrushchev was cashiered in 1964.[13] But of course no one, including him, knew that in October 1961.

In that respect, the Kekkonen of Memo 189, then in the penultimate year of his first term, could be said to be a work in progress. It certainly should not be taken as the last word on Kekkonen. Still, it is the closest thing we have to a verbal portrait of him, recorded in real time, interacting with another world leader, not in the sauna, but in the clear light of day. For all these reasons and more, the transcript of Memo 189, or one should say two transcripts—if we include Arthur Schlesinger's own unexpurgated account, which basically mirrors the official State Department stenographer's one, but contains some interesting omissions from the latter— together comprises a historiographical gold mine, and worth replaying at length.

The K and K tape (so to speak) can be broken down into several parts. In the first part, which takes up approximately the first third of the exchange, Kennedy, who had never met Kekkonen—or any other Finnish politician, as far as the author knows—at once forcibly states the American position on the matter which is uppermost on his mind, the Berlin crisis, while Kekkonen tries to play the role of devil's advocate. Whether or not Kekkonen expected Kennedy to ask him about Berlin right off the bat, no less so forcibly, is unclear—after all, the crisis was not Finland's problem, exactly, but he is game.

When the meeting begins, JFK is not present. Instead, Secretary of State Rusk sets the first item on the agenda, and the tone. The agenda is Berlin and the tone is urgent and alarmed. "The Secretary opened the meeting by outlining the Berlin problem as it stands today [from the US viewpoint]. He said that while there had been talks with Soviet foreign minister Andrei Gromyko] there was as yet no blue sky to be seen."

No blue sky. Now there was an American way of putting it. "Khrushchev," Rusk continued, "was continuing to call into question our vital interests on which we could not yield. The Secretary said that if [he] were to continue to press on these vital points, then we were all in for trouble."[14] By "we" did Rusk apparently meant the West—by which he apparently also meant Finland. Of course, Finland was not part of the West, nor did it necessarily wish to be, at least in this context. Finland was supposed to be neutral. Technically, Finland had not been one of "us" (i.e., the Western allies) since the Winter War.

In any case, Kekkonen, who may or may not have been upset at the president's absence, did not agree or disagree with Rusk's appraisal. His response was, well, neutral:

> President Kekkonen said that he had the opportunity of hearing Soviet views on Berlin since January 1959, when he talked with Khrushchev. Since then, he said, he had met Khrushchev once again, and had talks with President [*sic*] Brezhnev. He had tried to find some evidence of change in the Soviet attitude, but in vain, which was no surprise to him.[15]

Here we see the first instance of Slippery Urho. On the few occasions when Berlin comes up in his journals, including when the Berlin Wall went up the prior summer, Kekkonen seems to sympathize with the Soviet and East German position. Now, within the confines of the White House, the Finnish leader implies that he had repeatedly pressed his Russian friends to see if they had changed their position on Berlin. Had he really? Who knew?

Next Rusk says that there had been progress on several "procedural and not substantive" issues, as he termed them. Apparently the ever-cautious Soviet foreign minister said that Moscow was "prepared to consider" a four power agreement that would not require negotiation with the East Germans, as they previously insisted, and there was no absolute deadline for signing a peace treaty.[16] This was progress of a sort, he conceded. Nevertheless, Moscow was still hanging the sword of Damocles—its threat to cut off West Berlin—over the Western allies' heads unless and until they gave the USSR and the GDR (German Democratic Republic) satisfaction. However one termed it, Khruschev and Walter Ulbricht, Moscow's East German flunky, were extorting the West. Meanwhile, as anyone who read *The New York Times* could see, Moscow and its Warsaw Pact allies seemed to be making preparations to go to war.

Now Kekkonen took the devil's advocate role, rationalizing the Soviet position (which in fact he supported, as his journal shows):

> President Kekkonen said that Brezhnev had also told him that the Soviets were not prisoners of their own timetable [and] if there were to be real negotiations which were not merely a pretext for further delay.
>
> President Kekkonen said he had the impression that the Western Powers have not taken the Berlin problem as seriously as they should have since 1959, because Khrushchev had given up his [initial] six month ultimatum.[17]

Kekkonen continued to mix it up, albeit in a friendly way:

> [Kekkonen] said that West Berlin, as such, was not of great importance, but that it was the German question as a whole which was involved.
>
> He said he had gained the strong impression from what Brezhnev had said about the Germans that the Soviets in fact fear [West] Germany very much . . . and that they are apprehensive about the [West] Germans unleashing another war.[18]

Which as we know Kekkonen agreed with—or partly agreed with.

Meanwhile, President Kennedy had entered the Oval Office. Seating himself in the rocking chair he favored because of his bad back, a difficulty he had had since his student days, and had been compounded by the near-fatal injury he suffered when his ship, the PT (Patrol Boat) 109 was sunk by the Japanese in the South Pacific during World War II, he now joined the meeting. Kennedy, who had caught the tail end of the dialogue between Kekkonen and Rusk, quickly got to the point:

> President Kennedy summarized the importance of the German question for the West. He said we had done all we could to integrate [West Germany] into the rest of Europe, and whatever the outcome of the present crisis, Germany's ties to the West must not be impaired. Thus West Berlin was not the sole issue.[19]

Trying to ingratiate himself with his host, Kekkonen said he understood Kennedy's position, while conveying what he had learned from Brezhnev after he had "pressed" him during their recent meeting in Helsinki—even if the Soviet position did not quite make sense to him either.

> President Kekkonen said it was easy for Finland to understand the US point of view in this matter. If the West were to give up its

> position in West Berlin, the result [severing West Germany from the West] might well be along the lines suggested by President Kennedy.
>
> He said that he had tried to find out from Brezhnev what advantage a separate peace treaty held for the Soviet Union. He said that one could not be sure, but that he thought there was a 50% to 60% chance that after a separate peace treaty had been concluded, conditions would be clarified in such a way as to lead toward the unification of Germany.[20]

Not only had Kekkonen allegedly pressed Brezhnev on the Berlin issue, he said. He claimed that he had argued the West's position with him: "President Kekkonen had then pointed out [to Brezhnev in Helsinki] that the West considered acccess to Berlin vitally important." Be that as it may, the Soviet position remained unchanged: "Brezhnev had said that the Soviet Union was prepared to guarantee access but that the Ulbricht [East German] regime would have to be associated with such a guarantee, since the GDR was a sovereign state."[21]

At this point one imagines that JFK started rocking his chair, as he did when he was angry or frustrated—or both, as he was at that moment. Not that he was angry or frustrated with his guest, of course. His Finnish guest just was not telling him anything new.

"The President pointed out the very great difficulties that lay in the way of recognizing or dealing with the GDR, due to the fact that the Germans"—by which he presumably meant the peoples of both West and East Germany—"would then feel that the prospects of reunification had been fatally impaired." Furthermore, "he said our hope was that it might be possible to reach an agreement with the Soviets under which our rights would be unimpaired."[22]

"If the USSR will not do this," Kennedy continued, according to Schlesinger's parallel, unexpurgated record of the meeting, "we will maintain access until we are challenged." "And if a challenge comes," the US president asserted, "we will meet that challenge."[23] Thus the Berlin quagmire. The conversation had now come full circle.

Still playing devil's advocate the tall, bald man from Finland tried to get things going again. He certainly got Kennedy going, taking a dig at his predecessor, President Eisenhower, and the call to arms the latter had issued in 1952 at the start of the Cold War, when Moscow began clamping down on its vassal states: "President Kekkonen referred to the difficulties of relations with Eastern Europe. He recalled that President Eisenhower, at the start of his administration had spoken of [the] liberation of Eastern

European countries." "However," Kekkonen pointed out for the American's edification, "Germany could not be reunified by force."[24]

Kennedy started rocking again (metaphorically):

> President Kennedy said he could not recognize the GDR. To do so would provoke a very strong adverse [West] German reaction. This could be seen from the effect of the [Berlin] wall had had on West German opinion.[25]

"You must be aware of the melancholy state of mind induced by the Wall," Kennedy continued, according to Schlesinger's account. "We do not wish to spread that state of melancholy by legitimizing the East German regime and stimulating a nationalist revival in West Germany."

"Germany," Kennedy said, according to Schlesinger, "has been divided for sixteen years and will continue to be divided. The Soviet Union is running an unnecessary risk in trying to change this accepted fact into a legal fact. Let the Soviet Union keep Germany divided on its present basis and not try to associate us legally with that division and thus weaken our ties with West Germany and its ties to Western Europe."[26] "Germany should not be allowed to become isolated, for this would lead to the destruction of freedom in Europe," the official account of Kennedy's remarks continues, as the US president underlined the portentous stakes that the Berlin crisis entailed for the West.[27]

Now it was JFK's turn to co-opt his guest, or try to. "From your point of view," Kennedy pointed out to Kekkonen, underlining how and why he felt what happened in Berlin affected his country, in another passage which the State Department stenographer omits, "you [Kekkonen] should regard all such developments with concern."[28] "Finnish independence depends on the preservation of the balance of forces within Europe," the American asserted. (Quotes from Schlesinger henceforth in *italics*.)

For the third time JFK restated the US position:

> *He said that he hoped that the Soviets would be prepared to reserve our rights to access in any agreement, otherwise there might be war.*[29]

Now the two presidents began to mix it up a bit, so to speak, as Kekkonen tried to take the Soviet side: "President Kekkonen said that the Soviets always use the argument that the West doesn't really want the reunification of Germany." To which Kennedy immediately responded:

> President Kennedy said . . . that Germany was now divided, and that this was a fact. The Soviets were taking an unnecessary risk in trying

> to force us to associate formally with them in proclaimng this. To do so would bring about the end of NATO and of the European Community—and this would mean the end of freedom in Europe.

Once again Kennedy brought Finland back into the picture. "We were of the opinion that a strong Europe was a great help to Finland," he declared, "and that if the West collapsed this would be very harmful to Finland's own interests."[30] America's fight was Finland's fight, was it not?

Kekkonen seems to have been slightly taken aback here. Demurring from Kennedy's collective call to arms, the Finn said that he was only trying to be helpful. "President Kekkonen said he had been passing on to the President what he had been told from the Soviet side because he thought this would be of interest to us." He restated the Soviet position, inserting that Moscow meant business:

> Brezhnev had told him at the conclusion of their talk that when the Soviets had signed a peace treaty with the GDR, the Allies would have to reach an agreement with [Walter] Ulbricht, otherwise, should they try to pass, the Soviets would shoot down their planes as they did the U-2.[31]
>
> *Brezhnev said he had no choice.*[32]
>
> Kennedy meant business, too.
>
> *Of course there is a choice. If the USSR denies us our rights we have no choice but to resist, or to see our position in Europe disintegrate.*[33]
>
> President Kennedy said he had every intention of upholding [America's] rights [and that if] the Soviets followed the course just described, this would mean war.[34]

There, for the second time in several minutes, was that word again—war. The line had been drawn. "This issue was not like the Laotian problem but struck at the heart of our vital interests, and we could not give way, for if we did, Europe would be gone."[35]

Next Kekkonen stated the obvious: "President Kekkonen noted that both sides had remained exactly at the same position they had taken at the start, and that there had been no move forward by either side."[36]

His American host agreed, adding that "what was needed now was some leadership from the West Germans."

The conversation seems to have reached a temporary stasis at this point.

Kekkonen, waxing grandiose, felt that this was a good time to quote Carl von Clausewitz, the celebrated Prussian general and military theorist.

> President Kekkonen said that time was short. He referred to a maxim by Clausewitz [*sic*] to the effect that when there is an issue between one power and a group of allies, the single power has the advantage because it can decide on its own which concessions it is prepared to make.[37]

Now JFK started rocking again. It seems that he did not appreciate the maxim, or the implication that East Germany, presumably the single power Kekkonen was referring to, was in a position to demand concessions from the US and its allies, or that the latter were prepared to give any:

> President Kennedy said that we were not prepared to give concessions, in return for which we would merely be given the rights we already enjoy. Otherwise we would be giving away such things as the Oder-Neisse territories [a section of Germany which the Allies transferred to Poland after the war] and Berlin's ties to the West, and then Soviet pressures would start again. This would not be a bargain.[38]
>
> As [Rusk] told [Soviet foreign minister Andrei] Gromyko, we would be buying the same horse twice.

Not wishing to antagonize his guest, JFK struck a conciliatory note. "The problem was a difficult one because of the peculiarities of [Berlin's] location," he conceded. "But we *have* [author's italics] to stay there and we hoped the Russians knew it."[39] Pass it on to Moscow please: the Allies were in Berlin to stay.

> At this point Kekkonen decided to play devil's advocate again:
>
> President Kekkonen said the Soviets frequently defend their position in terms of internatonal law, referring to the sovereign right of nations and to the precedent of the peace treaty [the Allies had made in 1945] with Japan.[40]
>
> This got Kennedy mad again:
>
> President Kennedy refuted both arguments, saying that the Soviets had no right to give [away] parts of German sovereignty. With regard to Japan, the case was different. *This is an area that is vital to us. All Europe is at stake in West Berlin.*
>
> Japan was not divided and had its own government. If Germany and Japan were to be overrun, the road would lie open to the Soviets.
>
> [From Schlesinger's account] *If we do not meet our commitments in West Berlin it will mean the destruction of NATO and a dangerous situation for the free world*."[41]

"And this," Kennedy, clearly miffed, reiterated, "we would not permit."[42]

Now it was time for Kekkonen to turn it down a notch. He had played the devil's advocate role too well for his own comfort. "President Kekkonen said he felt that he was in an awkward position, because he had been relating what he had heard the Soviets say and it might be thought this represented his own views, which was not the case."[43]

Kennedy reassured his guest, while once again underlining the Allies' commitment: "President Kennedy reassured him. He added that he wished to stress the necessity of the United States meeting its commitments."[44]

Yes, he knew that Kekkonen was only the messenger, so to speak. Be that as it may the next time you see Leonid Brezhnev, Kennedy seemed to be telling Kekkonen, please tell him he should not f*** with the United States.

Now Kekkonen apparently tried to get back on his host's good side, broaching the Allies' other major issue with Moscow, its resumption of nuclear testing. "Turning to the subject of Soviet resumption of nuclear testing, President Kekkonen said he had told Brezhnev the bad effect throughout the world this had created, and asked him why the Soviet Union had resumed tests."[45]

Next Kekkonen vouchsafed the presumably confidential information Brezhnev had conveyed to him on that subject in Helsinki three weeks before, to the effect that only 30 percent of the tests had been conducted at that time: the Soviets had conducted their thirteenth test at that time. During the intervening three weeks, Moscow had conducted another half dozen tests. *The biggest tests were to come* (Schlesinger).

That was news to Kennedy and his advisors, if not necessarily news they wanted to hear: Schlesinger wrote a note to himself to remember to pass that explosive tidbit on to McGeorge Arthur Bundy, Kennedy's national security advisor, who was not present. The hastily typewritten note from Schlesinger to Bundy is in the Kennedy archives. "Another difficult moment," Schlesinger later recalled. "You could hear a pin drop." Not only was Moscow playing chicken on the ground; it was intent on doing the same in the stratosphere.[46]

Kekkonen reverted to helpful friend mode. He said that Brezhnev said that the Soviet Union knew that this was an unpopular thing to do.[47] Well, that was one way of describing girdling the Earth with a layer of lethal, radioactive fallout.

Clearly Kennedy was as put out by the nuclear issue as he was by Berlin, if not more so, particularly by what he felt was Moscow's duplicity regarding the matter.

> President Kennedy said that it was obvious that [the Soviets] had been preparing [the tests] for many months, during which converstions had been going on in Geneva between the West and the Soviet Union.

"Being a free society, it was not possible for us to test without inspection," he continued, "whereas the Soviet Union might complete their current series of tests and then call for an unpoliced moratorium on all tests."[48] Obviously Khrushchev was intent on making things as uncomfortable as possible for the US both on the ground, and in the heavens. What was it with That Man?

The presidential guest did his best to enlighten his perplexed American counterpart. "President Kekkonen said he had the impression that the resumption of tests had a connection with the German problem."[49] Put another way, the Russians were engaging in nuclear blackmail.

Now, remarkably, Kekkonen and Kennedy exchanged notes on what they thought *really* drove Khruschev, and what had made him so trigger-happy: "President Kekkonen said he had the impression that the Russians suffer from an inferiority climax and feel that they are not always treated in a manner appropriate to their power and importance." His host, recalling his embarrassing smash-up with the Soviet premier in Vienna four long months earlier, half-agreed, while offering his own assessment of the unpredictable top Red's psychological makeup. "President Kennedy said that in his talks with Khrushchev [in Vienna] he had sensed two contradictory feelings and attitudes on his part: first a feeling of not being quite sure of himself, and second, a feeling of great superiority."[50] "*These two forces exist within Khrushchev: a feeling of not having arrived, alongside a feeling of being better than anyone else.*"[51] "It was difficult to balance these two" conflicting impulses in the volatile Russian, JFK mused.[52]

Here, on this mid-fall afternoon in 1961, in the White House, the American and Finnish presidents were bonding over their mutual bafflement over That Man in Moscow, as their foreign ministers and adjutants listened in, and the White House stenographer dutifully typed away. Things were certainly getting interesting now.

Roughly an hour had elapsed.

Now that the two leaders had completed their mutual tour d'horizon, the subject turned to Finnish-Soviet relations, including the "third rail" EFTA-European Economic Community (EEC) issue. Now Kekkonen the metaphorical hostage of Moscow emerged. Unsurprisingly, this was the most difficult passage of the conversation for him.

What would be the effect on Finland if the United Kingdom joined the Common Market? President Kennedy wondered. Kekkonen backed into this part of the conversation a bit oddly, noting how much effort the Kremlin had expended in trying to persuade visiting Finnish officials how much better living conditions were in Russia than had been described by the West. Here was the inferiority complex Kekkonen had described. Strangely, the Finnish president seemed to understand why the Soviets were so keen to show off their *House Beautiful* homes.[53] Of course, he seems to imply, *of course* the Soviets wished to see how much nicer their homes were than had been described by the Western propaganda. Indeed, as Kekkonen later indicated to Dean Rusk in their somewhat bizarre follow on conversation the next day, the Russian people's homes and living conditions were *so* much nicer and better than had been described that he was worried that the USSR would eventually beat the West in that area, too.

Wisely, Kennedy let that ridiculous suggestion pass. He did not wish to recreate the Kitchen Debate with Kekkonen. What he wanted to know was just how difficult Moscow was making it for the Finns—not who had the nicer homes.

> President Kennedy asked President Kekkonen how he saw the future of Finnish relations with the Soviet Union.
>
> President Kekkonen said that the economic relationship wth the Soviet Union was stable. Exports to and from the Soviet Union were balanced at about 15% of Finland's total trade.[54]

Now Kennedy brought up the new EFTA-EEC imbroglio, whereupon Kekkonen described the political quagmire this had created for Finland and what would happen if Britain succeeded in merging EFTA with EEC, and the economic catatastrophe this would create for Finland.

Now Kekkonen, the hostage president, clearly began to dissemble. The US State Department stenographer noted his evasivesness.

> President Kennedy asked if Finland was in a position where she could sign the Rome treaty now.

> President did not reply directly, but referred to difficult politcal conditions.

Now came the Finn's first outright lie: "He said the Soviets had not exerted pressures on Finland." Kennedy, who knew otherwise, continued to press his untruthful guest.

> President Kennedy asked whether the Soviet Union was satisfied with the present form of government, or would they prefer a Communist regime [instead].
>
> President Kekkonen said he thought the Soviets were satisfied and that their primary consideration was one of security.[55]
>
> *Any attempt to create a Communist Finland would be far more trouble to* [the Soviets] *than it was worth it to them.*[56]

Fair enough.

Again, Kennedy returned to the EFTA-EEC issue, to Kekkonen's evident distress, explaining why he was a fan of the EEC and strongly suggesting that the United States would be happy if Finland joined it, while his Finnish counterpart tried to explain why he could not. "President Kennedy listed the reasons for the US support of the Common Market. He said that it would cost [the US] in trade, but would be a stabilizing force for Germany and for Europe if the UK were to join it." Kennedy said he was confident that "the other countries involved would recognize the special problems of other countries [and EFTA members], for example, Switzerland and Sweden."[57]

Kekkonen replied that "of course a great variety of interests were involved and that Finland would have to look out for its own. "Finland faced the problem of coming to terms both with the Common Market and with the Soviet Union," the Finnish president continued. "That," Kekkonen put it with finality, "is our Berlin."[58] Well put . . .

Kennedy continued to press Kekkonen, reminding him of the unhappiness with the concession that he had made to the USSR in order to get Moscow to allow Finland to join EFTA in the first place, which had raised hackles both among the EFTA members and the US, a point that was on the verge of being academic. "President Kennedy referred to Finland's most favored nation agreement with the Soviet Union, which had posed a problem to GATT [the 1947 General Agreement on Tariffs and Trade]. He said that this would be compounded if the UK joined the Common Market."[59]

Kekkonen begged for his host's understanding. "President Kekkonen said he hoped that the objections which had been formulated to the terms of Finland's agreement with the Soviet Union were more formal than substantial." Kennedy said that he understood. Still, he was not about to let his new Finnish friend completely off the hook: "President Kennedy reiterated the unhappiness which [Finland's] granting Most Favored Nation status to the Soviet Union had created in the United States," the official transcript continues, "and he hoped President Kekkonen would make use of this in resisting any attempting at encroachment by the Soviet Union."[60]

Now *that* was a bit rich, as JFK must have known. Did he really expect his guest to "use" the putative "unhappiness" the Finnish deal with Moscow vis-à-vis the EFTA had aroused amid the American populace (which was arguable, at best) to get the USSR not to give Finland a hard time if and when she indicated that it wished to join the Common Market? That was a convoluted argument, as well as a rather thin one. Still, at least the US president indicated that he understood that Finland was between a rock and a hard place, especially on this issue, and that the space between them was about to get narrower.

Yes Finland was in a difficult spot, its president conceded, as the second hour of his marathon discussion with Kennedy began. But, he protested, he had no complaints, nor did the Finnish people—a point that was arguable, of course: "President Kekkonen described Finland's position as a happy one compared with what it was in 1944."[61]

Happy? Well, that was one way of putting it, of one discounted the continuous pressure the Kremlin exerted over its neighbor.

Redonning his devil's advocate hat, Kekkonen tried to get his host to understand Moscow's point of view vis-à-vis its pesky neighbor and former grand duchy, citing the 1945 Yalta agreement that Joseph Stalin extracted from his American and British allies that Moscow had a right to expect the governments of neighboring countries to be friendly to the USSR.

That of course was a stretch. There was no formal agreement among the Allies that the governments of countries on the Soviet border *must* have friendly governments. There was, at best, only an understanding that it was preferable if said governments were friendly to Moscow.

JFK let that patently false argument pass. He did not want talk about Yalta. He wanted to know *specifically* the nature of the pressures that the Kremlin had applied and were continuing to apply now on Finland. Now the Night Frost, which had taken place while Kennedy was a senator, or "the frosty night" as he referred to that affair, came up: "President Kennedy recalled the Soviet pressures on Finland in 1958, which the Finns referred to as 'frosty night.' He asked what the pressures were which the Soviets had applied and what had caused them to raise those pressures."[62]

Now Kekkonen gave perhaps his most tortured, half-true, half-untrue answer of the afternoon: "President Kekkonen said that during his visit to Leningrad in 1959 he had asked Khrushchev the same question. Khrushchev had said that Finland and the Soviet Union had a common border of 1300 kilometers [800 miles] and that there was a substantial element of security in their relationship."[63] *True*, more or less.

According to Kekkonen, Nikita Khrushchev had told him that certain members of the Finnish Government had been doing things which impaired this "element of security," as he put it. [64] "*Actually our government had done nothing*," he continued, according to Arthur Schlesinger's record of the conversation, "*except for a few statements which might be considered threatening to Soviet security*," in another line from his translated remarks that Schlesinger caught, and that the State Department stenographer either did not catch or decided to omit.[65]

Now the Finn told a bald-faced lie: "President Kekkonen said that Finland had complete freedom to decide what government it should have, and that the Soviet Union had made no demands on Finland." Then he said something very revealing. "However," he continued, in rote mode, "Finland must take the Soviet position and attitude into account even when she disagrees with the Soviet Union." At the same time he confided, "*this was a difficult position for Finland which before 1944 had always been fully armed to defend itself against the Soviet Union*."[66]

Here Kekkonen was referring to the provision of the 1947 Treaty of Paris, the treaty which Finland signed following the final armistice with Moscow (and which preceded the 1948 Fenno-Soviet mutual assistance treaty) which emasculated the Finnish military, limiting it to a standing army of 42,000 and comparatively minuscule navy and air force.

It is not clear whether Kennedy was aware of that emasculating provision of the 1947 treaty, which many if not most Finns—including Kekkonen, obviously—found "difficult." It is possible he may not have been familiar with the treaty at all, which would not have been so surprising. JFK had been in his first term as Congressman in 1947. Finnish affairs were not particularly high on his agenda, nor that of his Bostonian constituents.

In any case, *this* Kennedy, the current president of the United States, who was in the midst of another face-off with Kekkonen's Soviet friends, wanted to know more about the Soviet-induced Night Frost, "or frosty night," as he termed it, which he *did* know about. "President Kennedy inquired what methods the Soviet Union had used to express its displeasure with Finland."[67]

Now Kekkonen was more forthcoming. More or less: "President Kekkonen said that [the Soviets] had recalled [their] Ambassador, who had left without saying good-bye to the President. Also they had caused trade difficulties." While Finland could have gone on this basis for some months he continued, "this would merely have made matters worse economically."[68] No argument there.

So much for the "frosty night," as Kennedy termed it. He seems to have been more or less satisfied with his guest's less than candid response. Easing up, JFK asked Kekkonen to peer into his crystal ball and tell him what he foresaw for the Communist world in the years to come. It was time for Kekkonen to propound his pet convergence-of-the-two-systems theory:

> President Kekkonen said he thought in 30 years, the capitalist system would gradually be transformed by various modifications and restrictions, and that the Communist system would be progressively liberalized, to a point where both systems would be so close to each other that it would be difficult to know what to quarrel about.[69]
>
> [Schlesinger's version: *I think in 30 years time the two systems will be virtually indistinguishable.*]

Kekkonen probably guessed that in thirty years' time he would be deceased, as the then late four term president-cum-sovereign would indeed be. One wonders, though, how he would have reacted if he had known that 1991 was also the year when the USSR would cease to be, along with Finland's special relationship with Moscow, which was his life's calling.[70]

Kennedy's response to Kekkonen's cloudy theory was a sharp one. In the closest thing to a flash of his famed wit he displayed that afternoon, he cracked, "I would be happy to make it to 1970."[71] Peering into his own somewhat less roseate crystal ball, according to the State Department, Kennedy "said he thought that we had witnessed an increasing strength of nationalist sentiment since 1945 and that this would prevent a major change in balance of power in the world, if we could prevent problems of the Berlin type from exploding."[72] Again, his assistant, Arthur Schlesinger, heard the president's response somewhat differently. "If we can prevent situations like Berlin coming to a final climax which would destroy both of our societies," Kennedy said, according to the latter's account, "then we can get over the next decade. But if the USSR forces us into a showdown over areas vital to our future [like Berlin] neither society will survive."[73]

Why the State Department stenographer wished to soften Kennedy's apocalyptic prediction is unclear, but there it is. Thus the value of Schlesinger's record.

Now it was time for Kekkonen to trot out his pet political figure eight theory again. "President Kekkonen said he thought that the economic systems of East and West were getting closer to each other." "But," he added, continuing his tour d'horizon, "Soviet support and exploitation of nationalist sentiment in areas such as Africa had the effect of increasing Soviet political strength."[74]

JFK, mindful of the ongoing uprising in Portuguese Angola, agreed that Kekkonen had a point: "President Kennedy said he felt it was important to support and encourage national sentiment in Africa, even though this occasionally brought us into conflict with some of our European Allies."[75]

Pleased to find a point on which he agreed, Kekkonen continued in the same vein: "President Kekkonen said that as long as countries like South Africa and Portugal pursued their present policies, this conferred a great advantage to the Soviet Union."[76]

Kennedy concurred, while underlining that it was not so easy for the US to criticize Portugal, for one, even if it wished to because of its treaty commitments, including the one allowing Washington to continue to use its naval base in the Azores: "President Kennedy said that the problem [of supporting nationalist movements in Africa] was a very difficult one. For example the Azores Base Agreement, which was coming up for renegotiation soon, was of very great importance to the United States, and that this had to be borne in mind."[77]

His Finnish counterpart indicated that he sympathized:

> [Kekkonen said] that he had become aware during the war how strongly United States policy had worked against colonialism, and he thought this was a wise policy.[78]
>
> *The two powers bear an enormous responsibility. We pray for your success.*[79]

For the moment the two leaders had reached a meeting of minds of sorts. "I'd like to see both nations survive long enough to see whether the USSR will surpass the US by 1970 as Khrushchev asserts," Kekkonen noted, by way of adding a hopeful fillip to their talk.[80] "I hope it is interested enough in that race," Kennedy cracked, according to Schlesinger, "not to end it all in three or four months."[81] The Cuban Missile Crisis, when Khrushchev came very close to doing just that, was a year away.

Well and good. It was time, Kennedy decided, to bring the discussion back to Topic A: Berlin. And so he did with a start.

> President Kennedy said that it was important that the Soviet Union distinguish between areas of secondary importance and primary importance. Even though Finland [had] problems, he [hoped] that she would realize that the object of United States policy with regard to Berlin was to keep Europe free, and that although Finland could not herself do much about it, she could understand that her fate was bound up with the outcome of the issue.[82]

Put another way, once again, America's fight was Finland's fight.

Well, not quite. At this point Kekkonen brought up the aforementioned reference to Article 2, the problematic clause of the 1948 treaty and Finland's "special position with regard to the Berlin problem." Was this proof, as some of the more conspiratorial-minded observers would later claim, that the shifty Finnish leader already *knew* that his Russian friends were already planning on invoking Article 2, as they would two weeks later, triggering the Note Crisis?[83] Impossible to say, writes Jukka Tarkka. In hindsight, the Finnish writer states, Kekkonen's reference to the mischievous proviso "can be seen as relying on the knowledge of the impending note or a hunch about it." "Of course," he adds, "it is possible that Kekkonen was thinking about some other unspecified matter."[84]

In any case, the Finn's reference to the explosive clause that would lead to the Note Crisis two short weeks later went past his American host. Evidently JFK's otherwise extensive preparation for the belated meeting had glossed over it. Article 2 was "not relevant," he said.[85]

A full two hours—roughly forty minutes more than President Kennedy had allocated for the conversation—had gone by at this point. President Kekkonen shifted back to devil's advocate mode now, trying to get the man sitting opposite him to see things from Moscow's point of view.

"President Kekkonen said that in 1939 the Soviets had asked for a strip of territory in East[ern] Finland in order to safeguard the security of Leningrad. This showed the USSR's concern for its security."[86]

Like much if not most of what Kekkonen said that afternoon, both regarding Soviet intentions and the special relationship, that, as anyone who was familiar with the Winter War knew, was half-true. As he or anyone else who knew the true history of the war knew, in 1939 Joseph Stalin was also keen to reincorporate Finland into Mother Russia. This false reference to the Winter War also seems to have gone by Kennedy.

Stirring, Kennedy wanted to make a point again. Once again, he underlined America's resolve. Perhaps Moscow was concerned about its "security." But that did not mean it could push America around:

> The President outlined the various steps which the United States has taken in order to create conditions for peace in the world. However in areas which were of vital interest to the freedom of the West and the security of the United States, our stake must be recognized by the Soviet Union.[87]

Kekkonen was still in devil's—or one should say, Moscow's advocate—mode: "President Kekkonen said that the Soviets have declared their plans openly and have committed themselves to them." Trying to be helpful, in his own "actively neutral" way, Kekkonen broached the possibility of bringing in the United Nations: "President Kekkonen said that possibly one way out would be for the United Nations to play a role in the solution. He had mentioned this to Brezhnev, who had agreed."[88]

At this point Kennedy began getting impatient again:

> President Kennedy said that when the Wall was built in Berlin, we had not interfered because we recognized that this was a matter of vital Soviet interest. The Soviets had the power, if they so wished, to sign a separate peace treaty, and to limit their objectives.
>
> He agreed that certain United Nations office could be set up in West Berlin, if this would help bring about a solution, but that he would not accept Soviet troops.[89]

Kekkonen tried to meet Kennedy's point. Perhaps Washington and Moscow were closer to a final resolution of the Berlin problem than the US president thought, as indeed would soon prove the case. President Kekkonen said that Brezhnev had used the phrase, "If the West had ingenious proposals the Soviet Union would always be prepared to consider them."[90]

And so the dialogue went on for some time in this vein: Kekkonen trying to show how "reasonable" Moscow really was, Kennedy disagreeing as politely as he could, while emphasizing American resolve.

And so it went for the remainder of the parley.

Finally JFK decided to bring the interesting, if somewhat frustrating—at least for him—conversation to an end. What the US president really wanted to know—what really mystified him—was why the expansionist-minded Soviets had acted so differently, or apparently differently vis-à-vis Finland:

> President Kennedy turned once again to the question of why President Kekkonen thought the Soviets had not used pressure to overthrow a free society in Finland on their own border when they [had] repeatedly gone to such efforts to expand throughout the world.
>
> He observed that with regard to Finland, the Soviets seemed to be following a purely nationalist rather than ideological line.[91]

And now, for a moment, the Finn dropped his guard: "President Kekkonen said that the case of Finland was a special one which Finland herself could not always understand. Ideological factors did not play a major role."[92]

Well, if Kekkonen himself did not understand, or fully understand That Man in Moscow, as the US press referred to Khrushchev, and what he wanted from Finland, how could he expect the American president to understand?

At any rate, JFK seems to have appreciated this final note of candor from his presidential guest. Perhaps he did not understand the Kremlin any better than he did before, but he better understood Finland's and its president's unique and excruciating predicament.

The next day, Kennedy told the press that he "had had a very fine talk with President Kekkonen."[93] It also was a very revealing one, both for Kennedy and Kekkonen scholars. Arthur Schlesinger summed it up in the unpublished, typewritten passage of his journal: "Kekkonen is a tough bald man, an old pro, self-contained and apparently sensible. JFK enjoyed the talk and it went on 40 minutes longer than scheduled."[94]

Urho Kaleva Kekkonen did, too. That the young American president, whom he had earlier underestimated, made a deep and lasting impression on him was clear from his stricken visage when he went on Finnish national television two years later to announce Kennedy's assassination on the evening of November 23, 1963.

But that then unimaginable event was still far into the future as the two leaders and their entourages wrapped up their first summit.

The next afternoon, October 17, 1961, Kekkonen had another conversation with Kennedy. Apparently that talk was not recorded.

He also had a lengthy meeting with Dean Rusk, the US secretary of state, for which the transcript also exists, in which the two went over more or less the same ground as Kennedy and Kekkonen had covered the prior day.

One gets the feeling that Kekkonen was somewhat bored with Rusk, who, after all, was not president. The fact is, the colorless if efficient career diplomat was, truth be told, somewhat boring.

The transcript of the interview between the two men reflects that. Kekkonen sounds bored. He is more forthright here, however. Less awed by Rusk, he also feels less need to dissemble, leading to a number of extraordinarily revealing and disquieting moments, two of which are worth recounting.

Perhaps the oddest and most revealing moment occurs when Kekkonen, unprompted, returns to the subject of the notional consumerist battlefront of the Cold War between the East and the West, the one he feared the Soviets was winning, and the impact the Soviets' progress in this area was supposedly having on his envious countrymen. Thus, after expressing appreciation for Rusk's concern about Soviet political pressure on his own country, Kekkonen confessed that:

> He sometimes thinks that the greatest internal danger for Finland lies in its inability to keep with the rate of progress in the standard of living in the USSR, which enhances the attraction of communism in his country. He said that although the standard of living in Finland is high there is currently nothing to fear, but with the [Soviets'] rate of progress the situation might be different ten or twenty years from now.[95]

How the Finnish president had managed to convince himself that living standards in the USSR had improved so rapidly as to endanger the future of capitalism on his side of the Finnish-Soviet border beggars belief. If anyone needed proof, or further proof, of how willfully blind Kekkonen was to the true state of affairs behind the Iron Curtain, here it was.

Less than a year later Soviet troops, acting on orders from the Kremlin, would fire on Russian workers demanding better living conditions and lower prices in the industrial city of Novocherkassk, murdering twenty-five and injuring eighty-five. And here, strangely, the putatively clear-eyed president of the one capitalistic country bordering the USSR with a manifestly better standard of living was worried that word of how well those same restive workers were supposedly doing would waft over the border and pose an "internal danger" to his comparatively deprived nation. The American foreign minister's startled and garbled riposte was just as strange:

> Secretary Rusk countered that he [was] not pessimistic about the ability of free world countries in this regard. He pointed to the rapid development [of the US] over the past forty years, citing as one example rural electrification and [the fact that] the US had added to its Gross Domestic Product since 1920 the equivalent of entire Soviet GDP.

"Some of the slogans of 19th century capitalism," Rusk pointed out to his guest, on a plaintive note, were still valid, including "private initiative."[96]

Another odd moment. Not that rural electrification, a landmark achievement of Franklin Delano Roosevelt's first term, was not a great achievement in its day, but one would have thought that Rusk had newer ammunition to counter Kekkonen's insipid comment.

At another point, while Rusk was discussing the Allies' difficulty in understanding why Moscow had suddenly gone nuke-mad, Kekkonen offered another insight into the method behind Khrushchev's nuclear madness which Harold Macmillan, the British prime minister, had conveyed to him during his visit to Great Britain the prior May.

The two leaders were discussing the threat of nuclear war at the time. According to Kekkonen, Macmillan remarked to Khrushchev that a nuclear war would mean the end of civilization. On the contrary, Khrushchev allegedly told the flabbergasted Brit, in the case of such a conflagration "large portions of Asia and Africa would not necessarily be destroyed."[97] Everything was relative in Khrushchev's world, nuclear holocaust included.

While they were on the subject of Brits and The Bomb, Kekkonen added that during Leonid Brezhnev's recent visit to Helsinki, the bearish Soviet official had also confided that Moscow was about to set off a fifty-megaton bomb large enough to destroy the entire United Kingdom—the very same Tsar Bomb that Khrushchev had just announced at the Communist Party of the Soviet Union Congress earlier that day.

So Kekkonen knew about the Tsar Bomb, too. What he did not know of course was when Moscow would actually detonate it.

Okay, but why? Rusk asked Kekkonen. What was the point behind the Kremlin's nuclear fixation? Evidently the latter responded, this was something that Moscow felt it had to do. Who knew? As Kekkonen had confessed the day before, he did not always understand the Soviets himself. Perhaps it had something to do with Berlin.

If nothing else, Kekkonen's story underscores the mad Strangelovian juncture humankind had reached in October 1961, just a year before production actually started on Stanley Kubrick's film *Dr. Strangelove, or How I Learned to Love the Bomb.*

The US Secretary of State concluded his somewhat fatuous dialogue with his distinguished Finnish guest with the anodyne observation that there were "no real issues between the US and the USSR and [that] only when the destinies of other countries became involved"—Berlin, for example—that friction arose. As far as Finnish-American relations were concerned, both men agreed, all was well.

Nevertheless Kekkonen had a serious point to add, one he hoped Washington would take to heart. Appearances notwithstanding, he said, Finland was "not selling its neutrality abroad, but was seeking the understanding of the greater powers." "Demonstrative support for that policy," he added, presciently, "would not be helpful."[98] Translation: we do not need America's arm around our shoulder.

When the Note Crisis hit two weeks later, and John Kennedy and Dean Rusk were deliberating the kind of support to offer the beset Finnish government in its moment of peril, as well as how to convey it, Rusk would understand what Kekkonen meant.

In the meantime, Nikita Khrushchev had given Kennedy, and Rusk, a lot to process with the nuclear-themed speech he gave in Moscow that very same day. On the one hand, regarding the issue of nuclear testing, the Soviet premier made it clear he was not backing down at all. Quite the contrary.

When it came to the Berlin crisis, however, the Soviet leader was now prepared to be more accommodating. "The western powers were showing more understanding of the situation," the Soviet premier told the delegates in the same marathon six-hour-long speech in which he unveiled the Tsar Bomb, "and were inclined to seek a solution to the German problem and the issue of West Berlin."[99] "If this were so," he continued, "we would not insist on signing a treaty absolutely before October 31st, 1961," the deadline he had earlier set.[100] Perhaps. The second Berlin crisis was suddenly over.

Still That Man in Moscow remained as maddening and mystifying as ever.

Thus ended Kekkonen's two-day-long exchange of views with the upper echelons of the Kennedy administration. Whether or not he provided as much insight into the Soviet mentality as Kennedy and Rusk had hoped for is debatable, however despite Kekkonen's strange belief that the USSR was winning the battle for the hearts and minds of not only the Russian people, but Finnish ones, too, he seems to have enhanced the Americans' understanding of and sympathy for Finland's unique geopolitical predicament, along with their recognition of Kekkonen himself as a formidable and canny player, if perhaps a somewhat blinkered one.

If it had not exactly been a meeting of minds, it certainly had been a meeting of friends, as the amiable joint communiqué issued at the end of the presidential guest's visitation made clear. No doubt there was some considerable gnashing of teeth in Moscow when Kekkonen's Soviet friends read it.

For the moment though, Kekkonen basked in the success of his visit. The lengthy tête-à-tête with Kennedy also enhanced Kekkonen's own regard and respect for Kennedy, whom he had earlier disparaged. "Of all the U.S. presidents he met, Kennedy was his favorite," says Jaakko Kalela, Kekkonen's future chief of staff.[101]

The two leaders would never meet again.

The Finnish head of state had still had one more engagement on the itinerary for his Washington visit, an appearance at the National Press Club the next day, October 17, one of the rites of passage for visiting heads of government. As is generally the case with high-ranking visitors to the half century old professional organization, Kekkonen did not try to make news with his deliberately low-key speech, nor did he wish to. However he did wish to make a few things clear.

Those in the audience for the Finnish leader's speech might well have recalled that the last Finnish official to speak at the club was Hjalmar Procopé, Finland's ambassador to Washington during World War II, including both the Winter War, which many if not most adult

Americans recalled, when the dashing Procopé was the toast of Washington; and the Continuation War, the war Americans wanted to forget, when the Finns were cobelligerents with the Germans, and culminated with Procopé being declared persona non grata and forced to leave Washington.[102]

There was no mention of Procopé and the Continuation War today in Kekkonen's address to the National Press Club. He had more important things to talk about. Taking place at the end of the first trip by a sitting Finnish president to Washington, DC, as well as at the renowned public forum, Kekkonen saw the address as nothing less than a mission statement for Finland, as well as his best chance to correct some of the impressions and misimpressions about Finland and its foreign policy circulating in the international press.

Kekkonen and his press secretary, Max Jakobson, considered the speech so important that they had began working on it months before in Helsinki. As Jukka Tarkka, Jakobson's biographer, recounts, the oration was a joint effort by the two men, with Jakobson creating the basic outline, and Kekkonen making a number of key additions and deletions. Kekkonen's key contribution, after considerable deliberation, was the passage that would become known, and celebrated, at least in Finland, as "the Finnish paradox." He wanted his address to include a sentence or catch phrase, as it were, which summed up Finland's hard-to-explain role, and existence, as the only democracy bordering the USSR, the same enigma that puzzled President Kennedy, as the latter confided during their meeting.

The answer was the Finnish paradox—the fact that the better Finland's relations were with Moscow, the better its relations could be with the West.

According to Jakobson, he also wanted to add a corollary sentence about how the greater the West's confidence in Finnish neutrality, the more improved its position would be vis-à-vis Moscow; however Kekkonen, ever aware of the political tightrope he was walking, particularly in relation to Moscow, scotched that. "Kekkonen rejected this statement of the obvious," writes Tarkka. "He wanted to say nothing that Moscow could interpret as a quest for western support against the Soviet Union."[103]

Tricky thing that Finnish neutrality. Kekkonen began by remarking about how surprised he was that his "little country," as American commentators also kept referring to it—a throwback to the days of the

Winter War, when Americans cheered for "Brave Little Finland"—had found itself on the front pages of again.[104]

Next he took his audience on a brief, if selective tour of Finnish history, including Finland's horrific experience during World War II and, pointedly excluding the Continuation War, the less glorious war that followed the glorious *Talvisota*, the debilitated image the country wound up having particularly in the West and how "few people in this country had much confidence in our ability to survive as an independent nation, not to mention the re-establishment of Finnish neutrality."[105] As Kekkonen proudly asserted, Finland *did* survive as an independent nation and fully functioning democracy, and Finnish neutrality *had* been reestablished, witness the success of his recent visits to both London and, now, Washington.

Moreover, if America and Britain had come to accept the course Finland had taken, so had Moscow, witness the 1948 Fenno-Soviet Treaty of Friendship Mutual Assistance and Cooperation. This time, unlike the day before, Kekkonen judiciously omitted mention of Article 2, the clause of that treaty Moscow would invoke thirteen days later, triggering the Note Crisis.

It was time to trot out the Finnish paradox. "Normally," Kekkonen observed, in fluent English, "it would seem that when in a border country between East and West, the influence of the Western world is on the increase, the influence of the East would correspondingly diminish.

> And in reverse, if the influence of the Eastern world grows, the West must retreat: Finland is one of the countries on the border of West and East. But in our case, the better we succeed in maintaining the confidence of the Soviet Union in Finland as a peaceful neighbor, the better are our opportunities for close co-operation with the countries of the Western world. For example, in 1955, the Porkkala base, leased to the Soviet Union by virtue of the Armistice Agreement of 1944, was returned to us.[106]

"Another example" of the putatively benign, "paradoxical," Fenno-Soviet relationship, Kekkonen continued, recalling his proudest foreign policy achievement to date, "is the fact that in 1960 Finland decided to associate herself with the European Free Trade Association." Left unsaid was the considerable effort Kekkonen had to go to get Moscow to acquiesce to the (now in doubt) EFTA milestone.

"But we have also found," the Finnish president self-confidently continued, "that when mutual confidence between Finland and the Soviet

Union for some reason is impaired and suspicions arise," Helsinki had to contract its relations with the West. Perhaps that was difficult for an outside observer viewing the Finnish scene from, say, Washington, or London to understand, but it made perfect sense when viewed from Helsinki.[107]

According to Kekkonen, all was basically well aboard the good ship *Finlandia* as she plowed the waves. All she asked for was some understanding of her "special" position. Regarding the health of Finnish democracy, "if anyone [had] doubts of the vitality of our democratic institutions," he added, in his sole reference to the current presidential campaign—the same one that his friends in Moscow would shortly throw a wrench into—"let him go to Finland to have a look at the vigorous presidential campaigning taking place there."[108]

One suspects that some of the members of the Finnish press in attendance might have raised their eyes at that remark. Although Olavi Honka, Kekkonen's opponent, was continuing to vigorously campaign, everyone knew—or at least Finns knew—that their esteemed president had thus far remained studiously aloof from the electoral business and had yet to deliver even a single speech.

According to Kekkonen, Finland was essentially just another peace-loving Nordic democracy: "Our political institutions, our legal system and social structure are similar to, and in some respects identical with those of the other Scandinavian nations."[109]

The speaker only mentioned the larger European security picture, including the Baltic region one that included the allegedly warmongering NATO members Norway and Denmark, which Moscow would soon cite as one of the reasons for the explosive demarche it would soon send whizzing in Helsinki's direction in passing:

> It is true that on the vital issue of security Scandinavia [is] divided: Norway, Denmark and Iceland are members of NATO, Sweden and Finland are neutral. But this does not prevent the foreign ministers of the five countries from meeting twice a year to exchange views.[110]

As far as Urho Kekkonen was concerned, all was well in his peaceable neighborhood including vis-a-vis the Neighbor to the East. And thus the Finnish guest of honor ended his speech to the National Press club to a round of appreciative applause.

As Max Jakobson recalls it, perhaps not so surprisingly, Kekkonen's address was an unalloyed success, with one journalist, Werner Imhoof from *Neue Zurcher Zeitung*, the leading daily of stalwart neutral Switzerland coming up to him afterward to congratulate him on this "breakthrough for Finnish foreign policy."

The write-up of the speech in *The New York Times* the following day by veteran reporter Russell Baker was respectful, if somewhat more underwhelmed. "The accent in public declarations during [Kekkonen's] visit has been mainly on Finnish neutrality," Baker wrote.

> President Kennedy has condoned and praised it and President Kekkonen, in his speech today, explained [that] neutrality [was] an imperative of Finnish national existence.
>
> Neutrality "is a way of solving our security problem," Mr. Kekkonen said. "It is not an ideological attitude."[111]
>
> However one described it, Kekkonen's tour of the New World was going swimmingly.
>
> So far.

Running alongside Baker's straightforward account of the speech in *The New York Times* was a surprisingly critical profile of "The Man in the News" section by the *Times* reporter who knew him and Finland best, Werner Wiskari. In many ways the detailed, Manichean picture that Wiskari drew of his subject resembled the mixed, if not unsympathetic one he had limned in his last profile of Kekkonen for his paper two years before, except that this time the borders between the lighter and darker areas were starker.

On the one hand, Wiskari made clear that the Finnish president was without peer as a master politician, as well as master of the Finnish political scene:

> Bald, nearly six feet tall and a most vigorous man of 61 years, he is generally recognized as the only powerful figure on Finland's splintered political scene, where eight parties squabble and bicker. Mr. Kekkonen, who is now near the end of his first six year term as President, after having been Premier five times, is accustomed to power.
>
> No one could look more a man of command than Mr. Kekkonen as he strides into a Finnish gathering, his heels biting the floor and his trim figure ramrod-straight.
>
> His manner of speech is hard-hitting, and his language, when directed at opponents of his Agrarian party, can be withering.[112]

On the other hand, as the reporter added, if Kekkonen was the most impressive figure on the Finnish political scene, he also was the most divisive in recent Finnish history.

> The first Finnish chief of state ever to see the New World while in office, he represents a country whose 793 miles of common frontier with the Soviet Union dictate a carefully neutral foreign policy. *He represents also a nation divided over himself for Finns cannot be neutral about him.* [author's italics].
>
> Charged by the Constitution with the conduct of Finnish foreign policy, the President is noted as a most flexible practitioner of what he deems possible. But his judgement, and the thinking behind it have been matters of sharp controversy.
>
> The Social Democrats and members of four other non-Communist parties agree with Mr. Kekkonen that, because of geography, Finland hopes to preserve her independence only through maintaining a relationship of friendship with the neighboring Russians. But they accuse the President of giving way too much to Moscow and of doing so with the aims of keeping his Agrarian Party [*sic*].[113]

The *Times*man did not pull any punches about the depths of the opposition to the Finnish leader. "So widespread is the hatred of him," he observed, in his only reference to the current presidential campaign, "and so strong the fear that he is playing a dangerous game that an unusual six party-drive is underway to defeat him in January's presidential elections." Nevertheless, despite the opposition to Kekkonen, Wiskari's money, so to speak, was on the current president.

"The betting here is that he will squeeze into office again with Communist support," he concluded.[114]

Chapter 13

The Great Healer (10/19–10/29/61)

> It is not for us to pass judgment or condemn. It is for us to diagnose and cure.
>
> —Urho Kekkonen's speech to the United Nations General Assembly, October 19, 1961
>
> In foreign policy, [Nikita Khrushchev's] grins in 1955, like his growls in 1961, have come with a suddenness and daring that bear the distinctive Khrushchev trademark.
>
> —Soviet scholar James Billington's psychological profile of Nikita Khrushchev, *The New York Times*, October 19, 1961

The following day, October 19, 1961, the first day of Urho Kekkonen's visit to New York, *The New York Times* devoted its lead editorial to its distinguished visitor. In contrast to Werner Wiskari's earlier somewhat mixed profile of the Finnish leader, there were no qualifiers in this piece, which invoked Americans' warmest memories of Finland, including the celebrated fact that of all the countries the United States assisted financially following World War I, she was the only one who paid her debt in full, and of course, the still vividly remembered Winter War:

> Finland is deeply admired in this country not only for the great contribution of Finnish immigrants to American life and civilization but, more specifically, for Finland's remarkable record of debt payment after World War I, when other countries were defaulting, and for her heroic fight against the Russian invaders in the Finnish-Soviet war of 1939–40.[1]

Skeptics aside, the paper insisted, Finland's post–World War II record, including dealing with its former enemy-now-turned-friend, was worthy of admiration, as well:

> No country has had more remarkable success in coping with problems growing out of the last war than Finland. She was saddled

> by defeat with heavy reparations to Russia and with nearly half a million refugees from territories seized by the Soviets.

"Yet," the paper's paean to Brave Little Finland, as she was called during the Winter War, continued, "little Finland in eight years marshaled more than a billion dollars of goods, services and money from war-shattered resources to meet external and internal obligations of wartime origin." Also, contrary to what some critics maintained, the *Times* insisted, Finnish democracy was no less robust than it had been before the war: "simultaneously [Finland] has been able to resist Russian intrigues and domestic Communist pressures and preserve her democratic political system."[2]

Even the much-maligned Fenno-Soviet "mutual assistance" treaty of 1948, the same one which Moscow would shortly invoke, triggering the Note Crisis, came in for praise:

> By accepting a limited mutual defense treaty with the USSR and maintaining a neutrality that contributes to Russia's frontier security, Finland has by now achieved a practical live-and-let-live basis of coexistence with her powerful Soviet neighbor.[3]

Withal, if Kekkonen wanted a ringing endorsement of *his* foreign policy here it was. The keys to the city, and to America's heart were once again Finland's, and his. Investors, too, were welcome:

> New York and the nation can welcome without reservations President Urho Kekkonen, who is in the United States on the first visit ever made here by a Finnish chief of state. He seeks no grants but would welcome normal trade credits. His mission is primarily one of goodwill; and this Americans accord with full measure to him and to his country.[4]

What a change ten months and Kekkonen's determined public relations campaign for his "new," active neutrality foreign policy had made.

That same day, October 19, 1961, Finland's eighth president addressed the United Nations General Assembly, the first Finnish head of state to do so since the country joined the world body in 1955, the year before he assumed the presidency, when Finland began to emerge from under the postwar Soviet umbrella.

Kekkonen's speech to the UN General Assembly was in the same conciliatory vein as his address to the National Press Club. If anything, it was slightly fuzzier, with a touch of grandiosity.

Finland's policy of neutrality, the president explained, was designed to "remove Finland from the realm of speculation." "Rather than judges," he said, somewhat obscurely, "we"—the Finnish people—"see ourselves as physicians."

Speculation? Whose speculation? What sort of speculation? Physicians? This was something new. "It is not for us to pass judgment or condemn," Kekkonen loftily asserted. "It is rather to diagnose and cure."

Fine, one could hear the puzzled delegates thinking to themselves. *Diagnose what?*[5]

Predictably Kekkonen avoided mentioning the more portentous ills the world was suffering from, namely the still festering Berlin crisis and Moscow's decidedly unhealthy, recently resumed atmospheric nuclear testing campaign. For the moment, the bespectacled six-foot-tall Finn just wanted it to be known that "Doc Finland" was on call.

Kekkonen's hear-no-evil, see-no-evil speech was greeted with perfunctory applause. It is not known whether the Soviet delegation joined in.

And so it went.

To be sure, by any measure, Kekkonen's trip to the New World *had* been a success. Not since the winter of 1939 had Finland enjoyed so much positive publicity on the other side of the Atlantic. Any hard feelings about the Continuation War or Finland's postwar cozying up to Moscow were forgotten as the jubilant Finnish president and his entourage continued their triumphant progress. Was Finland once again "America's sweetheart," as Christopher Isherwood, the British playwright, then living in Los Angeles, wrote in his diary during the Winter War. Not quite, but close.

In the meantime, *The New York Times* gave the Kekkonens' visit to the New York area the same scrupulous attention as it might accord a visiting high potentate. First, the paper reported, Kekkonen made the obligatory visit to the Empire State Building, "though the view was somewhat obscured by fog." His disappointment at the blocked view naturally lessened, however, after "Herbert R. Degnan, senior vice president of the Empire State Building, gave President Kekkonen a small silver replica of the building."

That afternoon, the Finnish head of state entertained a group of UN representatives at a luncheon at the posh St. Regis Hotel. Then the Kekkonens returned to their suite at the Waldorf Astoria Hotel, where New York State Governor Nelson Rockefeller and Senator Jacob Javits stopped by the famed, luxurious hostelry to pay their respects.[6] Then it was on to the mayor's residence, Gracie Mansion, where Mayor Robert Wagner presented Kekkonen with a gold medal. And so it went.

Over the next few days, the *Times* continued to report the Kekkonens' progress in almost clinical detail. Thus on October 22, the paper noted that the presidential couple made three stops in the Westchester-Connecticut area, including a visit with Kekkonen's friend, Samuel Pryor, the vice president of Pan American Airways, and his wife, in Greenwich, Connecticut, to "inspect an international collection of dolls," before crossing back into New York state to lunch at the Mount Vernon home of their son, Taneli, now a member of the Finnish UN delegation, and see their grandson Timo.[7]

Finally, on October 22, the Kekkonens were off for the remainder of their US tour. After the excitement surrounding Kekkonen's meeting with John F. Kennedy, and his heavily publicized visits to Washington and New York, the rest of his trip would, perforce, be somewhat anticlimactic—or at least was intended to be. According to the itinerary which the Finnish Foreign Ministry had carefully worked out, the plan was for the Kekkonens to tour the three central states with the largest populations of Finnish descent, Michigan, Minnesota, and Wisconsin, before continuing on to San Francisco.

Then the Kekkonens and their entourage, which included Ahti Karjalainen, who had been promoted foreign minister in June, Richard Seppälä, Helsinki's ambassador to Washington, and Max Jakobson, were scheduled to fly to Honolulu for a few days of rest and relaxation, where they were guests of Pryor, the aforementioned airline executive with the impressive doll collection.

Then the visitors were due to return to the mainland, for the final engagement of Kekkonen's US tour, a speech at the World Affairs Council in Los Angeles, on November 1, before finally returning to Finland, after wrapping up their three-week trip, by far the longest Kekkonen had undertaken thus far, with or without Sylvi.

That was the program.

And for the next week everything basically went according to program. Predictably, the attention the US press paid to the Kekkonens also trailed off, if not entirely. News of the Finns was harder to find now in the leading US newspapers, and that was just fine with the Finnish president. As much as the surprisingly intense coverage of his visit to the US, including his amiable meeting with Kennedy and the warm reception at the White House gratified him, it also likely made him nervous, and quite possibly was one of the factors behind the diplomatic missile the Kremlin was preparing to send his way, according to Max Jacobson's biographer, Jukka Tarkka. "The purpose of the note was to prevent Finland from distancing itself from the Soviet sphere in its quest for neutrality," Tarkka writes in his book about the hardworking Jakobson, who wrote no less than thirty-four speeches for his boss during for his North American tour. "Moscow felt that Kekkonen's trips to the West had significantly increased this risk."[8]

On October 22, *The New York Times* reported that the Kekkonens had flown to Detroit, Michigan, to kick off their tour of the Great Lakes region. Two days later, another bottom-of-the-page dispatch noted that the couple had stopped in Duluth.

In the meantime, while the Kekkonens were paying their respects to their émigré forebears in the upper reaches of the American Midwest, the two major international crises—the looming confrontation on the ground between the US and the USSR over Berlin, and the mushrooming one in the stratosphere between the two nuclear powers, continued to becloud the world's consciousness.

One could literally hear the two-part drumbeat to war every day in the *Times*, as Moscow ratcheted up tensions. To wit:

> **10/21 6 NATIONS IN U.N. BID SOVIET CANCEL 50-MEGATON TEST**
>
> Six countries in the direct path of Soviet fall out asked today that the General Assembly "solemnly appeal" to Moscow to abandon its plan to explode a fifty megaton nuclear bomb.[9]

The six aforementioned aggrieved countries were Denmark, Sweden, Norway, Iceland, Japan, and Pakistan. Significantly, if perhaps not surprisingly, Finland, the other Nordic country most directly in the path of the fallout from the new round of Soviet atmospheric nuclear tests opted not to join the appeal.

Thus Finnish self-censorship. Evidently this was one malady which Finland's UN delegation decided would be best to let its neighbors "diagnose and cure," in Kekkonen's words. It was one thing for the Finns to question the wisdom, or morality, of the USSR's decision to resume the poison-spewing tests, behind closed doors, as Kekkonen did (or claimed he did) with Leonid Brezhnev in September, before he left for the US. It was quite another for Finland to do so at the UN, even if it meant forsaking Kekkonen's vaunted Nordic unity. Active Neutrality, it seems, had its limits.

10/22 GILPATRIC WARNS U.S. CAN DESTROY ATOM AGGRESSOR

The United States is so strong and its power so well deployed that an aggressor making a sneak nuclear attack would invite self-destruction, an Administration spokesman said tonight. Roswell L. Gilpatric, Deputy Secretary of Defense, said the Government's confidence in its ability to deter Communist action or resist Communist blackmail was based on an appreciation of the military power of each side.[10]

The so-called missile gap that JFK had campaigned on—the belief that the USSR was more militarily powerful than the US was, the Kennedy administration now knew, was false. And Khrushchev knew that it knew, which only made him angrier and determined to prove that his country really *was* stronger and just as capable as ever of vanquishing the capitalist foe, as he boasted to the vociferously clapping delegates at the recent conclave of the Communist Party of the Soviet Union.

The next day it was the Berlin crisis, which had entered its most fraught phase, which took the most prominent place on the front page of the *Times* and the US press, after an American diplomat who was probing the recently walled up and fortified border between East and West Berlin was stopped by East German police, prompting an American response.

10/23 9 AMERICAN M.P.'S CROSS BERLIN LINE TO FREE OFFICIAL

Soldiers With Rifles Enforce Right of U.S. Diplomat to Enter City's East Zone

Tanks Support Move

Nine armed United States soldiers moved into East Berlin twice tonight to enforce the right of an American diplomat to enter the Communist-held sector. The diplomat had been stopped by East German border guards.

It was the first time armed United States troops had crossed into the Communist sector of Berlin during the current crisis.

In the meantime four M-48 tanks and two M-59 armored personnel carriers moved into position 500 yards south of the Friedrichstrasse checkpoint. It is the only crossing point available for passage into East Berlin by Western officials.[11]

Checkpoint Charlie, the site of the imminent confrontation between American and Soviet forces, was about to have its day in the bleak Cold War sun.

The next day, October 24, 1961, it was bombs away again, so to speak, as Moscow, disregarding its fallout-wary neighbors' appeal, sans mute Finland, went ahead and dropped the biggest bomb ever dropped above ground along with a smaller underwater device.

10/24 SOVIET FIRES RECORD BOMB OF 30–50 MEGATON RANGE; CLAIMS ANTI-MISSILE GAIN

2 Blasts in Arctic

One Test Under Water—U.S. Wary on Big Explosion's Force

The Soviet Union conducted the largest man-made explosion in history early today by detonating a thermonuclear bomb with a force equal to 30,000,000 or more tons of TNT.

Two hours after this atmospheric explosion, a small atomic device was detonated beneath the water, the first underwater Soviet explosion to be announced. Both explosions, the twenty second and twenty third by the Soviet Union since it resumed testing on September 1, were conducted in the vicinity of Novaya Zemlya, the Soviet testing ground between the Barents and Kara Seas.

The Soviet explosion was twice as large as any previously conducted by man since he unleashed the power of the atom nearly two decades ago.[12]

To illustrate the danger of the latest Soviet superbomb, the *Times* feature was accompanied by a large map of the world looking down on the North Pole, and the site of the latest Soviet test, including a band indicating the countries that would experience the initial fallout, showing that Finland would be first in line to be hit by the new wave of radioactivity.

The next day Moscow reaped the rhetorical whirlwind of the world's wrath.

10/25 SOVIET ASSAILED IN MANY NATIONS OVER SUPERBOMB

Reaction in Non-Communist is Bitter—Most of Red Bloc Unaware of Test

A storm of indignation, protest and condemnation swept the non-Communist world yesterday over the explosion Monday by the Soviet Union of the largest nuclear bomb ever tested. Only in the Communist world was there no public outcry against the fall out danger. . . .

Prime Minister Jawaharlal Nehru of India condemned the Soviet explosion as a "horrible thing" and a sign of "exhibitionism. . . . Such tests not only contaminate the atmosphere but pollute the hearts and minds of people everywhere."[13]

The Nordic countries, led by Halvard Lange, the Norwegian foreign minister—the same obstinate Norwegian whom Kekkonen had tried to bully on Moscow's behalf during his visit to Oslo earlier in the year—joined the storm of protest, the *Times* reported:

> Foreign Minister Halvard Lange of Norway said he had hoped world opinion would cause Premier Khrushchev to call off the explosion, "but we know he does not heed protests." In Stockholm Prime Minister Tage Erlander cabled an appeal to Premier Khrushchev to cancel further "horror" tests.[14]

Finns spoke up, too—at least their newspapers reportedly did: "Helsinki newspapers said the fall-out would reach Finland in a week and criticized the Russians' 'dangerous playing with life, health, and values,'" according to the *Times*.[15]

Meanwhile, in distant Minnesota, far removed from the terrestrial and stratospheric furies, the Kekkonens and entourage arrived in Duluth, the state's third largest city, on the shores of Lake Superior, for "two days of touring on the Minnesota iron range," as a small dispatch from the Associated Press on the bottom of page two recorded.[16]

Now it was the escalating Berlin crisis that took center stage in the news again, as Moscow decided to match the American show of force at Checkpoint Charlie with one of its own.

> **10/27 RUSSIAN TANKS GO INTO EAST BERLIN; U.S. SHOWS FORCE**
>
> 33 Vehicles Are Mile From Crossing Point Used by Americans
>
> Thirty three Soviet medium tanks, manned by Soviet troops, moved into the center of East Berlin tonight.
>
> It was a show of military power clearly calculated to counter the force displayed by the United States to assert the right of free entry into the Communist sector of the city.
>
> The tanks were manned by black-uniformed Soviet troops believed to be from the Twentieth Guards Division stationed near Berlin.
>
> The tanks were tentatively identified as T-54s, the latest-model Soviet medium tank, which mounts a long-barreled 100 millimeter gun. They were accompanied by jeeps and personnel carriers with troops.[17]

Meanwhile at the flashpoint crossing the US Army made a conspicuous show of arms for the third time in five days, as the *Times* reported:

> Just after 3 P.M., the [US] tanks rumbled up to the border, three of them right to the line on the Friedrichstrasse. Their engines were kept running and their guns were pointed straight down the street into East Berlin.[18]

Next, on Moscow's orders, ten of the hulking Soviet T-55 battle tanks rumbled up to the checkpoint, stopping just one hundred and fifty to three hundred feet away. The US tanks parked nearby turned back, stopping an equal distance from it on the American side of the boundary, their turrets pointed at the Soviets.

Was World War III about to break out? For the next two days it certainly looked like it. For sixteen fraught hours, between October 27 and 28, 1961, American and Soviet gunners faced each other, prepared for a Dodge City shootout. Both groups of tanks were loaded with live ammunition.

The alert levels of the American garrison in West Berlin, followed by the rest of the US armed forces including SAC, the Strategic Air Command, the nuclear-armed wing of the US Air Force, were subsequently raised to Defcon (Defense Condition) III, the highest level of readiness since World War II.

Both groups of tanks facing each other at Checkpoint Charlie had orders to fire on each other.

It was the closest that the fifteen-year-old cold war of nerves between East and West had come to a hot shooting war. And of course if that happened it was anyone's guess when those SAC B-52s forming up for their heavenly nuclear skirmish line started doing their thing, or their H-bomb armed Soviet Tupolev counterparts theirs.

Who, the world wondered, would blink first?

At the same time, on October 27, the high-flying Finnish president flew to San Francisco, where he delivered a speech on Finnish foreign policy to the Commonwealth Club, the noted public affairs forum.

All eyes, including those of most Finns—including presumably those of the Finnish presidential party—remained fixed on the Berlin showdown.

> **10/28 U.S. TANKS FACE SOVIET'S AT BERLIN CROSSING POINT**
>
> United States and Soviet tanks confronted each other for the first time. They were less than one hundred yards apart on the narrow Friedrichstrasse crossing point on the border between West and

East Berlin. As they remained in position with their guns pointing at each other, the situation was described by a responsible American source as fraught with danger.[19]

And then, suddenly after a hurried spate of phone calls between the White House and the Kremlin, and their respective minions in the field, it was over. With the aid of Georgi Bolshakov, a Soviet military intelligence officer working undercover as a journalist in Washington helping to expedite things, the US and Soviet leaders jointly agreed to reduce tensions and withdraw their respective forces.

This time it was President Kennedy who blinked first. With Bolshakov, the GRU (Main Intelligence Directorate) officer acting as intermediary, JFK agreed not to further push the issue of who could enter East Berlin provided that the Soviets removed their tanks from the scene first. And so they did.

Regarding the detested, two-month-old Wall which separated East and West Berlin, Kennedy remarked, “It’s not a very nice solution, but a wall is a hell of a lot better than a war.”[20] A year later, during the Cuban Missile Crisis, it would be the Soviet leader who would stand down but of course no one knew that then.

At any rate there would be no Dodge City shootout in Berlin, as readers of the *Times* read to their relief when they picked up their papers the following day, October 29.[21]

10/29 U.S. AND RUSSIANS PULL BACK TANKS FROM BERLIN LINE

Withdrawal from Crossing Point Cuts Tension After 16-Hour Confrontation

Soviet Units Go First

United States and Soviet tanks pulled back today from Berlin’s dividing line today after facing each other for 16 hours through a chilly, drizzly night.

They did not go far, but their withdrawal from the Friedrichstrasse crossing point on the border between West and East Berlin helped lower the tension caused by confrontation of the wartime allies. The Russians left first.[22]

That same day, as per his schedule, the Finnish president and his party flew to Honolulu for their putative vacation.

Once again, there was no mention of Finland or its president in the *Times*, not even a small bottom-of-the-page dispatch. Why should there be? Finland was no longer news, at least in the West.

That was about to change. Unbeknownst to the world, the Kremlin had decided to initiate a new crisis in its ongoing war of nerves with the West, one that did not involve troops or tanks, but which definitely involved nerves—especially Finnish, as well as American ones.

The previous day, Saturday October 28, 1961, Andrei Gromyko, the Soviet foreign minister, left a message with the Finnish embassy in Moscow that he wished Eero Wuori, the Finnish ambassador, to meet him at the Foreign Ministry, on Monday the thirtieth.

Nothing was mentioned about the purpose of the visit, other than that it was important.

That same day, Sunday the twenty-ninth, *The New York Times Magazine* coincidentally published a psychological profile of Nikita Khrushchev by noted Sovietologist James Billington. Entitled "Five Clues to the Khrushchev Riddle," the article purported to help readers better understand that mystifying Man in Moscow, and the motives behind his reckless behavior.[23]

In the article Billington pointed out that perhaps Khrushchev's apparently irrational obsession with Berlin perhaps was not so irrational at all when viewed in the context of the very real Russian Germanophobia that was the legacy of the wars Russia had fought over the years, particularly the horrific last one. "The choice of Berlin as the focal point for the present crisis has certain psychological as well as strategic advantages," the scholar pointed out.

"By clouding the real issues and manipulating Germanophobia, he can hope to arouse considerable popular support in Russia and other sections of Eastern Europe," Billington wrote"[24] Perhaps, there *was* a method to Khrushchev's madness after all.

At the same time, the Soviet leader's supposed dementia was also part of his method, according to Billington. "By turns a liberalizing and terrifying force," Khrushchev reveled in his unpredictability. "In foreign policy," the analyst wrote, "[Khruschev's] grins in 1955, like his growls in 1961, have come with a suddenness and daring that bear the distinctive Khrushchev trademark."[25]

Put another way, That Man in Moscow, as the ever-mystifying Soviet leader was known, *enjoyed* crises.

And evidently so he did, as the Western world, including his distressed Finnish neighbors discovered the next day. Nikita Khrushchev, it turns out, was just getting started.

CHAPTER 14

The Postman Always Rings Twice (10/30/61)

> This was the big one all right.
>
> —A British scientist's comment after the Soviet Union's fifty-megaton atmospheric nuclear test, October 31, 1961

> The Note Crisis hit the American embassy like a bomb.
>
> —James Ford Cooper

The front page of the *Times* of London on Monday, October 31, 1961, said it all.

> **RUSSIAN BOMB PUT AT OVER 50 MEGATONS**
>
> **BRITAIN DEPLORES LATEST ARCTIC TEST**
>
> **"WANTON DISREGARD OF HUMANITY"**
>
> The Russians yesterday exploded in the Arctic a nuclear device of at least 50 megatons, the biggest man-made explosion on record. The test took place in the Novaya Zemlya region.
>
> Western European recording centres began picking up shock waves soon after 8:30 a.m., GMT [Greenwich Mean Time], and some said it was two, three or even four times as great as last Monday's 30 megaton blast.
>
> After the shock had been recorded at Kew Observatory, an official said, "This was the big one all right."
>
> Asked about the reports, a Foreign Ministry spokesman in Moscow said: "We cannot say anything about it. No information."[1]

What was there to say? The latest mega explosion, to paraphrase Marshall McLuhan, was its own message. No further information was needed.[2] "A wide margin of uncertainty" indeed. That seems to have been one of the points of the latest Soviet horror.[3] What *was* the point? Perhaps that *was* the point.

Meanwhile, as a look at the adjoining column on the *Times* of London's front page revealed, Moscow had another surprise:

> **MOSCOW SHOCK FOR FINLAND**
>
> **TALKS ON GERMANY DEMANDED**
>
> **PACT INVOKED**
>
> The Soviet Foreign Minister, Mr. Gromyko, handed a note to the Finnish Ambassador in Moscow in which the Soviet Government proposes, "in view of the threat with which West Germany and the countries allied with West Germany, negotiations in accordance with the Soviet-Finnish pact of mutual friendship and assistance."[4]

Eero Wuori, the longtime Finnish minister, had already been ambassador to the USSR for six years. It is reasonable to presume that his meeting with Gromyko, the famously deadpan Soviet foreign minister, on the morning of October 30, the first day of the Note Crisis, as it soon became known, was the greatest shock of his tenure, if not his public life.

Once again, as it had three years before at the start of the Night Frost, the Kremlin had decided to drop the boom on Helsinki. And this one came with a nuclear blast wave.

> The Soviet Note calls the Finnish Government's attention to "increasing militarism in West Germany" and speaks in hard terms of Norwegian and Danish membership of NATO.[5]

Once again, as Khrushchev had done two years before at his supposed friend Urho Kekkonen's sixtieth birthday party, Norway and Denmark, the two Nordic NATO members, were denounced for participating in what Moscow claimed was the restoration of the military potential of West Germany.

Additionally, Moscow warned the two Scandinavian NATO members against establishing a joint command with the allegedly revanchist West German regime, as they had indicated they would do. "The realization of the plan to establish a joint command in any form whatsoever would signify a new step in subordinating the armed forces of the Scandinavian

NATO members of the revenge-seeking designs of West German militarism," the bellicose Soviet communiqué warned.[6]

Now, too, Finland's neutral neighbor, Sweden, which also happened to be one of Europe's largest arms manufacturers, also caught some of the Kremlin's buckshot, *The New York Times* noted:

> [The Soviet note] also refers to "Swedish indifference" towards German militarism, and mentions, among other things, deliveries of arms by Sweden to West Germany.[7]

Stockholm beware, the Kremlin knew all about those Bofors arms shipments the famous Swedish firm was making for West Germany.

As far as their Finnish neighbors were concerned, oddly, the only criticism the note contained for them, per se, sounded almost like an afterthought, confined to a paragraph near the end of the windy dispatch, wherein Moscow took to task "certain circles of the Finnish press . . . which actively supported the dangerous preparations of the NATO countries and thus contribute to whipping up war psychosis which is contrary to Finnish foreign policy."[8]

Technically the Finns themselves got off comparatively easy in the note. Nevertheless, the fact remained that it was the Finns to whom the weaponized demarche was directed, and it was they who were now being ordered to negotiate with Moscow on the basis of the putative West German military threat.

For better or worse, "little Finland" was back in the news in a big way. And so was Urho Kekkonen.

"The Finnish Foreign Ministry immediately informed President Kekkonen, who is at present in the United States," *The New York Times* noted. "The Soviet Note has come as a complete shock to Finland."[9]

And so it did to Finland's friends in the West, as well, particularly the American government. "The Note Crisis hit the American embassy like a bomb," writes James Ford Cooper, the former US deputy ambassador to Helsinki, in his trenchant memoir, *On the Finland Watch: An American Diplomat in Finland During the Cold War.*

The same could be said for the other Allied embassies in Helsinki, as they took in the explosive news.[10] One thing was clear: the two Soviet blasts, including both the epistolary and the nuclear ones, were definitely connected. The Soviet note was a clear political action "to the accompaniment of the big explosions," Halvard Lange, the outspoken

Norwegian foreign minister, then in Paris, noted drily to the *The New York Times*. "He said it had to be regarded in the framework of the entire international situation."[11]

The US State Department was in no doubt that the two events were insidiously connected too. "The USSR note to Finland is a typical effort by the Soviet Union to sow confusion and divert activities," the department noted in its first official statement about the crisis:[12]

> The explosion of the 50 megaton bomb in contempt of world opinion and the Soviet posture toward Germany and Berlin have made it abundantly clear that the Soviet Union is the source of the present world tension.

The by now familiar charges about German militarism were, rightly, dismissed as so much Soviet bombast. Although the West German Army, the *Bundeswehr*, did contain several former high-ranking Wehrmacht officers, contrary to the note's authors, the Bonn government had no designs on its neighbors.

"We find it repugnant that the Soviet Union should seek to involve Finland in its diversionary propaganda activities, especially in view of Finland's chosen policy of neutrality," the US communiqué ended.

At the White House John F. Kennedy, faced with yet another crisis, pondered how to respond.[13] Why Finland? Why now? Why, just as the Berlin crisis seemed to be winding down had Moscow decided to trigger another one, no less one involving Finland now?

C. L. Sulzberger, the former *New York Times* correspondent in Moscow, now its top Kremlinologist, also felt that the two explosions, as it were, were connected.[14] "Mr. Khrushchev is trying to frighten somebody with its ghastly superbombs, but it is not yet clear just whom," the analyst asserted on November 1.[15] "The Soviet Premier appears to be seeking some objective by his horror program. Something drove him to this ghastly step and we can only speculate what," Sulzberger continued. "Note the coincidence in timing: superbomb explosions, increasingly public rift with China, the final disgracing of Stalin, whose monument is now made an un-monument, *vicious new pressures on Finland* [author's italics], and preparations for a new party purge."

"Surely these events must be connected," the *Times*man declared.[16] But how?

In Washington Max Frankel, the newspaper's diplomatic correspondent, was also stumped. "The Soviet note to Finland, with its sweeping attacks on 'some quarters' in Finland, Sweden, Norway and Denmark [about] the West Germans and with its appeals to latent Scandinavian suspicion of the Germans," he wrote that same day, "was thought by officials here to be wild in substance."[17]

Frankel's British counterpart, the diplomatic correspondent of the *Times* of London, thought that the answer to what was really behind the verbal attack could be found in the fact that their Finnish friends had not accorded official recognition to Moscow's East German protectorate. "If she [Finland] could be induced to recognize East Germany and to sign the proposed peace treaty with Germany," the (unsigned) British correspondent speculated, "this could be some encouragement to a number of other neutral states to follow suit."

So that was it? Moscow wanted Helsinki to recognize the glorious GDR. But, if that was so, why was the Kremlin calling for military negotiations?

There were also rumors that Nikita Khrushchev was on the verge of starting a new purge.[18]

One thing was certain, wrote Frankel, as Western observers struggled to make sense of Moscow's *billet de boom*. "The Soviet Note was thought by officials here to be wild in substance but nonetheless accurately fired to cause a great deal of trouble."[19]

And so it did.

Evidently, if perhaps not so surprisingly, both journalists were so focused on analyzing the diplomatic missile Moscow had "fired" in the context of the larger, strategic European picture, and the "trouble" Moscow wished to cause for Germany and its Nordic friends and partners, that they overlooked the specific "trouble" or impact the Khrushchev and his cronies intended it to have on Finland.

Neither mentioned what was assuredly one of the "tactical" objectives of the note, if not its principal one: to ensure the reelection of its Finnish friend, Urho Kaleva Kekkonen. Or what was also almost certainly its corollary objective—to take the edge off Kekkonen's successful US tour, and remind him that Big Brother Nikita was watching.

One can be fairly sure that both objectives were on the minds of the Finnish president's visibly shocked entourage as they gathered on the beach at Maui to hear his press secretary's summary of the note, after he had been called to the phone by a lifeguard.

How shocked *was* Kekkonen by the note? In point of fact, if one looks closely at the aforementioned photograph, his expression can probably more accurately be described as one of chagrin.

Which, come to think of it, would actually make sense. What part of that chagrin was real and what part was acting? We shall never know for certain. However, it is fair to conclude that he wasn't particularly happy at that moment.

What *was* Urho Kekkonen's true reaction to the Soviet bombshell?

His journal, for which he recorded only several short entries during the twenty-four days he was traveling in Canada and the United States, as was his form when he was abroad, is not very helpful in this regard.

There is one interesting entry for October 15, his last day in Canada, in which Kekkonen writes about a function at the Soviet embassy in Ottawa that he attended the night after his first meeting with President Kennedy. In that notation Kekkonen recalls that at the party, at which a number of Soviet diplomats from other countries were present, the Soviet ambassador, Arnazasp Arutyunyan, had said to him, "It's good that you are here. You can make known Soviet foreign policy in the right way here."

To which Kekkonen replied, "But this"—promoting Soviet foreign policy—"is your business." "I heard later that my reply was passed around from man to man," he adds.[20]

Could Kekkonen's remark have helped trigger the note? Who knows? It certainly could not have pleased Moscow.

At any rate, there are no further entries until October 30, 1961, the day of Ambassador Wuori's fateful meeting with Andrei Gromyko in Moscow, on day 1 of the sudden crisis. "Soviet note to Finland about following the second article of the [1948] friendship agreement," the terse entry says.[21] Apparently Kekkonen was still processing the attack. Not so surprising: there was, after all, a lot to process.[22]

Meanwhile the Finnish government and he had an immediate decision to make: how were they to respond to the Soviet demand for negotiations, more specifically that the alleged threat from West Germany sufficiently serious to warrant consultations between the Russian and Finnish military establishments?

While Kekkonen was absorbing the explosive note, the perception of Finland in the West had already shifted—which presumably was *also* one of its objectives—from the "deeply admired" neutral nation and hero of the Winter War depicted in *The New York Times* editorial of October 19 to the newly captive nation of the present day.[23]

Now, to the considerable distress of Kekkonen and his advisors the Winter War was being cited in America not as the occasion of Brave Little Finland's heroic fight against the Russian invaders, but rather for the threatening communication that preceded it, as well as the other ones that Joseph Stalin sent the three, soon-to-be-swallowed Baltic states in the fall of 1939 during the run up to the *Talvisota*.

Thus, on November 1, the *Times* of London ominously declared in an editorial titled "Finnish Barometer":

> Putting pressure on Finland is a well tried Russian move in the battle of nerves. The latest Soviet Note is clearly intended to recall the precedents. In 1939 the demands that led to the Winter War came hard upon the dismemberment of Poland and the forcing of defense treaties on the Baltic States.[24]

That also corresponded with how the Swedish correspondent of the *Times* of London interpreted it. "The apparent ending of many years of calmness in Finnish-Russian relations and the fact that the other Scandinavian countries together with Germany are being made more or less scapegoats justifying the Russians in their Finnish move has created some alarm here," the British paper's correspondent reported from Stockholm.

> It is remembered that the Russian Note to Finland in 1939 also calling for Finnish sacrifices for the defence of Russia against a German threat was the first foreboding of grim years for the Scandinavian people.[25]

Needless to say, this was the last thing Kekkonen and his image-conscious press chief—no less the Finnish people—desired to read.

What exactly *was* Moscow trying to achieve with that troublesome missive?

What was its true objective? Or did it have more than one objective?

The latter, according to the aforementioned 1972 CIA report, which contains probably the most accurate, as well as succinct, analysis of the Note Crisis. "The note claimed that West Germany had become a danger to peace in Europe and that it was naive to assume that German ambitions could be kept under control without NATO." "The Soviet action caused alarm in Finland and throughout the West and was seen as a pretext for putting pressure on Finland," the report continues. "The Soviets probably had more than one objective," the anonymous authors continued, before discussing the "strategic" implications/ramifications of the note, especially in the context of the Berlin crisis:

> A series of Soviet threats had culminated in 1961 in an ultimatum that unless an all-German treaty was signed by the end of the year the Soviets would conclude a separate peace treaty with Germany. Both sides had engaged in military build-ups, and the building of the Berlin Wall in August 1961 sharply exacerbated tension.[26]

Of course, without interviewing the actual authors of the notorious dispatch, the CIA could only offer its most informed speculation about their motives; however, seven decades later its breakdown still sounds on the mark: "In preparing the demarche to Finland, the Soviets may have hoped that their note would impress the West with which they viewed the situation."[27]

At the same time, because the Berlin crisis had actually just been defused by the time Moscow fired it off, the authors discount that "strategic" objective as Khrushchev's primary motivation:

> By the time the note was handed to the Finns, however, Khrushchev had already begun to back away from his ultimatum [about forcing the West to sign a peace treaty with the GDR]. Khrushchev should have known that as he [and Kennedy] retreated, the situation would be defused and therefore, the note to the Finns would gain him little in terms of East-West confrontation.[28]

Hence the general bewilderment about the timing of the demarche: if Khrushchev intended the epistolary missile to strengthen his hand vis-à-vis the standoff over Berlin, it would have made more sense to launch it while those American and Soviet tanks were facing off on Checkpoint Charlie several days before, not afterward.

Which pointed towards the "tactical," Finnish-specific objectives of insuring Kekkonen's reelection, while simultaneously negating some of the positive publicity of his American tour, as most likely being uppermost in Khrushchev's mind when he signed off on the troublesome directive: in addition, and probably at least equally important, the USSR was probably concerned by Kekkonen's visit to the United States, fearing that the advancement of Finnish relations with the West would endanger the "special relationship" between Moscow and Helsinki.

Then, too, there was the Olavi Honka factor, and the fact that the reelection of Moscow's man in Helsinki, i.e., Urho Kaleva Kekkonen, was by no means assured: "Soviet trust in Finnish intentions had been further undermined by [Honka's] challenge to Kekkonen's leadership."[29] The only thing that was clear was that the issue of Finnish neutrality was now seriously in doubt. "Whatever its motivation," the CIA report continues, "the Soviet October 1961 note presented a serious challenge to Finland's embryonic neutrality" as well as to Urho Kekkonen himself."[30]

In the author's view, if the Night Frost created the basic template for Finland's relationship with the USSR from 1958 forward—as well as Kekkonen's relationship with Moscow, and what became the Kekkonen regency—the Note Crisis supplied the finish. Indeed, if one believes, as do many Finnish scholars and historians, that one of the principal "tactical" motives behind the Note in the first place—if not *the* principal motive—was to help ensure Kekkonen's reelection, as the aforementioned CIA report also suggests, it is not clear that firing that note was really necessary.

As Werner Wiskari, the most experienced Western correspondent in Helsinki noted in his profile of Kekkonen in *The New York Times* that he published on October 18, 1961, following Kekkonen's extraordinary meeting with Kennedy, "the betting" among informed circles in the capital was that, for all the charged emotions Kekkonen aroused among Finnish voters, he would nevertheless manage to "squeeze" into his second term on his own and without any direct Soviet pressure.[31] Wiskari's view coincides with that of Bernard Gufler, the current US ambassador to Finland.

> Thus, a month later, on November 16, Day 18 of the crisis, while the country was waiting to see whether Kekkonen's seemingly precipitate decision to dissolve the Parliament would appease Moscow, the envoy cabled Washington that in his opinion "[the] intention behind Soviet action may have included some small element of desire to help re-elect Kekkonen, *though difficult* [*to*] *believe in view his re-election almost certain* [author's italics]."[32]

In short, if the primary objective of the Soviets, who quite possibly *did* give Kekkonen some sort of head's up that they were thinking of invoking Article 2—witness his odd reference to it during his earlier meeting with Kennedy—*was* in fact to enable his reelection, the diplomatic cluster bomb that Gromyko handed the Finnish ambassador, Wuori, on October 30—was redundant.

At any rate, as Jukka Tarkka observes, "Whatever the background of the note it involved the most fundamental questions [regarding] Finnish foreign policy."[33] It also presented Kekkonen—and Finland—with a conundrum, as Tarkka succinctly puts it: "To [agree] to consultations would have implied acceptance of the Soviet view that West Germany had aggressive intentions. This would have [weakened] western faith in Finnish neutrality."[34]

On the other hand, he continues, "Finland could have responded too with a note disputing the existence of a threat. However such a response would have shifted the crisis onto Finnish-Soviet relations and Finland's eastern border would have become a segment of the Cold War exacerbated by the Berlin crisis."[35]

How Kekkonen resolved that conundrum, he knew, or must have known, would determine Finland's immediate geopolitical future, not to mention his own political one.

Little wonder that in that iconic photograph the Finnish leader looks surprised. As Tarkka notes, it is possible, if not indeed likely that Kekkonen expected some sort of support from Moscow for his election. After all in April he *had* reportedly discussed the possibility of dissolving parliament to help ensure such an outcome with his friends at the Soviet embassy, a move his "friends" are said to have supported.

But certainly not this!

Little wonder that he looked as flabbergasted as the rest of his entourage that day on Maui beach.

Doubtless he was.

"Kekkonen may well have expected *some* [author's italics] kind of support from Moscow but he was gravely surprised when it came in such heavy-handed form," Tarkka continues. "He was so enthusiastic about the success of his trip that he scarcely would have wanted to spoil his triumph by arranging a note to Finland that overnight [destroyed] the good will he had engendered."[36]

Meanwhile there was still a conundrum—and a crisis—to solve.

To be sure, the basic timeline of the roller-coaster, four-week-long crisis, is well known. The following abbreviated timeline, based on the one provided by Viktor Vladimirov, the top KGB man at the Soviet embassy, who witnessed in his 1993 memoir, *Näin se oli* (This is how it was), will suffice for the moment.

10/28 Soviet Foreign Minister Gromyko indicates that he wishes to meet Finnish ambassador Wuori.

10/30 Gromyko hands over the note.

11/1 UKK [Kekkonen] is informed [of note], but does not leave immediately. He sends [Ahti] Karjalainen back to Finland in his stead.

11/1 UKK gives a speech in the United States, and tries to calm everyone down, basically saying that even though it's a serious situation, it's important not to panic.

11/3 UKK returns to Finland.

11/5 UKK gives a TV and radio speech regarding his visit to the US and the note.

11/11 Foreign Minister Karjalainen meets Gromyko, who says that the note was brought about, by, among other things, a "serious" anti-Soviet political faction in Finland.

11/14 UKK dissolves the parliament [announces that] new elections are to be held in February, approximately the same time as the presidential elections.

11/17 UKK discusses Note with closest advisors. Military not invited.

11/18 Government proposes that UKK should meet with Khrushchev in person.

11/19 The USSR agrees to meeting between leaders.

11/22 UKK's train leaves for Moscow. To avoid the press he drives to another train station to get there.

11/23 The visibly nervous Finn arrives in Moscow, but seems to calm down after he meets with his friend, V. Kotov [Mikhail Kotov, former Helsinki KGB agent], before he is to meet with Khrushchev.

11/25 Communiqué confirms crisis has been resolved.

11/26 UKK gives a speech on TV and radio about the crisis.[37]

All this is well known, of course.

Meanwhile, feverish speculation about the Kremlin's true motivations in behind the Note continued, particularly among Finland's unsettled Scandinavian neighbors, which may in fact have been one of the reasons why the Kremlin sent it in the first place. In this respect, it could well be seen as a form of disinformation—or "fake news" in today's parlance.

"Soviet note appears to be seriously jarring Sweden, Norway and Denmark," an internal State Department memo continued. "Together with callous Soviet testing note may serve to bring home to Scandinavians fallacy of believing Soviets will leave Scandinavia [alone]." Just how shaken up those countries were could be seen in the headlines of some of their newspapers that week.[38]

Thus, from Denmark, came this weird editorial from *Det fri Aktuelt*, the Danish Social Democratic daily, suggesting that the 1948 treaty with which Moscow was now trying to "blackmail" Finland was no longer valid because it was, in effect, an antique:

> In Nordic opinion the Russian reasoning of the note is misrepresented and without basis in realities, although that in no way makes it less serious as a danger signal. The present Soviet government ought to consider that the agreement with which Moscow now tries to exploit as blackmail against Finland and us was forced upon Finland by [Soviet foreign minister Vyascheslav] Molotov during the highest period of power of the criminal Stalin.[39]

If Stalin was so discredited that Khrushchev could now order Uncle Joe's coffin's removal from Red Square, the Danish paper suggested, why not throw the 1948 treaty in with it?

Put that in your pipe!

In Norway, which shared a border with the USSR, and already had a tense relationship with Moscow, there was anger at the note. There the weaponized Soviet letter backfired, setting off a discussion about whether the government ought to revisit its standing policy about not allowing nuclear-armed US bombers to use Norwegian bases, as *Bergens Tidende*, Bergen's leading daily warned:

> In Norway it is recognized that respect for Finland is a condition, perhaps the most important, of our special policy on bases. A Soviet pressure against Finland might have the effect that our base policy must be revised.[40]

Across the border, in Sweden, *Stockholms-tidningen*, the Swedish Social Democratic daily, decided that the nuclear-tipped Note was really not meant for *any* of the Nordic countries, including Finland, but for West Germany:

> The connection between latest nuclear explosions and the new [Soviet] diplomatic offensive is obvious. Actually the note from Moscow is not aimed at Finland but at West Germany.[41]

Perhaps, to paraphrase Marshall McLuhan's famous saying, the mayhem the Note created *was* the message. It certainly shook up a lot of people in the neighborhood. One thing is certain: regardless of how much or how little advance warning Kekkonen had about the infamous Soviet note, he and his aides now had a very volatile and unpredictable crisis on his hands.

CHAPTER 15

Stay Calm and Carry On (11/1/–11/11/61)

> Foreign newsmen will be offended but I am again forced to tell them, don't sell the bearskin before the beast has fallen.
>
> —Urho Kekkonen in a speech to the nation in which he dismissed the importance of the Soviet note, November 5, 1961

> Finland decided today to send Foreign Minister Ahti K. Karjalainen to Moscow to ask what the Russians really had in mind in requesting defense consultations.
>
> —*The New York Times*, November 8, 1961

Having gotten over his initial shock at Moscow's troublesome epistolary gambit, Urho Kekkonen had decided that, whatever the Kremlin's intentions were, the Soviet note was definitely *not* meant for him. The note, he wrote in his journal on November 1, 1961, "is aimed more at NATO, Denmark and Norway than at Finland, which is only a post box for it."[1] Then again, as we know, Kekkonen was a man who was quite good at taking a blinkered view of things if the situation required. And the situation required.

The fact remained, however, that the Kremlin *was* insisting on military negotiations not with West Germany, nor Norway nor Sweden for that matter, but with Finland. In his journal, Kekkonen sounds resigned to the fact that some sort of negotiations with the USSR "may have to go through." He added, however, rather wishfully, "[they] probably will have no effect on Finnish neutrality."[2]

What was a hostage president to do? Withal, Kekkonen's reaction reminds one of Queen Wilhemina of the Netherlands' reaction after World War II broke out. "Act as if nothing will happen," she advised her nervous subjects in the fall of 1939, after Nazi Germany invaded Poland, "and nothing will happen."[3]

As we know, something *did* happen to the Dutch: the following spring Germany *did* invade the Netherlands.

And so, not a few Finns believed too during those nerve-racking weeks of November 1961. Perhaps Moscow was not necessarily planning to *invade* Finland again.

Nevertheless, something was definitely happening.

Meanwhile the Finnish president acted as if he didn't have a care in the world.

Another fascinating thing that emerges from reviewing the wide-ranging and diplomatic fallout from the Soviet note are the roles and viewpoints of several hitherto forgotten or overlooked players in the three-and-a-half-week-long drama. One of these is Bernard Gufler, the relatively clear-eyed US ambassador, who was Washington's eyes and ears in Helsinki during the crisis. Gufler's daily stream of detailed, well-written dispatches, including the reports of his meetings with the key Finnish dramatis personae, including Kekkonen and Ahti Karjalainen, his foreign minister, comprise a fascinating, relatively objective, if not entirely accurate, running commentary on the crisis.

Gufler, a career Foreign Service officer who had served as assistant chief of the US mission in West Berlin at the start of the Berlin crisis in 1958, before departing to become ambassador to Ceylon (as Sri Lanka was then called) had a particular perspective on the crisis. He was actually forced to leave the Berlin post by the Eisenhower administration because of what his superiors considered his strong anti-Soviet bias, quite something for an administration that was not known for being soft on Moscow to begin with.

The hardened anticommunist seems to have calmed down by time he was posted to Helsinki. Although he was not as hawkish as his predecessor, John Hickerson, he was not a great fan of Kekkonen, nor vice versa (Kekkonen later called him "an idiot").[4] Still, Gufler, who would remain ambassador for another year and a half, had already developed a strong affection for Finland and was clearly moved by its plight.

Another forgotten figure who emerges from these documents is Jaakko Hallama, the director general for political affairs of the Ministry of Foreign Affairs, who was then also serving as head of office for Karjalainen, the traveling foreign minister. Hallama, who later served as secretary of state during Kekkonen's second term (1962–67), and Finnish ambassador to Moscow during this third one (1967–70), unfortunately, is perhaps best remembered as the cuckolded husband of Anita Hallama, who later became Kekkonen's mistress. Meanwhile, his laudable and not inconsiderable role in the crisis, has been forgotten. If the Note Crisis has a forgotten hero, it may well be the cool-headed Hallama. As Gufler describes in his detailed dispatch of November 1, 1961, the third day of the affair, it was Hallama who advised Kekkonen not to panic and fly home but to proceed with his previously planned program—which is exactly what Kekkonen did.

As Gufler's dispatch makes clear, Moscow was keen for the Soviet demarche to be publicized as soon and as widely as possible, without regard for Finnish sensibilities.

Thus, from Gufler's telegram to the State Department of November 1:

> Called this morning on Hallama, Acting Secretary General of Foreign Office, who is in effect acting Foreign Minister. Hallama gave me the following information:
>
> [Soviet Foreign Minister Andrei] Gromyko delivered his note to the Finnish Ambassador in Moscow on Monday, saying it could be released to press Tuesday or Wednesday [as it was].[5]

As Gufler writes, Hallama, still reeling from the thunderbolt note, was cautiously optimistic, while not dismissing the seriousness of the situation.

> Hallama has not had time to think out implications [of the] note but believes it motivated by something more than mere desire accomplishment [of] Soviet aims in Finland. He thinks it part of over-all efforts Soviet Union. Now the note contains no strictures against Finland or its government and concentrates its main attacks on Germany, its NATO Allies with special attention to Scandinavia.[6]

As Gufler observes, Hallama discounted his concern, which may have been based on rumors the former had heard or was simply a figment of his imagination, that Moscow intended to invade Finland.

> Hallama does not think that Soviets now mean to push for an occupation of Finland or even for bases in Finland. He thinks that if something drastic with regard to Finland it would have been done suddenly when note presented.
>
> Hallama thinks Finland should go slowly and play for time, while showing enough activity to give Soviets feeling that matter

> not being taken lightly. He advised President Kekkonen by telephone not to return immediately but to carry on planned program.[7]

Instead, it was agreed that Karjalainen, the foreign minister, would return first.

Go slowly and play for time, the cool-headed Finnish diplomat advised.

Which basically describes the course of action the Finnish government took for the first ten days of the twenty-four-day crisis.

At the same time the clear-headed acting secretary of state, who understood that Helsinki could not play for time forever and would have to talk to Moscow, had gamed out how Kekkonen—or whomever was representing him in the eventual talks—ought best to respond:

> Hallama is convinced that Finland cannot refuse invitation [to] enter into conversations with Soviets or it must do so within framework of "policy of friendliness" . . . Hallama believes however that accepting invitation consult does not constitute automatic admission contentions of Soviet note. Finns will insist that their territory is not menaced and that Soviet Union is not menaced through Finnish territory.

Hallama was confident that although Finland could not dismiss the Soviets' contention that "war tension exist[ed] elsewhere," the country would able to thread the needle and emerge with its independence intact.[8]

November 2 (Day 4)

If Urho Kekkonen had been prostrated by Nikita Khrushchev's Halloween surprise, he did not look or sound like it when he touched down in Los Angeles on Tuesday evening, where the Kekkonens were once again given the VIP treatment. If New York could roll out the red carpet for the flying Finns, so could Los Angeles. The difference, of course, as anyone who read the papers knew, was that now Kekkonen and Finland were caught up in the crisis triggered by the Soviet note.

Sam Yorty, the recently elected mayor, greeted the Kekkonens as they stepped off their plane from Hawaii as a Finnish-American choir burst into song.

Once again, as in 1939, the eyes of America were on Finland. "I know you are representing the case of freedom," Yorty declared in his somber welcoming remarks.[9] Not to worry, scoffed Kekkonen. At the packed speech he gave next evening for the World Affairs Council at the Ambassador Hotel, the final engagement of his American tour, the Finnish president recalled the stout-hearted words of defense of Finnish democracy—and, implicitly, his stewardship of it—which he had tendered to the bearish Khrushchev a year before, on the occasion of the latter's uproarious visit to Helsinki for his sixtieth birthday party.

> **KEKKONEN CALM ON SOVIET'S MOVE**
>
> President Urho K. Kekkonen of Finland reaffirmed tonight his country's dedication to democracy. In a speech here he recalled that a year ago he had told Premier Khrushchev that "even if all the rest of Europe were to turn Communist, Finland would stand on her traditional northern democracy so long as the majority of our people want it."
>
> "With these words," Mr. Kekkonen said, "I wish to express my profound confidence in the strength of Finnish democracy and in Finland's freedom and independence."
>
> "Faith in the future of Finland is today as firm as it was then."[10]

Pretend as if nothing has happened, and nothing will happen, as Queen Wilhemina once put it.

Crisis? What crisis? There was nothing new about Article 2 according to the Finnish president: "As far as Finnish-Soviet relations are concerned," Kekkonen told his Fennophile listeners, "the proposal to have consultations does not introduce a new principle." At the same time, he conceded, "it reflects the very grave tension that exists in Europe."[11]

Go slowly, play for time.

As far as Urho Kekkonen was concerned, the US tour had been a great success. The shocking Soviet note took nothing away from that, or so he publicly claimed. Max Jakobson, who was busy running interference for his boss with the nosy American press, seconded Kekkonen's apparently nonchalant attitude. Thus, when an inquiring reporter asked him whether the president was concerned about the Soviet note the press aide airily replied, "Emperors never sleep badly," he jested, paraphrasing a remark attributed to Otto von Bismarck.[12]

Lo! Now his boss was an emperor!

At all events, he and Jakobson insisted, Finland was determined to go it alone.

The day before, as the Finnish leader wrote in his journal, he had received a telegram from President Kennedy about the developing crisis in which the latter underlined his regard for Finland. Sometime later, according to the diary, an American agent, possibly from the CIA—Kekkonen does not identify him—evidently came to his hotel in Los Angeles to get his response.

Kekkonen's aide-de-camp, Major Urpo Levo, who apparently received the American, asked how they should respond to the unexpected intercession.

His charge did not hesitate: "Levo asked [me] how he should reply to Kennedy, who has sent a man to ask how USA could help Finland in the matter of the note." Kekkonen's answer was short and to the polite: "thank him and respond: nothing."[13]

It was not the last time the White House would offer to help, as will be seen.

November 3 (Day 5)

Stay calm and carry on. That was the Finnish government's unspoken motto as the upbeat head of state returned to Helsinki the next day, November 3. One of the diplomats waiting to greet the Kekkonens at the airport was Aleksey Zakharov, the faithful Soviet ambassador. If the Finnish president had hard feelings toward his Soviet friends for turning his life upside down, he did not show it, according to *The New York Times*:

> He joked at the airport with Premier Martti Miettunen. He had smiles for other members of the Government and for the diplomats who had turned out to greet him—especially for Ambassador Aleksei Zakharov of the Soviet Union.
>
> There was no mention during the welcome ceremony of the Soviet note of last Monday.[14]

Unrecorded was how or whether Kekkonen greeted Gufler, the American ambassador, who had attended the October 16 meeting at the White House with President Kennedy and who also was one of the diplomats waiting to greet the Finnish president.

Meanwhile an angry Max Jakobson let loose on the US press about how it had depicted the new Fenno-Soviet affair in Winter War terms. "Mr. Jakobson said he had been stunned by 'the wild speculation in the press in the United States' over what would happen to Finland now."[15] Jakobson was just doing his job, as Tarkka, his biographer, writes: "Jakobson did his utmost to show that there was no crisis and [that] everything would work out in complete accord. He insisted that the Finns were taking the crisis calmly."

Of course, Jakobson, "knew, as everyone else did, that people were worried."[16]

So was the rest of the Finnish government as the US ambassador noted in the distinctly downbeat cable he sent the State Department following his meeting that morning with Ahti Karjalainen.

> Called on Foreign Minister this morning. He thanked me most cordially for warm reception and hospitality he and President had enjoyed in the US. With reference to Soviet note, he made the following remarks:
>
> The Soviet note came as a great shock but more shock than surprise as some Finns have feared Soviet action of that sort.[17]

The government was still deliberating how to respond to the note, Karjalainen told Gufler. Finland's top diplomat admitted that his government did not have any idea what Khrushchev wanted. The Finnish government had "no idea at the moment what [the] Soviets intend to demand from it," the sympathetic American envoy wrote.

Mum was the word at the Soviet embassy. Evidently Ambassador Zakharov and his colleagues were happy to keep Kekkonen and Karjalainen in suspense about the endgame.

Did that explain Zakharov's Cheshire Cat–like grin at the airport when he greeted Kekkonen?

Meanwhile Kekkonen, exhausted from the long trip and the new crisis, was temporarily incommunicado. In his conversation with Gufler, Karjalainen, the disconsolate foreign minister, conceded that the premise of the note, that the USSR was actually threatened by West Germany, was absurd: "Finland does not feel it is menaced by NATO and does not accept the premises of Soviet note [Kekkonen told Gufler]. It does not feel menaced by West Germany either." Karjalainen had spoken to the president the previous night, he told the jowly, fifty-eight-year-old envoy. Kekkonen "is keeping cool and optimistic," he maintained. "He hopes that President's optimism will be justified," Karjalainen, clearly in a funk himself, added.[18]

Moved by the Finnish official's distress, the American tried to buoy him up. "I remarked that, as he could see from reception Finnish party had received in America, the American people have a genuine liking for Finland and the US wants nothing but a genuine maintenance of its neutrality." At this point, according to Gufler, Karjalainen "sighed and said with real feeling, 'that is exactly what we want to maintain.'"[19]

Meanwhile, just as they had twenty years before during the tense run-up to the Winter War, a pack of scoop-hungry Western journalists had descended on the Finnish capital to cover the recrudescent Fenno-Soviet tensions. Once again, the Foreign Ministry's press department found itself giving briefings for them at Helsinki's most famous hotel, the venerable Hotel Kämp. There, however, Jakobson and his colleagues stressed, the similarity with 1939 stopped. "Journalists seeking Winter War atmosphere looked for it in vain," writes Tarkka.[20] For one thing, Jakobson took pains to point out, Finland had made no preparations for military preparations.

This was partly true. The fact was, as Tarkka also notes, "[Finnish] defense forces [did] prepare for military consultations. However, Kekkonen kept them at arm's length."[21]

November 4 (Day 6)

For his part, Olavi Honka, the president's opponent in the upcoming election, and his backers, were still carrying on. In that respect, the Soviet disinformation campaign had not been effective in gagging Finnish democracy—yet, according to *The New York Times*:

> **FINNISH CAMPAIGN REMAINS INTENSE**
>
> Kekkonen Enemies Keep Up Pressure to Defeat Him
>
> The bitterly fought Presidential campaign is continuing without a let-up as Finland awaits the mutual defense consultations requested by the Soviet Union.
>
> Regardless of what the Soviet move portend—most Finns believe the outlook is not threatening—there has been no change in the campaign to defeat President Urho Kekkonen.[22]

Although Kekkonen continued to remain mute, his backers, including V. J. Sukselainen, the disgraced former premier, who had managed to retain chairmanship of the Agrarian League despite his forced resignation because of the Kela housing scandal, did not.

> Former Premier Veino J. Sukselainen, chairman of the Agrarian Party [*sic*], denounced the President's foes today as so blinded by hatred that they could not see the national interest.
>
> Olavi Honka, Dr. Kekkonen's rival candidate, was campaigning near by. Mr. Honka, who emphasizes that he is seeking to unite the Finns, does not attack the President.

> But his chief sponsors have been saying that the Soviet note smashes the Agrarian "myth" that the President gets along well with the Russians, [and] that he alone can protect Finland.
>
> It is widely believed that the consultations will strengthen the President's chances for re-election if they go well, but damage them if Finland's independence should be threatened.[23]

Would there actually be consultations? *Would* they go well?

Who knew?

Once again, this was a moment for the resolute Finns to use their vaunted *sisu*, the peculiar Finnish word that roughly translated as grit. At any rate, if one of the tactical objectives of the Soviet summons was to cause domestic political mayhem for the Finns, it certainly had achieved that.

Ad interim, the psychological shrapnel from the note was still ricocheting around the diplomatic community, as Ambassador Gufler confirmed in a cable he sent Washington that day, after a conversation he had had with the French ambassador. "French ambassador expressed to me opinion on following lines: main motivation Soviet note [was] desire to make absolutely certain Kekkonen [was reelected] president by frightening Finnish public and then permitting Kekkonen to 'save' Finland," he wrote.[24]

Which, of course, is exactly what happened.

The US diplomat disagreed with the precognizant Frenchman, however: "French embassy views are out of line with other information received by the embassy, although some opponents of Kekkonen are circulating similar stories about Kekkonen's alleged advance knowledge of Soviet intention to act and Soviet intention to use the note to assist his re-election."[25]

What "information" was fake, and what was real? *Who knew?*

Day 7 (November 5)

Now Kekkonen and his advisors decided that it was time for him to step out of the shadows for the sake of the country's morale, as well as his reelection campaign.

And so the Finnish leader did in a dramatic radio and television address to the nation. The ostensible purpose of the address was to discuss his lengthy trip. After all, he had been away for twenty-four days, the longest trip of his presidency.

And yes, there was the matter of The Note, as the Finnish press was beginning to call it.

It did not really mean a thing, he assured his worried audience:

> **KEKKONEN HOLDS NOTE IS NO PERIL**
>
> Says Soviet Bid for Parley Respects Finns' Neutrality
>
> President Urho K. Kekkonen told Finland tonight that a recent Soviet request for defense talks did not herald the slightest danger to Finnish independence or neutrality.
>
> In a confident and often angry speech, which included a bid for re-election, he stressed that the Soviet note, delivered last Monday, had reiterated Moscow's recognition of Finnish neutrality.[26]

Kekkonen himself sounded anything but calm on the subject of the scaremongering foreign press. This was no Night Frost, he assured his listeners—just a cold snap, if that.

> He spoke in especially sarcastic tones in dismissing the additional speculation that the Soviet Union was about to demand bases on Finnish soil and that Finland could expect pressure for some kind of shift in government.

"Foreign newspaper men will be offended," Kekkonen seethed, referring to some of the "vultures" (as some Finns called them) of the foreign press who were congregated around town seemingly waiting and hoping for a replay of 1939, "but I am again forced to tell them, don't sell the bearskin before the beast has fallen."[27]

The cause of Finnish neutrality had been his life's work he, asserted. "If I see that I am not succeeding in this task," the head of state said with no little emotion, "then I shall leave my office to those who think they have better possibilities."[28]

Then the aroused speaker, his hubris showing, proceeded to take a distinctly unpresidential swipe at his opponent, Olavi Honka: "Without naming him, the President dismissed Mr. Honka as 'a political dilettante' and said times were too grave for Finland to be entrusted to such a man."

Kekkonen added that Finland's reply to the Soviet note had not yet been determined. Still to be decided was whether "the threat of an armed attack" actually existed.[29]

Perhaps Moscow would forget about the whole thing!

The next day the Finnish press generally praised the president's performance, particularly his passionate reassertion of Finnish neutrality. At the same time, several took him to task for his surprising and unpresidential attack on his opponent.

Meanwhile, the fact remained, Kekkonen still needed to figure a way to answer the note.

Day 8 (November 6)

Finally, on November 6, 1961, more than a week after the incendiary summons had been delivered, Zakharov, the Soviet ambassador, decided it was time to break the ice and pay a visit to Karjalainen, the seemingly omnipresent foreign minister, according to *The New York Times*.

> **RUSSIAN AND FINN CONVERSE ON NOTE**
>
> Direct contacts between the Finns and the Russians have begun over the Soviet Union's request for defense consultations.
>
> Aleksei V. Zakharov, the Soviet ambassador, called this afternoon on Foreign Minister Ahti K. Karjalainen. Their conversation was described as general and preliminary in nature. . . .
>
> It was reported that the Finns did not expect to dispute openly the view expressed in the Soviet Note that West Germany and its allies posed a threat of war. The Finns, it was said, plan only to indicate they do not consider the situation quite so grave and then listen to what the Russians propose.[30]

Days 9–10 (November 7–8)

Things began moving now.

Slowly.

Evidently the conversation between Karjalainen and Zakharov was an amicable one. However, after all, Zakharov was only ambassador. It was not clear whether the Soviet envoy knew what Moscow really wanted from the Finns. Nor would he presume to speak for Moscow (at least in this case). According to Tarkka, Zakharov also privately assured Jakobson that the demarche was a gambit to insure Kekkonen's reelection.

But *was* it? The Kremlin's demand for military negotiations, as per Article 2 of the 1948 treaty, was on record. Further clarification about the matter, it seems, would have to come from the Kremlin itself.

It was agreed: Karjalainen would go to Moscow to clarify things.

For his part, Eero Wuori, the understandably frazzled Finnish ambassador to Moscow, who had since returned to Helsinki, was sure what the ultimate result of The Note would be. The shaken envoy, who Andrei Gromyko had handed the slow-fused diplomatic bombshell two long weeks before on October 30, setting off the crisis, was "extremely pessimistic," according to Tarkka. "He said that consultations were unavoidable [and] that the Soviet Union would probably have to be granted bases and even that Finnish radar surveillance might have to be merged with Soviet airspace control."[31]

Fortunately for the Finnish government, Wuori's pessimistic augury did not leak.

Meanwhile, in America the crisis was still big news in *The New York Times*, along with the rest of the US press:

> **FINNISH FOREIGN CHIEF TO DISCUSS NOTE IN MOSCOW**
>
> Will Explore Soviet Request for Defense Consultations
>
> Finland decided today to send Foreign Minister Ahti K. Karjalainen to Moscow to ask what the Russians really had in mind in requesting defense consultations.
>
> This decision, the Foreign Ministry said, has the effect of postponing a Finnish reply to the Soviet note, which was delivered Oct. 30.
>
> Although Mr. Karjalainen is ready to leave, he is not expected to depart before Thursday. Today and tomorrow are Soviet holidays. His mission was described as exploratory. He would have to seek instructions from Helsinki, it was said, before he could agree to consultations.[32]

The wheels of diplomacy were turning.

Slowly.

Of course Helsinki regarded the note as serious, Max Jakobson, continuing to hold the line, while maintaining the government's basic line said, at his latest briefing at the Hotel Kämp. "Any note that talks of the threat of war could not be a lighthearted matter," he said, according to *The New York Times*.

> However, Mr. Jakobson cautioned against regarding the note as "a Soviet attack on Finland's position." He said this was a "basic fallacy" that had caused a recent wave of "scare stories" in the world's press about Finland's fate.[33]

Fake news!

The next day, November 8, it was announced that the Soviet foreign minister, Gromyko, had agreed to receive Karjalainen, his Finnish counterpart, for "exploratory talks" in Moscow three days hence, on Saturday, November 11.[34]

Apparently there was no rush. Karjalainen, it was announced, would be leaving for the Soviet Union on Friday morning by train. Accompanying him would be his cool-headed top aide, Jaakko Hallama.

"Mr. Vuori [*sic*] the Finnish ambassador in Moscow is expected to be present at the discussions."[35]

CHAPTER 16

In the Shadow of the Note (11/14–11/21/61)

> President Kekkonen's decision to dissolve the Finnish Parliament and call for new elections indicates that a political crisis has arisen in Finland in the wake of last Saturday's talks between the Finnish and Soviet Foreign Ministers.
>
> —*The New York Times*, November 15, 1961
>
> Finns are faced with disturbing puzzle by enigmatic Soviet statement that "if proper political guarantees [are offered] military consultations may be avoided." As late as yesterday afternoon [Jaakko Hallama] made further unsuccessful efforts to obtain definition.
>
> —US ambassador Bernard Gufler, cable sent to Washington, November 15, 1961

November 14 (Day 16)

In the event, as we know, Andrei Gromyko made it clear to Ahti Karjalainen during their meeting at the Kremlin on November 11, 1961, that the time for playing for time was over. As the Finnish government announced, somewhat belatedly, the Monday following Karjalainen's return after it had digested the flying diplomat's electric report, "the Soviet government would like assurance as quickly as possible that the present foreign policy of Finland will continue." "And," the statement continued, "that nothing will prevent the development of friendly relations between Finland and the Soviet Union."[1]

Anyway, it was time for Urho Kekkonen to provide such "assurance" by putting the plan for dissolving the parliament, the same plan he had allegedly discussed with Aleksey Zakharov in April, when he and the Soviets began worrying about his reelection, into action, as the *Times* of London reported:

> **RUSSIA WARNING TO FINLAND**
>
> **SWIFT ASSURANCE DEMANDED OF FOREIGN POLICY**
>
> **PARLIAMENT DISSOLVED IN HELSINKI**
>
> A Russian statement that military consultations between Finland and Russia might be avoided if Finland could give a swift assurance that its foreign policy will remain unchanged was made at the recent meeting in Moscow of the two countries' Foreign Ministers it was revealed today by the Finnish Government.
>
> Publication of a statement on the Moscow meeting was followed by the dissolution of Parliament by President Kekkonen, who referred to "increased international tension."[2]

As noted earlier, whether or not Urho Kekkonen and the Kremlin had a firm understanding that he would take this dramatic step, or had merely discussed it, is somewhat unclear.[3]

Anyway, it was done. The wheels of politics were turning faster now. Too fast, for some Finns:

> Publication of details of Mr. Karjalainen's and Mr. Gromyko's talks caused activity in Finnish political circles which received the news if not with shock than with astonishment.

Nevertheless the government denied that anything untoward had occurred:

> To a question about the speed of the timetable, a Foreign Ministry spokesman replied: 'I would not call it an emergency.'[4]

The prime minister, Martti Miettunen, who had the thankless assignment of announcing the dissolution of parliament, did not sound very happy when he spoke to the nation about the shock move. Clearly his speech was as addressed as much to Moscow as it was to the Finnish people:

> In a grave voice, Mr. Mieuttenen [*sic*] tonight spoke to the nation on radio and television. He said it was possible that northern Europe could not in the future enjoy the role of bystander as before.

> The decision to have premature general elections is taken in order to safeguard Finland's position in case the international situation gets worse.[5]

The Finnish government might not consider the situation a crisis, but the Swedish government did, or at least appeared to do so, according to an article on the same page of the British newspaper:

> **SWEDISH READINESS FOR WAR**
>
> Within 24 hours essential military forces can be organized in different parts of the country, and within a few days the main part can be mobilized, Mr. Erlander, the Prime Minister, said in Riksdag [Swedish parliament] today in response to a question about Swedish military readiness.

The Swedes were not taking any chances, Tage Erlander, the Swedish prime minister, confirmed: "He also said that there were detailed plans for the evacuation of the Government in the event of war."[6]

November 15 (Day 17)

Back in Helsinki, the Finnish government had no plans to evacuate—or if it did it was not publicizing them—however, according to *The New York Times,* the Social Democratic backers of Olavi Honka, Kekkonen's opponent, had taken the hint and were discussing having him exit the race:

> **SOVIET MOVE SEEN AS AID TO KEKKONEN**
>
> The Finnish Presidential race appeared substantially altered today in President Urho Kekkonen's favor.
>
> With the Soviet position being interpreted as a demand for the re-election of President Kekkonen, leading sponsors of the candidacy of Olavi Honka from five parties met tonight to consider the prospects.
>
> There was some sentiment for ending the drive on behalf of Dr. Honka.[7]

President Kekkonen, who had dismissed the garrulous, bowtie-wearing jurist as a "dilettante," had no problem with this sentiment, as the terse entry in his diary for November 15 reveals: "Hakala," he notes, referring to Jaakko Hakala, the veteran editor-in-chief of *Aamulehti,* the

Tampere-based daily, and prominent Conservative politician, "informed [Kalle] Kaihari—a businessman who was a friend of Kekkonen—"that Honka would was withdrawing his candidacy today."[8]

The writer was jumping the gun somewhat here. In the event, the supposedly "dilettantish" ex-judge, who was clearly enjoying the fight, resisted taking the hint and did not give up his candidacy for another nine days. Still, just the fact that Honka's resignation was now on the table underscored how serious the situation had become. For its part, the *Times* had no qualms about terming the situation a crisis, as per its editorial that day:

CRISIS IN FINLAND

President Kekkonen's decision to dissolve the Finnish Parliament and call for new elections indicates that a political crisis has arisen in the wake of last Saturday's talks between the Finnish and Soviet Foreign Ministers.

So far as is known Mr. Gromyko made no explicit demand for Soviet military bases in Finland or for the stationing of Soviet troops there, possibilities implicit in the original Soviet note two and a half weeks ago.

But the hard fact is that after Finland's President received his Foreign Minister's report about the Moscow conversation he decided that a new Parliament must be elected soon because the present international situation demands decisions that cannot wait.[9]

"That statement," according to *The New York Times*, "cannot help but arouse grave anxiety for the future among the Finnish people and among Finland's friends abroad." The paper continued, "The memories of what happened to Finland after a not-dissimilar sequence of events in 1939," referring to the run-up to the Winter War, when the Finns engaged in a series of frustrating conversations with the Soviets that culminated with a Soviet invasion, "will not lessen this anxiety," it continued.[10]

Despite the fast-moving developments, most Finns, while understandably anxious about the crisis, seemed to be keeping their nerve.

FINLAND STUDYING MOVE

Finnish political circles today began a calm study of the new political picture caused by yesterday's drastic movements which culminated in President Kekkonen's decision to dissolve Parliament.

> The parliamentary parties held meetings today discussing the new situation but the Government had no extra session.
>
> Members of the Government were meeting tonight, which is the normal procedure.[11]

"The general feeling in Finnish political circles," concurred the *Times* of London, "is that nothing new is to be expected—at least not during the next few days."[12] Of course, the issue of meeting the Russian military for consultations, as the original communiqué of October 30 demanded, remained unresolved.

Urho Kekkonen himself seemed to be calm, or relatively calm, at least on the evidence of his journal. "Press reaction has been quite calm," the president wrote on the evening of November 15.[13]

In point of fact, the clips from the Finnish newspapers Kekkonen included in his journal sounded anything but:

> "HS [*Helsingin Sanomat*]: If the Agrarian League's leadership had previously taken a position on other democratic parties in an understanding and factual manner, the current situation would scarcely have been reached.

Anyway it is clear why the president was "calm," as it is known that he had been privately planning to dissolve the parliament for months ever since he and Karjalainen first secretly broached the notion with the Soviet embassy six months before.

Perhaps, as Kekkonen evidently hoped, his Soviet friends, mollified by the aforementioned "drastic movements," including the dissolution of the *eduskunta*, would wait until the duly scheduled election in three months before bringing any more pressure to bear.

One could always hope.

November 16–17 (Day 19–20)

'Twas not to be.

Next, as we know, all hell broke loose. No, dissolving parliament would not cut it for the Politburo. The request for military consultations with the Finns still stood, according to the message that Vasili Kuznetsov, the deputy Soviet foreign minister, handed to Wuori, the jittery Finnish ambassador, who had since returned to his lonely post at the Finnish embassy in Moscow.

Moreover, the Soviets were no longer asking for consultations. They were insisting on them.

> **SOVIETS BIDS FINNS DISCUSS DEFENSE IN MOSCOW "SOON"**
>
> Parley to Meet Bonn Threat Termed "Unavoidable"—Timing Is Stepped Up
>
> The Soviet Union wants Finland to send a delegation to Moscow "as soon as possible" for mutual defense talks. Such discussions were said by the Russians to be "exceedingly unavoidable."[14]

Although the Berlin crisis had been resolved, or apparently resolved, to Moscow's satisfaction, the supposedly dire threat posed by the putatively revanchist West German government, the requisite condition for invoking the dread Article 2 of the 1948 Fenno-Soviet Treaty, had not been removed.

On the contrary, according to Moscow.

As proof, the next Soviet note—for this, above all, was an affair of notes—cited the current visit to Norway of Franz Josef Strauss, the West German defense minister, to discuss the joint command that Germany and Denmark reportedly had in the works, as well as possible joint maneuvers.

All these things poised "*an immediate threat to Soviet and Finnish security* [author's italics]," according to Kuznetsov.[15]

Now Moscow was referring to its security and supposedly neutral Finland's security as the same quantity. *That* was certainly new.

In any event, time was up: Nikita Khrushchev and his comrades were insisting on having those dread talks.

To be sure, this second note was just as maddeningly worded as the first one. It also contained an out or possible out for the beset Finns.

The Politburo was insisting on bilateral talks now.

On the other hand, the new Russian ukase also declared that "if proper political guarantees are given military consultations may [be] avoided."

What exactly did *that* mean? "The Finns have been jolted several times in recent weeks by demands from Moscow," Werner Wiskari wrote in *The New York Times*. "They have reacted calmly, clinging stubbornly to an optimistic outlook, but uneasiness has grown."[16]

It certainly sounded that way in the telegram that Ambassador Bernard Gufler sent Washington that afternoon.

Even the steady-as-she-goes Jaakko Hallama, the Finnish secretary of state, seemed to be losing his head now.

For one, the Finnish embassy in Moscow was having difficulty getting its act together the US envoy cabled: "Saw Hallama this morning. He was greatly disturbed that Finnish Embassy Moscow leaked to press news of Wuori's call on [the deputy foreign minister] Kuznetsov and that information had become known to public with bad results even before it reached the Finnish government."

Even though Kekkonen had, presumably, already planned to dissolve the parliament in order to appease Moscow, Gufler reported, the move had not worked:

> President and Foreign Minister both deeply shocked by latest Soviet action. President apparently fears that calling of elections done too hastily. He had apparently decided before Soviet note [to do] some such thing and grasped at this already prepared action as possibly beneficial in situation created by note.[17]

At any rate, if indeed there had been a prearranged script between Kekkonen and the Kremlin, by continuing to press for negotiations, the Kremlin was now revising it.

And, the stressed out Hallama told Gufler, the fact that it did so was proof that the rumors that the putative crisis was a game, and that his boss, Kekkonen, was in on "the game," were false:

> Hallama feels latest Soviet action should disprove unfair rumors that have had wide circulation that Kekkonen in any way leagued with Soviets or tied to them by secret agreements.
>
> Hallama was also annoyed that Olavi Honka and his obtuse Social Democratic backers hadn't taken the hint, withdrawn his candidacy and rallied around The President.
>
> He believes that it is high time for other parties to rally around Kekkonen and for Honka to withdraw his Presidential candidacy.[18]

Finland's hour of decision had clearly arrived. Or had it?

As Gufler also notes, the Soviet note renewing its request—make that demand now—for talks with Helsinki, also included a possible and puzzling out exit ramp for Helsinki: "Finns are faced with disturbing puzzle by enigmatic Soviet statement that 'if proper political guarantees military consultations may [be] avoided.'"

Apparently Zakharov, the reliably helpful Soviet ambassador, was not being very helpful this time in decrypting his superiors' message:

> As late as yesterday afternoon, Hallama made further unsuccessful efforts [to] obtain [clarification of Moscow's terms] from Zakharov. Zakharov implied that it was up to Finland to [clarify] terms and to offer guarantees which Moscow would define as acceptable or unacceptable only after they were offered.[19]

November 18–19 (Days 20–21)

"Finns are faced with disturbing puzzle by enigmatic Soviet statement," wrote Gufler.[20] There was that familiar word–enigmatic.

In October, 1939, shortly before the Winter War, that celebrated Kremlin watcher and Soviet critic Winston Churchill famously described the Soviet Union as a "riddle wrapped in a mystery inside an enigma."

Now once again, after supposedly achieving a successful live-and-let-existence with the Soviet bear, Finland had, once again, ran headlong into that enigma.

Who best to solve it? Who else? Little mystery there, as the headline of the *Times* of London on the November 19, the twenty-first day of the greatest crisis in postwar Finnish history, announced:

> **DR. KEKKONEN TO VISIT RUSSIA THIS WEEK**
>
> Siberia Talk With Mr. Khrushchev
>
> President Kekkonen of Finland is to meet Mr. Khrushchev [in] Novosibirsk Siberia, on Friday to discuss the Soviet request for negotiations under the 1948 mutual assistance pact.[21]

It had all happened quickly. The day before, the eighteenth, the Finnish cabinet, acting on Kekkonen's own hasty request after getting the word from his envoy, Wuori, that this was the best and indeed only means of resolving the situation, had met and decided to ask Kekkonen if he would go to Moscow to meet Khrushchev to talk things over.

Khrushchev, unsurprisingly, had agreed. Somewhat less graciously, however, the Soviet premier declared that he would not meet his Finnish friend in Moscow, but in Siberia, where he was on a tour of Soviet agricultural communes. The top Red agreed to interrupt his tour in order to see his erstwhile Finnish friend, however if the latter wished to meet him he would need to make the three-thousand-mile trek by plane then train to come to him.

Not a problem, the obliging Finnish president signaled. So it was set: the two leaders were to meet in Novosibirsk on Thursday, November 23. The exact location was not clear.

So be it, Kekkonen resolved. If the mountain would not come to Muhammad, then, just as he had done two years before when he had voyaged to Leningrad to meet Khrushchev to resolve the Night Frost—once again, he, "Muhammad" Kekkonen, would journey to the Soviet mountain. Except that this time the "mountain" was several thousand miles further away.

In the meantime, while he was contemplating his pilgrimage to Siberia, the Finnish president had some time to kill. The following day, November 19th, the now visibly anxious Finnish politician gave a campaign speech in the east central city of Jyväskylä.

It was an odd campaign speech. Part report, part confessional, the address began on a straightforward note, as Kekkonen explained the moves he had made thus far to avoid the military negotiations the Soviets were demanding.

"When word came that the conversation between Foreign Ministers Karjalainen and Gromyko had included a hint of the possibility that military negotiations might be avoided if assurance could be quickly given that the present friendly foreign policy would continue," Kekkonen explained, "the Finnish Government had three alternatives:

> Either we could accept the proposal and begin military negotiations or deny the existence of any threat of war and refuse to enter any talks. Or the third choice was to dissolve Parliament so that we could obtain as quickly as possible the answer to the question whether we [could] continue a friendly policy [towards= the Soviet Union] or not. The Government chose the last alternative.

Unfortunately, the speaker conceded, that strategy "does not appear to have brought the hoped for result." As Kuznetsov, the deputy Soviet foreign minister, had told Wuori: "tension had increased so much in the Northern European Soviet region that an immediate threat to Finnish and Soviet security existed."[22] Consequently, "the Soviet government had come to the conclusion that speedy negotiations were unavoidable."

As he later admitted, the next passage of his speech was as much for Moscow's benefit as for his immediate Finnish audience, as Kekkonen launched into something of a diatribe against West Germany and its insensitive Norwegian and Danish NATO allies, especially Strauss, Bonn's defense minister, who was visiting Oslo at the time.

"Here we are," he declared. "I have no knowledge of what [West German Defense] Minister Strauss has done in Norway—scarcely anything extraordinary," Kekkonen declaimed. "But," he vented, "the mere visit at a time when we live in the shadow of the note is an unbelievable disservice to us."[23]

In the shadow of the note. A melodramatic phrase and an apt one. To be sure, if one were making a film about the Note Crisis of 1961, that would make as good a title as any.

In closing, the visibly discomfited head of state asked his fellow citizens in Jyväskylä to have faith as he steered through the ship of state through the diplomatic rapids: "We do not know what tomorrow will bring. If I am asked now what must be done, I would say we must preserve our presence of mind and remain calm."

"I am strongly confident that we can continue our policy of neutrality," Kekkonen asserted. "But," he continued, growing emotional again, "this requires recognition of the facts, or in other words, a national realism and unanimity on this point. Defiance and fanaticism are now a national peril [author's italics]."[24]

Whose defiance exactly was Kekkonen alluding to? The Social Democrats? The press? Who were these fanatics he was referring to? His bête noire, Väinö Tanner? Kari Suomalainen, the impish cartoonist? The shaken president did not say.

Ad interim, on the information warfare front, Moscow continued to press the attack. Thus, the balderdash expounded by the so-called Soviet Information Bureau that same day: "Who can now guarantee that West German nuclear rockets will not fly to Northern Europe and Scandinavia?"[25] *Nuclear rockets?* Since when did the West Germans have nuclear rockets?

"By forcing the Scandinavian countries into military cooperation with themselves, the leaders in Bonn are making an area of international tension and a nest of potential war conflict."[26]

Forcing the Scandinavian countries into military cooperation with themselves?[27]

In the West, speculation continued about who Moscow was really trying to scare, Finland's supposedly hapless Scandinavian neighbors who had been "forced into military cooperation with themselves," or just Finland, or the West in general, or all three.

There was no comment from Finland's Nordic neighbors, on which Helsinki had enforced "an enjoinder of silence," as noted American journalist Don Cook wrote in *The New Republic.* "The conviction now deepened in Scandinavia, which had been enjoined by the Finns to pursue a policy of unprovocative silence—that [Moscow's objective] was strategic and not political."[28] *Stay worried* was the message from Moscow—or one of them, according to Cook.

Sweden was certainly worried, he confirmed:

> Sweden, almost more scared than Finland and protecting its policy of unalterable neutrality at every opportunity, [continued to] put its armed forces on semi-alert status, shifted some units into strategic areas, and kept men in barracks while also distributing civil defense instructions.[29]

In the meantime, Moscow was still insisting on those military negotiations with Helsinki, as the new Soviet agit-prop machine continued its rolling barrage of disinformation.

November 20–21/Days 23–24

One thing was certain: Kekkonen and Khrushchev would have a lot to talk about when they finally met in faraway Novosobirsk. At the same time, unbeknownst to the world, the Kennedy administration wanted to make sure that Kekkonen knew that he did not walk alone . . .

Chapter 17

The Mission (11/21–11/25/61)

> On the eve of your departure for Novosibirsk I am sending you this private message so that you may in be in no doubt of the position of the United States.
>
> —Secret message John F. Kennedy dispatched to Urho Kekkonen before he left for Siberia

> [Kekkonen] had obviously lost weight and his skin looked slightly yellow. He aroused [a] feeling of sympathy for [a] sorely tried man, who though he made mistakes, is nevertheless trying to do what is best for his country.
>
> —US ambassador Bernard Gufler's report following his meeting with Kekkonen on November 21, 1961

Flash forward forty-eight hours to the afternoon of November 21, 1961, the day before Urho Kaleva Kekkonen was due to set out on his historic journey. That afternoon Bernard Gufler, the US ambassador to Finland, set off on a secret mission of his own. In the diplomat's pocket was a confidential message from President John F. Kennedy.

The message, the culmination of a memo from Dean Rusk, the American secretary of state, to JFK before it was dispatched to the US chancery in Helsinki under his name, signaled nothing less than a break with America's long established, hands-off policy vis-à-vis Finland, as enunciated by Dean Acheson, Harry Truman's secretary of state, a decade before, in 1950. "It would be most dangerous at the present time to make any efforts in the direction of Finland that would produce a reaction on the part of the Russians," Acheson wrote at the time.[1]

As we know, President Truman basically followed that hands-off policy toward Finland. So did his successor, Dwight D. Eisenhower and his hawkish secretary of state, John Foster Dulles, even though it was not popular at the State Department, or with the confrontation-minded ambassador to Finland, John Hickerson, who had urged Washington to challenge Moscow during the Night Frost.

So, it will be recalled, had Gerald Smith, the US assistant secretary for policy planning at the time, who had endorsed Hickerson's fervent plea for Washington to get more actively involved in backing the beset Karl-August Fagerholm's government, or else risk "losing the game" over Finland, as Hickerson put it. "The [Finnish] situation presents a good case of Western ability in assisting a free nation to withstand Soviet political and economic pressures," Smith wrote in his memo of October 23, 1958.[2] "It is also a test of [our] ability to move swiftly when the occasion requires. If we and our allies cannot or do not meet these in the psychologically important case of Finland, we must recognize that there are serious limitations in our ability to compete with the USSR in the cold war."

Secretary Dulles, however, had rejected Hickerson's and Smith's arguments. He, too, refused to open another front over Finland—not because he had any philosophical objection to doing so. Finland, it seemed was just too far away. Furthermore, Washington had too many other fronts or potential fronts with Moscow to worry about—Berlin. for example. For better or worse, as much as the top US diplomat and some of his hawkish colleagues in Washington would have preferred otherwise, the Finns would have to protect their neutrality and fend off the Communist threat without significant US support, beyond the limited economic and moral aid Washington had continued to provide Finland, and which Finland had chosen to accept since it opted out of the Marshall Plan after World War II.[3]

Now, on the eve of Kekkonen's Hail Mary trip to Siberia to resolve the Note Crisis, Kennedy's aggressive secretary of state, Dean Rusk, acting on the advice and consent of Gerald Smith and his other Fennophile colleagues at the US State Department, which was even more belligerent than that of his predecessor, Eisenhower, had decided that a change of course in American policy toward Finland was urgently in order, as Secretary Rusk noted in the memo he forwarded under his name to the White House on November 20.

First, Rusk urged, JFK had to send a message to Kekkonen *pronto*, before Kekkonen set off for Siberia: "The first and most pressing action recommended is a message from you to President Kekkonen," he urged. "President Kekkonen is meeting Premier Khrushchev in Novosibirsk on November 24 and will be leaving Helsinki on November 22 or November 23. *Therefore the message should be transmitted today, November 20th* [author's italics]."[4]

The days of regarding the Finnish-Soviet "problem" as an isolated affair were over, wrote Rusk. It was time to view Europe's northeastern corner as an active latest front in the Cold War, and one which necessitated a public, more active role for the United States. "If we continue to maintain a hands-off position," Rusk urged the president, "the Soviets are likely to achieve a good portion of their objectives."

"Thus," the fighting memo continued, "we believe it is necessary to accept a confrontation with the Soviets in Finland, despite all the advantages the USSR possesses in that area."

That line bears repeating: "*thus we believe it is necessary to accept a confrontation with the Soviets in Finland* [author's italics]." It was not necessary to go to war for the Finns, Rusk cautioned, if only because the Soviets themselves did not appear prepared to go to war with the Finns, at least as yet. Rusk felt, however, that the United States ought to be prepared to fight for the Finns, and alongside the Finns in every other way: "This would involve a readiness to assist Finland in the political, economic and propaganda spheres. We believe the Soviets are unlikely in the Finnish context alone to resort to military force."[5]

Put another way, if the USSR was willing to wage a hybrid war over its presumptive Finnish protectorate, as it would be called today, so was the US.

What about the recipient of Kennedy's message of support, the man in the middle of this imminent battle between East and West over Suomi, President Urho Kaleva Kekkonen? What was the intended effect of this message on *him?*

To encourage him of course. "The message to President Kekkonen is intended to strengthen his internal fortitude prior to his meeting with Khrushchev. While he has shown himself in our view overly pliable in the past in relations with the USSR, there seems to be no alternative but to place reliance in the first instance upon him," Rusk continued.[6]

Pliable. There was that word again. Put simply, Kekkonen might be too spineless for Rusk's taste; however at the moment he was all the Free World had.

Was it arrogant, as well as somewhat naive, for Kennedy and Rusk to presume that either Kekkonen or the Finnish people actually *wanted* the US to get more involved in the "game" with Moscow over Finland's future? No doubt. But that was the way Kennedy, Rusk, as well as many if not all Americans viewed the world at the start of the 1960s.

JFK had said as much in his inaugural address in January of that year, "Let every nation know, whether it wishes us well or ill," the thirty-fifth president had declared, "that we shall bear any burden, meet any hardship, support any friend, oppose any foe, in order to insure the survival and the success of liberty."[7] Now, Rusk was urging Kennedy to make good on that vow for our Finnish friends and support *them* and oppose the Soviet foe in order to insure the survival and success of *their* liberty.

And so on the afternoon of November 21, 1961, as had been arranged, Ambassador Gufler drove the five mile long distance from the US embassy to the presidential mansion, Tamminiemi, in order deliver Kennedy's staunch of support to his Finnish counterpart.

The instructions from the State Department regarding Gufler's subrosa visit, as well as how he was to handle JFK's telegram were straight out of the annals of spy craft: "Message should be conveyed orally and written communication not left," they stated. "Approach should be made inconspicuously. We wish to avoid public knowledge that American ambassador saw President immediately before his departure to meet Khrushchev."

Anxious not to make Kekkonen's job harder than it already was, as well as appreciative of his earlier stated wish to Rusk that the US downplay its support in case of such a contingency that the Finnish head of state had conveyed during their meeting the month before, the State Department emphasized that Gufler's visit was not to be publicized in any manner: "Should press learn of your meeting suggest you say only you called to obtain President Kekkonen's views. You should agree with Kekkonen beforehand on the line to be followed with press in case of queries or leaks."[8]

Kennedy's extraordinary telegram merits quoting at length. The US chief executive began by underlining the *entres nous* nature of his telegram:

> On the eve of your departure for Novosibirsk I am sending you this private message so that you may be in no doubt of the position of the United States. It will receive no publicity whatsoever, for I am mindful of your desire not to be embarrassed by public comments which might be misconstrued as infringements on Finnish neutrality.[9]

After reiterating his respect for Finnish neutrality as the basis for the American position on Finland, JFK also signaled that there had been an important change in that position. Now, in line with his new decision to be willing to confront Moscow over its pressure on of Finland, the

White House was also ratcheting up the pressure on Kekkonen: "You will appreciate that our concern in this matter derives not only from our great interest in the welfare of your country. We have placed on ourselves a solemn obligation to respect that neutrality at all times and in all ways."

"In our own national interest," the most remarkable line of Kennedy's message continued, "we have to expect that Finland will in fact be truly neutral."[10] That sentence, at once conveying the essence of the new American policy towards Finland *and* how that policy related to US security—*and* Washington's expectations of the accommodationist Kekkonen, whom it clearly did not entirely trust, merits analyzing.

"*In our own national interest*. . . ." Maintaining Finnish neutrality was now a matter of America's national interest, as well as that of the Free World. Kennedy had said something along the same lines in his meeting with his Finnish counterpart several weeks before when he said, in so many words, that America's fight was Finland's fight.

Now he reversed the equation, and made it explicit: Finland's fight was now America's fight. Consequently "*we have to expect that Finland will in fact be truly neutral* [author's italics]."

Message to Urho Kekkonen: buck up. The United States is depending on you. And so is the Free World.

Perhaps inevitably there was a reference to 1939, which no doubt grated on Kekkonen, as Gufler continued to read aloud from JFK's cable: "I realize the doubts and anxieties which you and the Finnish people are now suffering as the memories of 1939 return to you." Not to worry, the envoy continued, as his host listened, while the translator from the Foreign Ministry interpreted Kennedy's words for him, America had Finland's back.

Washington was not going to abide another Night Frost on his watch, not if he had anything to do about it:

> I want to assure you of the readiness of my country to give Finland our political and economic support in the event of economic pressure against Finland designed to secure political compliance. We are prepared, when opportune, to speak out firmly on behalf of Finland's security and independence.

The US would even be willing to take up Finland's cause in the United Nations, Kennedy declared: "We would be willing to carry to the United Nations actions seeming to threaten your country's independence, depriving you of the right to follow your own chosen course of neutrality."[11] All Kekkonen had to do was to say the word and Adlai Stevenson II, the plain-spoken former governor and two-time Democratic candidate for president whom Kennedy had chosen to be his ambassador to the United Nations, would take up Finland's cause in the Security Council.[12]

Kennedy's sub-rosa telegram ended on an upbeat note: "I am sure that the unity of all patriotic Finns, irrespective of their party when their country is threatened," the US envoy continued, as he paused for his chief's words to be translated, "is a source of strength underlying Finland's resolve to determine its own destiny."[13] Gufler finished delivering the secret message and waited for his host to respond.

Judging from the long cable Gufler sent to Washington that evening, Kekkonen's lengthy response to Kennedy's portentous message was gracious and well-considered. For someone who was under enormous pressure from both East and West, the Finnish leader seems to have been extremely calm when he replied via his interpreter.

One can imagine the maelstrom of emotions that the besieged Finnish president felt as the American envoy read Kennedy's note, or counternote, with its vow to publicly stand up for Finland, along with Kennedy's and his secretary of state's evident belief that he needed bucking up before he met his Russian friend.

There was nothing emotional about Kekkonen's reply, however. Nor is there any indication that he took offense at the White House's evident lack of confidence in him. Indeed, if one were looking for material proof that Kekkonen was equal to the grave moment he and the Finnish nation were facing his carefully worded reply to JFK will suffice. It was only after Kekkonen finished speaking, and Gufler took a hard look at the somewhat wan and shaken man facing him that the American ambassador wondered whether that was actually the case.

The gist of Kekkonen's response, like the earlier response he had given Kennedy three weeks before in Los Angeles after Moscow first sent its heat-seeking missive his way, can be captured in four words: thanks, but no thanks.

First, the Finnish president wished to express his gratitude for the lengths to which Kennedy had kept things under wraps. Actually, things were not quite as serious as Washington feared, the former noted with a trace of irritation, unable to resist several digs at the foreign press, with its dark invocations of 1939:

> I am very grateful for this expression of President Kennedy's consideration. I am also appreciative of the fact that this is just between us, because if the press were to get wind of your message my position in upcoming talk would be seriously damaged.
>
> As I said in my speech Sunday [in Jyväskylä] I will leave [for the USSR] with grave thoughts. We Finns are concerned about outcome of talks, but I do not personally believe that the situation is as serious as President Kennedy thinks. Perhaps some of the press speculation about Finland's difficulties may have influenced him.[14]

Next, read Gufler's memo, came Kekkonen's frank situation report, including the motives behind the steps he had taken thus far to pacify Moscow, and the admission of his failure to do so, at least thus far. "All Finns [*sic*] actions taken since receipt of note have had one aim in which we have not been not been successful. We want to avoid military discussions according to Article II of the 1948 treaty, because that would be tantamount to agreeing that [the] threat mentioned in note actually exists."[15]

Which, of course it did not, Kekkonen conceded, prior public protestations to the contrary. "That was why we sent [Ahti] Karjalainen to Moscow. We wanted to have a civilian rather than a military delegation, for latter would have been construed as tacit admission that threat exists."

"That was why we decided to dissolve Parliament," Kekkonen continued, somewhat disingenuously, conveniently omitting the fact that he had discussed taking that step with the Soviets in April. Kekkonen figured that in this way we could gain a three-month breather.

In the event, that breather had lasted only two days. "Now," he simply said, "the only alternative was to send me."

The Finnish leader said he was "hopeful" that he would be able to convince Khrushchev that it was "in the interests of the Soviet Union to permit Finland to retain its present position," he told his guest. If he could, all would be well. At the same time, he conceded that the worst was also possible. "Worst would be," he said, according to Gufler's memo, "if Khrushchev were to insist that Commies [*sic*] be put into positions of authority here in Finland."[16]

Commies? Was that contemptuous term the Russophobic Gufler's— or was it Kekkonen's and his means of ingratiating himself with the "Commie"-loathing ambassador, always a possibility with the shape-shifting Finn?

"I do not think that this is [a] realistic alternative," he added, "but in present situation all sorts of things go through one head." If worse *did* come to worse, as Kekkonen implied was entirely impossible, and Moscow continued to put the squeeze on him, then he would resign. He had worked fifteen years on the assumption that his difficult path of reconciling Moscow, which the former Russophobe had persuaded the country to take—was "right for Finland." "If it develops that I have worked in vain then I am not going to try to hold onto this job by hook or crook" and he would consider it his duty to resign, he told the Americans.[17]

The ruckus he had raised in Jyväskylä about the visit of Strauss, the West German defense minister in Oslo, was just so much smoke and mirrors, Kekkonen conceded:

> My statement about Strauss's visit to Norway was part of [an] effort to create favorable basis for negotiations with Khrushchev. I for my part don't care much what Strauss was doing in Norway, but I said what I did in order to create better atmosphere for talks with Soviets. [A] number of statements made in my earlier speeches, if taken out of context would be unsupportable.[18]

Noted!

On the other hand, Kekkonen added, with apparent sincerity, he felt the West ought not to dismiss the Soviet Union's Germanophobia altogether: "Actually, you know there is genuine fear in Soviet Union regarding West Germany. They are afraid that if present development continues West Germany will be so strong that it will be able to do what it wishes without worrying about its allies."[19]

At this point, the American visitor, who apparently had listened without comment until then, felt obliged to push back:

> With reference [to] President Kekkonen's statement regarding West Germany, I remarked that US had not helped form NATO and re-armed West Germany to support any military adventures by [her] or anyone else in NATO. I added that [the] West Germany of today was no longer Germany of Hitler either in size or spirit and it was contained within the framework of its Western allies.

The Soviets knew this was nonsense, Gufler pointed out, and *they* knew that *we* knew, but that was the game they were playing. "I gave my opinion that Soviets know this and that their expressions of fear represent propaganda rather than reality."[20] Kekkonen's response to Gufler's riposte is not recorded.

However, if the exchange was not exactly a meeting of minds, it was anything but contentious, as the American made clear in his cable to Washington that evening.

As far as President Kennedy's offer of economic assistance was concerned, the Finnish president "was grateful for his consideration, but [did] not believe that such assistance will in fact be required, because [he] did not expect any economic pressure." Translation: the Finn did not expect a reprise of the Night Frost. And even if that were to transpire, he implied, he would prefer to soldier the storm alone.

Thanks, but no thanks.

But *thanks*—and thanks for keeping this *entres nous*: "Once again I appreciate discreet way in which President Kennedy's message has been delivered and [he was] particularly grateful for wisdom and restraint shown by [the] US government in its attitude toward current crisis."[21] So, the president conceded, at least privately, it was a crisis, after all.

And so it went. Meeting adjourned.

Would Khrushchev display the same "wisdom and restraint" when the two met three days hence in Novosibirsk?

Personally Ambassador Gufler doubted it, he indicated in the postmortem he sent Washington.

At the same time he admitted that, frankly, he sympathized with the Finnish president. "At first glance President Kekkonen looked normal and reasonably cool," he wrote. "He began conversation in controlled, calm manner." When Gufler "had looked at him more closely, [however, he] was struck with [the] deterioration [in] his appearance since" he had last seen him at Helsinki's airport after the hard-pressed Finn had returned from the US eighteen long days before. Kekkonen "had obviously lost weight and his skin looked slightly yellow," Gufler continued, obviously moved.

> He looked drawn and heavily burdened with care. As he unfolded his thoughts, particularly when he referred to possible failure policy for which he [had] worked fifteen years, he revealed a strong undercurrent of emotion and some sense of desperation. [Kekkonen] aroused in both Youngquist of our Embassy, who served as interpreter, and I a feeling of sympathy for sorely tried man, who

> though he has made mistakes, is nevertheless trying to do what is best for his country.[22]

If the "crisis" was part of a prearranged charade, as some alleged at the time, and have since, the patently exhausted and debilitated man Gufler had just met was certainly a very good actor!

Nevertheless, even though the US envoy sympathized with the "sorely tried" Kekkonen, and even seems to have come to admire him, he was doubtful about the outcome of the latter's pending Siberian summit with the impulsive and enigmatic Soviet premier:

> President Kekkonen is apparently going on his mission intent on playing as his only card himself and his past record of dealing with Soviets and their leader.
>
> It is to be hoped that things go as he expects, but in the light of rebuffs experienced by Finns within past two weeks it appears more likely that he may encounter situation beyond his control.
>
> [Signed] Gufler.[23]

Urho Kekkonen had made up his mind. Or rather, more accurately, he had not changed his mind about whether he wished to accept the Americans' help, of either the moral or material kind.

No, he did not desire Finland to become a bone of contention between Washington and Moscow. He did not want Adlai Stevenson to take up Finland's cause in the Security Council. He did not want economic assistance. And he did not want the US Information Agency to go head-to-head with its Soviet counterpart, the Soviet Information Agency, on the propaganda front.

He did not want Finland to become a front—or, more precisely, an active front—of the Cold War, at all: *thanks, but no thanks.*

And on that note, Kekkonen bid Gufler and his Finnish-speaking aide adieu and prepared to receive his next guest, Con O'Neill, the British ambassador.

The latter proceeded to buck up Kekkonen by assuring him how much London respected him and Finnish neutrality, while underlining NATO's benign intentions. "O'Neill as my guest," the entry for the Finnish president's last fraught day before he departed for Siberia read. "England accept[ed]" Finnish neutrality, it continued. "NATO won't attack Finland." Not to worry: NATO—including West Germany—would not violate Finnish territory, as The Note had claimed.[24]

The Americans and the British had done their best to bolster Kekkonen, as well as disabuse him of the notion that either NATO or any of its members posed any sort of threat to Finland, as Moscow had alleged. The rest was up to him, really, and Nikita Khrushchev.

Nearly a year had passed since Kekkonen's and Khrushchev's last meeting in Moscow. Certainly the signals the Finn had received from Khrushchev's minions during the crisis, as best as he could decipher them, had been less than heartwarming. And that bomb he had dropped on Siberia, the radioactive fallout from which had just reached Finland, was not exactly designed to foster Finnish-Soviet relations either.

Also if Khrushchev still liked Kekkonen so much, why was he forcing him to make that hegira to Novosibirsk? Yes, it was good that Khrushchev wanted to meet him at all—but Novosibirsk? These, one imagines, were some of the thoughts that ran through the Finn's mind that night, as he steeled himself for his rendezvous in Siberia.

Was he really as "desperate" as Gufler thought? Perhaps not. Nevertheless, the American's description of how much Kekkonen had physically deteriorated over the last few weeks sounded authentic.

It also sounds like the Finnish government was desperate, according to the short dispatch that United Press International's Helsinki correspondent filed that night:

> HELSINKI, Finland, Nov. 21.
>
> The Government held a last minute conference today on the eve of President Kekkonen's trip to the Soviet Union to try to get Premier Khrushchev to ease his pressure on Finland.[25]

How the cabinet was supposed to assist Kekkonen, after it had already agreed to dispatch the esteemed president to Siberia to try to relieve the aforementioned pressure is not clear.

Max Jacobson's protestations to the contrary, things were beginning to feel very much like October 1939, when Juho Paasikivi, Kekkonen's mentor and predecessor, boarded the train for Moscow on three successive occasions to meet Joseph Stalin as crowds of his emotional countrymen gathered at Helsinki's Central Station to see their supposed savior off.

Which explains why Kekkonen had decided that he would *not* depart for Russia the next day from Central Station: that was *not* a scene he wished to recreate.

November 22 (Day 24)

And so the following morning, November 22, the eighth president of Finland and his entourage, including his wife, Sylvi, his foreign minister, Ahti Karjalainen, and Kekkonen's two military adjutants piled into the two limousines waiting for them outside Tamminiemi, and motored out of the capital without fanfare "and boarded the train at an unannounced stop near the Russian border," as Werner Wiskari reported in *The New York Times.*

> **KEKKONEN STARTS TRIP**
>
> President Urho K. Kekkonen began today a two-day journey to Novosibirsk to plead Finland's case with Premier Khrushchev.
>
> The president slipped out of Helsinki so as to avoid any mass demonstration of concern over the nation's future. He will see Premier Khrushchev Friday in the Siberian city in an attempt to find some way of sidestepping or at least minimizing the defense talks requested by the Russians Oct. 30.[26]

The *Times*man made clear in his report that he was no more optimistic that the Finn would succeed at his mission than his predecessor and mentor, Juho Paasikivi had done when the latter had journeyed to Moscow to "plead" Finland's case twenty-two years before:

> Government sources said it now looked as if Finland would have to enter some kind of military consultations with the Soviet Union. But they expressed hope that the President's prestige as a leader the Russians trust to pursue a policy of peaceful coexistence could be used to reduce the extent of such talks.[27]

All bets were certainly off about what would actually happen when the two leaders met in faraway Siberia. Anything was possible, wrote Wiskari:

> Fears that military talks might abridge the nation's neutrality underlined the Finnish efforts to keep the current crisis on a political rather than a military level. But there are also fears here that the Russians might say during the defense talks that the small Finnish military establishment needed Soviet "help."[28]

After four roller-coaster weeks, Finns, or at least many Finns, were as frightened as they had been that not so long ago on a late autumn day when Paasikivi left on his Mission Impossible, as Don Cook wrote in the *New Republic*:

> Kekkonen's departure was no less an emotional moment [as Paasikivi's had been]. In hundreds of inlets along the Finnish coast, small boats that normally would have been hauled out of the water for winter were still at their moorings. Finns were talking openly and writing to relatives about their plans to pack up and leave the country.[29]

In the event, while the Kennedy administration was standing down, as per Kekkonen's request, another Nordic leader had decided to stand up for Finland with Moscow. The leader in question? None other than Halvard Lange, the redoubtable foreign minister of Norway, as Seymour Topping also reported in *The New York Times* that same day.

Indeed, just as Urho Kekkonen's train was crossing the Russian border, Lange—the same Lange whom Kekkonen had tried browbeat on behalf of Moscow into forsaking nuclear weapons in March—was reportedly going head to head with Anastas Mikoyan, the gnarly Soviet deputy prime minister on behalf of Finland at a luncheon at the Norwegian embassy in Moscow:

> **NORWEGIAN REJECTS MOSCOW'S PRESSURE**
>
> Dr. Halvard M. Lange, Foreign Minister of Norway, who has had blunt talks with Soviet leaders, reaffirmed today the loyalty of his nation with the Atlantic alliance.
>
> The privately expressed differences between Dr. Lange and Soviet officials unexpectedly became public at a luncheon in the Norwegian Embassy attended by Anastas I. Mikoyan, Soviet First Deputy Premier, and Andrei A. Gromyko, Soviet Foreign Minister.

According to the veteran foreign correspondent who would later become the newspaper's managing editor, the Soviet official took the first shot:

> Mr. Mikoyan, rising to make the customary courtesy remarks, surprised the guests by denouncing what he described as the militarism of West Germany. The Soviet leader also berated Norway for having joined the North Atlantic Treaty Organization after Soviet troops had helped to liberate the country in World War II.[30]

By Topping's account, Lange gave back as good as he got, explaining why he felt it was only natural that Norway, which suffered a devastating

German occupation during the war, would seek to join the treaty alliance afterwards.

The Nordic diplomat also said that he "could not accept" what Mikoyan had said about West Germany, now Norway's ally. While he was at it, Topping wrote, the Norwegian decided to put in a word for his beset Nordic neighbor:

> Dr. Lange, alluding to Soviet demands on neutral Finland, said:
>
> "It is our hope that conditions we have arrived at in the Nordic area will continue without considerable changes. We feel that this will be to the advantage of all peoples cooperating for peace and friendship in our part of the world."
>
> Dr. Lange's allusion was made shortly before President Urho K. Kekkonen crossed the Soviet border on his way to Novosibirsk, where he is to confer with Premier Khrushchev.[31]

Evidently the Norwegian tried to disabuse Mikoyan and Gromyko of any notion that putting pressure on Finland would somehow affect Norway's and Denmark's allegiance to NATO. Topping alluded to the Lange factor in his update on Kekkonen's visit in the *Times* the following day, November 23, after the Finnish leader had completed his lengthy pilgrimage by train and plane to Novosibirsk.

> **KEKKONEN TO SEE KHRUSHCHEV TODAY**
>
> Finland's President Arrives in Novosibirsk—Seeks to Avert Defense Talks
>
> President Urho K. Kekkonen of Finland arrived in the Siberian city of Novosibirsk today to confer with Premier Khrushchev on the Soviet demand for military consultations between their countries.

The Soviets were reportedly impressed by Lange's intercession on behalf of the Finns:

> There was cautious speculation that Mr. Khrushchev might prove more conciliatory after the talks with Soviet officials that were completed in Moscow yesterday by Dr. Halvard M. Lange, the Norwegian Foreign Minister.
>
> *Dr. Lange was understood to have made it clear to Andrei A. Gromyko, Soviet Foreign Minister, that Soviet pressure on Finland would not disrupt the defense measures taken by Norway in the Baltic area within the framework of the North Atlantic Treaty Organization* [author's italics].

> It was believed that one of the reasons for the unexpected Soviet move toward Finland was an attempt to discourage Norwegian and Danish military cooperation with West Germany.[32]

The reporter noted that Moscow had put a blackout on press coverage of Kekkonen's trip: "Finnish and Western correspondents were denied permission to go to Novosibirsk to cover the Kekkonen-Khrushchev meeting."

Urho Kekkonen would have to walk the final mile through the long shadow of the Soviet note, in his memorable phrase, alone.

Apparently the Finnish president just missed Lange, who was en route to Tashkent after delivering his fiery words to Gromyko, Mikoyan et al.:

> After a brief rest in Moscow, Dr. Kekkonen drove to an airport to board a special Ilyushin-18 prop-jet airliner. He did not have an opportunity to confer with the Norwegian Foreign Minister, who left from the same airport shortly afterward for a tour of Tashkent.[33]

What, one wonders, would Kekkonen have said to Lange if they had had a chance to confer? Did Lange's putative pushback cause Khrushchev to think twice about his pressure campaign? Who knows? It is worth recalling, though, particularly in light of Lange's own resistance to Kekkonen's own pressure campaign on behalf of the Kremlin earlier in the year. In the end, that was apparently less important to the Norwegian. Maintaining Finnish neutrality—and Finnish independence—was more important, at least to him.

In the meantime Kekkonen and his small entourage continued on to Novosibirsk. According to Vladimir Vladimirov, the KGB man, before he boarded the plane for Novosibirsk Kekkonen had a brief meeting Mikhail Kotov, a key figure in the KGB whom he known since the days when the latter had served on the Allied Control Commission in Helsinki, and was now stationed in Moscow.

Gufler's impression that the Finnish president was under nervous strain was not a figment of his imagination, it seems. According to Vladimirov, Kekkonen *was* nervous.

His colleague, Kotov, managed to calm him down, however. And then, he, Sylvi, and their small coterie were off for their rendezvous with destiny, while the Finnish nation waited for the denouement with bated breath.

Chapter 18

Good Losers (11/26/61)

> The president slipped out of Helsinki to avoid any kind of mass demonstration of concern over the nation's concern.
>
> —*The New York Times*, November 24, 1961
>
> A careful reading of the note now shows it to be very understandable.
>
> —From Urho Kekkonen's speech to the nation on his return from Novosibirsk

What about the rest? The rest, as they say, is history. To reprise: within the space of forty-eight hours, between the evening of Friday, November 23, and the morning of Sunday, November 25, 1961:

—Urho Kekkonen had a "frank and friendly" three-hour meeting with Nikita Khrushchev.[1]

—Karl-August Fagerholm, the deposed former prime minister, now speaker of the parliament, and Kekkonen's co-father-in-law, proposed that Kekkonen's presidency should be prolonged by law.

—Olavi Honka, the Social Democratic candidate for the Finnish presidency, resigned his candidacy "for the sake of the Fatherland."

—Nikita Khrushchev decided that even though the putative resurgence of "German militarism" was still a threat, he would not press his friend, the Finnish president, for the military consultations he had demanded after all, provided that he did his best to suppress the "rightist elements" in Finland who threatened the special Finnish and Soviet relationship.

—Urho Kekkonen flew back to Moscow, where he boarded the overnight train to Helsinki.

Or as the *The New York Times* summed it up:

> **REPRIEVE FOR FINLAND**
>
> Last week, Finland's President Urho K. Kekkonen journeyed the 2,340 miles to confer with Soviet Premier Khrushchev who was on a tour of Siberian farmlands. Their talk in a forest cottage Friday—and related events in Helsinki on the same day—appeared to end the four-week crisis in Soviet-Finnish relations as suddenly as it had started.[2]

This time Kekkonen decided that it was all right for him to remain on the train bringing him, his wife Sylvi, and their aides with him back from Moscow all the way to Central Station, memories of 1939 be damned. After all, unlike his distinguished predecessor, Juho Paasikvi, after the latter's frustrated negotiations with Joseph Stalin, before the Winter War, he had succeeded in *his* peacekeeping mission.

The thousands of cheering Helsinkians who greeted Kekkonen when he arrived in Helsinki certainly thought he had triumphed. And so did the grateful Finnish nation, as Don Cook, the US journalist, wrote:

> Four days later on Sunday evening [November 26] the blue railway carriage pulled back into Helsinki station and this time it was the works: red carpet, the entire cabinet, speech of welcome and praise by the prime minister, diplomatic corps waiting to shake hands, military band and honor guard, and 5,000 or more Finns on hand to cheer.[3]

The Note Crisis was officially over.

Not quite. First the Finnish president had a speech to make.

It was quite a speech. Yes, he told the estimated two million Finns who were watching and listening in on their tv sets, thanks to their president's magnanimous Russian friend, Nikita Khrushchev, as well as his own not inconsiderable ministrations, he told them, Finland had received a reprieve. There would be no military consultations with Moscow after all.

From the looks of the videotape of the momentous speech, however, it took a while for the wan looking president to get to it. First, reading from his notes, the Finnish leader regurgitated some of the anti-Western propaganda he had been forced to swallow in Novosibirsk.

The speech was doubtless the most unctuous, as well as disingenuous one Kekkonen had given since the one he delivered in December 1958 following the resolution of the Night Frost crisis. Indeed, the two speeches were essentially of the same sycophantic piece.

To be sure, the first part of the address was really directed at Moscow.

First, Kekkonen, conceded, alluding to the hue and cry the by now infamous Soviet note had triggered, "this note aroused great attention throughout the world, and many interpretations were offered." But, if one really examined it from the Kremlin's point of view, he asserted, the mystifying demarche made utterly complete sense:

> A careful reading of the note now shows it to be *very understandable* [author's italics], if it is considered against the tense international situation. But it cannot be correctly understood unless one tries to assume the position of its sender, the Soviet government and to view the situation as it appears from Moscow.
>
> Every sensible person will realize that many things can only be clarified through honest and unprejudiced effort to see the reasons underlying political action.

Of course the Soviets had reason to fear West Germany, Kekkonen continued:

> The concern the Soviet Union feels because of the accelerated rearmament of West Germany is a fact and it is genuine—and in the light of history it is understandable.
>
> Every state tries to secure its safety by all available means and to take the necessary steps to prepare its against aggression.

Of course, the international situation was tense: "During this autumn I have had discussions with the leading statesmen of both West and East," Kekkonen blithely continued, referring to his meetings with Leonid Brezhnev and John F. Kennedy, "and they would have poorly understood what I heard were I to deny the danger of a European war."[4]

After all, the US president had used the word "war" several times while they were discussing the Berlin situation during their meeting, hadn't he, the Finnish leader explained, apologetically.

Clearly, this was not the same self-assured leader who had spoken to the nation upon his return from the United States three weeks before and urged his countrymen to keep calm and carry on. The Urho Kekkonen who spoke to the Finnish nation on the evening of Sunday, November 26, 1961, sounded considerably different from his self-assured pre-Novosibirsk self. He also looked different, as Werner Wiskari the *New York Times* reporter, wrote the next day: "Some observers noted that the President spoke without the forcefulness and apparent confidence that had marked his speech to the nation November 5."[5]

Plainly, the intervening ordeal, including the exhausting pilgrimage to Siberia had taken something out of the Finnish president.

Not that Kekkonen had minded having to make the trip. On the contrary he stated, he was very grateful to his friend Khrushchev for making time to see him:

> I wish to express, once more, my gratitude to N.S. [Nikita Sergeyevich] Khrushchev for his readiness to interrupt his important travel plans and reserve a day for discussions with me. Three thousand agricultural leaders had been convened in Novosibirsk for a conference and they had to wait for a day because of the discussions granted to Finland.

So good of him, don't you think?

Finally, after paying homage to the ever sensible, all-wise Khrushchev, the president got to the part the anxious nationwide audience was waiting for. The discussions he had had with Khrushchev while all those Russian farmers were patiently waiting around were indeed "frank and friendly and produced good results," he proclaimed.

The next passage showed that Kekkonen was aware that Finland's anxious Swedish neighbors were listening, too: "During the discussions I pointed out that the initiation of the proposed [military] consultations might cause anxiety and war psychosis in the Scandinavian countries."

War psychosis? Well, that was one way of putting it.

After all, the Swedes had been making preparations to evacuate their government.

> For this reason I suggested that the Soviet Union should not insist on the consultations it had proposed, and expressed the opinion that were the question settled in this way it would calm public opinion in the whole of Scandinavia and result in a reduced need for military preparations, not only in Finland and Sweden, but also in Norway and Denmark.

And thus, by his telling, the humble Finnish president had shown the all-wise and benevolent chairman of the Council of Ministers of the USSR the way forward, and the chairman agreed that it corresponded with Soviet security interests. "The result of the discussions was that

[Khrushchev] found he could agree to put off the military consultations proposed by the Soviet Government."[6]

So there it was: mission accomplished. There would be no military negotiations after all, no demands for bases, and no invasion.

Across Scandinavia and Finland there was a collective sigh of relief at those words. "[Khrushchev] said that if postponement of consultations was likely to relieve tensions among North European nations it was right to agree to a proposal to this effect."

To be sure, as with the Soviet reprieve that had resolved the Night Frost three years before, there were a number of explicit, as well as implicit conditions attached to the Kremlin's latest commutation.

For one, Kekkonen now agreed to keep an eye on the putatively tense situation in the Baltic Sea region for Moscow. The Soviet leader, he continued,

> expressed the wish of the Soviet Government that, bearing in mind the interest felt by both the Soviet Union and Finland in the safeguarding of their respective frontiers, the Finnish Government should closely follow the development of the situation in North Europe and the Baltic region and if need be, transmit its views to the Soviet Government on any measures that might be called for.

In short, Finland now agreed to be the USSR's trip wire.

This was new. Perhaps, as Jukka Tarkka and others have suggested, this new, demeaning clause, also disparagingly referred to as the "guard dog" clause, was Khrushchev's gesture to the hard-liners in his own military and the Politburo who would have preferred to see him squeeze Kekkonen further.

That was speculation. For the moment, outside observers only had Kekkonen's words to go by. Whatever exactly transpired at that cottage in Siberia, the Finnish head of state was singing a distinctly new tune now. Five days before, he had implicitly rejected President Kennedy's statement that neutral Finland manned the western border of the Free World. Now, remarkably, he had explicitly accepted the reverse. That was new—as well as news.

Bad news to American ears.

"It is most important to note that the Soviet Union, even in this tense international situation regarded Finland's policy of neutrality as an integral part of its own security policy," Kekkonen continued. "This must be regarded as a great achievement for Finland for it imposes on us, in the name of our own interests, the duty of conducting a foreign policy based on the confidence of the USSR."

There was more—much more. As he had in 1958, the Finnish head of state roundly chastised those who criticized the The Neighbor to the East, especially that great friend of Finland, Nikita Khrushchev. "As I said in my speech in the Kremlin yesterday," the nervous president continued, repeating himself:

> our negotiations in Novosibirsk were one of the most important meetings between Finnish and Soviet leaders. . . . [Nikita] Khrushchev now—like often before—showed great understanding for the position, views and wishes of Finland. Khrushchev is the leading statesman of the Soviet Union and naturally, in all his actions he primarily looks after his own country's interests, but at the same time he is a great friend of Finland, in the same way that many of his colleagues in the Government are.[7]

By this point of Kekkonen's discourse, there were doubtless heavy sighs at the US embassy.

"This should be remembered with gratitude in Finland," he blathered on. "I have noticed how readily people in Finland join in Western criticism of Khrushchev but my long-term experience assures me that the Finnish cause is not served by such an attitude."[8]

There was more. This time, unlike three years prior after the Night Frost, the Finnish president was not merely interested in stifling the domestic press. He also wanted to gag the opposition, as the headline of *The New York Times* blared the next day:

> **KEKKONEN URGES ANTI-REDS TO QUIT FINNISH POLITICS**
>
> President Says Retirement of Men Hostile to Soviet Would Aid Neutrality
>
> President Urho K. Kekkonen suggested that opposition leaders who had incurred the hatred of the Soviet Union should withdraw into private life for the good of Finland.
>
> Dr. Kekkonen made his suggestion in a radio and television report to the nation on his talks with Premier Khrushchev of the Soviet Union. The Finnish President spoke less than three hours having returned from Novosibirsk in Siberia, where Mr. Khrushchev had agreed to postpone the joint defense negotiations demanded by Moscow Oct. 30.[9]

Surprisingly or not Kekkonen, never known for his magnanimity, did not mention Olavi Honka's decision two days before to resign his candidacy for the presidency, virtually reassuring his own reelection to a second term.

Fine by me!

Now, if only some of Honka's misguided backers, like Väinö Tanner, he strongly implied, would also exit the Finnish political scene all would be well:

> If the politicians to whom the Soviet Union objects should retire, Dr. Kekkonen said, there would not be the "slightest doubt" that Finland could continue neutral "in all situations."
>
> No names were mentioned in the President's speech. It was regarded as clear that he meant principally the leadership of the Social Democratic party and especially Vaino A. Tanner, its vehemently anti-Communist chairman.
>
> "When they retire from the stage," Dr. Kekkonen said, "they know they will be fulfilling the highest duty of a citizen—safeguarding the security of their fatherland."[10]

That would also make that great friend of Finland, the wise and sensible Nikita Sergeyevich Khrushchev very happy:

> Mr. Tanner and his followers who have frequently been attacked by the Soviet Union, were denounced publicly by Premier Khrushchev Friday in Novosibirsk. At a luncheon in honor of President Kekkonen, Mr. Khrushchev charged that "the activities of the Rightists and Tannerites in Finland are aimed at smashing Soviet-Finnish friendship."[11]

Hopefully Moscow's bête noire, Tanner, would take the hint and follow the "dilettante" Honka out the door, he continued, as Bernard Gufler, the US ambassador, who had been so concerned about the overwrought president before he left for Novosibirsk, unhappily listened in, along with the rest of the distraught Western diplomatic corps.

Perhaps Nikita Khrushchev had not forced Urho Kekkonen to put "Commies" into his government as Gufler had called the unapologetically pro-Soviet Finnish Communist party—but what Gufler and British ambassador Con O'Neill, who had also tried to succor Kekkonen before his voyage to Russia and the other disheartened members of the Western diplomatic corps were hearing was nearly as ominous. Whether or not Kekkonen planned to insert that "suggestion" about forcing Tanner et al.

to retire in his extemporaneous speech is not clear, but out it came, along with the following extraordinary, bonkers passage:

> This journey has strongly confirmed my conviction that we now have every possibility, thanks to the good basis achieved, of successfully continuing our policy of national independence. The Soviet Union feels confident that we have the will to pursue the policy of friendship and the policy of neutrality.

And then came this part: "*If by our own actions we cause this confidence to cease, we have only ourselves to blame* [author's italics]." In other words, if Nikita Khrushchev, that great and sensible friend of Finland, decided once again to invoke the dread Article 2 of the 1948 Fenno-Soviet treaty because of the perceived threat of war it would entirely be Finland's own fault.

Put another way, it was now incumbent on Finland to help safeguard the USSR.

Then there was this: "*I appeal to the Finnish people and those who have not had confidence in Soviet friendship, to use a sports term, to be good losers* [author's italics]."

"In sport," Kekkonen droned on, "a good loser is often preferable to a bad loser."[12]

So now the Finnish president was asking Finns to be "good losers?"

So, the whole crisis had been a game after all.

Or had it?

And then, the weary head of state got back into his limousine and returned to Tamminiemi to collect his thoughts and catch up on his sleep and his reading, including the hundreds of letters that had poured in during the perilous passage.

To judge from a random selection of correspondence from November and December in the files of the Kekkonen archives, most of those letters, particularly those from his diehard rural followers, were favorable—even worshipful. Many of the missives had biblical references. It seems that the elderly woman who, two years before, had pointedly told Werner Wiskari that she believed in God, Kekkonen, and the Agrarian League—"in that order"—was not alone.

One letter Kekkonen received at this time, in the form of an epic poem, welcomed him home from his cumbersome journey praising him for "spreading the light of morning as an interpreter of justice and peace."[13]

Can one blame Urho Kekkonen for having delusions of grandeur after reading epistles such as these?

Yet another specifically referenced the Paasikivi-Kekkonen line, thanking him for making its value and importance clear to him again. "When I heard that You were going to Russia on account of the note, a shout came to me in prayer. Then I had a dream. I was standing on a high mountain."[14]

Praise be!

Nor were Finns alone among Kekkonen's grateful followers. The archives include numerous letters of praise and thanksgiving from followers from abroad, including Swedes. Witness a letter from a fan in distant Karlskrona congratulating the Finnish leader for his successful mission, while noting that his Finnish neighbors ought to be thankful for having such a "divinely honest and upstanding" president.

To be sure, there also were quite a few correspondents who decidedly did *not* worship Kekkonen and took strong issue with his obsequious, semicoherent speech, such as one self-described bitter resident of Hyvinkää, a small town north of Helsinki, who took Kekkonen to task for criticizing his political opponents, the Social Democrats, in all his speeches and implying that they were not as patriotic as he because they supposedly disrespected the USSR.

That was not the way to build harmony among the Finnish people, the infuriated correspondent alleged. The writer, for one, was unhappy that Olavi Honka had been forced to resign his candidacy. So were others.

And so it went.

Essentially Finns heard what they wanted to in Urho Kekkonen's speech. The true believers trusted and admired him found more reason to do so. Those who distrusted and disliked him found a new set of reasons to continue to do so.

In the meantime, with his reelection now virtually reassured, Finns in both camps began getting used to the idea that the eighth president would be around for a while. The political, and to some degree, spiritual template for the next two decades of the Kekkonen regency had been set. Now, with the apparently successful resolution of the Note Crisis, and the elimination of the last credible opponent he would ever face, the glazing for Kekkonen's grand design had been applied.

For the moment, most Finns seemed to be happy that the Soviet sword of Damocles hanging over their country that the threatened military consultations represented had been removed. “All of Finland now heaved a fervent sigh of relief,” wrote Don Cook. “All those boat owners who had left their boats at their moorings in case the Soviet sword fell and they needed to evacuate, now felt secure enough to haul them out of the water.”[15]

Yrjö Länsipuro, the noted Finnish journalist, recalls the feeling of euphoria that followed Kekkonen’s “triumphant” return from Novosibirsk. “The Note Crisis was one of the ways that Kekkonen became indispensable,” said Länsipuro, who had supported the Social Democratic candidate, Honka, before he exited the presidential race, as had his newspaper, *Amulehti*, the Tampere daily.

“There is no question about it. We were really scared.”

“It made a big impression on the country when he [Kekkonen] resolved it.”[16]

Chapter 19

Aftermath (10/28/61–1/1/62)

> Our admiration for the Finnish people remains. But Russia has committed another aggression and Finland has suffered another defeat.
>
> —*The New York Times*, October 28, 1961

> The ambassador agreed, adding that every responsible Finnish statesman would now also have in his mind more than ever the need to get along with the Soviets.
>
> —Memo about Finnish ambassador Rafael Seppälä's visit to the US State Department regarding the aftermath of the Note Crisis

Like many if not most Finns, the peoples of their country's Nordic neighbors, who had played an unwitting role in the Finnish–Soviet melodrama, also felt relief at the denouement of the drama, mixed with apprehension about Moscow's future intentions.

Thus the following reports from the Stockholm and Copenhagen correspondents of the *Times* of London which appeared on November 27, the day after the Finnish and Soviet leaders' Siberian powwow. First from Sweden:

> **GUARANTEE FOR ELECTION**
>
> Swedish observers believe that the Russian-Finnish agreement has afforded relief, perhaps only temporary, to the Finnish people, and it has increased President Kekkonen's authority before the election. The Russians, it is said, received a guarantee that Dr. Kekkonen will be re-elected, and the other Nordic countries have been given a warning as keen as any since 1939.
>
> The Soviet Union is obviously using Finland as a weapon against the western powers, according to newspaper comment. It is also said that the Russian attempts to frighten Denmark and

> Norway out of NATO will possibly be more intensive than before, and nobody doubts that the fate of Finland is to be used as a piece in that game.[1]

And from Denmark:

> **SPECULATION OVER BALTIC COMMAND**
>
> The outcome of the Novosibirsk talks has been received in Copenhagen with relief. The pro-Government newspaper sees as the reason for the apparent climbdown by Russia that Dr. Kekkonen will continue in office and the apparent persuasive powers of the President.

The American reaction to the surprising outcome of the crisis, including the apparently forced exit of Olavi Honka from the Finnish presidential race, and Urho Kekkonen's encouragement to his other domestic opponents and critics to follow suit and exit the stage, was anything but euphoric.

Thus the scathing editorial in *The New York Times* appeared on November 28, 1961, as the price which Nikita Khrushchev had exacted in return for pausing his demand for military consultations became alarmingly clear. No longer was the *Times* singing Finland's praises, or that of its sadly irresolute president:

> **UNDERMINING FINLAND'S FREEDOM**
>
> The outside world does not know what Premier Khrushchev said to Finnish President Kekkonen in their conversation at Novosibirsk. We do know that Mr. Kekkonen came home with an assurance that he would not have to humiliate himself now by having military talks with the Russians—that is, by ordering his military advisers to listen to while the Russians told them what to do.
>
> But this is not the end of the story. President Kekkonen returned to Helsinki to deliver a radio and television report to the nation in which he underlined Finnish neutrality "in all situations" and then—and here was the unhappy core of the bargain—called upon those Finnish politicians who were unpopular with Moscow to retire to private life. This he said, would be "fulfilling the highest duty of a citizen—safeguarding the security of their fatherland."

> The principal specific reference seemed to be to Vaino Tanner, who is the chairman of the Social Democratic party and hates communism.[2]

What exactly *had* happened at Novosibirsk? As Kekkonen later confided to Max Jakobson, Khrushchev's "performance" at that secluded cottage outside of Novosibirsk was "strangely equivocal," as Jukka Tarkka, his biographer recounts. In Khrushchev's speech at the start of the meeting, "he took a brusque military line, but in the negotiations that followed he was flexible and constructive," he writes.[3]

Again, the way Tarkka sees it, internal tensions within the Soviet Communist Party played a large role in the way the Soviet premier used the Note Crisis, as well as the way he resolved it at Novosibirsk, at least a larger role than was perceived at the time. "Having used the Note to show his firmness [to his internal audience]," Tarkka writes, "while at the same time having gained the upper hand with the Finns, the Russian leader felt free to soften his stance."[4]

Perhaps so. In any case, there was no question, in the view of America's leading newspaper, that Finland had suffered both a moral and political defeat, along with the Free World.

What a difference a month had made. Apparently Don Cook had undercounted the number of Helsinkians who flocked to Central Station to welcome the Great Man home. Cook estimated the crowd at 5,000. The *Times* thought the crowd was twice as large.

Not that it was impressed:

> The bands played and a crowd estimated at more than 10,000 welcomed Mr. Kekkonen from his brief but humiliating Siberian exile.

"Our admiration for the Finnish people of all parties remains," the gloomy editorial continued, once again invoking the memory of the Winter War, to the gnashing of teeth at the Finnish foreign ministry. "We believe that they would fight bravely now if they were attacked in force, just as they have done before. . . . But Russia has committed another aggression," the paper inveighed, "and Finland has suffered another defeat."[5]

That was also pretty much the way Dean Rusk, the US secretary of state, felt. The depressing outcome of the blacked out Siberian talks validated Rusk's apprehensions about Finland's timorous president, as America's top diplomat made clear in the telegram he sent to the US mission to

NATO in Brussels that same day, November 28, containing his "guidance" for discussing the Finnish situation, particularly with fellow NATO members Norway and Denmark.

"You," Rusk instructed Thomas Finletter, the US ambassador to NATO, "should endeavor [to] dispel [the] belief Novosibirsk talks have eased Finnish position. [The] sense of euphoria in Finland and idea [that] Kekkonen scored great triumph most disquieting as is [the] feeling of relief apparent in Scandinavia and in some other NATO countries."[6]

Any relief at the outcome of the talks, Rusk maintained, was delusory. And, just as many felt that by acquiescing to Soviet pressure in order to resolve the Night Frost crisis three years before, the pliant Finnish president had paid too high a price, so he felt, the latter had done again.

It was difficult to tell from Rusk's furious screed with whom he was more disappointed, Urho Kekkonen or his putatively naïve constituents. In any case, the American no longer believed that neither he nor they had the spine or the wits to discern or counter the perfidious Soviet moves against them. In one of the numerous remarkable lines of the telegram, he wrote: "*Finnish people and leaders are not necessarily in best position themselves to assess significance of Soviet people or steps which must be taken to counteract them* [author's italics]."[7]

Rusk then went on to enumerate the numerous ways the Novosibirsk "agreement" was a defeat both for Finnish independence and democracy and the Free World. As a consequence of the crisis, Rusk contended, the Soviets had:

– Ensured re-election [of] President Kekkonen by in effect causing withdrawal of leading opposition candidate.
–Demanded withdrawal from political life of Finnish political leaders and other elements considered by Soviets to be anti-communist; a demand reiterated publicly by Kekkonen in Finland.
–By their seeming magnanimous treatment of Finland given fillip to election prospects of Finnish communist party.
–Defined, in Kekkonen's words, Finnish neutrality as essential part of Soviet security policy.
–Elicited statement from Kekkonen to[the] effect that maintenance of Soviet confidence is not only Finland's responsibility but that loss of confidence would be "exclusively" fault of Finns.

–Obtained Kekkonen's concurrence that it is Finnish Government's duty in light [of] future developments to initiate military consultations with Soviets under Article II; onus is therefore on Finland to observe and interpret developments in Northern Europe in manner acceptable to Soviets.[8]

One gathers that Rusk had written off Kekkonen, if not Finland itself, as a lost cause. In any case it was incumbent on its stalwart Nordic neighbors to ignore its weak and duplicitous president, and awaken the Finnish people to the renewed danger of "satellization" they were in while also strengthening their resolve to resist it:

> According to Kekkonen-Khrushchev communiqué and Kekkonen's Nov 26 [statement] "relaxation" of Soviet pressure [is] dependent on Finnish performance on matters noted above and "easing of tensions in Northern Europe." Warning thus served on Sweden, Norway and Denmark [that] unless they relax their military posture and attenuate ties with NATO new Soviet demands on Finland will be made.
>
> Efforts [to resist Soviet influence in Northern Europe] will be greatly complicated unless Finns themselves are brought to understand significance of current developments and are prepared to stand up to Soviets.
>
> *In* [a] *sense Finland being used by Soviets as hostage for policies on part of Scandinavian countries deemed "proper" by Soviets* [author's italics].[9]

There was that word again: hostage. Except that not only was Moscow holding Kekkonen himself hostage in return for acting as it desired; now, according to Rusk, the Kremlin was also holding all of Finland hostage in return for getting all of Scandinavia to follow its will.

Withal, it was not a pretty picture. To fix it, Rusk cabled his NATO envoy, America's first task was "to strengthen Finnish resolve." "We hope Norway, Denmark and through them Sweden will take the lead," he continued.

Rusk was still anxious to confront Russia over Finland on the information warfare front, as well as other nonmilitary fronts, in order to prevent its further slide into "satellization," as he phrased it. However, Rusk, who would go on to become one of America's longest-serving secretaries of state, serving a total of eight years under both John F. Kennedy and his successor, Lyndon B. Johnson, no longer trusted the captive Finn nation, or its president to do this for themselves. The whole country needed bolstering, he felt and soon, or else the West might as well write it off.

In Helsinki, US ambassador Bernard Gufler's post-Novosibirsk prognosis about the state of Finnish democracy was nearly as pessimistic. Gufler also felt that the Soviet agreement to suspend the demand for military consultations was a bait and switch, and that Finland was being used as a hostage. He, too, had resoundingly lost faith in Urho Kaleva Kekkonen. "Soviets may think pause useful," he cabled the State Department in his postmortem on the debacle on December 2, 1961, because:

> 1. If they drive Kekkonen and his supporters too far too fast they might balk or by being too obedient lose their effectiveness for Soviet purposes.
> 2. Lull interested countries and circles in free world.
> 3. *Preserve Finland as usable hostage which still in danger* [*of*] *being strangled slowly or left alive more in appearance than fact* [author's italics].[10]

Usable hostage! Quite a phrase.

The envoy also had basically written off the Finnish president.

In the US ambassador's estimate, the grossly uneven post-Novosibirsk balance sheet was as follows: "Finland was given some fair words and postponement of military consultations which Soviets completely again [can] demand tomorrow."

In return, Gufler concluded, the Soviets received:

> 1. Kekkonen's firm commitment to concept that Finnish foreign policy and political leadership must always be acceptable to Soviets.
> 2. Reduction Finnish presidential election to empty formality amounting [to] Kekkonen's "reappointment."
> 3. Public acknowledgement by President Finland that:
>   a. Soviet note to Finland justified by international tensions.
>   b. Soviet fear [of] Germany genuine and understandable.
>   c. Khrushchev [is] great friend of Finland but must naturally look after his own interests.
>   d. Great achievement for Finland that Finnish policy recognized by Soviets as integral part of Soviet security system.
>   e. If Finland's neutrality and independence are lost, it will be Finland's fault.

f. Finland has duty of standing watch on Baltic [Sea region].
g. There must be no criticism of Khrushchev in Finland.

4. “Nation’s interests require that all in disagreement with foregoing remain quiet.”

All in all, not much of a reprieve.

According to the put-out diplomat, the possible consequences for captive Finland were:

1. [To increase] apprehensions about disagreements with Soviet Union in any field.
2. Freer field for Finland’s communists and increase[d] inhibition against attacking them as agents of Soviets.
3. [To] decrease general knowledge of what happening because [of] tendency [to] silence objective public discussion in press.
4. Greater disorganization than ever among anti-communist groups and parties.
5. Anti-communist voter apathy by sense [of] futility and fear that heavy anti-communist vote could produce immediate Soviet reprisals.
6. Communist [parliament] election gains could furnish basis demand [for] inclusion in government.[11]

In the event, many of Gufler’s fears proved unfounded. Kekkonen might be a lost cause, but Finnish voters were made of sterner stuff than he or Rusk feared. In the forthcoming 1962 parliamentary election, the SKDL, the Finnish Communist party, would actually lose votes. But he did not know that at that time.

At the same time, the US ambassador’s assessment of the state of the anticommunist, and implicitly, anti-Kekkonen opposition was not quite as bleak as that of his superior, Rusk:

> Despite gloomy situation above outlined there are in Finland active pro-democratic, anti-communist elements that even this soon after Novosibirsk have recovered enough hope and courage [to] continue struggle [to] preserve and reinforce country’s will to survive [as] genuinely neutral independent nation.[12]

Like Rusk, Gufler also recommended turning up the heat on the information front. The courage of the aforementioned patriots “gives justification for efforts to help on part of Finland’s friends,” he went on. “These efforts might take form [of] well considered public statements, quiet diplomatic actions designed [to] encourage Finnish will to resist and discreet offers [of] political or economic help at appropriate times."[13]

Nevertheless, and notwithstanding these qualifications, the disappointed diplomat, who would go on to serve another two years as ambassador to Helsinki, was just as downbeat about Finland's future as he had been before that remarkable meeting with Kekkonen the night before the latter departed for Siberia. At the very least, he felt, the Finnish president had forsaken the enormous good will and prestige his well-publicized US tour had generated.

But that seemed like a long time ago now.

America's almost audible volte-face regarding Finland led Richard Seppälä, the Finnish ambassador to Washington, to request an appointment at the State Department on November 28, 1961, the same day that the disgusted Rusk fired off the above philippic to Thomas Finletter, the US ambassador to NATO, in Brussels. The strongly adverse reaction to the result of the Novosibirsk talks in the US press understandably made him fear that Finland's relationship with the US, as well as its image in the Free World, was in the balance.

Now Seppälä wished to "Present His Country's Views on Finnish-Soviet Situation," as the headline of the memo following the anxious diplomat's visit read.[14]

The Finnish ambassador was right. As both that memo and the Rusk and Gufler telegrams well indicate, the Finnish-American relationship was very much in the balance on that fraught late November afternoon in 1961, as the figurative dust following Kekkonen's return from his fateful appointment in Siberia settled.

A summary of the extraordinary meeting that took place that day between Seppälä and the American diplomats U. Alexis Johnson, the deputy under the secretary of state, and Eiler R. Cook, the head of the department's Finnish desk at the State Department, and the latter's resultant memo, follows.

Seppälä, who had attended Kekkonen's historic meeting with Kennedy six weeks before and accompanied him for the remainder of his continental Grand Tour, was keen to restore the good will it had generated, which he now feared had been lost because of the pejorative way the crisis and its outcome was being depicted in the press:

> The Finnish Ambassador opened the conversation by stating that [Helsinki] considered the problem to be solved to [the Finnish

> government's] entire satisfaction. There had been interpretations in the press of the Fenno-Soviet talks, and these interpretations had not all been correct.

Seppälä said he "understood that many journalists [were] friends of Finland, but their conclusions, however, are not necessarily the correct ones." How much had changed in six weeks. In October Seppälä had proudly watched on as President Kennedy gave his president and his country their respectful due in the White House. Now here he was, several blocks away, sheepishly defending his president's actions and that of his "small country" to a senior State Department functionary.[15]

The ambassador also wanted to dispel some of the misunderstandings circulating abroad about the actual meaning of the joint communiqué issued after Kekkonen's meeting with Khrushchev in Novosibirsk. Contrary to what *The New York Times*, or anyone else thought, Seppälä insisted, the overblown crisis had indeed been resolved to Finland's satisfaction.

> On the basis of his telephone conversation with Foreign Minister [Ahti] Karjalainen yesterday Finland considers the problem solved and does not agree with the point of view expressed by many that the whole matter is still hanging over Finland, so to speak.
>
> Ambassador Seppala [*sic*] referred specifically to the penultimate paragraph of the Novosibirsk communique where Khrushchev had stated "that the Soviet Government finds it possible to postpone for the time being the military consultations it had suggested."

Khrushchev had put no pressure on his Finnish friend to do anything whatsoever, Seppälä blithely maintained. Nor had there been any change either in Finland's relationship with Moscow, or in Finland's strictly neutral foreign policy. Perhaps the notion of Finland as a bridge builder between East and West had to be put on hold for a while, nevertheless Finnish neutrality was still authentic.

> From the Soviet side there had been no pressure nor were there secret arrangements or requests. President Kekkonen had stated this clearly in his November 26 speech to the people of Finland following his return from Novosibirsk. The Finnish ambassador

> went on to say that his Government feels that this intermezzo has not changed Finland's political situation nor has it changed the policy of neutrality which they [the Finns] so sincerely wish to follow. Ambassador Seppala [*sic*] said that he hoped this would be understood here and in other countries.[16]

Intermezzo? Come to think of it, the crisis did have a musical quality to it, albeit a discordant one.

Next the evidently stressed Finnish envoy turned to the sticky, and supposedly misunderstood matter of Olavi Honka's resignation from the presidential race. The fact that Honka's decision occurred on the same day that Kekkonen met Khrushchev in Siberia was purely coincidental, Seppälä insisted. In fact, the veteran diplomat, who would continue in his Washington post for four more years, until 1965, when he was appointed ambassador to France, insisted, the timing of Honka's resignation—which the latter announced just prior to Moscow's decision to suspend its demand for military consultations, and which Andrei Gromyko, the Soviet foreign minister had explicitly indicated was a precondition for same—was an "unfortunate" coincidence.

No one had pushed Honka out of the race. He had jumped, Seppälä continued with a straight face.[17]

> Ambassador Seppala [*sic*] next turned his attention to the resignation of Mr. Honka from the presidential race. Mr. Karjalainen had told the Ambassador that the Finns had known nothing of this until the news came over the wires. Mr. Honka had made his own decision—admittedly arrived at on the basis of the situation as it existed.

"Karjalainen did not know why [Honka] timed his resignation when he did actually," the Finnish ambassador said.[18]

Having done his best to point out that everything was well and that "the problem," as Seppälä kept calling the crisis, had been amicably solved without any undue Soviet pressures or damage to Finnish democracy, the stammering Finn then blithely went on to contradict himself: "The Finnish Ambassador next turned to Nikita Khrushchev's comments on certain rightist elements in Finland," the memo of the conversation continues.

Now Seppälä began to depart from the script he had arranged with his foreign minister. "He admitted that one could interpret

[Khrushchev's comments] as interference in Finnish internal affairs"—this after denying that the Soviets had exerted any untoward pressures of any kind. Of course, he said, Khrushchev was referring to Väinö Tanner. Tanner "was by no means a radical, or anything else bad," the envoy conceded:

> [Seppälä] recalled the important and patriotic role Mr. Tanner had played during the war years. However he had come into bad grace—it was too bad but that was a fact. What Finns think of Mr. Tanner did not matter. It was the opinion of their neighbor that was important.[19]

Thus was Seppälä's explanation of President Kekkonen's suggestion that certain political leaders step out of the political pressure.

That line bears repeating: *What Finns might think of Tanner did not matter. It was the opinion of their neighbor that was important.*

No, Novosibirsk had not changed anything at all. After all, hadn't the Kremlin always exercised veto power over who participated in Finnish political life?

Johnson's response to the artificially roseate picture that the Finnish ambassador drew was predictably a bemused one. Both Johnson and Seppälä agreed that the principal Soviet motive behind the troublesome note had been strategic. They also agreed that Finland had been used, by Moscow, if not exactly as a hostage, then at least as a convenient decoy for the USSR's greater, regional ambitions:

> Johnson thanked the Ambassador very much for his extremely interesting presentation of the views of his Government. It of course again raised the question what the whole purpose of the whole Soviet exercise was.
>
> Ambassador Seppala [*sic*] answered that the Soviets had used the 1948 treaty as an opening to discuss the threat of war, particularly as it involved Germany. The Finnish Ambassador viewed the note as directed not so much against Finland as in a larger context.
>
> Mr. Johnson agreed, adding that it seemed that Finland was being used. The Ambassador agreed.

Once again, the jumpy Finn repeated that his government was "glad that the problem was settled."[20]

Johnson responded, apparently with tongue in his cheek, that his government was glad too, if not quite as glad: "Mr. Johnson said that we [the United States] were also pleased, but not as pleased as Finland seemed to be." "He realized that Finland must also be relieved," the American added, soothingly.

At this point Seppälä, anxious for Johnson to drop his mask, asked his fellow diplomat what he *really* thought about the situation: "Ambassador Seppala [*sic*] wondered what we thought of the recent happenings."

So Johnson told him: "It was his own reaction that the Soviets had demonstrated that they could crack the whip. Every Finn, politician or citizen, would have this in the back of his mind from now on."

To which Seppälä, wearying of the charade, dropped *his* mask:

> The Ambassador agreed, adding that every responsible Finnish statesman would now also have in his mind more than ever the need to get along with the Soviets. [author's italics]
>
> He also agreed that something new had been added to Finnish relations with the USSR [author's italics].[21]

In fact, when it came down to it, there did not seem to be all that much difference between the way Johnson really viewed the Finnish situation and how Seppälä saw it, besides the degree to which each was "relieved" that "the problem" had been solved.

In fact, truth be told, the Finnish envoy did not really seem relieved at all. One imagines that his discomfiture was similar to that experienced by other Finnish ambassadors in the West at this time.

The unexpectedly revealing meeting ended on a friendly note, and why not? Finland and the United States were still friends, after all. It's just that the former now had a very visible gun aimed at its head—a Soviet gun. The memo summarizing the meeting concluded:

> In closing Mr. Johnson once again thanked the Ambassador for his frank presentation and told him that he would see to it that the Secretary and the President heard of this Finnish assessment of the situation, as they were both much interested in Finland.

Ambassador Seppälä said that he believed his account of the Finnish position to be quite accurate.[22]

We know from Rusk's furious communiqué, quoted earlier, that *he* still very much desired America to do something about Finland and that *he* wanted to strengthen the Finns' dormant will to fight back against Moscow by every possible means short of war.

How did JFK feel about the matter? In the event, Finland's relationship with the US—and, to some degree, its relationship with the West—hung in the balance. Did President Kennedy still believe, as he indicated in that note he had had Bernard Gufler read aloud to Kekkonen the day before he set off for Siberia that America's national security depended on Finland's stalwart maintenance of its neutrality?

Put another way, where exactly on the map of the "East-West conflict"—as it was often called in those anxious days—was Finland situated? Did it form part of the northeastern most border between the Free World and the Communist bloc, as Kennedy had asserted—or was it the other way around, as Kekkonen had strongly implied after he had returned from Siberia?

And if so, what did Kennedy wish to do about it, now? Perhaps Finland's uncomfortable new moment in the international spotlight was not over yet.

Chapter 20

Intermezzo

> The presidential election was held in Novosibirsk.
>
> —Helsinki taxi driver, *The New York Times*, November 29, 1961
>
> I wonder how that objection [the lack of political choice] might apply to Finland, where it appears that the only anti-Soviet candidate has been forced to leave the presidential race.
>
> —Question put to President John F. Kennedy at his November 29, 1961, press conference
>
> He wanted to help Kekkonen, of course.
>
> —Sergei Khrushchev, interview by author

As it happened, the world found out how John F. Kennedy felt about Finland, or more precisely, what he intended to do about Finland—or not—at his next press conference, the following day, November 29, 1961. One assumes that, like Dean Rusk, his secretary of state, JFK was also disappointed with the performance of his Finnish counterpart, for whom he had rolled out the White House red carpet six weeks and a seeming eternity before.

Still, Kennedy had not said anything about it in public about the Finnish debacle—nor, in point of fact, had any US official.

Had the official US policy toward Finland, including confronting Moscow over its "aggression" against Finland, as *The New York Times* had archly put it and as Rusk, ardently desired, changed? If Kennedy was looking for an opening for a new front with Moscow over Finland here it was, while the West was still reverberating from the shock waves of the mushroom cloud-enshrouded crisis the Soviets had suddenly precipitated.

The Finnish and Nordic Washington correspondents amongst the 372 reporters present that afternoon in the auditorium of the State Department were particularly interested in hearing what Kennedy had to say on the matter.

Everything hinged on the president's opening statement.

In the event was no mention of Finland in the statement. Kennedy's focus, as it had been at all of his recent press conferences that fraught autumn, was the East–West conflict. His principal concern within that context, and the front he was mostly focused on, he indicated, continued to be Berlin.[1] Despite the end of the standoff between American and Russian forces at Checkpoint Charlie, the president declared, there continued to be "a direct clash of interest in a major area which is Berlin and West Germany." It was for that reason, he said, that his administration had called up US reserve forces and increased preparedness for conventional warfare.

There also was a new front Kennedy was increasingly concerned about, in South Vietnam, where there had been increased fighting between US-backed forces and North Vietnamese-backed Communist one. Just two weeks before, on November 14, 1961, Kennedy had made the fateful decision to increase the number of US advisers in Vietnam from 1,000 to 16,000 over the next two years.[2]

Still no mention of Finland.

Then the pensive-looking Kennedy took questions.

Perhaps inevitably, Finland *did* come up.

In the event, in one of the few upbeat notes in the US–Soviet conflict, just a few days before the press conference, Kennedy had been offered and had given an interview to *Izvestia*, the official organ of the Supreme Soviet of the Soviet Union. Surprisingly, the wide-ranging interview with the paper's editor-in-chief, which actually contained some criticism of the USSR and the Soviet system, was published in full. One of the reporters at the conference—it is not clear whom from the transcript of the conference that was published the following day *in The New York Times*—decided to use one of Kennedy's more pointed answers, in response to a question about what he most objected to about the Soviet system, as a way of getting him to comment on the outcome of the Novosibirsk summit, specifically Olavi Honka's apparently forced exit from the Finnish presidential campaign.

"In your interview with Izvestia," the inquiring reporter asked, "you said that the thing you objected to most about the Soviet system was the lack of political choice." "I wonder," the questioner continued, "how you would describe how that objection might apply to Finland, where it appears that the only anti-Soviet candidate for president was forced to leave the race?"[3]

Kennedy hesitated for a moment, but only a moment. "I would prefer to make that as a general statement," he responded, refusing to be drawn in, "rather than apply it to any particular country, because some countries are having difficulties at this time and I am not sure that any statement I might make at this time would be of assistance to them."[4]

And there, in a nutshell, it was: JFK had decided *not* to confront Moscow over Finland. He had too many other fronts, or potential fronts, to worry about: Berlin, Vietnam, and Cuba.

Now he was pulling the US back to the Acheson-Dulles line on Finland, Dean Rusk's fulminations notwithstanding.

American policy regarding Finland had been reset, and so, essentially, it would remain for the next thirty years, through the remainder of Urho Kekkonen's presidency until the fall of the USSR.

And that, except for the occasional, well-meaning statement of support from one American official, was essentially that.

Thus the well-meaning statement the American representative to the North Atlantic Council made in a private session of the organization on November 30, 1961. "This," he said, referring to the Note Crisis, "is not a separate event but part of a global struggle," blustered Rusk. "We need to keep in mind the enormous power of the West, especially the US Air Force's Strategic Air Force," he went on, referring to America's mighty strategic nuke-wielding bomber arm. "We should make it clear that we will not allow the Soviet Union to use the Finnish hostage in future adventures."[5] To be sure, as we know, a year later, the US, including those ominous Strategic Air Command bombers, did go toe-to-toe with Moscow again during the Cuban Missile Crisis; however by then Finland had receded from the headlines.

Meanwhile, back in Helsinki itself, the same day, November 29, 1961, that Kennedy was officially giving the Finnish affair a wide steer, the euphoria of the Soviet "reprieve" was wearing off, and "bitterness at the shattered state of Finnish politics" was setting in, according to Werner Wiskari's sober report in the *Times*:

> **SOVIET DIMS JOYS OF FINNISH YULE**
>
> Note on Arms Talk Likened to an Atomic Cloud
>
> Christmas trees were on sale today in the marketplace in front of the Presidential Palace, for next Sunday is Little Christmas, the usually happy start of the Yule season. But this year there is a tinge of uneasiness here.
>
> It stems from a new element in Finnish life—the Soviet note of October 30. As one Finn put it, the note hangs like an atomic cloud over Finland.

In the words of the then popular American television show, Finns realized that, geopolitically, their country was back in the twilight zone, a Western democracy in the shadow of the Soviet bear, and fated to stay that way indefinitely—as well as fated to have the same Soviet-friendly president for some time. The feared conflagration following the delivery of the explosive note might have been averted, but the political fallout remained.

> President Urho Kekkonen managed better than anyone had expected in his conversation in Novosibirsk last week. But the military consultations the note had demanded are only "postponed." The note remains.[6]

No doomsayer, the reporter put the best possible spin on the situation.

No, the sky had not fallen, exactly. But it was still pretty dark.

Nevertheless the Finns had not completely lost their *sisu* according to Wiskari:

> Still there is no hand-wringing here. "Naturally," a prominent Finn commented, "it must be recognized that the Soviet [Union] has further narrowed Finland's freedom of maneuver."
>
> But clinging tenaciously to optimism, he and others point out that they have been in far worse situations before. Despite two wars with the Soviet Union and numerous crises, next Wednesday is the forty fourth anniversary of Finland's freedom of maneuver.

It sounded as if Wiskari, who would remain on the Nordic beat for three more years before returning to New York City to join the editorial staff of his newspaper, was himself of two minds about what had actually transpired.

> A Helsinki taxi driver, asked for his analysis of the Finnish political situation, responded by first invoking the name of Satan, as Finns do if they want to add earthy emphasis to their remarks.
>
> "The presidential election," he said, "was held in Novosibirsk."

"In various emergency meetings around town, politicians spoke with equal bitterness," the veteran reporter continued, "of the shattered state of Finnish politics in the aftermath of the Soviet note."[7]

To paraphrase Kekkonen himself, Finland continued to walk in the shadow of the note. And so it would for the next three decades.

As Don Cook, one of the "bad weather birds"—as Finns called the Western reporters who flew into Helsinki every time things looked dark—who had covered the Note Crisis, observed in the sage, and still valid, postmortem he wrote the *The New Republic*, "although all of Finland heaved a fervent sigh of relief, something about the whole episode seemed contrived. Finns began to ask themselves what had really happened, why it had happened and who except for their president and the Russians had really gained."[8]

And so they have been asking ever since.

More than seven decades later, the Note Crisis remains the most controversial episode of modern Finnish history.

As I have noted, I feel that the controversy, while deserved, has been somewhat misconstrued

As Urho Kekkonen's biographer, my principal interest in the crisis is in how it shaped his presidency, as well as his character. To me, both of these things are clear, and really, ought to be clear to an objective, well-informed observer.

As I have suggested, the true significance of the Note Crisis vis-à-vis Kekkonen's presidency is as the second act of a two-hander that began with the Night Frost of 1958, when that "great friend of Finland," N. S. Khrushchev—as Kekkonen called him in his address to the Finnish nation of November 26, 1961—decided to test the limits of the "special relationship" between Moscow and Helsinki by forcing out a Social Democratic government not to its liking, and, at the same time, to test Kekkonen, the Finn who he entrusted to manage that relationship for him, by seeing how willing and able he was to do Khrushchev's bidding.

As we know Kekkonen certainly was willing, and although it took longer than Moscow would have liked, and the Fagerholm cabinet proved more resilient than either he or Moscow expected, while Khrushchev kept a stranglehold on Fenno-Soviet trade, and the hard-pressed Finnish president fumed and sputtered and basically made a fool of himself, he ultimately was able to execute Kremlin's wishes and the Western-oriented Social Democratic cabinet was forced out.

After the Night Frost, along with Kekkonen's tortured, disingenuous exegesis of the crisis and the supposedly manifest, "understandable" reasons for Moscow's economic extortion Khrushchev and the Politburo knew that he was "their man." The Note Crisis, along with Kekkonen's no less (if not more) disingenuous exegesis of the outcome of that episode, including the forced—or all but forced—resignation of his opponent, Honka, simply confirmed that.

Once again, as I have posited, if the Night Frost created the template for both Kekkonen's first term, both insofar as the degree he was willing to abase himself to accommodate the Kremlin, and tamper with Finnish democracy, the Note Crisis—during and after which he essentially did the same—provided the finish.

What I have tried to do herein as the reader has hopefully seen, is to clarify that, while also placing the Note Crisis in the additional context of the annals of information warfare, of which it was unquestionably an extraordinary success, witness the trouble it created not just for Kekkonen, but for the entire region and the Western Allies. There is also no question in my mind that the timing of these linked crises was also linked to Moscow's larger ambitions. It was no coincidence that that supposed "good and great friend of Finland, N.S. Khrushchev," as Kekkonen put it in his speech after he returned from Novosobirsk, timed the first act of his Finnish two-hander with his decision to instigate the second Berlin crisis.

Nor was it, nor can it be a coincidence that he dropped the boom on Helsinki again three years later at the same time when he was trying to—and did—force a resolution to the parallel, ongoing German crisis, while also testing the West's and the world's nerves in the heavens with his megaton atomic tests.

Amongst other things, Khrushchev was a master dramatist, even if he does not seem to have quite thought out exactly how his multiple-front war with the West would ultimately play out. He would find that out a year later when he found that his strategy of pushing the United States to the limit backfired during the Cuban Missile crisis, and the Soviet premier was forced to remove the nuclear missiles he had surreptitiously placed in America's backyard.

Finland was always a subplot of that larger play, but it was an important subplot to him, and one that he took a personal interest in because of his fondness for Kekkonen, if not necessarily for Finland. In that sense, one could say, the Note Crisis was indeed an intermezzo in the Cold War, in Richard Seppälä's memorable phrase, and not an entire movement, as it briefly threatened to become—and doubtless would have become if Kennedy had decided not to engage the Soviet (as the USSR used to be called) over Finland, as his hawkish secretary of state, R[illegible], had urged.

But what a revealing intermezzo it was.

As far as Kekkonen's character was concerned, of course, that, including his ability to thrive under pressure, as well as fool whomever needed fooling—including himself— had already been shaped before the crisis. One cannot really say that the crisis really changed him, but, as we have seen those four roller-coaster weeks in the penumbra of the note certainly showed him as both his best, as well as his worst.

Nevertheless the controversy revolving around the crisis continues, and it would be remiss of me not to address it, preferably with the aid of those who actually knew the parties involved, including Kekkonen and Khrushchev themselves.

One of the more credible witnesses among those who knew Kekkonen, both in this writer's opinion as well as a number of Kekkonen's surviving entourage, is Jaakko Kalela. Kalela, who joined Kekkonen's staff as foreign policy advisor in 1973 during his third term, rose to become his special advisor for foreign policy, continued to work for him for the remainder of his presidency, and probably knew Kekkonen as well as anyone among his extant staff. Although Kalela, who later became secretary general of the office of the president of the republic for Kekkonen's successors Mauno Koivisto (1981–94), Martti Ahtisaari (1994–2000), and Tarja Halonen (2000–2012) perforce could speak with more authority about the issues and questions he and his former boss dealt with after 1973, he also has given considerable thought to the Note Crisis, as did all of Kekkonen's close advisors, who, perforce, labored in the shadow of The Note, both at that time and thereafter.

In any case, much, if not most of what Kalela says about Kekkonen—of whom he remains fond, but certainly not worshipful—makes sense, at least to me, even if departs from the popular revisionist view of that murky interlude, so the reader will indulge me if I quote from my interviews with him, as well as our correspondence, at length.

According to the Finnish president's former confidante, the still radioactive controversy stemming from the crisis can basically be divided into two questions, neither of which can be definitively answered: "One," writes Kalela, "what were the Kremlin's—and Khrushchev's—motives in instigating the crisis in the first place—the Berlin crisis, the conference of the CPSU [Communist Party of the Soviet Union] that was being held at the time of the crisis, guaranteeing that Kekkonen would be reelected, etc."[9]

"Two—how much did Kekkonen know [about the crisis] in advance: nothing, some information for [*sic*] a warning; or full knowledge and joint planning with the Soviets."

"The Soviet archives are not open enough to give a final answer to either question," Kalela continues, "nor do Kekkonen's archives nor any other archives." Kalela then goes on to dissect the much-discussed analysis of both of these questions by one of the Russians who was closest to the scene, Viktor Vladimirov, the KGB station co-chief, who, as we have seen, frequently met with Kekkonen during his first term. Vladimirov writes about the crisis at length in his 1993 memoir.

Kalela then goes on to explain why what the former KGB lieutenant general writes about the crisis, which created quite a stir when his book was published, must be taken with a large grain of salt:

> Vladimirov who was then No. 2 or 3 in the Helsinki [embassy] wrote in his memoirs that the sole motive was to guarantee the continuation of Finland's foreign policy line and to help Kekkonen. He denies that the international situation was a factor—which is not objectively true.
>
> He [Vladimirov] argues that the initiative for the note was made by his boss [*sic*], [Vladimir] Zhenikov. This may be partly true, but he also seems to be over-estimating the role of the KGB and the Helsinki residence. It is obvious that in this way the KGB wanted to elevate their role and importance in the record.

"Vladimirov definitely denies that Kekkonen took any initiative or participated in the planning of the note," Kalela observes. "But Vladimirov argues that Kekkonen was warned but also assured that the crisis would be resolved without harming Kekkonen's interests."[10]

As noted and discussed above, and which the author believes is clear from an objective evaluation of the evidence, including *all* of the wheels that were turning at the time, both in Finland and abroad at that fraught moment of the East–West conflict, The Note, as well as the decision to deliver it to the Finnish government *at that time* was motivated by a multiplicity of motives on the part of the Kremlin, including assuring Kekkonen's reelection.

Did Kekkonen have a head's up that Moscow was thinking of invoking Article 2 of the 1948 treaty?

He probably did, Kalela thinks, and so does this author. Kekkonen's mention of Article 2 during his meeting with Kennedy at the White House, which took JFK by surprise, would seem to confirm that. Nevertheless the former presidential aide insists that, regardless of the Kremlin's motives, the actual timing of the Soviet demarche, while Kekkonen was in the US, was a surprise to him. The shocked look on Kekkonen's face in that famous photo of him and his lei-adorned entourage in Hawaii was, he believes, was *not* feigned. I also think his shock was real.

What *were* Khrushchev's motives in firing off the note? To answer that question, I also asked another Russian who was close to the scene who I thought might have something to say about that—the Soviet premier's son, Sergei Khrushchev.

Sergei, who died in 2020, emigrated to the US in 1991, the year the USSR collapsed. He went on the author of several books about his father, most notably the biography, *Nikita Khrushchev and the Creation of a Superpower*. Khrushchev also was a senior fellow at the Watson Institute of Brown University before he retired in 2015.

Fortunately I was able to get ahold of him before he passed.

It was not easy.

Suffice to say that one afternoon in 2016 there the author was in the Soviet memorabilia-lined den of Sergei Khrushchev, who looked uncannily like his father, asking him what he recalled about the Note Crisis and Nikita Khrushchev's motives in sending that multiple mayhem-making demarche at that time.[11]

Did he remember the affair at all? "Of course I remember it," Khrushchev junior said immediately, as if he was insulted by the question.[12] "I remember it well." Then what *was* his father's motive in sending The Note?

"He wanted to help Kekkonen, of course, father said. We must do something to help Urho."

And how much, if any warning did his father give Kekkonen that he was going to deliver the note at that time? "That I don't know," Khrushchev replied.[13]

He must have known something, Khrushchev said, but he was not sure.

So there it was. I had my answer. Sort of.

In the end does it really matter what the senior Khrushchev's motives really were? Jaakko Kalela asks.

"As a whole, to my mind, it is quite obvious that no matter what the Kremlin's motives were The Note affair was humiliating and negative for Kekkonen," Kalela wrote me in a long letter. "In 1961," according to Kalela, who later became ambassador to Estonia, "Kekkonen wanted to show that he was a great foreign policy leader, that he could master relations with the USSR but at the same time be welcome and respected in Washington and the West and have his policy of active neutrality validated."

"The image that he was trying to create was totally ruined by the Note," Kalela continued. "Khrushchev basically told Kekkonen,

'We are prepared to resolve this, but I am inspecting *kolkhozes* in Novosibirsk, so why don't you come here.' And then Kekkonen has to travel 5,000 kilometers [actually it was 4,580 kilometers or 2,845 miles] to meet the Great Leader because he can't stay one more day in Moscow to deal with the issue. Kekkonen was forced to undertake a penitential journey."

"Critics are still saying that Kekkonen ordered the Note to create a heroic tale for himself. I don't think that this is a heroic tale at all. I do think history will see it see [the crisis] this way, eventually. Of course it was a surprise to him, especially at *that* time.

"Kekkonen went too far, and got slapped on the fingers [*sic*] by the Kremlin. I suppose he suspected that his friend, Khrushchev, was going to try do something to help him, but certainly not at that time and in that way."[14]

The former presidential assistant believes that his boss had two options for resolving the crisis, once the Soviet premier "invited" him to Novosibirsk. To wit: "He could step down as president, which I believe he considered"—and as indeed had given serious thought to, as he told Bernard Gufler on the eve of his departure. "Or," Kalela, says, "he could suffer the humiliation."

"So," he concludes, "he decided to suffer the latter."

Anyway, what really matters, Kalela continues, with an audible note of admiration, is what Kekkonen made of situation. "He made the best of it really, or the best he could. He returned from Novosibirsk, gave a statement that Finnish neutrality had been saved."

Kalela continues, flashing forward, Kekkonen "won the presidential elections"—as indeed Kekkonen did on January 15, 1962—"inflicted a staggering defeat upon the opposing coalition, *as well as the Communists* [author's italics]—as indeed Kekkonen also did three weeks later, "formed a government to his liking and pulled himself up again."

"It's quite a feat, if you think about it."[15]

In his biography of Max Jakobson, Jukka Tarkka agrees with that complimentary assessment. "Kekkonen had come a long way from Helsinki to Novosibirsk," he notes, "but he had achieved what he set out to do. There were to be no negotiations." "Neutrality," which, as Tarkka points out, was really Kekkonen's code for Finnish independence—even if it was a constricted form of independence—"was [achieved] according to Kekkonen's [formula], not by defying the Soviet Union but by achieving accord with it."

To be sure, the former parliamentarian continues, the protean Finn "might not have won the Nobel Prize" for the bobbing and weaving manner with he succeeded in maintaining Finnish neutrality and Finnish independence, "but he deserved an Oscar for masterful acting."[16] Indeed.

Was Kekkonen in fact capable of planning the entire crisis with the Soviets, including that humiliating trek to Siberia to resolve the matter?

No doubt. Whether he *actually did* so—which the evidence, including Ambassador Gufler's eyewitness account of Kekkonen's "desperate" appearance on the eve of his pilgrimage to Novosibirsk, at least to this writer, persuasively argues *against*—is more or less beside the point, at least as far as how things turned out.

To be sure, whatever one thinks of Urho Kekkonen's performance during the Note Crisis, which has taken on renewed interest in light of the revived Fenno-Soviet tensions following Finland's decision to join NATO following Russia's invasion of Ukraine, including whether or not it was a "feat" as Kalela maintains, or something else—the end result, at least as far as the "shattered" Finnish political scene, as Werner Wiskari, the astute *New York Times* correspondent put it, was, and is, inarguable.

Kekkonen now towered over that scene as Don Cook of *The New Republic* wrote in his prescient, and essentially accurate, postmortem. Indeed he was now Finland's "only man," the American wrote: "Kekkonen, at the center of this web of emotion and politics," the American reporter concluded, in a voice of mixed admiration and dismay—which essentially is how most Finns now regarded him, "*is without question not only Finland's 'strong man,' but practically its only man* [author's italics]. He dominates the Finnish political scene and stands far above any other Finnish politician in ability."

> Kekkonen is also extremely controversial in Finland, violently condemned by many. He is politically ruthless. He plays the complete lone-wolf with his government and his people. He consults nobody, confides in nobody [and] is capable of the most unpredictable tricks and maneuvers.[17]

Still, Cook conceded, Kekkonen was fated to be Finland's "only man" for quite a while.

And so he would be.

For a very long while—twenty years more to be precise—with the result that Kekkonen wound up being the longest-serving democratically elected executive in the world. In any case, the template for what would ultimately become a quarter century facsimile regency had been set; the glazing had been applied.

And so it would for the "special" relationship, including both its written codicils, particularly the problematic Article 2 of the 1948 treaty which triggered the Note Crisis, as well as the various unwritten ones which were confirmed during Kekkonen's formative first term (see Finnish self-censorship), which would remain in effect for the rest of the Finnish magnifico's tenure, through the breakup of the USSR in 1991 and the scrapping of the 1948 treaty, and beyond.

And now, thanks to Vladimir Putin's invasion of Ukraine, triggering memories of Joseph Stalin's invasion of Finland in 1939, Finland is actually a member of NATO, something that was unimaginable until recently.

And what, one wonders, would Khrushchev, no less Kekkonen, make of that?

THE END.

Notes

Prologue

1. Bernard Gufler (1903–73), career US diplomat, American ambassador to Finland (1961–63).

2. "Telegram from the Department of State to the Embassy in Finland," November 20, 1961, in *Foreign Relations of the United States, 1961–1963*, vol. 16, *Eastern Europe; Cyprus; Greece; Turkey* (Washington, DC: Government Printing Office, 1994), document 199.

3. In December 1961, Anatoliy Golitsyn, a KGB officer with the rank of major serving under the cover of vice consul at the Soviet embassy in Helsinki, defected to the United States.

4. Halvard Lange (1902–70), Norwegian foreign minister (1946–63). Werner Wiskari, "Scandinavians Are Calm," *New York Times*, November 1, 1961, 3.

5. "Memorandum by the Secretary of State," February 9, 1950, in *Foreign Relations of the United States, 1950*, vol. 4, *Central and Eastern Europe; The Soviet Union* (Washington, DC: Government Printing Office, 1980), document 307.

6. "Memorandum from Secretary of State Rusk to President Kennedy," November 20, 1961, in *Foreign Relations of the United States, 1961–1963*, vol. 16, *Berlin Crisis, 1961–1962* (Washington, DC: Government Printing Office, 1993), document 214.

7. "The Embassy in Finland to the State Department," October 28, 1958, Department of State.

8. "Memorandum from Secretary of State Rusk," November 20, 1961.

9. "Department of State to the Embassy in Finland," November 20, 1961.

10. "Department of State to the Embassy in Finland," November 20, 1961.

11. Juhani Suomi, *Urho Kekkosen paivakirjat 1, 1958–62* [*Urho Kekkonen's Diaries 1, 1958–62*] (Helsinki: Otava, 2001), 443.

12. "Department of State to the Embassy in Finland," November 20, 1961.

13. "Department of State to the Embassy in Finland," November 20, 1961.

1. Stormy Weather (2/56–1/57)

Epigraph 1. "A Faustian Pact," *Books from Finland*, 1997, 218–19.

Epigraph 2. Urho Kekkonen, *Puheita ja kirjotuksia*, 1: *Puheita vuosita 1936 – 1956* [Speeches and Writings, 1: Speeches from 1936–1956] (Helsinki: Weilin + Göös, 1967), 142.

Epigraph 3. Juha Engstrom, interview by author, March 2016. Juha Engstrom (1942–), aide-to-camp to the president (1976–85).

1. David Kirby, *A Concise History of Finland* (Cambridge: Cambridge University Press, 2006), 256.

2. Sergei Khrushchev, interview by author, March 2016.

3. "Finland's New President," *New York Times*, March 3, 1956, 18.

4. "Finland's New President."

5. Henrik Meinander, the noted historian, believes that Kekkonen's "fixation" on Karelia was another one of his many political feints.

6. Otto Wille Kuusinen (1881–1964), the Finnish politician turned Soviet functionary. Kuusinen is the only native Finn who is buried in the Kremlin Wall.

7. Kliment Voroshilov (1881–1969). Voroshilov is buried in the mausoleum in Red Square.

8. "Voroshilov to Finland," *New York Times*, August 20, 1956, 2.

9. "Voroshilov Leaving Finland," *New York Times*, August 26, 1956, 6.

10. Kauko Sipponen (1927–2019), legal scholar, president's chief of staff (1973–76).

11. Sergei Khrushchev, interview by author.

12. Kauko Sipponen, interview, interview by author, March 2016.

13. Imre Nagy (1896–1958), Hungarian communist politician, prime minister (1953–55), leader of Hungarian revolution 1956.

14. Vesa Vares, *Foes Who Grew Better with Time: The Image of János Kádár and Urho Kekkonen in the West from 1956 to the End of the 1960s* (Jyväskylä, Finland: University of Jyväskylä, 2002), 43.

15. Kekkonen also instructed the Finnish delegation to the United Nations, which Finland had just joined, with Moscow's acquiescence, to abstain on a Security Council declaration underlining Hungary's right to self-determination.

16. Dmitri Shepilov (1905–95), foreign minister of Soviet Union 1956–57; Arvid (Arvo "Poika") Tuominen (1894–1981), Social Democratic parliamentarian (1958–61).

17. "'Liberation' Pledge to Finland," *Times* (London), June 30, 1958, 10.

18. "Suomolaiset communist odottavat 'Kadar-kulmaa" [Finnish Communists Await 'Kadar-Corner], *Helsingin Sanomat*, June 29, 1958, 7.

19. Uuno Johannes (Jussi) Kekkonen (1910–62). A major in the Continuation War, Kekkonen was ambushed with his troops in Kiimasjarvi in July 1941, wounded badly in the head and wound up losing his sight. After the war he worked as a businessman.

20. Viktor Vladimirov (1922–95), Soviet lieutenant general, KGB station chief in Helsinki. Viktor Vladimirov, *Nain se oli: muistelmia ja havaintoja kulissientakaisesta 1954–84,* [This Is How It Was: Memories and Observations of Diplomatic Activity in Finland 1954–84], trans. Arnold Hiltunen (Helsinki: Otava, 1993), 65–66.

21. Jaakko Kalela (1944–), foreign policy adviser (1973–83). Jaakko Kalela, interview by author, May 2014.

22. Bulganin and Khrushchev had hoped to make the trip the first stop on a grand tour of Scandinavia; however, the governments of Sweden, Norway, and

Denmark, angry over the Soviet crackdown in Hungary, made it clear that they were not welcome.

23. "Speech of the President of the Republic," *Helsingin Sanomat*, June 8, 1957, 13.

24. "President Kekkonen: Doubts and Misunderstandings Have Evaporated," *Helsingin Sanomat*, June 8, 1957, 13.

25. Drew Middleton, "Finns Unswayed by Russian Talk," *New York Times*, June 8, 1957, 8.

26. Middleton, "Finns Unswayed."

27. "Finns Unswayed."

28. "Finns Want Closer Ties to the West," *Business Week*, June 15, 1958, 121.

29. Jaakko Iloniemi (1932–), Finnish diplomat, ambassador to Washington (1977–83). Jaakko Iloniemi, interview by author, June 2015.

30. Vladimirov, *Nain se oli*, 65–66.

31. Vladimirov, *Nain se oli*, 65–66.

32. Eugene Lyons, "The Many Faces of Nikita Khrushchev," *Reader's Digest*, August 1959, 50.

33. Sergey N. Khrushchev, *Nikita Khrushchev and the Creation of a Superpower* (University Park: Pennsylvania State Univerity Press, 2001), 235.

34. Khrushchev, *Nikita Khrushchev and the Creation of a Superpower*, 235.

35. Molotov found himself the new ambassador to Mongolia. Kaganovich was given directorship of a small potassium factory in the Urals. Bulganin was banished to Stavropol, where he ended his working life as deputy director of the regional economic council.

36. Khrushchev, *Nikita Khrushchev and the Creation of a Superpower*.

37. Khrushchev, *Nikita Khrushchev and the Creation of a Superpower*.

38. Ivan Serov (1905–90). In 1958, Khrushchev, still irritated with Serov, removed him from the KGB, whence he became head of the GRU, the Soviet military intelligence agency.

39. Khrushchev, *Nikita Khrushchev and the Creation of a Superpower*, 236

40. Fabian Steinheil (1762–1831), Russian governor general of Finland (1810–24).

41. Antti Hackzell (1881–1946). Typical of this benighted period of Finnish history, the luckless Hackzell, who suffered a stroke during the arduous Moscow negotiations, only led the government and the peace delegation in name at that point. The negotiations were consummated by his foreign minister, Carl Enckell.

42. Johan Wilhelm (Jukka) Rangell (1894–1982), wartime prime minister of Finland.

43. Kekkonen ordered his planning staff to keep Helsinki small, or relatively small, according to Jukka Petäjä, literary critic for *Helsingin Sanomat*, whose father was a city architect.

44. Donald S. Connery, *The Scandinavians*, trans. Heidi Järvenpää (London: Eyre & Spottiswoode, 1967), 492.

45. Wilson was incapacitated in October, 1919, at the height of his arduous, and ultimately unsuccessful, campaign in support of the Versailles Treaty.

For the remaining eighteen months of his presidency his affairs were effectively managed by his wife, Edith, and his top advisor, Colonel Edward House.

46. Letter from the archives of Urho Kekkonen.

47. Letter from the archives of Urho Kekkonen.

2. A Brusque Intervention (6/57–10/58)

1. "A Tightrope to Coexistence," *Times* (London), December 14, 1959, 11.

2. "Soviet Rebuffs Finland; Calls off Trade Talks and Attacks Tanner as Leader," *New York Times,* October 25, 1957, 7.

3. "Telegram from the State Department to the Embassy in London," September 2, 1958.

4. Anastas Mikoyan (1895–1978), Soviet deputy prime minister.

5. George Maude, *Aspects of Governing the Finns* (New York: Peter Lang Publishing, 2010), 230.

6. Kekkonen's inaugural visit to the Soviet Union was the first of the twenty-seven official or state visits he was to make during the course of his presidency. The average length was three days. The longer visits tended to coincide with East–West crises. The longest, fourteen days, took place in October 1962, on the eve of the Cuban Missile Crisis.

7. Sergei Khrushchev, interview by author, March 2016.

8. The French ambassador to Moscow from 1956 to 1964, DeJean would suffer far worse, falling victim to an attractive woman "swallow" in a KGB honey trap. He was later recalled. William J. Jorden, "Voroshilov Cool to De Gaulle Bid," *New York Times,* May 29, 1958, 3.

9. Janos Kadar (1912–89), Hungarian communist leader (1956–88).

10. Juhani Suomi, *Urho Kekkosen paivakirjat 1, 1958–1962* [Urho Kekkonen's Diaries 1, 1958–1962] (Helsinki: Otova, 2001) 66.

11. Eino Kilpi (1889–1963), journalist and socialist parliamentarian.

12. Named after Sergo Ordzhonikidze, a longtime associate of Stalin who died in 1937 under mysterious circumstances. The cruiser's fierce reputation was enhanced in 1956, when a British frogman named Lionel Crabb died while surreptitiously inspecting it when docked in Portsmouth harbor.

13. Werner Wiskari, "Russians Sail In, Finns Sail on through Another Political Day," *New York Times,* August 8, 1958, 6.

14. John Hickerson (1898–1989), American ambassador to Helsinki (1955–59).

15. "Telegram from the Embassy in Finland to the Department of State," August 30, 1958, in *Foreign Relations of the United States, 1958–1960,* volume 10, part 2, *Eastern Europe; Finland; Greece; Turkey* (Washington, DC: Government Printing Office, 1993), document 183.

16. Väinö Leskinen (1917–72), social democratic politician, minister of social welfare (1958–59); Olavi Lindblom (1911–90), social democratic parliamentarian (1954–66).

17. Johannes Virolainen (1914–2000), Center Party politician, prime minister (1964–66).

18. Donald S. Connery, *The Scandinavians*, trans. Heidi Järvenpää (London: Eyre & Spottiswoode, 1967), 491.

19. Urpo Levo (1921-98), general and second adjutant of the president (1955-62), later first adjutant (1965-74), and promoted to major general.

20. Suomi, *Urho Kekkonen's Diaries 1*, 96.

21. Suomi, *Urho Kekkonen's Diaries 1*, 84.

22. Rainer von Fieandt (1890–1972), financier, prime minister (1957-58); Veikko Vennamo (1913-97), politician, founder of the Rural Party; Suomi, *Urho Kekkonen's Diaries 1*.

23. Viktor Lebedev (1900-68), Russian ambassador to Helsinki (1951-58).

24. Connery, *Scandinavians*, 489.

25. The so-called Stockholm syndrome refers to a 1977 bank robbery-cum-hostage taking in which some of the civilian hostages wound up sympathizing with the robber-captors.

26. Viktor Vladimirov, *Nain se oli: muistela ja havaintoja kulissientakaisesta diplomaatiitoiminnnasta Suomessa* [This Is How It Was: Memories and Observations of Diplomatic Activity in Finland 1954-84], trans. Arnold Hiltunen (Helisnki: Otava, 1993), 65-66.

27. Suomi, *Urho Kekkonen's Diaries 1*, 109.

28. Suomi, *Urho Kekkonen's Diaries 1*.

29. Kekkonen relied on a number of Russian-speaking staffers to translate for him during his meetings with the Russians. Perhaps the best known—or at least the most prominent—of these during his first term was Kustaa Loikkanen.

30. It is worth noting here that in October 1958, a loan of 400 million rubles—the same amount that Moscow had offered Helsinki—was extended to the putatively neutral, Soviet-friendly government of Egypt in order to assist with the building of the Aswan Dam. The loan, which was gratefully accepted by the government of Gamal Nasser, was considered a major Soviet coup in the East-West propaganda war.

31. Hertta Kuusinen (1904-74), communist parlamentarian.

32. Suomi, *Urho Kekkonen's Diaries 1*, 109.

33. Suomi, *Urho Kekkonen's Diaries 1*, 109.

34. 1897-1961. The publication of Leino's memoirs, scheduled for 1958, was canceled because of Soviet pressure and the entire run of 12,000 books was destroyed.

35. Then again, Kekkonen had little regard for most of the eleven US ambassadors who served during his presidency. Suomi, *Urho Kekkonen's Diaries 1*, 109.

36. "Despatch from the Embassy in Finland to the Department of State," May 12 1958, in *Foreign Relations of the United States, 1958–1960*, volume 10, part 2, *Eastern Europe; Finland; Greece; Turkey* (Washington, DC: Government Printing Office, 1993), document 179.

37. "Telegram from the Embassy in Finland to the Department of State," September 2, 1958, in *Foreign Relations of the United States, 1958–1960*, volume 10, part 2, *Eastern Europe; Finland; Greece; Turkey* (Washington, DC: Government Printing Office, 1993), document 184.

38. "Embassy in Finland to the Department of State," September 2, 1958.

39. Evidently Hickerson got his intelligence about the Finnish communists from the ardently pro-Kremlin Finnish communist press. If the American embassy had reliable contacts within the SKDL, which apparently it did not, he would have learned otherwise.

40. "Embassy in Finland to the Department of State," September 2, 1958.

41. "Memorandum of Conversation," September 4, 1958, in *Foreign Relations of the United States, 1958–1960*, volume 10, part 2, *Eastern Europe; Finland; Greece; Turkey* (Washington, DC: Government Printing Office, 1993), document 185.

42. Charles Cabell (1903-71). An Air Force general, Cabell was deputy director of the CIA from 1953 to 1962. He was forced to resign by President Kennedy after the Bay of Pigs debacle. Christian Herter (1895–1966), US secretary of state (1959-61).

43. "Memorandum of Conversation," September 4, 1958.

44. Lebedev's vacation turned out to be permanent. Moscow did not send his replacement, Aleksey Zakharov, until January 1959.

45. "Signs of Coolness," *Times* (London), September 17, 1958, 8.

46. Suomi, *Urho Kekkonen's Diaries 1*, 109.

47. Suomi, *Urho Kekkonen's Diaries 1*, 109.

48. In 1957, Finland took a first step toward membership in the OEEC when it signed the so-called Helsinki Club protocol with the OEEC allowing easier payment arrangements irritating Moscow.

49. Suomi, *Urho Kekkonen's Diaries 1.*

50. Werner Wiskari, "Finland's Cooling on Soviet Hinted," *New York Times*, October 10, 1958, 2.

51. Wiskari, "Finland's Cooling on Soviet Hinted," 2.

52. Wiskari, "Finland's Cooling on Soviet Hinted."

53. Wiskari, "Finland's Cooling on Soviet Hinted."

54. I. V. Spiridonov (1905–80). Also first secretary of the Leningrad Regional Party.

55. Suomi, *Urho Kekkonen's Diaries 1*, 72.

56. Suomi, *Urho Kekkonen's Diaries 1.*

57. Invited to join the UN in 1955, Finland generally abstained in votes that pitted the West against the communist bloc. Suomi, *Urho Kekkonen's Diaries 1*, 109.

58. One of the means Kekkonen used was to show the notes he was receiving from Wuori, the Finnish ambassador to Moscow, indicating the Kremlin's distress to Virolainen, but not to Fagerholm.

59. Suomi, *Urho Kekkonen's Diaries 1*, 109.

60. "Telegram from the Embassy in Finland to the Department of State," October 13, 1958, in *Foreign Relations of the United States, 1958–1960*, volume 10, part 2, *Eastern Europe; Finland; Greece; Turkey* (Washington, DC: Government Printing Office, 1993), document 190.

61. Gerald Smith (1922–98). Career US diplomat.

62. "Memorandum from the Assistant Secretary of State for Policy Planning (Smith) to Acting Secretary of State Herter," October 23, 1958, in *Foreign*

Relations of the United States, 1958–1960, volume 10, part 2, *Eastern Europe; Finland; Greece; Turkey* (Washington, DC: Government Printing Office, 1993), document 193.

63. "Memorandum from Smith to Herter," October 23, 1958.

64. Suomi, *Urho Kekkonen's Diaries 1*, 109.

65. "Telegram from the Embassy in Finland to the Department of State," November 6, 1958, in *Foreign Relations of the United States, 1958–1960*, volume 10, part 2, *Eastern Europe; Finland; Greece; Turkey* (Washington, DC: Government Printing Office, 1993), document 194.

66. "Embassy in Finland to the Department of State," November 6, 1958.

67. "Embassy in Finland to the Department of State," November 6, 1958.

3. The Boom Drops (11/58–1/59)

Epigraph. Jaakko Hautamäki, "Ystävien kesken" [Among Friends], *Helsingin Sanomat*, April 6, 2008, https://www.hs.fi/sunnuntai/art-2000004560314.html.

1. Central Intelligence Agency, "'Finlandization' in Action: Helsinki's Experience with Moscow," Freedom of Information Act Reading Room, 1972, https://www.cia.gov/readingroom/docs/esau-55.pdf.

2. Eino Uusitalo (1924–2015), parliamentarian of the Center Party (1955–83), minister of interior (1971, 1976–82); *Helsingin Sanomat*, April 23, 2010.

3. Hautamäki, "Among Friends."

4. Juhani Suomi, *Urho Kekkosen paivakirjat 1, 1958–1962* [Urho Kekkonen's Diaries 1, 1958–1962] (Helsinki: Otava, 2001), 138.

5. Suomi, *Urho Kekkonen's Diaries 1*, 140–41.

6. Ahti Karjalainen (1923–90), minister of trade and industry (1959–61), foreign minister in various cabinets between 1961 and 1975, and prime minister (1962–63, 1970–71). Suomi, *Urho Kekkonen's Diaries 1*, 143.

7. Urho Kekkonen, *Puheita ja kirjotuksia, 2: Puheita presidenttikaudelta 1956–1967* [Speeches and Writings, 2: Speeches from the Presidential Period 1956–1967] (Helsinki: Weilin + Göös, 1967), 71.

8. Telegram from the Department of State to the Embassy in Finland, November 25, 1958, in *Foreign Relations of the United States, 1958–1960*, vol. 10, part 2, *Eastern Europe; Finland; Greece; Turkey* (Washington, DC: Government Printing Office, 1993), document 196.

9. Dean Acheson (1893–71), US secretary of state (1949–53).

10. "Memorandum by the Secretary of State," February 9, 1950, in *Foreign Relations of the United States, 1950*, vol. 4, *The Soviet Union* (Washington, DC: Government Printing Office, 1980), document 307.

11. Dean Rusk (1909–1994), US secretary of state (1961–69).

12. Khrushchev, *Khrushchev Remembers*, 338.

13. Khrushchev, *Khrushchev Remembers*, 338.

14. Suomi, *Urho Kekkonen's Diaries 1*, 143.

15. "Strain in Finnish Cabinet Grows," *The Times* (London), November 26, 1958, 8.

16. Arvo Korsimo (1901–69), party secretary of Agrarian League (1950–60)

17. Suomi, *Urho Kekkonen's Diaries 1*, 149.

18. "Telegram from the Embassy in Finland to the Department of State," December 3, 1958, in *Foreign Relations of the United States, 1958–1960*, vol. 10, part 2, *Eastern Europe; Finland; Greece; Turkey* (Washington, DC: Government Printing Office, 1993), document 198.

19. Edvard Benes (1884–1948), president of Czechoslovakia (1935-38, 1945–48). His second presidency ended after a Soviet coup.

20. Suomi, *Urho Kekkonen's Diaries 1*, 151.

21. James Ford Cooper, *On the Finland Watch: An American Diplomat in Finland During the Cold War* (Bloomington, IN: Author House, 2001), 65.

22. Cooper, *On the Finland Watch, 65;* James Ford Cooper, *Finland as a Homeland: An American Diplomat in Finland during the Cold War* (Helsinki: Tammi, 1998), 228.

23. Jaakko Iloniemi interview.

24. Paavo Laitinen (1931–2004), Finnish diplomat.

25. Taneli went on to have a distinguished career with the foreign service, serving as ambassador to Athens, Rome, Malta, Warsaw and Tel Aviv. However his alcoholism, which led to his recall from his last post in Tel Aviv, would destroy him. He committed suicide in 1985, a year before his father's death.

26. James Ford Cooper, *Finland as a homeland: An American diplomat in Finland during the Cold War* (Helsinki: Tammi, 1998), 229.

27. Kekkonen, *Speeches and Writings 2*, 66–74.

28. "Telegram from the Embassy in Finland to the Department of State," December 11, 1958, in *Foreign Relations of the United States, 1958–1960*, vol. 10, part 2, *Eastern Europe; Finland; Greece; Turkey* (Washington, DC: Government Printing Office, 1993), document 203.

29. Kauno Kleemola (1906-65), Finnish politician.

30. Cooper, *Finland as a Homeland*, 227.

31. Suomi, *Urho Kekkonen's Diaries 1*, 450.

32. Suomi, *Urho Kekkonen's Diaries 1*, 157.

33. Erik Tawaststjerna (1916–93), musicologist, biographer of Jean Sibelius.

34. From an unpublished letter by Tawastjerna to Kekkonen, Kekkonen archives.

35. Pekka Lähteenkorva and Jussi Pekkarinen, *Kirjeta myllarille, 1956–1981* [Letters to the Miller, 1956-1981], (Helsinki: Otava, 2000), 63-64.

36. Suomi, *Urho Kekkonen's Diaries 1*, 161.

37. Suomi, *Urho Kekkonen's Diaries 1*, 178.

38. Suomi, *Urho Kekkonen's Diaries 1*, 179.

39. Suomi, *Urho Kekkonen's Diaries 1*, 180.

40. Rolf Törngren (1899-1961), prime minister (May 5-October 20, 1954), foreign minister (1953–54, 1956–57, 1959–61).

41. Suomi, *Urho Kekkonen's Diaries 1*, 185.

42. "Finns Moving Closer to Russia," *Times* (London), January 22, 1959, 9.

43. Max Jakobson, *Finland in the New Europe* (Westport, CT: Greenwood, 1998), 71.

44. Jakobson, *Finland in the New Europe*, 71.

45. David Kirby, *A Concise History of Finland* (Cambridge: Cambridge University Press, 2006), 250.

4. A Clever Man (1/59–7/59)

Epigraph. "Finns' Realistic Chief," *New York Times*, January 24, 1959, 4.

1. Urho Kekkonen, *Puheita ja kirjotuksia, 2: Puheita presidenttikaudelta 1956–1967* [Speeches and Writings, 2: Speeches from the Presidential Period 1956–1967] (Helsinki: Weilin + Göös, 1967), 80.

2. "Finns' Realistic Chief."

3. "Finns' Realistic Chief"; interestingly, *Don Quixote* was also one of Khrushchev's favorite novels.

4. Unpublished letter.

5. Pekka Lähteenkorva and Jussi Pekkarinen, *Kirjeta myllarille, 1956–1981* [Letters to the Miller, 1956–1981] (Helsinki: Otava, 2000), 74–76.

6. Lähteenkorva and Pekkarinen, *Letters to the Miller 1956–1981*, 77.

7. Jouko Loikkanen, Kekkonen's former secretary (1952–60).

8. Timo Kekkonen, interview by author, October 2014.

9. Timo Kekkonen, interview by author.

10. Donald S. Connery, *The Scandinavians*, trans. Heidi Järvenpää (London: Eyre & Spottiswoode, 1967), 512.

11. Paul Reynaud (1878–1966), prime minister of France (March–June 1940). Hélène de Portes (1902–40), Reynaud's mistress.

12. "Author and President's Wife," *Times* (London), May 1, 1961, 15.

13. Juhani Suomi, *Urho Kekkosen paivakirjat 1, 1958–1962* [Urho Kekkonen's Diaries 1, 1958–1962] (Helsinki: Otava, 2001), 62.

14. Timo Kekkonen, interview by author.

15. "Author and President's Wife," 15.

16. "Author and President's Wife."

17. Joiko Loikkanen, interview by author, May 2014.

18. Kari Suomalainen, *Maxi-Kari: 1000 piirrosta 1951–85* [Maxi-Kari: 1,000 Drawings, 1951–85] (Helsinki: Otava, 1985), 87.

19. *New York Times*, January 29, 1959, 6.

20. Suomalainen, *Maxi-Kari*, 96.

21. Aleksey Zakharov, Soviet ambassador to Finland (1959–65).

22. Suomi, *Urho Kekkonen's Diaries 1*, 242.

23. *Associated Press*, February 12, 1959.

24. Werner Wiskari, "Finland President Cites Neutrality," *New York Times*, March 5, 1959, 4.

25. Wiskari, "Finland President Cites Neutrality."

26. Wiskari, "Finland President Cites Neutrality."

27. Suomi, *Urho Kekkonen's Diaries 1*, 205.

28. Wiskari, "Finland President Cites Neutrality."

29. Suomi, *Urho Kekkonen's Diaries 1*, 218.

30. Suomi, *Urho Kekkonen's Diaries 1*, 227.

31. Spiro Agnew (1918–96), US vice president (1969–73).

32. Suomi, *Urho Kekkonen's Diaries 1*, 250.

33. Suomi, *Urho Kekkonen's Diaries 1*, 205.

34. Werner Wiskari, "Khrushchev Calls Off Plan for a Visit to Scandinavia," *New York Times*, July 21, 1959, 1.

35. Central Intelligence Agency, "'Finlandization' in Action: Helsinki's Experience with Moscow," Freedom of Information Act Reading Room, 1972, https://www.cia.gov/readingroom/docs/esau-55.pdf.

36. Central Intelligence Agency, "'Finlandization' in Action."

37. Kaarlo Pitsinki (1923–2015), Finnish politician.

38. "Finnish Socialists Annoy Russia," *Times* (London), May 5, 1959, 5.

39. "Finnish Socialists Annoy Russia."

40. "Can Finland Remain Independent?," *Times* (London), July 18, 1959, 5.

41. "Can Finland Remain Independent?"

42. "Despatch from the Embassy in Finland to the Department of State," June 4, 1959, in *Foreign Relations of the United States, 1958–1960*, vol. 8, part 2, *Eastern Europe; Finland; Greece; Turkey* (Washington, DC: Government Printing Office, 1993), document 206.

43. "Embassy in Finland to the Department of State," June 4, 1959.

44. "Embassy in Finland to the Department of State," June 4, 1959.

45. "Embassy in Finland to the Department of State," June 4, 1959.

5. Scylla and Charybdis (7/59–12/59)

1. "Telegram from the US Embassy to State Department," July 15, 1959.

2. "US Embassy to State Department," July 15, 1959.

3. Juhani Suomi, *Urho Kekkosen paivakirjat 1, 1958–1962* [Urho Kekkonen's Diaries 1, 1958–62] (Helsinki: Otava, 2001), 254.

4. "US Embassy to State Department," July 15, 1959.

5. "US Embassy to State Department," July 15, 1959.

6. "Telegram from the State Department to the Embassy in Great Britain and Finland," September 2, 1959.

7. "State Department to the Embassy in Great Britain and Finland," September 2, 1959.

8. "National Security Council Report," October 14, 1959, in *Foreign Relations of the United States, 1958–1960*, vol. 10, part 2, *Eastern Europe; Finland; Greece; Turkey* (Washington, DC: Government Printing Office, 1993), document 213.

9. "National Security Council Report," October 14, 1959.

10. Edson O. Sessions (1902–87), US ambassador to Helsinki; "Despatch from the Embassy in Finland to the Department of State," February 2, 1960, in *Foreign Relations of the United States, 1958–1960*, vol. 10, part 2, *Eastern Europe; Finland; Greece; Turkey* (Washington, DC: Government Printing Office, 1993), document 216.

11. "Mikoyan Brought Greetings from Khrushchev and Voroshilov," *Helsingin Sanomat*, October 23, 1959, 7.

12. "Mikoyan in Finland Warns on Tradie Tie," *New York Times*, October 23, 1959, 3.

13. Suomi, *Urho Kekkonen's Diaries 1*, 275.

14. "Memorandum of Conversation," October 23, 1959, in *Foreign Relations of the United States, 1958–1960*, vol. 10, part 2, *Eastern Europe; Finland; Greece; Turkey* (Washington, DC: Government Printing Office, 1993), document 214.

15. "Memorandum of Conversation," October 23, 1959.

16. "Memorandum of Conversation," October 23, 1959.

17. "Memorandum of Conversation," October 23, 1959.

18. In 1960 the Swedish-speaking population of Finland was 330,000 or approximately 7.5 percent of the total Finnish population of 4,430,000.

19. May 5 to October 20, 1954. Törngren also ran against Kekkonen in the 1956 presidential election.

20. Suomi, *Urho Kekkonen's Diaries 1*, 450.

21. Suomi, *Urho Kekkonen's Diaries 1*, 285.

22. Leland Stowe (1899–1994). Famous American World War II journalist, war correspondent and author.

23. Leland Stowe, "The Finns Fight for Freedom," *Reader's Digest*, September 1959.

24. Stowe, "Finns Fight for Freedom."

25. Stowe, "Finns Fight for Freedom."

26. Suomi, *Urho Kekkonen's Diaries 1*, 288.

27. Werner Wiskari, "Finns Celebrate Freedom Today," *New York Times*, December 6, 1959, 42.

28. Wiskari, "Finns Celebrate Freedom Today."

29. Wiskari, "Finns Celebrate Freedom Today."

30. Werner Wiskari, "Bitterness Rises in Finns' Politics," *New York Times*, December 8, 1959, 3.

31. Wiskari, "Bitterness Rises in Finns' Politics."

32. Wiskari, "Bitterness Rises in Finns' Politics."

33. Suomi, *Urho Kekkonen's Diaries 1*, 295.

34. Suomi, *Urho Kekkonen's Diaries 1*, 295.

6. Seventy-Seven Kilograms (1/60–5/60)

Epigraph. "Despatch from the Embassy in Finland to the Department of State," February 2, 1960, in *Foreign Relations of the United States, 1958–1960*, vol. 10, part 2, *Eastern Europe; Finland; Greece; Turkey* (Washington, DC: Government Printing Office, 1993), document 216.

1. "Presidentin uudenvuodenpuhe taloudesta ja kouista" [President's New Year Speech on the Economy and Schools], *Helsingin Sanomat*, January 2, 1960, 14.

2. Juhani Suomi, *Urho Kekkosen paivakirjat 1, 1958–1962* [Urho Kekkonen's Diaries 1, 1958–1962] (Helsinki: Otava, 2001), 306.

3. The Anglophobic French had prevented the British from joining the European Community.

4. Suomi, *Urho Kekkonen's Diaries 1*, 313.

5. Wolfgang Leonhard (1921–2014), German political author and historian.

6. The new passes were issued. The crisis continued.

7. "Embassy in Finland to the Department of State," February 2, 1960.

8. "Embassy in Finland to the Department of State," February 2, 1960.

9. "Embassy in Finland to the Department of State," February 2, 1960.

10. "Embassy in Finland to the Department of State," February 2, 1960.

11. Nevertheless it may well have been on his mind. Interestingly, in the journal entry for February 12, when he was in the hospital, Kekkonen includes a number of clippings from Finnish newspapers mentioning Eisenhower's plan on skipping Finland during his projected trip to the USSR in the spring, so the fact that he had turned down his invitation to stop over was clearly on his mind.

12. "Embassy in Finland to the Department of State," February 2, 1960.

13. "Embassy in Finland to the Department of State," February 2, 1960.

14. Suomi, *Urho Kekkonen's Diaries 1*, 323.

15. Suomi, *Urho Kekkonen's Diaries 1*, 329.

16. "National Security Report," October 14, 1959, in *Foreign Relations of the United States, 1958–1960*, vol. 10, part 2, *Eastern Europe; Finland; Greece; Turkey* (Washington, DC: Government Printing Office, 1993), document 213.

17. "National Security Report," October 14, 1959.

18. "National Security Report," October 14, 1959.

19. Revealingly, a previously scheduled visit by the Finnish commander in chief had been postponed, according to the memo. "National Security Report," October 14, 1959.

20. "National Security Report," October 14, 1959.

21. Hubert Beuve-Méry (1902–89), French journalist, founder and editor of *Le Monde* (1944–69).

22. Suomi, *Urho Kekkonen's Diaries 1*, 325.

23. Suomi, *Urho Kekkonen's Diaries 1*, 330.

24. Suomi, *Urho Kekkonen's Diaries 1*, 331.

25. Zakharov served as Soviet ambassador to Finland from February 1959 through January 1965.

26. Sakari Simelius (1900–1985), Finnish general, commander-in-chief of the defense forces (1959–65).

27. Suomi, *Urho Kekkonen's Diaries 1*, 332.

28. Khruschev had already angered the Soviet military in January by reducing the size of the army by a milion men.

29. William Taubman, *Khrushchev: The Man and His Era* (Helsinki: Art House, 2007), 466–67.

30. Taubman, *Khrushchev*, 469–70.

31. Taubman, *Khrushchev*, 471.

32. Suomi, *Urho Kekkonen's Diaries 1*, 337.

7. A Party to Remember (5/60–9/60)

Epigraph. Urho Kekkonen, *Puheita ja kirjoituksia*, 2: *Puheita presidnttikaudelta 1956–1967* [Speeches and Writings, 2: Speeches from the Presidential Period 1956–1967] (Helsinki: Weilin + Göös, 1967), 68–118.

1. Juhani Suomi, *Urho Kekkosen paivakirjat 1, 1958–1962* [Urho Kekkonen's Diaries 1, 1958–1962] (Helsinki: Otava, 2001), 353.

2. Werner Wiskari, "Khrushchev Lauds Finns on Arrival," *New York Times*, September 3, 1960, 1.

3. Wiskari, "Khrushchev Lauds Finns on Arrival."

4. "Mr. Khrushchev in Finland," *Times* (London), September 3, 1960, 6.

5. Wiskari, "Khrushchev Lauds Finns on Arrival."

6. "Coalition Effort Fails in Finland," *New York Times*, June 23, 1960, 12.

7. Kekkonen, *Speeches and Writings, 2*, 117–19.

8. "Khrushchev Presses the West for U.N. Disarmament Summit," *New York Times*, September 4, 1960, 1.

9. "Khrushchev Presses the West."

10. "Khrushchev Presses the West."

11. "Khrushchev Presses the West."

12. "Khrushchev Presses the West."

13. Konrad Adenauer (1876–1967), German statesman, chancellor of the Federal Republic of Germany (1949–63).

14. "Khrushchev Presses the West."

15. "Khrushchev Presses the West."

16. "Khrushchev Presses the West."

17. "Khrushchev Presses the West."

18. Suomi, *Urho Kekkonen's Diaries 1*, 356.

19. Suomi, *Urho Kekkonen's Diaries 1*, 356.

20. Suomi, *Urho Kekkonen's Diaries 1*, 356.

21. Suomi, *Urho Kekkonen's Diaries 1*, 356.

22. Suomi, *Urho Kekkonen's Diaries 1*, 356.

23. Suomi, *Urho Kekkonen's Diaries 1*, 357.

24. "Grappling with Politics within the Shadow of Russia," *Times* (London), November 21, 1960, 10.

25. Erik von Frenckell (1887–1977), sports administrator, politician of the Swedish People's Party; Suomi, *Urho Kekkonen's Diaries 1*, 359.

26. Michel Werboff (1896–1990), Russian American portrait painter.

27. Suomi, *Urho Kekkonen's Diaries 1*, 363.

28. A. M. Rosenthal, "U.N. Chief Warns Katanga of Force," *New York Times*, September 24, 1960, 13.

29. William Taubman, *Khrushchev: The Man and His Era* (Helsinki: Art House, 2007), 481.

30. Suomi, *Urho Kekkonen's Diaries 1*, 363–64.

31. Khrushchev's wild performance was later cited as one of the reasons for his removal by the Soviet Central Committee in 1964.

32. Suomi, *Urho Kekkonen's Diaries 1*, 364.

33. Torsten Steinby (1908–96), editor at *Hufvudstadsbladet* (1960–74); Suomi, *Urho Kekkonen's Diaries 1*, 365.

34. Karl Overbeck (1909–72), German diplomat.

35. Suomi, *Urho Kekkonen's Diaries 1*, 366.

36. Toivo Rapeli (1903–95), evangelist, author.

37. Suomi, *Urho Kekkonen's Diaries 1*, 366.

38. Suomi, *Urho Kekkonen's Diaries 1*, 364–65.

39. Arvo "Poika" Tuominen (1894–1981), Finnish journalist, Social Democratic member of parliament; Suomi, *Urho Kekkonen's Diaries 1*, 368.

40. Suomi, *Urho Kekkonen's Diaries 1*, 369.

8. The Gordian Knot (11–12/60)

Epigraph. Central Intelligence Agency, "'Finlandization' in Action: Helsinki's Experience with Moscow," Freedom of Information Act Reading Room, August 1972, https://www.cia.gov/readingroom/docs/esau-55.pdf.

1. Juhani Suomi, *Urho Kekkosen paivakirjat 1, 1958–1962* [Urho Kekkonen's Diaries 1, 1958–1962] (Helsinki: Otava, 2001), 369.

2. Suomi, *Urho Kekkonen's Diaries 1*, 369.

3. "A Rising Star in Finnish Politics," *Times* (London), October 25, 1960, 7.

4. The prediction was accurate: Karjalainen assumed his first prime ministership in April 1962. "A Rising Star in Finnish Politics."

5. Central Intelligence Agency, "'Finlandization' in Action."

6. Suomi, *Urho Kekkonen's Diaries 1*, 372.

7. Suomi, *Urho Kekkonen's Diaries 1*, 376.

8. Suomi, *Urho Kekkonen's Diaries 1*, 372.

9. "Finns' Bid Is Endorsed," *New York Times*, November 24, 1960, 8.

10. Central Intelligence Agency, "'Finlandization' in Action."

11. "Kekkonen Terms Neutrality Vital," *New York Times*, October 18, 1961, 14.

12. "Kekkonen Terms Neutrality Vital."

13. Max Jakobson, *Finland in the New Europe* (Westport, CT: Greenwood, 1998), 71.

14. Jakobson, *Finland in the New Europe*, 71.

15. Jakobson, *Finland in the New Europe*, 72.

16. Jakobson, *Finland in the New Europe*, 72.

17. Jakobson, *Finland in the New Europe*, 72.

18. Jakobson, *Finland in the New Europe*, 72.

19. "Moscow Approves Finns' Trade Plan."

20. "Moscow Approves Finns' Trade Plan."

21. Suomi, *Urho Kekkonen's Diaries 1*, 378.

22. The society, Finland's oldest foreign policy association, still exists.

23. "Moscow Approves Finns' Trade Plan."

24. "Moscow Approves Finns' Trade Plan."

25. "Moscow Approves Finns' Trade Plan."

26. "Moscow Approves Finns' Trade Plan."

27. Suomi, *Urho Kekkonen's Diaries 1*, 378.

28. "Moscow Approves Finns' Trade Plan."

29. "Despatch from the Embassy in Finland to the Department of State," December 3, 1960, in *Foreign Relations of the United States, 1958–1960*, vol. 10, part 2, *Eastern Europe; Finland; Greece; Turkey* (Washington, DC: Government Printing Office, 1993), document 228.

30. "Embassy in Finland to the Department of State," December 3, 1960.

31. "Embassy in Finland to the Department of State," December 3, 1960.

32. "National Security Council Report," December 30, 1960, in *Foreign Relations of the United States, 1958–1960*, vol. 10, part 2, *Eastern Europe; Finland; Greece; Turkey* (Washington, DC: Government Printing Office, 1993), document 229.

33. "National Security Council Report," December 30, 1960.

34. The 1948 Fenno-Soviet Friendship Mutual Assistance and Coopertion Pact only recognized Finland's desire to remain outside great power conflicts. It did not, however, recognize Finnish neutrality. Instead Moscow considered Finland to be "striving to be neutral," as indeed it would.

35. Suomi, *Urho Kekkonen's Diaries 1*, 381.

36. Suomi, *Urho Kekkonen's Diaries 1*, 379.

37. Jakobson, *Finland in the New Europe*, 70.

38. "National Security Council Report," December 30, 1960.

39. "National Security Council Report," December 30, 1960.

40. Suomi, *Urho Kekkonen's Diaries 1*, 381.

9. The Bridge Builder (1/61–3/61)

Epigraph. "'1961 Was One of the Most Favorable Years for the Economy': The President's New Year's Resolution," *Helsingin Sanomat*, January 1, 1961, 6.

1. Richard Rafael (R. R.) Seppälä (1905-97), ambassador to Washington (1958-65).

2. Veikko Hakulinen (1925-2003), cross-country skier, threefold Olympic champion.

3. "Kennedy Greets Finnish President on Visit to Capital," *New York Times*, October 17, 1961, 1.

4. "Despatch from the Embassy in Finland to the Department of State," January 11, 1961.

5. "Embassy in Finland to the Department of State," January 11, 1961.

6. "961 Was One of the Most Favorable Years for the Economy.'"

7. Tuure Junnila (1910-99), Finnish economist and politician, member of Parliament from National Coalition Party. Juhani Suomi, *Urho Kekkosen paivakirjat 1, 1958–1962* [Urho Kekkonen's Diaries 1, 1958-1962] (Helsinki: Otava, 2001), 399.

8. Suomi, *Urho Kekkonen's Diaries 1*, 397.

9. Interestingly, the *Sanomat* later reported that the idea for the visit came from Kennedy.

10. "Memorandum from the Secretary of State to the President," March 23, 1960, in *Foreign Relations of the United States, 1958–1960*, vol. 10, part 2, *Eastern Europe; Finland; Greece; Turkey* (Washington, DC: Government Printing Office, 1993), document 220.

11. Sakari Tuomioja (1911-64), Finnish politician and diplomat, governor of the Bank of Finland 1945-55.

12. "Neutral in Neutral Land," *New York Times*, November 25, 1961, 2.

13. "Neutral in Neutral Land."

14. Olavi Honka, *Memories and Opinions* (Helsinki: WSOY, 1972), 269.

15. According to Tanner's biographer, Lehtinen, the prime mover behind Tanner's nomination was Tanner's acolyte, Kaarlo Pitsinki.

16. David Kirby, *A Concise History of Finland* (Cambridge: Cambridge University Press, 2006), 256.

17. Suomi, *Urho Kekkonen's Diaries 1*, 408.

18. Suomi, *Urho Kekkonen's Diaries 1*, 409.

19. Suomi, *Urho Kekkonen's Diaries*, 409.

20. Suomi, *Urho Kekkonen's Diaries 1*, 410.

21. At least if they did, they not tell the press.

22. Suomi, *Urho Kekkonen's Diaries 1*, 410.

10. The Perfect Storm (3/61–9/61)

Epigraph. Juhani Suomi, *Urho Kekkosen paivakirjat,* 1: 1958–62 [Urho Kekkonen's Diaries, 1: 1958–62] (Helsinki: Otava, 2001), 436.

1. Veikko Vennamo (1913–97). Chairman of the Finnish Rural Party (also known as the Finnish Small Peasants' Party, 1959–79). Suomi, *Urho Kekkonen's Diaries 1*, 411.

2. Suomi, *Urho Kekkonen's Diaries 1*, 414–15.

3. "Finnish Candidate for Presidency," *Times* (London), March 18, 1961, 6.

4. "Finnish Candidate for Presidency."

5. "Finnish Candidate for Presidency."

6. Reino Kuuskoski (1907–65). Jurist, Finnish prime minister (April–August, 1958).

7. Suomi, *Urho Kekkonen's Diaries 1*, 413.

8. Becky Little, "JFK Was Completely Unprepared for His Summit with Khrushchev," *History*, July 13, 2018, https://www.history.com/news/kennedy-krushchev-vienna-summit-meeting-1961.

9. Walter Ulbricht (1893–1973), East German Communist Party head (1950–71).

10. Arthur M. Schlesinger, Jr., *Journals 1952–2000* (New York: Penguin Books, 2007), 134.

11. Schlesinger, *Journals 1952–2000*, 134.

12. Suomi, *Urho Kekkonen's Diaries 1*, 419.

13. Suomi, *Urho Kekkonen's Diaries 1*, 432.

14. Suomi, *Urho Kekkonen's Diaries 1*, 433.

15. Suomi, *Urho Kekkonen's Diaries 1*, 436.

16. Suomi, *Urho Kekkonen's Diaries 1*, 415.

17. Matti Valtasaari (born 1907), Finnish official, chairman of the Paasikivi Society (1967–75). Suomi, *Urho Kekkonen's Diaries 1*, 421.

18. Suomi, *Urho Kekkonen's Diaries 1*, 436–37.

19. *Economist*, May 13, 1961, 30.

20. *Economist*, May 13, 1961, 30.

21. *Economist*, May 13, 1961, 30.
22. *Economist*, May 13, 1961, 30.
23. *Economist*, May 13, 1961, 30.

11. The View from Tapiola (10/61)

1. Werner Wiskari, "Finnish Election Worrying Soviet," *New York Times*, October 8, 1961, 6.
2. Wiskari, Finnish Election Worrying Soviet."
3. Wiskari, "Finnish Election Worrying Soviet."
4. The conflict over Laos, where Washington and Moscow backed opposing sides in the communist insurgency there, was Kennedy's first foreign policy crisis.
5. "President Sees Gromyko 2 Hours," *New York Times*, October 7, 1961, 1.
6. "Gromyko Session Deemed Failure," *New York Times*, October 8, 1961, 3.
7. Willy Brandt, (1913–92), mayor of West Berlin (1957–66), later chancellor of West Germany. "Brandt May Ask New Berlin Arms," *New York Times*, October 10, 1961, 1.
8. David Binder, "Soviet Building Up Forces in Germany for Maneuvers," *New York Times*, October 11, 1961, 1.
9. "Brandt May Ask New Berlin Arms."
10. "Memorandum of Conversation," October 16, 1961, in *Foreign Relations of the United States, 1961–1963*, vol. 16, *Eastern Europe; Cyprus; Greece; Turkey* (Washington, DC: Government Printing Office, 1994), document 189.
11. Martti Miuttunen (1907–2002), prime minister (1961–62, 1975–77).
12. Wendy Hall, *Times* (London), December 6, 1961, 15.
13. Hall, *Times* (London).
14. Hall, *Times* (London).
15. Hall, *Times* (London).
16. Hall, *Times* (London).
17. Hall, *Times* (London).
18. Hall, *Times* (London).
19. Hall, *Times* (London).
20. Hall, *Times* (London).
21. Hall, *Times* (London).
22. Hall, *Times* (London).
23. "President Sees No Easy Solution for Berlin," *New York Times*, October 12, 1961, 1.
24. Kennedy was paraphrasing the saying, "better Red than dead" often attributed to Bertrand Russell, the pacifist philosopher, and antinuclear activist. "President Warns of Long Struggle with Communism," *New York Times*, October 13, 1961, 1.
25. "Reds Again Fire over Berlin Line," *New York Times*, October 14, 1961, 1.
26. "Soviet Aim Seen to Humiliate U.S.," *New York Times*, October 15, 1961, 1.

27. Llewellyn E. Thompson Jr. (1904–72), American diplomat, ambassador to Moscow (1957–62, 1967–69).

28. "U.S.-Canada Test of Air Defense a Success," *New York Times*, October 16, 1961, 1.

12. Two Days in Washington (10/16–17/61)

Epigraph. "Kennedy Greets Finnish President on Visit to Capital," *New York Times*, October 17, 1961, 1.

1. "Memorandum from the Secretary of State to the President," March 22, 1961.

2. "Memorandum from the Embassy in Finland to Department of State," January 11, 1961.

3. "Kennedy Greets Finnish President."

4. Those in attendance were, representing the United States, President Kennedy; the secretary of state Rusk; Bernard Gufler, the ambassador to Finland; and William R. Tyler, the acting assistant secretary of state for European affairs. Representing Finland were President Kekkonen; the foreign minister Ahti Karjalainen; Richard R. Seppälä, the ambassador to the United States; and Max Jakobson, whose title is listed on Memo 189 as "Chief of the Press Bureau."

5. "Memorandum of Conversation," October 16, 1961, in *Foreign Relations of the United States, 1961–1963*, vol. 16, *Eastern Europe; Cyprus; Greece; Turkey* (Washington, DC: Government Printing Office, 1994), document 189.

6. The author studied history with Schlesinger at the City University of New York in the early 1980s. Arthur M. Schlesinger Jr., interview by author, 2005.

7. Arthur M. Schlesinger Jr., *A Thousand Days* (Boston: Houghton Mifflin Co., 1965), 379.

8. Becky Little, "JFK was completely unprepared for his summit with Khrushchev," *History*, July 13, 2018, https://www.history.com/news/kennedy-krushchev-vienna-summit-meeting-1961.

9. Jukka Tarkka, *Max Jakobson: Finnish Diplomacy in the Cold War* (Helsinki: Otava, 2013), 91.

10. Jakobson also recreated the conversation from notes he took at the time twenty years later in his book *Veteen pirretty viiva* (A line drawn in the water). The meeting was obviously a highpoint for him as well.

11. Tarkka, *Max Jakobson*, 141.

12. Jakobson also recreates the second, "off the record" conversation between Kennedy and Kekkonen on October 17, 1961, as well as the one between Kekkonen and Rusk in his 1981 book.

13. Khrushchev was forced into retirement by the Politburo in October 1964.

14. "Memorandum of Conversation," October 16, 1961.

15. "Memorandum of Conversation," October 16, 1961.

16. "Memorandum of Conversation," October 16, 1961.

17. "Memorandum of Conversation," October 16, 1961.

18. "Memorandum of Conversation," October 16, 1961.
19. "Memorandum of Conversation," October 16, 1961.
20. "Memorandum of Conversation," October 16, 1961.
21. "Memorandum of Conversation," October 16, 1961.
22. "Memorandum of Conversation," October 16, 1961.
23. Arthur M. Schlesinger, Jr., unpublished diary, 1961.
24. "Memorandum of Conversation," October 16, 1961.
25. "Memorandum of Conversation," October 16, 1961.
26. Schlesinger, unpublished diary.
27. "Memorandum of Conversation," October 16, 1961.
28. Schlesinger, unpublished diary.
29. Schlesinger, unpublished diary.
30. "Memorandum of Conversation," October 16, 1961.
31. "Memorandum of Conversation," October 16, 1961.
32. Schlesinger, unpublished diary.
33. Schlesinger, unpublished diary.
34. "Memorandum of Conversation," October 16, 1961.
35. "Memorandum of Conversation," October 16, 1961.
36. "Memorandum of Conversation," October 16, 1961.
37. Carl von Clausewitz (1780–1831), Prussian general and military theorist who stressed the "moral" aspect of war. "Memorandum of Conversation," October 16, 1961.
38. Oder-Neisse territories refer to the territories west of the Oder and Neisse Rivers, which Germany was forced to cede to communist Poland, to which East Germany readily acceded, but which West Germany objected to. Ultimately Bonn acquiesced to the Oder-Neisse cession in 1970.
39. "Memorandum of Conversation," October 16, 1961.
40. "Memorandum of Conversation," October 16, 1961.
41. Schlesinger, unpublished diary.
42. "Memorandum of Conversation," October 16, 1961.
43. "Memorandum of Conversation," October 16, 1961.
44. Memorandum of Conversation," October 16, 1961.
45. "Memorandum of Conversation," October 16, 1961.
46. Schlesinger, interview by author.
47. "Memorandum of Conversation," October 16, 1961.
48. "Memorandum of Conversation," October 16, 1961.
49. "Memorandum of Conversation," October 16, 1961.
50. "Memorandum of Conversation," October 16, 1961.
51. Schlesinger, unpublished diary.
52. Memorandum of Conversation," October 16, 1961.
53. Now defunct, *House Beautiful* was a popular American housekeeping magazine.
54. "Memorandum of Conversation," October 16, 1961.
55. "Memorandum of Conversation," October 16, 1961.
56. Schlesinger, unpublished diary.
57. "Memorandum of Conversation," October 16, 1961.
58. "Memorandum of Conversation," October 16, 1961.

59. GATT refers to General Agreement on Tariffs and Trade, the 1947 international agreement aimed at reducing tariffs and trades. "Memorandum of Conversation," October 16, 1961.
60. "Memorandum of Conversation," October 16, 1961.
61. "Memorandum of Conversation," October 16, 1961.
62. "Memorandum of Conversation," October 16, 1961.
63. "Memorandum of Conversation," October 16, 1961.
64. "Memorandum of Conversation," October 16, 1961.
65. Schlesinger, unpublished diary.
66. "Memorandum of Conversation," October 16, 1961.
67. "Memorandum of Conversation," October 16, 1961.
68. "Memorandum of Conversation," October 16, 1961.
69. "Memorandum of Conversation," October 16, 1961.
70. Schlesinger, unpublished diary.
71. Schlesinger, unpublished diary.
72. "Memorandum of Conversation," October 16, 1961.
73. Schlesinger, unpublished diary.
74. Schlesinger, unpublished diary.
75. "Memorandum of Conversation," October 16, 1961.
76. "Memorandum of Conversation," October 16, 1961.
77. "Memorandum of Conversation," October 16, 1961.
78. "Memorandum of Conversation," October 16, 1961.
79. "Memorandum of Conversation," October 16, 1961.
80. "Memorandum of Conversation," October 16, 1961.
81. Schlesinger, unpublished diary.
82. "Memorandum of Conversation," October 16, 1961.
83. "Memorandum of Conversation," October 16, 1961.
84. Tarkka, *Max Jakobson.*
85. "Memorandum of Conversation," October 16, 1961.
86. "Memorandum of Conversation," October 16, 1961.
87. "Memorandum of Conversation," October 16, 1961.
88. "Memorandum of Conversation," October 16, 1961.
89. The wall "was not a very nice solution," Kennedy said at the time the wall went up to his advisor, Walt Rostow, "but better a wall than a war." "Memorandum of Conversation," October 16, 1961.
90. "Memorandum of Conversation," October 16, 1961.
91. "Memorandum of Conversation," October 16, 1961.
92. "Memorandum of Conversation," October 16, 1961.
93. "Kennedy Greets Finnish President."
94. Schlesinger, unpublished diary.
95. "Memorandum of Conversation," October 16, 1961.
96. "Memorandum of Conversation," October 16, 1961.
97. "Memorandum of Conversation," October 16, 1961.
98. "Memorandum of Conversation," October 16, 1961.
99. Schlesinger, *A Thousand Days*, 400.
100. Schlesinger, *A Thousand Days.*

101. Kekkonen met four of the six presidents—or future presidents—who held office during his tenure: Kennedy; Lyndon B. Johnson, who he met when he was vice president in 1963, before Kennedy's assassination; Richard Nixon, who he met during his second official visit to Washington in 1970; and Gerald Ford, who he met at the 1975 Helsinki Accords. Jaakko Kalela, interview by author, June 2015.

Kekkonen revealed how he felt about Kennedy in the speech to the nation he gave after JFK's assassination. "He was a strong political leader, both mentally and physically, whose grasp of international affairs was marked by certainty and knowledge. Even though Finland was on the sideline of the most pressing concerns of international politics, and the United States President had many urgent and critical matters to attend to, he took great interest in matters regarding Finland. . . . Apart from being a skilled and realistic political leader, he also represented the American idealism in its purest form. He had great ambitions. He was a great man."

102. Hjalmar J. Procopé (1889–1954), Finnish ambassador to Washington (1939–44). Procopé, a member of the Swedish People's Party, was a minister in several interwar cabinets. After the war he served as the defense counsel for the president Risto Ryti during the 1945 to 1946 Soviet-mandated, so-called War Responsibility Trials.

103. Tarkka, *Max Jakobson*, 92.

104. Werner Wiskari, "Finnish Election Worrying Soviet," *New York Times*, October 8, 1961, 6.

105. Wiskari, "Finnish Election Worrying Soviet."

106. Wiskari, "Finnish Election Worrying Soviet."

107. Wiskari, "Finnish Election Worrying Soviet."

108. Urho Kekkonen, *Puheita ja kirjotuksia, 2: Puheita presidenttikaudelta 1956–1967* [Speeches and Writings, 2: Speeches from the Presidential Period 1956–1967] (Helsinki: Weilin + Göös, 1967), 148.

109. Kekkonen, *Speeches and Writings, 2.*

110. Kekkonen, *Speeches and Writings, 2.*

111. Wiskari, "Finnish Election Worrying Soviet."

112. Wiskari, "Finnish Election Worrying Soviet."

113. Wiskari, "Finnish Election Worrying Soviet."

114. Wiskari, "Finnish Election Worrying Soviet."

13. The Great Healer

Epigraph 1. Urho Kekkonen, *Puheita ja kirjoituksia, 2: Puheita presidenttikaudelta 1956–1967* [Speeches and writings, 2: Speeches from the Presidential Period 1956–1967] (Helsinki: Weilin + Göös, 1967), 155.

Epigraph 2. James H. Billington, "Five Clues to the Khrushchev Riddle," *New York Times Magazine*, October 29, 1961, 297.

1. "Visitor from Finland," *New York Times*, October 19, 1961, 34.
2. "Visitor from Finland."
3. "Visitor from Finland."

4. "Visitor from Finland."

5. Urho Kekkonen, *Speeches and Writings, 2*, 155.

6. "Visitor from Finland."

7. Samuel Pryor (1898–1985), aviation pioneer, associate of Charles Lindbergh, the vice president of Pan American Airways, and lifelong Fennophile; Taneli Kekkonen (1928–85), one of the Kekkonen's two sons, Finnish diplomat. Ambassador to Yugoslavia, Greece, Italy, Malta, Poland, and Israel. Died by suicide (1985); Timo Kekkonen (1957–), son of Brita and Tanneli Kekkonen. Finnish nongovernmental organization officer.

8. Jukka Tarkka, scholar, member of parliament (1995–99); Jukka Tarkka, *Max Jakobson: Finnish Diplomacy in the Cold War* (Helsinki: Otava, 2013), 139.

9. Kathleen Teltsch, "6 Nations in U.N. Bid Soviet Cancel 50-Megaton Test," *New York Times,* October 21, 1961, 1.

10. Joseph A. Loftus, "Gilpatric Warns U.S. Can Destroy Atom Aggressor," *New York Times,* October 22, 1961, 1.

11. Gerd Wilcke, "9 American M.P.'s Cross Berlin Line to Free Official," *New York Times,* October 23, 1961, 1.

12. John W. Finney, "2 Blasts in Arctic," *New York Times,* October 24, 1961, 1.

13. "Soviet Assailed in Many Nations over Superbomb," *New York Times,* October 25, 1961, 1.

14. Tage Erlander (1901–85), Swedish politician, leader of Social Democratic party, longtime prime minister (1946–69); "Soviet Assailed in Many Nations over Superbomb."

15. "Soviet Assailed in Many Nations over Superbomb."

16. "Soviet Assailed in Many Nations over Superbomb."

17. Sydney Gruson, "Soviet Advance," *New York Times,* October 27, 1961, 1.

18. Sydney Gruson, "U.S. Tanks Face Soviets at Berlin Crossing Point," *New York Times,* October 28, 1961, 1.

19. Sydney Gruson, "U.S. Tanks Face Soviets at Berlin Crossing Point," *New York Times,* October 28, 1961, 1.

20. James M, Markham, "A Lot Better than a War," *New York Times,* February 8, 1987, 21.

21. Dodge City, Kansas, a famous Wild West outpost, was noted for its gunfights.

22. Sydney Gruson, "U.S. and Russians Pull Tanks from Berlin Line," *New York Times,* October 29, 1961, 1.

23. James Billington (1929–2018), prominent American academic, founder of the Kennan Institute of Advanced Russian Studies at Princeton University, thirteenth librarian of Congress (1987–2015).

24. Billington, "Five Clues to the Khrushchev Riddle."

25. Billington, "Five Clues to the Khrushchev Riddle."

14. The Postman Always Rings Twice (10/30/61)

Epigraph 1. "Russian Bomb Put at Over 50 Megatons," *Times* (London), October 31, 1961, 10.

Epigraph 2. James Ford Cooper, *Finland as a Homeland: An American Diplomat in Finland during the Cold War* (Helsinki: Tammi, 1998), 61.

1. Cooper, *Finland as a Homeland.*

2. Marshall McLuhan (1911–80), Canadian philosopher and author, best known for his 1967 book, *The Medium Is the Massage.*

3. Cooper, *Finland as a Homeland.*

4. "Moscow Shock for Finland," *Times* (London), October 31, 1961, 10.

5. "Moscow Shock for Finland."

6. "Nootti 30.10.1961 Neuvostoliiton hallitukselta Suomen hallitukselle" [From the government of the Soviet Union to the government of Finland], Wikiaineisto, accessed January 27, 2020, https://fi.wikisource.org/wiki/Nootti_30.10.1961_Neuvostoliiton_hallitukselta_Suomen_hallitukselle.

7. Werner Wiskari, "Scandinavians Are Calm," *New York Times*, November 1, 1961, 3.

8. Bofors is a major Swedish arms manufacturer, best known for the Bofors antiaircraft gun that was a mainstay with Allied navies during World War II. "Nootti 30.10.1961 Neuvostoliiton hallitukselta Suomen hallitukselle."

9. "Move Surprises Finns." *New York Times,* October 30, 1961, 2.

10. Cooper, *Finland as a Homeland*, 61.

11. Wiskari, "Scandinavians Are Calm."

12. Cooper, *Finland as a Homeland*, 73.

13. Cooper, *Finland as a Homeland*, 74.

14. C. L. Sulzberger (1912–93), foreign correspondent, *The New York Times.* A friend of Kennedy, JFK once trusted him to deliver a note for him to Khrushchev.

15. C. L. Sulzberger, "Mr. K's Policy of Peaceful Co-Extinction," *New York Times*, November, 1, 1961, 38.

16. Sulzberger, "Mr. K's Policy of Peaceful Co-Extinction."

17. Max Frankel (1930–), correspondent, editor, *The New York Times*; Max Frenkel, "West Concerned at Soviet Demand for Finnish Talks," *New York Times,* November 1, 1961, 1.

18. "Moscow Shock for Finland."

19. Frankel, "West Concerned at Soviet Demand."

20. Juhani Suomi, *Urho Kekkosen paivakirjat 1: 1958–62* [Urho Kekkonen's Diaries 1: 1958–62] (Helsinki: Otava, 2001), 442.

21. Suomi, *Urho Kekkonen's Diaries 1*, 443.

22. Kekkonen was probably also taking in the news that the Soviets had also dropped their fifty-megaton nuclear bomb—the same one he had mentioned to Dean Rusk at their meeting—that morning. What, one wonders, was his reaction when he read about that literal explosion in *The Honolulu Advertiser*?

23. "Visitor from Finland," *New York Times*, October 19, 1961, 34.

24. "Finnish Barometer," *Times* (London), November 1, 1961, 11.

25. "Finnish Barometer."

26. Central Intelligence Agency, "'Finlandization in Action': Helsinki's Experience with Moscow," Freedom of Information Act Reading Room, August 1972, https://www.cia.gov/readingroom/docs/esau-55.pdf.

27. Central Intelligence Agency, "'Finlandization in Action.'"

28. Central Intelligence Agency, "'Finlandization in Action.'"

29. The otherwise authoritative report makes one serious omission: it neglects to mention the bomb Moscow dropped the same day Gromyko handed

Wuori the explosive note. It also overlooks the role that the very real tensions within the Communist Party at the time might have played in Khrushchev's decision to okay the note by way of helping to assuage those hard-liners who might have been disappointed by his "climbdown" as Tarkka puts it—a partial climbdown, which is probably the most accurate way of putting it—over Berlin.

30. Central Intelligence Agency, "Finlandization in Action."

31. Werner Wiskari, "Finnish Election Worrying Soviet," *New York Times*, October 8, 1961, 6.

32. "Telegram from the Embassy in Finland to the Department of State," November 16, 1961, in *Foreign Relations of the United States, 1961–1963*, vol. 16, *Eastern Europe; Cyprus; Greece; Turkey* (Washington, DC: Government Printing Office, 1994), document 194.

33. Jukka Tarkka, *Max Jakobson: Finnish Diplomacy in the Cold War* (Helsinki: Otava, 2013), 93.

34. Tarkka, *Max Jakobson.*

35. Tarkka, *Max Jakobson.*

36. Tarkka, *Max Jakobson.*

37. Viktor Vladimirov, *Nain se oli: muistelmia ja havaintoja kulissientakaisesta 1954–84* [This Is How It was: Memories and Observations of Diplomatic Activity in Finland 1954–84], trans. Arnold Hiltunen (Helsinki: Otava, 1993), 116–21.

38. "Memorandum of Conversation," November 1, 1961, in *Foreign Relations of the United States, 1961–1963*, vol. 16, *Eastern Europe; Cyprus; Greece; Turkey* (Washington, DC: Government Printing Office, 1994), document 191.

39. "Finnish Barometer."

40. Frankel, "West Concerned at Soviet Demand."

41. Frankel, "West Concerned at Soviet Demand."

15. Stay Calm and Carry On (11/1/–11/11/61)

Epigraph 1. Urho Kekkonen, *Puheita ja kirjotuksia, 2: Puheita presidenttikaudelta 1956–1967* [Speeches and Writings, 2: Speeches from the Presidential Period 1956–1967] (Helsinki: Weilin + Göös, 1967), 161–69.

Epigraph 2. Werner Wiskari, "Finnish Foreign Chief to Discuss Note in Moscow," *New York Times*, November 8, 1961, 2.

1. Juhani Suomi, *Urho Kekkosen paivakirjat 1, 1958–1962* [Urho Kekkonen's Diaries 1, 1958–1962] (Helsinki: Otava, 2001), 443.

2. Suomi, *Urho Kekkonen's Diaries 1.*

3. Gordon F. Sander, *The Frank Family That Survived* (London: Hutchinson, 2004), 84.

4. Suomi, *Urho Kekkonen's Diaries 1*, 450.

5. "Telegram from the Embassy in Finland to the Department of State," November 1, 1961, in *Foreign Relations of the United States, 1961–1963*, vol. 16, *Eastern Europe; Cyprus; Greece; Turkey* (Washington, DC: Government Printing Office, 1994), document 190.

6. According to Timo Soikkanen, the author of the official history of Finnish Foreign Ministry, Hallama also appealed to Gufler to ask NATO for moral

support. There is no indication of this panicky request, however—which might well have ended Hallama's career if it got out—in Gufler's voluminous cables. "Embassy in Finland to the Department of State," November 1, 1961.

7. "Embassy in Finland to the Department of State," November 1, 1961.

8. "Embassy in Finland to the Department of State," November 1, 1961.

9. Sam Yorty (1909–98), US politician, mayor of Los Angeles (1961–73). "Good Will Held Goal of Kekkonen," *Los Angeles Times*, November 2, 1961, 28.

10. Gladwin Hill, "Kekkonen Calm on Soviet's Move," *New York Times*, November 2, 1961, 13.

11. "Good Will Held Goal of Kekkonen."

12. Jukka Tarkka, *Max Jakobson: Finnish Diplomacy in the Cold War* (Helsinki: Otava, 2013), 93.

13. Suomi, *Urho Kekkonen's Diaries 1*, 442–43.

14. Suomi, *Urho Kekkonen's Diaries 1*, 442–43.

15. Suomi, *Urho Kekkonen's Diaries 1*.

16. Tarkka, *Max Jakobson*.

17. "Telegram from the Embassy in Finland to the Department of State," November 3, 1961, in *Foreign Relations of the United States, 1961–1963*, vol. 16, *Eastern Europe; Cyprus; Greece; Turkey* (Washington, DC: Government Printing Office, 1994), document 192.

18. "Embassy in Finland to the Department of State," November 3, 1961.

19. "Embassy in Finland to the Department of State," November 3, 1961.

20. Tarkka, *Max Jakobson*, 133.

21. Tarkka, *Max Jakobson*.

22. Werner Wiskari, "Finnish Campaign Remains Intense," *New York Times*, November 5, 1961, 17.

23. Wiskari, "Finnish Campaign Remains Intense."

24. "Telegram from the Embassy in Finland to the Department of State," November 16, 1961, in *Foreign Relations of the United States, 1961–1963*, vol. 16, *Eastern Europe; Cyprus; Greece; Turkey* (Washington, DC: Government Printing Office, 1994), document 194.

25. "Embassy in Finland to the Department of State," November 16, 1961.

26. Werner Wiskari, "Kekkonen Holds Note Is No Peril," *New York Times*, November 6, 1961, 11.

27. Wiskari, "Kekkonen Holds Note Is No Peril."

28. Kekkonen, *Speeches and Writings 2*, 169.

29. Kekkonen, *Speeches and Writings 2*, 169.

30. Werner Wiskari, "Russian and Finn Converse on Note," *New York Times*, November 7, 1961, 3.

31. Tarkka, *Max Jakobson*, 134.

32. Wiskari, "Finnish Foreign Chief to Discuss Note," *New York Times*, November 8, 1961, 2.

33. Wiskari, "Finnish Foreign Chief to Discuss Note."

34. "Finn-Soviet Talks Set," *New York Times*, November 9, 1961, 11.

35. Wiskari, "Finnish Foreign Chief to Discuss Note."

16. In the Shadow of the Note (11/14–21)

Epigraph 2. "Telegram from the Embassy in Finland to the Department of State," November 17, 1961, in *Foreign Relations of the United States, 1961–1963*, vol. 16, *Eastern Europe; Cyprus; Greece; Turkey* (Washington, DC: Government Printing Office, 1994), document 195.

1. Seymour Topping, "Talk of Soviet Bid on Berlin Traced," *New York Times*, November 15, 1961, 4.
2. "Russia Warning to Finland," *Times* (London), November 15, 1961, 14.
3. Juhani Suomi, *Urho Kekkosen paivakirjat 1, 1958–1962* [Urho Kekkonen's Diaries 1, 1958-1962] (Helsinki: Otava, 2001), 445.
4. "Russia Warning to Finland."
5. "Russia Warning to Finland."
6. "Russia Warning to Finland."
7. "Soviet Move Seen as Aid to Kekkonen." *New York Times*, November 16, 1961, 19.
8. Jaakko Hakala (1912–64) editor of *Aamulehti* (1956–64); Kalle Kaihari (1899-1989), Finnish businessman; Suomi, *Urho Kekkonen's Diaries 1*, 446.
9. "Crisis in Finland," *New York Times*, November 15, 1961, 42.
10. "Crisis in Finland."
11. "Crisis in Finland."
12. "Finland Studying Soviet Move," *Times* (London), November 16, 1961, 11.
13. Suomi, *Urho Kekkonen's Diaries 1*, 446.
14. Werner Wiskari, "Soviet Bids Finns Discuss Defense in Moscow 'Soon,'" *New York Times*, November 18, 1961, 1.
15. Wiskari, "Soviet Bids Finns Discuss Defense."
16. Wiskari, "Soviet Bids Finns Discuss Defense."
17. "Embassy in Finland to the Department of State," November 17, 1961.
18. "Embassy in Finland to the Department of State," November 17, 1961.
19. "Embassy in Finland to the Department of State," November 17, 1961.
20. "Embassy in Finland to the Department of State," November 17, 1961.
21. "Dr. Kekkonen To Visit Russia This Week," *Times* (London), November 19, 1961, 9.
22. Vasili Kuznetsov (1901-90), longtime Soviet politician. Deputy foreign minister (1955-77), first deputy chairman Supreme Soviet (1977-90).
23. Urho Kekkonen, *Puheita ja kirjoituksia, 2: Puheita presidenttikaudelta 1956–1967* [Speeches and Writings, 2: Speeches from the Presidential Period 1956-1967] (Helsinki: Weilin + Göös, 1967), 173-74.
24. Kekkonen, *Speeches and Writings 2*, 176.
25. Werner Wiskari, "Kekkonen to See Khrushchev Friday," *New York Times*, November 20, 1961, 1.
26. Wiskari, "Kekkonen to See Khrushchev Friday, "*New York Times*, November 20, 1961, 11.
27. President Kennedy demolished this line of attack at his prior news conference of November 8, 1961.
28. Don Cook, *New Republic*, November 22, 1961, 7.
29. Cook, *New Republic*, November 22, 1961, 7.

17. The Mission (11/21/61)

Epigraph 1. "Telegram from the Department of State to the Embassy in Finland," November 19, 1961.

Epigraph 2. "Department of State to the Embassy in Finland," November 21, 1961, in *Foreign Relations of the United States, 1961–1963*, vol. 16, *Eastern Europe; Cyprus; Greece; Turkey* (Washington, DC: Government Printing Office, 1994), document 200.

1. "Memorandum from the Secretary of State to the President," February 9, 1950, in *Foreign Relations of the United States, 1950,* vol. 4, *Central and Eastern Europe; The Soviet Union* (Washington, DC: Government Printing Office, 1980), document 307.

2. "Memorandum from the Assistant Secretary of State for Policy Planning (Smith) to Acting Secretary of State Herter," October 23, 1958, in *Foreign Relations of the United States, 1958–1960* vol. 10, part 2, *Eastern Europe; Finland; Greece; Turkey* (Washington, DC: Government Printing Office, 1993), document 193.

3. Finland opted out of the Marshall Plan, the American initiative to provide economic aid to Western Europe in 1948, out of fear of antagonizing the Soviet Union.

4. "Memorandum from Secretary of State Rusk to President Kennedy," November 20, 1961, in *Foreign Relations of the United States, 1961–1963*, vol. 16, *Eastern Europe; Cyprus; Greece; Turkey* (Washington, DC: Government Printing Office, 1994), document 198.

5. "Memorandum from Rusk to Kennedy," November 20, 1961.

6. "Memorandum from Rusk to Kennedy," November 20, 1961.

7. "President John F. Kennedy's Inaugural Address (1961)," U.S. National Archives Administration, February 8, 2022, https://www.archives.gov/milestone-documents/president-john-f-kennedys-inaugural-address.

8. "Telegram from the Department of State to the Embassy in Finland," November 20, 1961, in *Foreign Relations of the United States, 1961–1963*, vol. 16, *Eastern Europe; Cyprus; Greece; Turkey* (Washington, DC: Government Printing Office, 1994), document 199.

9. "Department of State to the Embassy in Finland," November 20, 1961.

10. "Department of State to the Embassy in Finland," November 20, 1961.

11. "Department of State to the Embassy in Finland," November 20, 1961.

12. Adlai Stevenson II (1900–65), American politician, governor of Illinois, two-time Democratic Party nominee for president, US ambassador to the United Nations. Stevenson had no qualms about confronting the USSR in the Security Council, as he would famously illustrate the following year during the Cuban Missile Crisis when he confronted the Soviet ambassador.

13. "Department of State to the Embassy in Finland," November 20, 1961.

14. "Telegram from the Embassy in Finland to the Department of State," November 21, 1961, in *Foreign Relations of the United States, 1961–1963*, vol. 16, *Eastern Europe; Cyprus; Greece; Turkey* (Washington, DC: Government Printing Office, 1994), document 201.

15. "Embassy in Finland to the Department of State," November 21, 1961.

16. “Embassy in Finland to the Department of State,” November 21, 1961.
17. “Embassy in Finland to the Department of State,” November 21, 1961.
18. “Embassy in Finland to the Department of State,” November 21, 1961.
19. “Embassy in Finland to the Department of State,” November 21, 1961.
20. “Embassy in Finland to the Department of State,” November 21, 1961.
21. “Embassy in Finland to the Department of State,” November 21, 1961.
22. “Embassy in Finland to the Department of State,” November 21, 1961.
23. “Embassy in Finland to the Department of State,” November 21, 1961.
24. Letters to the president after the trip to Novosibirsk, 1961, box 1/37, Archives of Urho Kekkonen, Orimattila, Finland.
25. *United Press International*, November 21, 1961.
26. Werner Wiskari, “Kekkonen Starts Trip,” *New York Times*, November 23, 1961, 6.
27. Wiskari, “Kekkonen Starts Trip.”
28. Wiskari, “Kekkonen Starts Trip.”
29. Don Cook, “Finland’s Perilous Neutrality,” *New Republic*, January 1, 1962.
30. Seymour Topping, “Norwegian Rejects Moscow’s Pressure,” *New York Times*, November 23, 1961, 1.
31. Topping, “Norwegian Rejects Moscow’s Pressure.”
32. Seymour Topping, “Kekkonen to See Khrushchev Today,” *New York Times*, November 24, 1961, 1.
33. Topping, “Kekkonen to See Khrushchev Today.”

18. Good Losers (11/26/61)

Epigraph 2. Urho Kekkonen, *Puheita ja kirjotuksia 2: Puheita preisidenttokaudelta 1956–1967* [Speeches and Writings from the Presidential Period 2: 1956–1967] (Helsinki: Weilin + Göös, 1967), 177.

1. Kekkonen, *Speeches and Writings 2*, 179.
2. “Reprieve for Finland,” *New York Times*, November 26, 1961, 8.
3. Don Cook, “Finland’s Perilous Neutrality,” *New Republic*, January 1, 1962.
4. Kekkonen, *Speeches and Writings 2*, 177–78.
5. Werner Wiskari, “Kekkonen Urges Anti-Reds to Quit Finnish Politics,” *New York Times*, November 27, 1961, 4.
6. Kekkonen, *Speeches and Writings 2*, 179.
7. Kekkonen, *Speeches and Writings 2*, 180
8. Kekkonen, *Speeches and Writings 2*.
9. Wiskari, “Kekkonen Urges Anti-Reds to Quit Finnish Politics.”
10. Wiskari, “Kekkonen Urges Anti-Reds to Quit Finnish Politics.”
11. Wiskari, “Kekkonen Urges Anti-Reds to Quit Finnish Politics.”
12. Kekkonen, *Speeches and Writings 2*, 181–82.
13. Kekkonen, *Speeches and Writings 2*.
14. Kekkonen, *Speeches and Writings 2*.
15. *New Republic*, January 1, 1962.
16. Yrjö Länsipuro, interview by author, June 2014.

19. Aftermath (10/28/61–1/1/62)

Epigraph 2. "Memorandum of Conversation," November 28, 1961, in *Foreign Relations of the United States, 1961–1963*, vol. 16, *Eastern Europe; Cyprus; Greece; Turkey* (Washington, DC: Government Printing Office, 1994), document 205.

1. "Guarantee for Election," *Times* (London), November 27, 1961, 10.
2. "Undermining Finland's Freedom," *New York Times,* November 28, 1961, 36.
3. Jukka Tarkka, *Max Jakobson: Finnish Diplomacy in the Cold War* (Helsinki: Otava, 2013), 135.
4. Tarkka, *Max Jakobson,* 135.
5. "Undermining Finland's Freedom."
6. "Undermining Finland's Freedom."
7. "Telegram from the Department of State to the Mission to the North Atlantic Treaty Organization and European Regional Organizations," November 28, 1961, in *Foreign Relations of the United States, 1961–1963*, vol. 16, *Eastern Europe; Cyprus; Greece; Turkey* (Washington, DC: Government Printing Office, 1994), document 206.
8. "Department of State to the Mission," November 28, 1961.
9. "Department of State to the Mission," November 28, 1961.
10. "Memorandum of Conversation," November 28, 1961.
11. "Memorandum of Conversation," November 28, 1961.
12. "Memorandum of Conversation," November 28, 1961.
13. "Memorandum of Conversation," November 28, 1961.
14. "Memorandum of Conversation," November 28, 1961.
15. "Memorandum of Conversation," November 28, 1961.
16. "Memorandum of Conversation," November 28, 1961.
17. "Memorandum of Conversation," November 28, 1961.
18. "Memorandum of Conversation," November 28, 1961.
19. Memorandum of Conversation," November 28, 1961.
20. "Memorandum of Conversation," November 28, 1961.
21. "Memorandum of Conversation," November 28, 1961.
22. "Memorandum of Conversation," November 28, 1961.

20. Intermezzo

Epigraph 2. "Transcript of the President's News Conference on World and Domestic Affairs," *New York Times,* November 30, 1961, 14.

1. "Transcript of the President's News Conference."
2. "Transcript of the President's News Conference."
3. "Transcript of the President's News Conference."
4. "Transcript of the President's News Conference."
5. "Transcript of the President's News Conference."
6. Werner Wiskari, "Soviet Dims Joys of Finnish Yule," *New York Times,* December 3, 1961, 13.
7. Wiskari, "Soviet Dims Joys of Finnish Yule."
8. Don Cook, *New Republic,* January 1, 1962, 3.

9. Jaakko Kalela, letter to author, September 30, 2013.

10. Jaakko Kalela, letter to author.

11. Oddly enough, Khrushchev asked the author if he would not mind accompanying him to his podiatrist where he was having a special shoe made for him, inevitably triggering memories of his father's shoe tantrum at the United Nations in 1960. Sometimes life *is* stranger than biography.

12. Sergei Khrushchev, interview by author, March 2016.

13. Khrushchev, interview by author.

14. Kalela, letter to author.

15. Kalela, letter to author.

16. Jukka Tarkka, *Max Jakobson: Finnish Diplomacy in the Cold War* (Helsinki: Otava, 2013).

17. Cook, *New Republic.*

Index